RICHARD HALLIBURTON'S
BOOK OF MARVELS

RICHARD HALLIBURTON'S

Complete

BOOK OF MARVELS

THE BOBBS-MERRILL COMPANY

Indianapolis PUBLISHERS *New York*

CONTENTS OF THE OCCIDENT

Dear reader:

When I was a boy in school my favorite subject was geography, and my prize possession my geography book. This book was filled with pictures of the world's most wonderful cities and mountains and temples, and had big maps to show where they were. I loved that book because it carried me away to all the strange and romantic lands. I read about the Egyptian Pyramids, and India's marble towers, about the great cathedrals of France, and the ruins of ancient Babylon. The stories of such things always set me to dreaming, to yearning for the actual sight and touch of these world wonders.

Sometimes I pretended I had a magic carpet, and without bothering about tickets and money and farewells, I'd skyrocket away to New York or to Rome, to the Grand Canyon or to China, across deserts and oceans and mountains . . . then suddenly come back home when the school bell rang for recess.

I often said to myself: "I wish my father, or somebody, would take me to all these wonderful places. What good are they if you can't *see* them? If *I* ever grow up and have a son, we are going traveling together. I'll show him Gibraltar and Jerusalem, the Andes and the Alps, because I'll want my boy not only to study geography—I'd like for him to live it, too."

Well, I'm grown up now. But as yet I haven't any son or any daughter to go traveling with me. And so, in their places, may I take you?

Your friend,

Richard Halliburton

MAP showing location
of Marvels in the
UNITED STATES
and the route we follow
to visit them.

chapter
1. San Francisco Bay Bridge
chapter
2. Golden Gate Bridge
chapter
3. Yosemite
chapter
4. Grand Canyon
chapter
5. Boulder Dam
chapter
6. Niagara
chapter
7. New York
chapter
8. Washington D.C.
chapter
9. Fort Jefferson

THE OCCIDENT

CHAPTER I

A MARVELOUS BRIDGE

Where shall we start?

I'm writing this book in a house on the top of a high hill in San Francisco. From my window I can see the two biggest bridges in the world—one red, one silver—stretching across the beautiful bay below. Why not start right here, on our journey across the world in quest of its marvels? For surely these bridges are among the most marvelous achievements in human history.

The silver bridge leads eastward across the bay to link San Francisco with the cities on the opposite shore. The bay here is five miles wide. But to this five miles of bridge over the water, the approaches over the land at both ends add another three. So from end to end this giant among bridges measures eight miles long. This is four times the length of the famous George Washington Bridge across the Hudson River at New York (which, previously, was the greatest in the world), and seven times the length of the historic Brooklyn Bridge.

Have you ever walked eight miles? Were you tired? How long did it take? Unless you walked very fast it took perhaps three hours. Now imagine walking and walking and walking for three hours—all on the same enormous bridge. And for three of the miles the roadway is two hundred feet and more above the water. If you have a sixteen-story skyscraper in your town, and if you have been on the roof and looked over the edge, you will know how far the roadway is above the waves.

As you will see from a look at the picture, this Bay Bridge is made in two sections not at all alike. One section leads from San Francisco to a small island in the middle of the harbor, while the second section leads from the island to the eastern shore. The roadway of the first half is held up by two great steel cables

3

San Francisco and its famous bay taken from an airplane at 16,000 feet. This picture show clearly the location of the city's two wonder-bridges. The right-hand one, divided by the islan is the Bay Bridge. It stretches eight miles from San Francisco to Oakland, the city in the upp right corner. The part of the bridge suspended from cables—the part reaching from San Fran

cisco to the island—is two miles long. On the other side of the picture is the Golden Gate Bridge, soaring across the mile-wide entrance to the bay. The span of this bridge—over 4000 feet—is by far the greatest in the world. At the lower left corner the Pacific Ocean breaks in white waves upon the beach. Golden Gate Park lies in a long black strip across the city.

which have been stretched out over the tops of steel towers that reach as high as fifty-story buildings. These cables are just like sagging tight-ropes on which you've seen circus acrobats dance— only a thousand times bigger. Hanging straight down from these tight-ropes are hundreds of smaller ropes, also of steel. And from the down-hanging ends of these, the roadway is suspended, high in the air. This road is a double-decker, one level above for automobiles, and one below for trains and trucks.

The second section, leading from the island to the eastern shore, mostly over shallow water, is built like an ordinary steel railroad bridge.

You would think that such a colossal framework, weighing thousands and thousands of tons, would be stiff and too firm to be moved. But this is not true—especially of the suspension part. Here, the monster cables, steel though they are, swing in the breeze like any other rope. If we cross this part of the bridge during a high wind, we can feel the roadway, crowded with trucks and automobiles and electric trains, very gently rising and falling.

So huge is this bridge, and so wide the bay it spans, engineers say it may remain the biggest in the world for a thousand years to come, for no larger body of water exists where the traffic is likely, within that time, to make necessary a greater effort.

Now that I've told you about the Bay Bridge, we shall cross over it ourselves. We'll have to go by automobile, as eight miles would take too long to walk. The sloping approach itself is over a mile in length, because it has to climb from the streets of San Francisco to the bridge floor, two hundred feet above.

We start up. Our rising concrete road soars above great warehouses and docks and churches. Now we're higher than most of the skyscrapers and can look down upon them. How tiny the people appear to be on the streets below!

Now we're on the bridge itself, and over the Bay. White ferry

San Francisco Examiner.

The Bay Bridge on a busy day. The roadway shown here is for passenger automobiles only. Below, on the lower deck, is the roadway for trucks and electric trains. The top deck is 200 feet above the water. The great concrete pier, supporting the center of the bridge, is a mile away.

boats sail far below us, and a big freight boat. If we had an apple we could toss it down the freighter's smoke-stack to the stokers.

Notice the steel cables, side by side, from which our roadway hangs. Each one is over two feet thick (Can you imagine a steel rope *two feet thick?*), and contains seventeen thousand strands of wire. Each wire is as big as a pencil and will lift our automobile and all of us in it, and not break. Just one foot-length of these big cables weighs two thousand pounds. But they *have* to be strong, for they must hold up millions and millions of pounds. At a crowded hour there may be as many as three thousand automobiles, five hundred trucks, and two dozen electric trains, all rushing across the suspended part of the bridge at once, and all weighing down the two cables. Yet all this traffic put together does not weigh even one-tenth as much as the two steel and concrete roadways over which the traffic moves.

And now we have come to the first of the giant towers on the tops of which the cables rest, and through which our roadway runs. These towers, four in all, stand upon concrete piers that go down 240 feet below the surface of the water. These piers themselves are taller than the average New York office building.

Such a vast undertaking, where brave men had to work so far down in the water and so high above it, was not finished without a tragic loss of life. In all, twenty-four workmen were killed, some by dynamite explosions deep in the rock foundations, some by falling from the towers or the roadway into the bay. And every time a workman perished, all work was stopped for the rest of that day. So on twenty-four days, during the construction of the bridge, work stood still, as a sign of respect to the twenty-four victims.

One morning when the bridge was half completed I was being led across it by an engineer. Suddenly word began to pass along from workman to workman that one of their fellows had just fallen to his death. "That makes the twentieth," somebody said.

8

San Francisco Examiner.

The Bay Bridge is as beautiful as it is wonderful. The huge towers, painted silver, rise 350 feet above the roadway. The cables from which the roadway is hung measure two feet thick. If the traffic is heavier on one side of the tower than on the other, the tower-top may bend as much as three feet toward the heavier side.

Without a word all the two thousand bridge-workers put down their tools, and walked in silent lines to the shore, and home.

We have now traveled two miles along this mighty swinging roadway, and come to what seems the end of it—to the far shore. But it's not the far shore—we're not yet in the middle of the bay. It's a rocky island called Yerba Buena, and right through it, through the widest tunnel in the world, still nearly two hundred feet above the water, the double-decker roadway passes.

This isn't a long tunnel, only about six hundred feet. But it's so high and wide that a six-story building could be pulled through it and have room to spare. All this height is necessary because of the two decks—automobiles upstairs and trains downstairs.

In a burst of light we emerge from the tunnel and see ahead of us the second section of the bridge—a section even longer than the first. But it is not so interesting as the suspended part. It looks more like a railroad trestle made of steel girders. Slowly it runs downhill over the shallow water of the East Bay until it comes to the Oakland end, eight miles from the starting point in San Francisco.

Oakland is the city where the early pioneers left their covered wagons behind and climbed aboard sail-boat ferries for the trip across the bay. And this trip might take, with stubborn winds and tides to face, half a day. What would these pioneers think now if they could return and see this marvelous silver-colored bridge soaring far above them, and hear the whir of a thousand motor cars speeding across from Oakland to San Francisco in fifteen minutes?

CHAPTER II

THE GOLDEN GATE

Isn't it remarkable that San Francisco should have not only the biggest bridge, but the *two* biggest bridges, in the world? And of the two, some people think that the shorter one—the red one—is the more wonderful. This one swings over the Golden Gate, the entrance to San Francisco Harbor, and so is called the Golden Gate Bridge.

It is likewise of the suspension type—hung on cables. But whereas the Bay Bridge is made of several spans linked together, the Golden Gate Bridge makes just one mighty leap across—one single span four-fifths of a mile long, a span almost *twice* as long as any single span on the Bay Bridge. Its towers, 750 feet high, are half again as high as the Bay Bridge towers. Beneath it the tides race in and out through the Golden Gate, and great Pacific liners pass, liners that are dwarfed by the shining steel web which seems to float as if by magic far above the tallest masts of the greatest ships.

On the other hand, the red bridge has only one roadway—for automobiles and trucks. There are no tracks for elevated trains.

And now we are going to visit *this* bridge, and see which of the two we think is the greater.

Just where the mile-wide "gate" is narrowest, a little peninsula juts out from the San Francisco shore. On this peninsula's point, in 1854, the United States Army built a brick fort called Fort Winfield Scott, after the famous American general of that name. The guns of this fort were of the largest size ever made up to that time and could shoot all the way across the channel—over a mile—and prevent any hostile battleship from entering the harbor.

One of the army officers stationed in the fort in 1879 was a colonel named Sydney Taylor. His wife and his ten-year-old son, Sydney, Junior, lived there, too. One day little Sydney asked

11

Across the Golden Gate, the entrance to San Francisco's harbor, swings this marvelous bridge. Its 4000-foot span is twice as long as the Bay Bridge spans. Its towers, painted red, are 750 feet high—high as the Woolworth Building. The cables, three feet thick, hold the single-deck roadway 260 feet above the waves. The ship passing beneath the center of the bridge is not a tug, but

a great passenger liner. The Pacific, on the left-hand side, fades away into the haze. When the sun sinks into the western ocean, and shines straight against this brilliant-colored bridge, it sets the red towers on fire. The cables gleam; the vast white concrete piers at either end turn gold. This bridge at sunset is a glorious sight.

a gunner what that powder was which he packed into the muzzle of the big guns to fire them. The gunner, thinking it amusing to make fun of the little boy's ignorance, said *charcoal powder.*

Straightway Sydney thought to himself: "If it's only charcoal powder, perhaps *I* can fire the big guns." So he pounded up a big basketful of charcoal and, when nobody was looking, stuffed this grit into the mouth of the biggest gun and used a ramrod to pack it tight. Then he set a match to it and plugged his fingers into his ears to keep out what he thought was going to be a terrific explosion.

But the charcoal grit crammed into the gun wouldn't even burn. Disgusted, Sydney left it as it was, and went off to some new adventure.

Then, a few days later, great excitement swept over the fort. A ship carrying Ulysses S. Grant was entering the Golden Gate. This was the world-famous General Grant who had led the northern armies to victory over the southern Confederacy, the General Grant to whom Robert E. Lee had surrendered, the General Grant who had twice been President of the United States, and was now on a triumphant trip around the world. He must be given a twenty-one-gun salute—and quickly—for his ship was sailing swiftly by, with the incoming tide.

The gunners prepared to man the biggest gun. . . .

It was full of charcoal grit!

And by the time this grit had been cleaned out, and gunpowder put in, Grant's ship had disappeared around the corner of the harbor.

The General's companions were indignant, and all San Francisco ashamed, that the fort had failed to salute one of the greatest living American soldiers, and the most celebrated person who had, up to that time, ever come to California.

But why do I tell this story? I tell it because Sydney continued to grow up in that fort, gazing across the rushing waters of the Golden Gate, wondering if, someday, giants might build a bridge across it . . . how wonderful it would be . . . a bridge soaring from side to side!

14

But he not only dreamed—he planned and worked too. And, thanks in part to his vision and enthusiasm, the bridge was built, not by giants but by American engineers. And to Sydney Taylor went the office of traffic-master, the official who has control of all bridge traffic.

So now he speeds across his dream bridge and looks down, 240 feet, right on top of Fort Winfield Scott—for one section of the bridge arches protectingly over the old fort, deserted now but still standing. And there below he sees the rusty old cannon that once failed to greet Ulysses S. Grant.

And we, too, having climbed on foot along the sidewalk of the long winding ramp, can now look over the edge—down into the courtyard of the fort. Behind us on the shore are strewn the batteries and the barracks of the modern army post, and before us stretches the most marvelous bridge-span on earth, suspended from the two parallel three-feet-thick cables. The concrete supports are big as the walls of Babylon; the two enormous red towers high as the Woolworth Building; the cables half again as big as those on the Bay Bridge. Indeed this bridge *does* seem to have been built by giants, but by giants who loved great beauty as well as great size; for with all its overpowering magnitude this red rainbow of steel has the grace of flight, and the rhythm of a poem.

We're in the middle of it now, at the point where the cables sag down to touch the roadway. At this point we are 2100 feet (a distance as great as two *Queen Marys*) from either tower. And though we are 260 feet above the waves of the Golden Gate, the towers rise nearly another 500 feet above.

I was allowed to climb one of these towers long before the roadway had been added. And while I stood on top of it, braced against the never-ending wind, and marveling at the glorious view—the bay, ringed with its hills and cities to the east, the open ocean to the west—a great bank of dense fog rolled in from the Pacific and blotted out all the earth below. The ocean, the bay, the Golden Gate, the hills on either side, all disappeared, and left nothing visible but the massive red tops of the two soaring towers

15

From a painting by Chesley Bonestell

One of the steel spans of the Golden Gate Bridge arches protectingly over old Fort Winfield Sco
This fort was built in 1854 at a point where the Golden Gate is narrowest. It was in this fort th
the commander's nine-year-old son, Sydney Taylor, Jr., in 1879, stuffed the biggest cannon so full
charcoal dust that it was unable to fire a salute when General U. S. Grant passed by.

—my tower and its twin, four thousand feet away. All the rest of the world was fog and sky. Would you like to have been there, too?

The best time to cross the bridge is at sunset. Then the sun dips into the ocean just out there beyond the entrance to the Golden Gate. It shines straight against the brilliant-colored bridge, and sets its red towers on fire. The cables gleam; the vast white concrete piers at either end turn gold. Behind, the sunset beats upon the spires of San Francisco, lights up the deep-blue water of the bay, and illuminates brightly the cities on the eastern shore, stair-stepping up the mountain side.

And perhaps as we watch, a great ocean liner, far down below, sails swiftly beneath us, headed straight for that flaming sunset—and on to China; or America's biggest battleship, coming home from the sea, glides below the rainbow and into the bay—a watch-dog, a guarantee of safety, for this incomparable monument to the courage and the genius of man.

The author visits the top of a tower during construction of the Golden Gate Bridge. The steel helmet had to be worn by all visitors and workmen as a protection against falling bolts.

CHAPTER III

THE HIGHEST WATERFALL

Where shall we go next on our wonder-tour?

There is Mount Rainier, not too far away, in the state of Washington—the most beautiful and graceful mountain in America.

There is the forest of giant trees in California's Sequoia Park —trees three hundred feet high and three thousand years old.

But even more marvelous, to me, among the wonders of the Pacific coast, is Yosemite Valley. And Yosemite is less than two hundred miles from San Francisco. Let's go there.

Up to the year 1851, ten years before the American Civil War, no white man knew that Yosemite existed. It was lost in the heart of the Sierra Nevada, and its secret guarded by peaks and canyons.

But the Indians knew. For centuries Indians had lived in this miraculous valley, hidden from the world by the mile-high precipices that walled them in.

This peace and security came to an end in 1851. Two years earlier, gold in vast quantities had been found in California, and thousands of gold-seekers came struggling across the continent by ox-cart to share the new-found wealth.

These miners and adventurers had no consideration for the welfare and happiness of the Indians. The invaders mistreated them, slaughtered the game and destroyed the fish. The Indians fought back. They killed the white men and burned their log houses, and ran away into the depths of the mountains.

To capture and punish one such party of Indian raiders, a company of white volunteers, under the leadership of Major James Savage, in March, 1851, struck out along snow-covered trails that led straight into the enemy's country, trails along which no white man had marched before.

Their path, winding through dense forests, suddenly brought the party to the edge of a precipice. Major Savage, at the head

18

of his column, looked over the brink. And what he saw made him forget all about the Indians.

For he beheld a great gorge in the mountains, floored with forests and meadows, and surrounded by cliffs and rock-towers that rose thousands of feet—rose so sheer and smooth that not even the smallest tree could find a crack in which to grow. And plunging down into the valley from the tops of these giant cliffs were waterfalls the like of which no white man in all the history of the world had ever before seen.

Near the spot where Major Savage stood, a river rushed to the edge of the wall, and fell six hundred feet through space—nearly as great a fall as *four* Niagaras. And as it fell it was torn into spray and mist so that it seemed to float in white and lacy folds down to the rocks below. Undoubtedly Major Savage thought: How much it looks like the veil of a bride!

Bridal Veil is its name today.

Quickly the Major led his men down the steep trail to the river at the bottom of the canyon. Opposite, they beheld a gray granite precipice three thousand feet high, smooth and clean, and shining in the sun. And so boldly did it thrust up its soaring face into the sky, the discoverers named it El Capitan—The Captain.

But what was that strange thundering the soldiers heard higher up the valley? Had the Indians received a supply of cannon?

To find out, the scouting party hurried on. They moved cautiously through the trees, nearer and nearer the booming. Now they were just below it. They pushed aside the underbrush. . . . And stared before them! No cannon here. No angry god. Only another waterfall. But *such* a waterfall! It came tumbling down at them from a point *2600 feet above!* Can you imagine that?—a waterfall *sixteen times* as high as Niagara? You say there is no such thing—it's impossible. That's what Major Savage said.

But it was real. He felt the spray blowing in his face. He heard the thunder of the water, and felt the rocks tremble. He

was looking at the highest and most spectacular waterfall on earth.

Because he was so close he didn't realize that this amazing cascade was not all one great leap. Not until he crossed the valley to the other side could he see that the river made three leaps to reach the canyon floor. The first was fifteen hundred feet—higher than two Bridal Veils. Then came eight hundred feet of cataracts. And then, seething and racing and foaming, the river plunged one last time, in a frenzy of spray, three hundred feet more.

Marveling, the explorers moved deeper into this wonderland. Straight ahead, blocking out the sky, they now noticed an extraordinary peak—a perfect half-dome of mountainous rock rising nearly a mile above them, with its flat, sliced side facing the valley. Some of the soldiers thought this curious half-mountain even more remarkable than the great cascade.

By night the company still had found no Indians. But they had found four more waterfalls ranging from three hundred feet to sixteen hundred feet. They had found trees thirty feet thick. They had found a secret treasury where Nature had collected her rarest gems of beauty. They had found, for the world, the valley without an equal—Yosemite!

And everything that this company found we can see today. Scarcely a tree or a stone has been changed.

On our own visit to this famous valley we have reached the narrow entrance. Guards stop us and ask if we have any cats or dogs. No cats or dogs are allowed, because, as everybody knows, Yosemite has become a National Park and a wild-game preserve where birds gather by the thousands, and where herds of deer graze beside the road, protected and unafraid. Cats might kill the birds and dogs attack the deer.

We travel on through a tunnel of trees between overhanging rocks. Suddenly the tunnel opens into a wide glade beside a lake. We are on the very spot where Major Savage pitched his camp. El Capitan raises its smooth, glowing granite face straight above us. And on the opposite side Bridal Veil Falls, soft and serene,

22

Yosemite Falls, the highest waterfall in the world. From the top of the cliff to the canyon floor is a drop of 2600 feet. The river's first leap is 1500 feet. Then comes 800 feet of cataracts (not seen in the picture). The last plunge is 300 feet. The total is *sixteen times* higher than Niagara.

Half Dome Mountain, in Yosemite Park. The top of this wonderful mountain is 9000 feet above the sea, and 5000 feet above the valley floor. The precipice drops 2000 feet. So smooth and steep is the curve of the half-dome, that this mountain was long considered unclimbable. But in 1875, Captain Anderson, a Scotchman, amazed all California by conquering the curve and the slickness. He drove iron pegs into the rock crevices, one peg above the other, and by means of

Courtesy Agfa Ansco.

these pegs pulled himself up. Since then a ladder has been built by which you and I climb to the summit. On top we look over the edge of the cliff where the mountain was sliced in half. It's like flying. The thunder of the cascades is only a murmur now. The forests, a mile below, are soft green mats. Every foot of this marvelous Yosemite Valley is unrolled beneath.

swaying and singing, trails its six hundred feet of mist-folds down the cliff.

Soon we, too, hear that strange thunder ahead—the same thunder Major Savage heard. But *we* know what it is. We turn a corner of the drive—and come face to face with the highest of all waterfalls. We see it as it first flows over the rim of the valley a half-mile above, as it tumbles fifteen hundred feet in one great, white, ever-widening plume of foam, as it plunges on downward, around and over the rocks, as it makes its final leap, to end in a roaring, boiling cauldron of spray and rainbows right beside us.

And as we watch, fascinated by this astonishing sight of flying water and mighty granite wall, the wind beats upon the falls as upon a sail. It blows the entire plume in a great curve far to one side, then to the other side, then lures it out from the rock face only to dash it back against the cliff with an explosive roar that shakes the valley.

I climbed once to the brink of this great waterfall, and stretched flat on the rock and looked over the edge, out upon the falling plume. I watched it being torn to pieces by the wind as it plunged down into the abyss. And the roar that rises fifteen hundred feet up the falling column of water from the unyielding rocks is a hundred times louder and wilder than the noise heard from below. It is an awesome sight and a terrifying sound.

But this time we are not going to climb to the rim of the Great Falls because we have an even more interesting climb ahead—to the top of Half Dome.

For twenty-five years after Major Savage and his party discovered Yosemite, people tried to climb Half Dome. But they couldn't. The curve of the dome was too steep, and the surface, worn smooth by wind and snow, too slick. Chipmunks and squirrels could climb it. These little animals lived happily on top, and laughed because human beings only slid down every time they tried to crawl up.

But in 1875 a Scotchman named Captain Anderson amazed all California by conquering the curve and the slickness. When he claimed to have climbed Half Dome, alone, nobody would believe him. So he took several friends and showed them how he had driven iron pegs into the rock crevices, one peg above the other. By means of these he pulled himself up, for the last thousand feet, over the curve of the dome to where it was flat on top.

From that day to this the chipmunks and squirrels have had a bad time of it, for Captain Anderson's series of pegs led to the building of a ladder, which today has steel cables on either side for hand rails. These rails help you to pull yourself upward and keep you from sliding off the slick surface of the dome.

To climb this thousand-foot ladder is not easy. But it's a fine adventure. Are you wearing rubber-soled shoes? You'll need them. Are you a good rider? We must first ascend eight miles of mountain trail on horseback to get to the base of the curving cliff.

Now we start the final struggle, pulling ourselves up the almost vertical ladder by means of the cables. At first our arms do all the work, while our feet just try to keep up with us. We slip and slide, but the rungs of the ladder prevent our falling all the way down. We can understand very well how this slick, steep dome defeated all climbers, Indians and white men alike, for so long. We express a silent thanks to Captain Anderson. Without the cables and the ladder we wouldn't be able to move ten feet upwards.

We're getting tired—our arms ache—the cables chafe our hands. But the higher we go the less steep the curve of the dome becomes—and less steep, and less steep, until it's almost flat—and we're on top.

We are 9000 feet above sea-level, and 5000 feet above the valley floor. From the topmost point a great projecting rock hangs over the 2000-foot precipice-side where the mountain was sliced in half. We stand on this overhang and look down. It's like flying. The thunder of the cascades is only a murmur now, and far away. The forests, a mile below, are soft green mats. The snowy Sierra rises about us. Every foot of this glorious valley is unrolled beneath. We know now how Major Savage felt when, pursuing that band of Indians, he burst upon this hidden paradise of peak and waterfall; and we can understand why the Indians, driven from this happy hunting ground out into the barren plains, died of homesickness for Yosemite.

CHAPTER IV

THE DEEPEST CANYON

Did you ever hear the story of the Seven Cities of Cibola?

It is an old legend that has been told in Spain for a thousand years.

A thousand years ago the Moors, crossing the Straits of Gibraltar from Africa, conquered Spain and made it part of their great Moslem empire. Many Christians fled from the country, among them a Catholic bishop and his followers, who sought refuge, so the legend says, in a land far to the west—across the Sea of Darkness. There these refugees founded seven cities, called the Seven Cities of Cibola, which became (as the legend improved with the telling) the richest cities in the world.

And so when Columbus discovered America, people were sure this new "India" was really Cibola to which the bishop had fled five hundred years before, and that the Seven Cities would soon be located. In fact the early gold-hungry Spanish explorers marched thousands of miles and endured great hardships looking for them.

From Mexico, in 1539, the Spanish Viceroy sent an expedition into what is now New Mexico, still hoping to locate the gold of Cibola. Indians assured the explorers that "seven large cities" would be found thirty days' march to the north.

Undoubtedly—thought the Spaniards—these are the very goals we are seeking. Soon we'll all be rich!

They hurried on. To explore the trail in advance, the captain sent ahead a Spanish scout along with an Indian guide. And sure enough the scout did find seven cities—only to be killed by the inhabitants.

But the Indian guide escaped, and fled back to his on-marching comrades with the story that Cibola had indeed been found, but could not be taken without an army.

The Grand Canyon of the Colorado, the deepest, the widest, the vastest, the most marvelous canyon on our earth. In northern Arizona the swift-flowing Colorado River has dug this enormous gulch, 5000 feet deep and ten miles wide. The rim of the plateau is 7500 feet above sea level, the river only 2500 feet. The rock walls are brilliantly colored. Many people consider this Canyon the first wonder of the world.

The captain rushed to Mexico to report. Promptly the Viceroy dispatched the great explorer, Coronado, to go and seize the cities and all their gold.

Coronado, overcoming great hardships, reached the land which the Indian guide had said was Cibola. But all the Spaniards found were seven poverty-stricken Indian pueblos, not far from the present site of Gallup, New Mexico.

The Indian inhabitants, probably to get rid of him, told Coronado that if it was gold he wanted, he'd find it "to the west"—and a great and wonderful river, too, a river that flowed deep in the earth between gold walls.

And so Coronado, excited by this new tall tale, sent one of his officers named Don López de Cárdenas with twelve men to investigate.

Cárdenas marched west, mile after mile, across burning, bright-colored deserts, and over barren mountains. He and his men were scorched by the sun. They grew desperate from thirst. How they prayed for the sight of that river! Whether or not it had gold walls didn't matter. If only it had water!

But the desert rolled on.

Then, as unexpectedly as a clap of thunder on a sunny day, they came upon it——

The Grand Canyon of the Colorado—the deepest, the widest, the vastest, the most marvelous canyon in the world. Cárdenas and his men stood and looked at each other, silent, on the brink of the abyss.

This was in 1540—eighty long years before the Pilgrims came to America in the *Mayflower*.

The walls—a mile deep—were not made of gold as the Indians had said, but of rock that in places looked like gold and shone like gold. And along with the yellow shades were bands of red, and blue, and green, all swimming in a lilac mist.

The Spanish historian who wrote the narrative of this famous expedition tells us more about it:

"Cárdenas and his twelve men spent three days on the rim looking for a passage down to the river. From above, the river looked no more than *six feet across,* though the Indians said it was fifty times that wide. Three of the men made an attempt to descend at the least difficult place, but soon returned and said it was impossible to go more than one-third of the way, so steep were the cliffs. Those who stayed above had thought that some rocks on the sides of the cliffs seemed about as tall as a man, but those who went down swore that when they reached those rocks they were bigger than the great cathedral tower of Seville."

It's this gash in the earth's crust we are going to visit next on our quest for marvels.

All of us have read stories and seen pictures of the Grand Canyon. These do not help us understand what the Canyon is really like. It's as if we tried to understand music just from reading about it, or from seeing pictures of a piano and a violin. The Canyon may look even rather dull in photographs. But when you see the real thing with your own eyes, the sight strikes you speechless—that mile drop to the river—that ten-mile void across to the other brink—those color-splashed temples and towers and pyramids of rock that swell up from the terraced walls—that yawning sea of painted splendor falling away into bottomless mysteries.

The Grand Canyon is too huge for us to measure by any scale we know. I'm sure it must have been intended originally for the great planet Jupiter, or for Saturn, and got shipped to our little globe by mistake. But by whatever chance it came to be here, the first sight of the Canyon, when the sunset is filling it with burning glory, or the moon with dark enchantment, is enough to overwhelm the most hardened traveler that ever lived.

But I believe I just said that writing about the Grand Canyon was a waste of time! . . . Let's have a *look* at it.

Like Cárdenas' men we must travel for miles across a high and barren plateau to reach the Canyon. And like Cárdenas, we come upon it all at once.

31

In the year 1540—eighty years before the Pilgrims landed in New England—a Spanish captain named Don López de Cárdenas, looking for a river which the Indians said had "walls of gold," came upon the Grand Canyon. He and his company were the first white men ever to see it. The walls, a mile deep, were not made of gold but of rock that in places looked like gold and shone

Photograph by Ernst Schwarz, Courtesy Agfa Ansco.

like gold.   And along with the yellow shades were bands of red and blue and green, all swim-ming in a lilac mist.   When we see the Canyon for ourselves, it seems too huge for us to measure by any scale we know.   We feel it must have been intended originally for the great planet Jupi-ter, or Saturn, and got shipped to our little globe by mistake.

Strange, isn't it, how we, too, stand silent? There's nothing to say. Nothing we could say would mean anything. A guide tells us how deep the great chasm is, and how wide, and how long. We don't listen. We don't *want* to listen. All we want is wings.

Instead we have to accept donkeys in order to explore the abyss. Riding these patient little beasts we start to descend the trail toward the Colorado River, five thousand feet below. The trail twists and zigzags down the cliffs . . . and on every side of us the painted rock-temples rear up their wind-sculptured domes and pinnacles.

These temples have taken ten million years to build. All these years the river has been grinding its channel deeper into the plateau, and the rainstorms and the winds have been carving into the rugged banks on either side.

The weather was cold at the seven-thousand-foot rim. Now, half-way down, it's warm. And at the bottom it's sweltering. The temperature has risen fifty degrees; for the walls, soaring three, four, five thousand feet above us, are close together here at the bottom, and reflect the heat.

We'd like to go for a swim and cool off. But the river roars past with its cargo of rocks and sand and mud, making a hideous din. And this on-rushing flood, thick as liquid cement, is three hundred feet wide—not "six feet" as Cárdenas estimated. In it a swimmer would be crushed to death.

And yet people *have* navigated this angry river from end to end, in tough little boats, and, struggling along in the muddy flood, raced past this very spot.

The first and most famous of all the river conquerors was Major Powell of the United States Army. The date of his exploit was 1869. This Canyon fascinated him. He wanted to explore and study every inch of it. Perhaps he might find a way to harness and control the treacherous stream. Though he had only one arm (having lost the other in the Civil War), he resolved to launch a boat in the headwaters of the river, and travel down the entire length of the Canyon.

Everybody tried to persuade him not to go. Trappers, looking from the rim, had noticed places where the river took great leaps to lower levels. The Indians assured him that the river disappeared completely at times into underground channels. They said no human being could possibly live, once seized in the Colorado's savage embrace.

But Powell was deaf to all warnings.

With three boats and nine men he pushed off from the shore, far to the north, in the state of Wyoming, hundreds of miles above the Canyon—on what was to be a truly heroic adventure.

For ninety days this brave little fleet floated hopefully on, right into the jaws of the terrible chasm. Through whirlpools and rapids, over waterfalls, the little boats were carried by the wild and merciless current. The roar of the water never ceased. The threat of disaster never departed. The boats were overturned. The men, with all their equipment, and all their food supplies, remained water-soaked for days on end. A hundred times the explorers escaped from what seemed certain death. But there could be no turning back. And who would hear them if they cried for help?

The nine men accompanying Major Powell were not all so iron-willed as their leader. Three of them, after twelve weeks of this constant battle to keep alive, came to the end of their strength and courage. They announced that they were going to quit, that the strain was driving them crazy, that they would try to climb the mile-high cliffs and take their chances on reaching the desert above, rather than continue another foot down that murderous river toward *sure* death with the party.

Major Powell let them go, and watched them crawling up the Canyon wall until they disappeared.

The three deserters, with desperate effort, actually reached the top. They had escaped! How beautiful and friendly the flat dry desert seemed!

But their happiness was brought to an abrupt and terrible end. Indians, distrusting all white men, and believing these were only three more who had come to rob them, seized the exhausted and helpless deserters, and put them to death.

And the very day they died, Major Powell and his six faithful followers fought their way around a great bend in the chasm, and were suddenly shot out of the south entrance of the Canyon into the quiet waters of the lower river—safe.

CHAPTER V

THE GREATEST DAM

I'm going to ask you a question:

Which is the largest natural lake in the world?

You answer, properly, Lake Superior—among the fresh water lakes; the Caspian Sea—among salt lakes.

But which is the largest *artificial* lake?

Very few of you may know the answer.

It's Lake Mead. This is the vast reservoir formed by the Colorado River backing up behind Boulder Dam.

And Boulder Dam, as all the world knows, is the biggest dam in the world. It's built across the Grand Canyon thirty miles below the point where Major Powell ended his famous expedition in 1869.

Major Powell was not the only member of his family to fall in love with the Colorado River. In 1861, a boy named Arthur Powell Davis was born to Major Powell's sister. At the time Major Powell explored the Canyon little Arthur was eight years old. Naturally he heard his famous uncle tell about the wonderful adventure.

The boy became so interested in the river that he resolved to be an engineer in order that he might carry on Major Powell's dream of harnessing and controlling this mighty current, and making it irrigate the deserts through which it flowed.

As he grew up he was sent to the best engineering schools in the country. And all the time, that romantic Colorado, rushing headlong in its mile-deep canyon, kept haunting him. The older he grew, the more he felt a challenge in this wild giant's evil behavior—allowing its banks, for a thousand miles, to become a desert, and then overflowing the fertile valleys near its mouth. What a splendid contribution to the American people it would be, young Davis kept thinking, if he could change all this, if he could dam up this runaway river, control the floods on the lower delta,

37

store the water, and use it to turn the desert into gardens of flowers and fields of grain.

In 1914 Arthur Davis became director of the United States Reclamation Service. He promptly presented to the government a definite plan for the construction of a Colorado River dam 300 feet higher than engineers had ever dared build a dam before. The site he had chosen was Black Canyon. Here the natural rock walls, only 350 feet apart at the water line, rose 2000 feet on either side.

Thirteen years were spent surveying the site. Then in 1931, when Arthur Davis was seventy years old and retired from service, he saw the dream of his boyhood coming true. He saw five thousand laborers descend into Black Canyon with picks and dynamite; he saw one of the greatest engineering projects ever conceived begin to take form. How sad that death overtook him in the midst of the construction work and kept him from seeing his bold vision carried through to the end!

First, the engineers, to build a dam across the bottom of the canyon, had to get rid of the river that rushed through it. So they built a temporary barrier of earth and rocks upstream. This blocked the flow. But the flow had to go *somewhere*. So they dug four tunnels each fifty feet in diameter into the rock sides of the canyon walls. These tunnels, called "by-passes," carried the entire river around the site of the great dam and emptied the water back in the canyon at a point farther down. Here a second temporary barrier was built to keep the river from backing upstream again to flood the dry stretch where the foundations were being laid.

Never in the history of the world have there been such foundations, for never before had such a weight been placed by man upon the earth—seven million tons of concrete. This was a weight heavier than the Great Pyramid of Egypt. To support this burden

38

Boulder Dam—the biggest dam ever built—rises to block the flow of the Colorado River. This monster dam, 730 feet high and 1300 feet along the crest, was one of the greatest engineering projects in history. Over 7,000,000 tons of concrete were piled up to hold back the river—a weight greater than the Great Pyramid of Egypt. This picture shows only a small part of the huge wall. Halfway down, on the right-hand edge, you can see four workmen standing on a cat-walk. Their tiny figures give some idea of the dam's vast size.

and hold back the millions of tons of water behind it, the dam had to be made *660 feet thick* at the base—as thick as a city block is long.

Upon this vast base, 2000 feet below the desert rim, the dam began to rise. The higher it climbed the wider it had to stretch to either side as the rock walls of the canyon leaned farther and farther away from each other. At last, 730 feet above the canyon floor, the engineers decided to stop building up their concrete. The thickness was now only 45 feet, but the length along the crest had increased to 1300.

Can you picture a dam with such a height—730 feet? The highest in the world, heretofore, was one in France—the wonder-dam of Europe—just 450 feet high!

When everything was ready, the by-passes were blocked up, and the river allowed, once more, to flow in its own bed. It rushed against the great white monster in its path. But the monster was as immovable as the canyon walls. Blockaded and helpless, the river could only rise against the barrier. At the same time it backed up in the canyon until the water measured over 600 feet deep at the dam, and made a lake 115 miles long stretching upstream—Lake Mead. Then, locked fast in this lake (named for the late Commissioner of the United States Bureau of Reclamation who held office at the time), part of the water was allowed to flow down huge steel tubes into power-houses where electric power could be generated in unlimited quantities and distributed to all the cities of the Southwest. The surplus water was discharged from outlets high above the power-houses and sent leaping, two hundred feet through the air, in jets eight feet thick.

We can better understand the quantity of this water when we learn that, if all discharge from the reservoir into the lower canyon were cut off (which of course must never happen), it would take *two years' constant flow* of the Colorado River to fill Lake Mead. But as part of the water must always flow on into the lower river, it has taken much longer than two years to fill the lake.

Wide World.

Boulder Dam during construction, from the upstream side. While concrete was being poured, work went on day and night—Sunday, Christmas, Fourth of July —non-stop with never a moment's rest. There had to be a constant flow of concrete *every minute for two years.* At midnight there was just as much activity as at midday. After sunset, powerful electric lamps flooded the dam and the canyon with light.

From the Grand Canyon it's an easy journey, in our automobile, to follow the stream down to Boulder Dam. (Though it certainly wasn't for Major Powell in his row-boat.) We motor across the desert, and with no more warning than we had at the Grand Canyon, we stumble upon another of the world's truly great sights. Suddenly, as our road leads over a rocky ridge in the burning wilderness, we see Lake Mead hundreds of feet below, held back by the huge white wall of concrete curving across the canyon;

41

Behind Boulder Dam a great artificial lake, called Lake Mead, backs 115 miles up the canyon. Right at the dam the water is over 600 feet deep. This lake contains as much water as Lake Ontario. Locked fast in the enormous reservoir, part of the water is allowed to flow down huge steel tubes into power-houses where electric power is generated in unlimited quantities. The overflow water is discharged from outlets high above the power-houses, and sent leaping 200 feet through the air in jets eight feet thick. If all discharge from the reservoir into the lower canyon were

*Spence Air Photos, Los Angeles.*

off (which of course must never happen) it would take *two years' constant flow* of the Colo-
do River to fill Lake Mead. But as part of the water must always flow on into the lower river, it
taken much longer than two years to fill the lake. Most of the electric power from this dam
es to Los Angeles and Hollywood. Thanks to the dam, there need never be another flood to
destroy the farms further down stream.

and on the lower side of this wall we see the canyon falling away, revealing the power-houses and the jets of leaping, roaring water —all seven hundred feet below the lake.

It was my good fortune to see Boulder Dam, the first time, during its construction. From this same point of view, at the canyon's rim, I could look down upon the section of dry river bed, and upon the two barriers—one upstream, one downstream—that held back the river. The dam was just half built, with buckets, each holding sixteen tons of concrete, constantly releasing their cargoes onto the rising white wall. High above everything, cables were stretched from cliff to cliff across the canyon, and along these cables wooden cages, big enough to hold thirty workmen, glided back and forth. Several times I went riding in these cages, and could look down a thousand feet onto the dry canyon floor where three thousand men, with trucks, and trains, and derricks, and electric shovels, all struggled and strained to heighten the cement mountain towering above them. This regiment of workers seemed unconcerned with the fact that the river, shut off by dykes upstream and down, had risen fifty feet above their heads, or that it was seething through its rock tunnels on either side of them.

The work went on day and night—Sunday, Christmas, Fourth of July—non-stop with never a minute's rest. There had to be a constant flow of concrete *every minute for two years* in order that the mass might be knit together in one piece.

At night the whole intensely busy scene was bathed with floodlights. In those days you could come, guided by the stars, to the edge of the abyss, at three o'clock in the morning, and peer far down to where the canyon floor glowed with light and throbbed with activity. And there, towering over the ant-like workers, the glittering vision of the dam's unfinished bulk leaped out of the darkness. That was a wonderful, a sensational picture, and one that we shall never behold again.

Now, however, our automobile rolls right across the crest of Boulder Dam, for the main highway uses it as a bridge. We can look over the upstream side and see the water of the lake close

At its base, Boulder Dam is 350 feet wide, and *660 feet thick*. At the top, where there is little or no water pressure, it's 45 feet thick. Half-way between the top of the dam and the right-hand edge of the picture, we find a concrete-lined basin (and a second one at the upper left-hand corner). In case of sudden flood, these basins, called spillways, will receive the overflow and send the flood waters through tunnels around the dam. Note the long lines of parked automobiles at the upper right corner.

at hand; and over the other side we can gaze upon the power-houses hundreds of feet below.

An elevator which descends right through the center of the dam drops us down to these power-houses. In them we find enormous rooms containing the biggest turbines and electric generators ever built. Beneath them and around them the entire Colorado, compressed in strong steel tunnels, roars like a chained monster—roars because it is in bondage and forced to turn with never-ending labor the tons and tons of giant machines.

But, thanks to the river's enslavement, it will now provide water miles away to thousands of acres of once-desert land. It will never again flood the farms and valleys near its mouth. It will provide heat and light to much of southern California. Perhaps the next orange you eat will have been grown on land reclaimed by Boulder Dam, and the next motion picture you see will have been made on sets lighted by electricity from the same source.

Few of the communities blessed by this engineering triumph will remember that it was Arthur Powell Davis who first had the vision of Boulder Dam. But lack of public praise did not concern the great engineer. The only reward he asked was to know that, thanks to his vision, there would be flowers and orchards growing where there had been only sand; that towns would rise where there had been only sage brush and rattlesnakes; and that the Colorado River, which he had found one of the most untamed and destructive forces in the land, had been tamed at last, and changed into one of America's richest resources.

CHAPTER VI

NIAGARA

I once asked a geography class of young people to name for me the biggest waterfall in the world. Without hesitation they all said Niagara.

And they found it difficult to believe when I told them that two other falls, Iguazu in South America, and Victoria in southern Africa, also have been called the greatest.

The fact is that of this trio, which together form a group ranking far above all others, each has a strong claim on the title.

Niagara, without doubt, has the greatest amount of water. Nearly half of the fresh water in the world is collected in the upper four of the Great Lakes, and the chief outlet is over Niagara Falls. For this reason Niagara's flow is always steady (except when it's frozen in winter) and always vast. Iguazu and Victoria are seasonal. In the wet season, after several weeks of tropical rains, their flow of water may be *sixty feet deep,* just twice the average depth of the Niagara River. At such times Iguazu and Victoria present terrifying spectacles. And a visitor coming upon either of them, then, would be convinced that the one before him is the most wonderful of all. But in the dry season, their waters may be so shallow at the brink that they dwindle almost to a trickle.

As for the width of the falls:

Niagara's rim is about 5300 feet wide—slightly more than a mile.

Victoria's rim is 5700 feet.

The brink of Iguazu extends for *10,000 feet.*

Niagara likewise has the least height of the three—167 feet. Victoria has the greatest, with 400 feet. Iguazu comes in between with 220 feet.

Niagara Falls. Over this 167-foot cataract plunges the Niagara River, the chief outlet for Lake Superior, Lake Michigan, Lake Huron and Lake Erie. Lake Ontario lies below the Falls. This world-wonder is divided between the United States and Canada. The section at the left of the picture is on the American side; the section in the distance, on the Canadian. Over the American Falls flows six per cent of the water; over the Canadian, ninety-four per cent. But the Canadian section is often hidden by spray, while the entire sweep of the American section can be clearly seen at all times.

But there are other things that make a waterfall wonderful, besides length and height. You must be able to *see* it. And of the three, Niagara, as a whole, is the most visible. From a score of dramatic viewpoints, Niagara reveals its entire crest (though the water-curtain itself, at the center of the Canadian Falls, is often obscured by mist). There is no one place from which even half of Iguazu can be seen. And as for Victoria, at the flood season when the flow should be most impressive, the clouds of spray rising from the foot of the Falls are so dense that they hide the scene completely, for days at a time.

On the other hand, Iguazu, in the depths of a tropical jungle, has the most beautiful setting. All about it Nature is still as wild and unspoiled as a thousand years ago. You can't even buy a postcard there! Victoria, too, has been only slightly "improved"; but Niagara, alas, suffers sadly from close contact with bridges and hotels and power-plants.

So it is easy to understand why, for years, arguments have raged as to which of these three giants is the greatest.

The chances are you have seen Niagara already, or so many pictures of it that you can describe it as well as I can, for it is the most visited and most photographed cataract on earth. Over two million people go there each year. (Perhaps ten thousand a year see Victoria. Scarcely two hundred a year reach Iguazu. When I looked upon Iguazu there was not another person in sight, except my Indian guide.) But however familiar Niagara may be, it must go high on our list of world-wonders. In foreign countries it is considered by many people the *first* wonder of this continent. When visitors come to America from England or China or Mexico, what is the one thing they most want to see? Niagara Falls. Even the Grand Canyon has to wait.

Those of us who have not already been there can expect a thrill that will never be forgotten. Those who have been, will be eager to go again.

The first white man to discover and describe Niagara was Father Hennepin, in 1678. It is too bad that cameras were not

For volume of water, Niagara Falls is without a rival in the world. The mighty flood flo[w]
over the brink has an average depth of thirty feet. We stand on the rocks at the foot o[f]
American Falls, and watch this curtain of water—thousands and thousands of tons of it—hu[rls]
itself over the precipice, and plunging down toward us from the plateau, 167 feet above.

is deafening. We are drenched in spray. By day, this wall of falling water is astonishing
gh, but at night, when the colored floodlights play upon it, the Falls are doubly wonderful
and beautiful.

known and that the good Father couldn't take for us a photograph of the scene as he found it. For since then the appearance of the Falls has changed tremendously. The Canadian brink, formed like a horseshoe, over which flows ninety-four per cent of the water, has been destroying itself ever since Hennepin's day. Geologists claim that the horseshoe was only a shallow curve in 1678, and that in the years which have passed since, the center has been worn back over one thousand feet. It is still retreating two or three feet each year. As a result, in quite recent times, the deep well inside the horseshoe has become so filled with clashing waters that, as at Victoria, the rising cloud of mist, if there is no wind to drive it away, hides a part of the Falls from view. The American section, which by right should be the less impressive, makes a much finer display—simply because its whole sweep can be seen easily at all times.

If Niagara seems marvelous to us, how much more marvelous it must have seemed to Father Hennepin! When he came upon it no sign of mankind intruded, except perhaps an Indian wigwam. Forests of oak and evergreens pressed to every brink. No unsightly steel bridges broke the view down the lower gorge. No power-houses, with their drab walls, offended the eye and stole from the Falls vast quantities of water. There were no streetcars, no soot and smoke, no guides, no sounds but the roaring music of the Falls and the murmur of the wind in the hemlocks. We can see, now, at the Grand Canyon, *exactly* what Cárdenas saw. But at Niagara the vista of dazzling natural beauty that burst upon Father Hennepin has undergone many an unhappy change.

Yet even today, Niagara can be enjoyed from a dozen fine viewpoints. We stand first on the brink of the American Falls, and watch the water, thousands and thousands of tons of it, hurling itself over the precipice. The basin, filled with seething whirlpools and foam, lies 170 feet below. Someone shows us where, in 1860, on the occasion of the visit of the Prince of Wales (later Edward VII), a tight-rope walker named Blondin stretched a wire across this boiling chasm from the American to the Canadian side and performed amazing feats upon it.

We cross to Goat Island, which separates the two sections of the Falls, and approach as close as possible to the cloud-drenched horseshoe. The roar here is deafening. We are bathed in spray. We are told that on several occasions daredevils have encased themselves in stout steel barrels and plunged over the Canadian Falls, where there is water instead of rock on which to land, and have lived. Does anyone in this party want to try *that* for fun? I'll just watch.

Crossing to the Canadian side, on the International Bridge, we put on raincoats and splash through a tunnel which leads us *behind* the Falls. Through a window in the rock we can stretch out our hands and touch the under surface of the thirty-foot-thick curtain of falling, howling water. The mist is so dense that we can scarcely breathe or see. No use trying to speak.

Next we go riding on the *Maid of the Mist*. This brave and famous little boat takes us out upon the angry flood below the Falls, and pushes forward toward the cliff until the spray almost hides her.

Then we go a mile down the rim of the gorge and take an aerial car which slides out on a cable high above the lower rapids, and look down upon the raging river which here shoots through the gorge at such dizzy speed that it piles up thirty-foot waves.

But we haven't seen everything *yet*. At night, with a billion candle-power in searchlights turned upon the Falls, they are even more astonishing, even more beautiful. The light changes in color. Now the falling water is rose color, and the clouds of mist are rosy clouds. Now the color is blue, now orange. On a clear summer night, this vision of rainbow waters hurling themselves out of the darkness into a glitter of light, and rushing into darkness again down into the black and fearsome canyon, is like a stupendous stage-set—the most gorgeous and spectacular stage-set ever seen.

53

Niagara's Horseshoe Falls, on the Canadian side. When Father Hennepin discovered Niagara in 1678, the curve of this section of the Falls was not nearly so sharp as it is today. Since Father Hennepin's time the center of the crescent has been worn back nearly a thousand feet. The rim is still retreating about three feet every year. In another three hundred years the Falls may

have moved another thousand feet up the river. Unfortunately, the deeper the curve becomes, the more spray there is to hide the water-curtain. Even so, of all the world's great waterfalls, Niagara is still the most visible. (See picture inside rear cover.) It can be enjoyed from a dozen viewpoints, but no other viewpoint is so fine as from the air.

In winter Niagara sometimes freezes solid. Then the thousands of tons of falling water turn to thousands of tons of gleaming ice. The roar of the Falls is stilled into a vast white silence. Then people clamber over the ice-castles at the bottom of the cliff, and look up at the hundred-foot icicles clinging to the rock.

And if you like cold weather you can come back in February, when the thermometer is down to zero and the Falls are frozen solid, and watch the colored lights playing on a million tons of frosty fairy castles instead of foam.

And so we've seen the first of the giant waterfalls. You're saying: This one *must* be the greatest of the three. It's impossible that any other falls could be so huge, so impressive, and so glorious. We cast our vote for Niagara right now.

But don't decide too soon. You may wish to change your mind when you see Iguazu. Remember, it's waiting for us in the jungles of South America. We'll get there in good time. And as for Victoria, we may go there, too, in another book.

CHAPTER VII

NEW YORK

If an inhabitant from another planet should come to our earth to visit us, which city would most interest and astonish him?

I'm sure it would be New York.

He would admire the grace and loveliness of Paris. He would respect London's gray and solid dignity. He would write home about Istanbul's matchless location, and Rio de Janeiro's harbor.

But his heart would leap the highest when he beheld New York.

His heart would have to be made of lead *not* to leap at the sight of this sky-aspiring city. For where else do such towers scrape the clouds? Where else have so many millions of people built such a hive in which to live? Where else do such floods of traffic flow through the streets, or such fleets of ships pour out their cargoes from every corner of the globe? The roar, the glitter, the wealth, the hard, sharp beauty, the magnitude of New York make it a marvel of marvels, without a rival in its field.

Nor does the fascination of this giant metropolis ever grow commonplace. For months, I once occupied an apartment in the very shadow of the Empire State Building. And yet when, at unexpected moments, I'd catch sight, down a narrow cross street, of that soaring shaft with the morning sun full on it, I'd be stopped in my tracks every time. And every time, its vertical bands of shining steel would lead my eyes helplessly up to the lantern, over twelve hundred feet above.

Countless times at night I've seen, from Central Park, the wall of light-flooded spires towering along Fifth Avenue and piercing the night sky. And the last time I saw them, like the first, I was profoundly moved by such a spectacle.

Once I tried to write a book in a house that overlooked New York Harbor. I finally had to move elsewhere because I spent all

58

Ewing Galloway.

The tallest structure in the world is the Empire State Building in New York— 1200 feet above the street. On its summit is a beacon light that can be seen for many miles by ships at sea. On the tip of the beacon is a hitching-post for dirigibles. No dirigible, however, has ever been anchored to it. If one ever *were* attached, it would look like this.

As we sail up New York Harbor from the sea, this glorious picture of Manhattan Island (take from Governor's Island) unfolds before us. Clustered around lower Broadway and Wall Stre these cloud-piercing towers make a dazzling sight. The two tallest ones seen here are nearly

thousand feet high. Each of the others seems to be straining to lift its head higher than its neighbors. If a visitor were to come to our earth from another planet, such views as this would make him certain that New York was the most interesting and astonishing city on our globe.

my working hours gazing out the window at the procession of great ocean liners that kept sailing in and out under my nose.

But no sooner do you get accustomed to a favorite view, in New York, than it's torn up to make way for a bigger and better view. The story is told of a citizen who was taking a visiting Londoner for a sightseeing tour down Park Avenue. The Londoner exclaimed about the size of the Grand Central Station.

"Well, you'd better have a good look at it now," said the New Yorker; "it may not be here when we come back:"

All aboard for this extraordinary city!

We'll take a ship to approach it first, and sail up the Bay from the Atlantic. Manhattan juts toward us like an arrow-head, flanked by the Hudson and the East River. Upon the tip of this arrow, rising tier on tier, are piled a forest of those colossal towers, each straining to lift its head higher than its neighbors, towers that would make King Cheops, who built the Pyramids, blink with astonishment.

And there's the Statue of Liberty, far grander and more beautiful than its pictures.

And there's the famous old Brooklyn Bridge gracefully arching the East River to Long Island. And several miles up the Hudson we catch sight of the pale gray web of the George Washington Bridge, the longest in the world until San Francisco spanned the Golden Gate.

And there's the *Normandie* coming toward us. Perhaps we'll see the *Queen Mary,* or the *Rex,* or the *Europa,* being pushed toward their docks by a swarm of tugs.

We're past the tip of the island now, and into the broad Hudson. The entire sweep of the lower Manhattan skyscraper-wall confronts us. We can pick out the Woolworth Tower, which was once the tallest. Now, however, there are a number of towers much higher. We glance north. There's the Empire State Building, dwarfing everything else. From the top of it one can look down upon all New York, and for miles beyond. Within the range of our eyes is a district where ten million people live.

63

Manhattan Island from three miles high. At the upper left corner we see the George Washing
Bridge spanning the Hudson River and joining New York to New Jersey. On the right is
East River dividing Manhattan from Long Island. The large dark patch near the upper end
the island is Central Park. Countless ships bringing their cargoes to New York's three hund

New York at night! When the city's million lights start gleaming on early evenings in winter, the skyscrapers of Manhattan offer a scene of unbelievable beauty. In this picture, the Chrysler Building, with its black spire and big shining windows, tops all the others. Just to this side of it is the Chanin Building. Near the lower left-hand corner we see half the front face of Grand

Central Railroad Station. Park Avenue runs into this station and around both sides of it. On the right-hand page, the tall building adorned with black vertical bands is the office building of the New York *Daily News.* Across the East River glitter the lights of Brooklyn and Long Island.

We've landed, and are swept into a stream of traffic. Every square foot of every street seems covered with automobiles. We pass the busy entrance to the Holland Tunnels. These are a pair of huge tubes sunk beneath the mud and water of the Hudson, tubes through which a never-ending stream of motor cars, rushing along at forty miles an hour, roll right under the river from New York to New Jersey.

But trying to get anywhere by motor car in New York is slow business, so dense and congested is the traffic. We'll take the subway, and fly along beneath the crowded streets.

What a bewildering place—a subway station! If it's at Times Square we are deafened by the roar of a score of trains—above us, below us, dashing around all sides of us. Did you ever push over an ant hill and see the ants rushing frantically this way and that? A New York subway station is just like a disturbed ant hill . . . thousands of people rushing frantically about.

If it's five o'clock the hubbub is indescribable. Endless lines of express trains draw alongside the platform. The doors roll back and disgorge tons and tons of people. They pour out of the cars the same way water pours out of an opening in the wall of a dam when the water-gate has just been raised.

But just as many people pour in again. And then this train of cars, jammed full of passengers, roars along at a dizzy speed. Flash—flash—flash, the local stations go whizzing by. Suddenly there is a cold wind. We're under the East River. On we go. Presently the train stops. We've traveled three miles in five minutes. We're in Brooklyn. Or, if we got on the wrong train we may plunge out of the dark tunnel into sudden light, and find ourselves moving along the floor of a great suspension bridge. We look up through the windows. There are those ever-soaring sky-scrapers. We look down. We're 150 feet above the river boats. Then into the darkness we plunge again. We wonder where we'll come up this time.

I don't want to give the impression, however, that New York

is just a whirlpool of noise and traffic and congestion. Several million people enjoy living here and wouldn't live anywhere else. One reason they love New York is that it is the center of the nation's culture. Music, art, the theater flourish here. The best orchestras and the best opera company in the world can be heard in New York. Some forty thousand people a day, in the winter season, attend its theaters (apart from the movies). In its museums are collected art treasures from every country. Is it entertainment you want? Is it serious study? Is it opportunity? In *this* city you can find *everything*.

And New York at night! Seen from the harbor after an early winter sunset, with a thousand times a thousand lighted windows shining in the gloom, the skyscrapers of Manhattan offer a scene of unbelievable beauty. All the stars in the heavens seem to have been collected here, and to have been woven in countless ropes that hang from the tower-tops hundreds of feet up in the dark sky.

After nightfall we go to the summit of the seventy-story Radio City building, and look down from the roof. The whole world below is strewn and spangled with shining jewels. Above Times Square the electric signs turn night into day. The forest of steel and stone around Grand Central throbs with light. Broadway, winding north as far as we can see, is a white-hot streak. In the midst of this burning sea, Central Park spreads its patch of velvet shadows. And down the rivers, and across the harbor, the ferry-boats move over the black waves like far-off comets, all ablaze.

In Europe I once listened to a citizen of a foreign nation (who had never been out of his own country) ridiculing America and belittling its accomplishments. I showed him a photograph of New York taken at night when the glitter of the lights was at its highest—a photograph taken from the same high point on which we stand. He looked at it wide-eyed. "I never dreamed there could be any place on earth like that," he said.

And he was never heard to mock America again.

New York in the moonlight. From the top of the Empire State Building on a clear moonlight evening we look south toward the tip of Manhattan, and on toward the lower bay and the sea. Wall Street's black towers stand out against the bright waters of the harbor. The Hudso

Ewing Galloway.

gleams like silver. The whole world below is strewn and spangled with jewels. The streets are white-hot streaks. And upon the shining rivers the ferry-boats, all ablaze, move like far-off comets.

A corner of New York's Central Park. In the midst of this city's roar and congestion, there are quiet and lovely spots like this, where the swans float on the lake, and the trees flower in the spring.

CHAPTER VIII

WASHINGTON

One of the brightest memories of my boyhood was my first trip to Washington. Age fifteen.

Woodrow Wilson was then President, and to my delight, as a special favor, I was taken to the White House, right into the President's office, and introduced to him. My fingers trembled a little when we shook hands . . . to me he was the greatest man in the world. He was *the President*.

He asked me where I went to school.

I told him: "At Lawrenceville, New Jersey." New Jersey was his state. He had been its Governor.

"And are you going to college?" I was hoping he would ask me about this, too.

"Yes—yes. To Princeton," I answered eagerly, "—*your* college!"

Woodrow Wilson had been a student there, had been on the faculty, had been its president.

After a few words about Princeton he asked if he could do anything to help me enjoy my visit to Washington.

"Let me see the rest of the White House," I replied promptly.

He called for a secretary, and I was taken into every room the public is allowed to view. I thought of all the Presidents who had lived and worked here—of President Madison, who had to flee when the British seized Washington and gutted the White House with fire—of the high-spirited Andrew Jackson, always in a fight—of Lincoln, and the four tragic years he resided in this mansion, struggling to preserve the Union—of Ulysses S. Grant, and the misfortunes of that great soldier when he was made the nation's Chief Executive by a worshipful people—of Cleveland, who moved out after one term of office only to come back again—of Teddy

73

The heart of the city of Washington is the Mall, stretching from the Washington Monument to the Capitol. No city in any country offers a grander or more beautiful vista. This two-mile prospect is bounded by stately government buildings. At the extreme left, the first of the row of white buildings (with only the corner showing) is the Department of Commerce. Then comes the

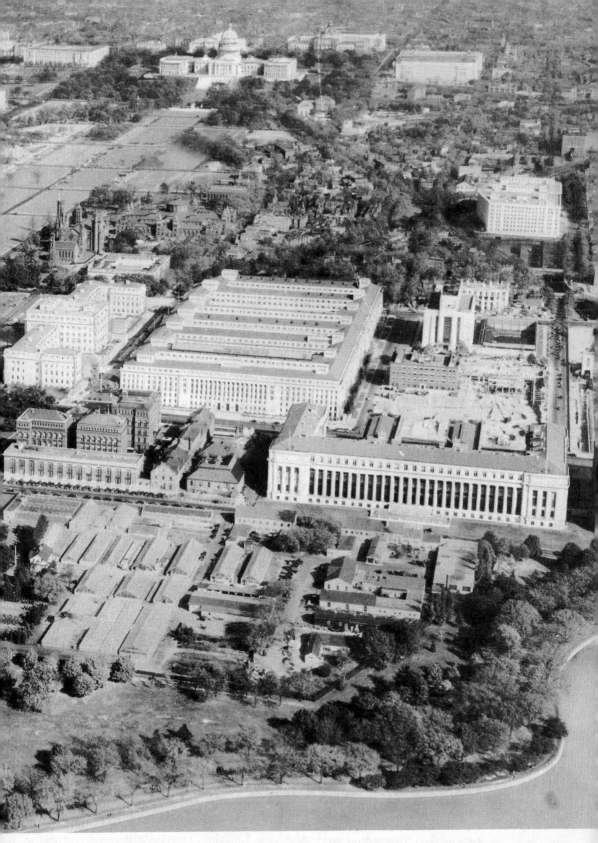

Post Office Department, followed by the Department of Justice and the Archives Building. Standing alone in the Mall is the National Museum. At the far end looms the majestic Capitol. The three large buildings on right—hand side are occupied by the Department of Agriculture and the Bureau of Engraving. Above everything soars the gleaming white monument to George Washington.

Fairchild Aerial Surveys.

Roosevelt's colorful years. And now Woodrow Wilson. I did not know that before many more months had passed, Wilson, in that very room where we'd met, would be reliving Lincoln's unhappy rôle—directing the nation into, and through, all the horrors and all the heartbreak of a great war.

From the White House I went to the Capitol, and watched the Senate in session. One of the Tennessee senators, a friend of my father's, took me out to lunch. We sat at a big table in the Senate dining room. Four more senators joined us. When they learned that I'd had an audience with the President they asked me all about it. One senator said:

"I've been trying for weeks to see that man—and this schoolboy is allowed to walk right in. Dick, the next time you call on the President will you take me?"

I thought these statesmen very jolly—not nearly so stern as I'd expected. Every time another senator passed by, my Tennessee host, who seemed to know them all by their first names, would say: "Hello, Joe—come on over. I want you to meet a young friend of mine. He's just seen the President, and thinks he's all right." And I'd shake hands with another famous personage around the Capitol. I must have met twenty or more senators. Ten of them gave me cigars!

And then I went to Mount Vernon and stood before George Washington's tomb and walked through the rooms where he had walked. Last of all, and best, I climbed 555 feet right to the top of the Washington Monument, and looked down on all the stately buildings that housed the government of our country.

Boy! Was I proud that day to be an American!

This was years ago. Since then I've returned to Washington time and time again. But each time, as I have watched it grow in splendor and in beauty, I have received fresh inspiration, and been proud, all over again, to be an American.

Fairchild Aerial Surveys.

To George Washington and Abraham Lincoln, America's greatest heroes, a grateful nation has raised these two wonderful monuments in our national capital. The Lincoln Memorial, built in the form of a Greek temple, is of marble. The Washington Monument, 555 feet high, is of granite. The Capitol Building (with its dome hidden behind the Monument) lies a mile beyond.

Washington celebrates the Fourth of July. Skyrockets burst near the Monument and cast their reflections in the water-mirror. The tip of the Monument, bathed in floodlights, shines against the dark sky. On the horizon we can see the illuminated dome of the Capitol. Washington is

wonder-city that should be visited by every American. Its beauty and dignity will make him love his country more. He will have a greater reverence for its past, and a greater confidence in its future. No one should write about the marvels of the world and leave out Washington.

Keystone.

No one should write about the wonders of the world, and leave out Washington.

From New York it isn't far, especially if we go by plane.

One should see our capital city from the air—from *high* in the air. Only then can one appreciate how carefully and ably it was planned, and how faithfully these plans have been carried out. The city, as much as the Monument, is a memorial to George Washington. It was he, almost alone among the leaders of his time, who looked forward to the enormous growth of this country and saw the necessity of a great Federal capital suitable to a great nation. It was he who selected the site. It was he who appointed the French engineer, L'Enfant, to design plans for a city that he visioned as magnificent as Paris. And it was he who laid the cornerstone of the Capitol.

How filled with joy and satisfaction George Washington would be if he could see his city now, with all his hopes and visions come to pass; if he could see his Capitol, a building unsurpassed in the world for noble and majestic beauty. How his eyes would stare at the new blocks of marble architecture facing the Mall, at the Supreme Court's shining Greek temple, at the purity and perfection of the Lincoln Memorial, at the graceful marble bridge that spans the Potomac, linking the city with his own Virginia!

No city in any country offers a grander or more beautiful vista than the Mall—that sweep of parkway from the Lincoln Memorial to the Washington Monument and on to the Capitol. Clear of all obstruction—except the Monument—adorned with green lawns and reflecting pools, bounded by trees and splendid government buildings, this two-mile prospect is truly one of the great sights of the world. Whether we climb to the dome of the Capitol and look toward the Memorial, or stand beneath the marble columns of the Memorial and look toward the Capitol, we enjoy an inspiring view that should be seen by every American. It will make him love his country more. He will have a greater reverence for its past, and a greater confidence in its future.

The Capitol from the air. George Washington laid the cornerstone for this noble building. He planned it to be the center of the great Federal city, suitable to a great nation. How filled with joy he would be if he could see his city now, as we see it! How proud he would be of the Supreme Court's Greek temple (near the upper right-hand corner), of the magnificent Library of Congress (next to it); and of the splendid buildings providing offices for the Senate (upper left corner), and of the House of Representatives (lower right corner)!

The great granite pillar rising in the middle of the Mall dominates all else. Though it is a monument to his own glory, I believe George Washington would say that this soaring shaft was the most impressive and the most beautiful of the national structures. How pleased he would be that it has been designed on such simple lines—straight, tall, self-contained, unadorned.

In my opinion, it belongs high on the list in our book of marvels, partly because of its heroic size, and partly because, more than any other monument to the memory of a man, it expresses the nature of that man. "Build it to the skies," exclaimed an American patriot; "you cannot outreach the loftiness of George Washington's character. Found it upon the massive and eternal rock; you cannot make it more enduring than his fame."

I've seen the Monument many times myself—on bright days when the sun beat hot upon it and lifted it boldly away from the background of blue summer sky. I've seen it on gray days—pale, pearl and serene, floating with the clouds, linking the heaven and the earth; and at night, with the flood-lights in full play transforming it into a great column of flame reaching toward the stars.

It is a most familiar sight, but never once, no matter what its mood, have I been other than inspired by this towering granite sword, by its strength and integrity. From time to time, I have feared that greed, and ignorance, and injustice, were threatening to destroy our country, feared we were losing all the ideals George Washington bestowed upon us. But just one look at his Monument has given me, and thousands like me, new faith in America and in the American creed that I learned as a child. It rises into the sky as a defender of noble standards, of honest dealing in public affairs, and as a defiance to every enemy who would drag down the institutions that have made our country great.

No monument was ever built to better purpose than this one, for as long as it guards our capital we can be sure that honor and justice, order and sanity, will prevail.

Build George Washington's monument to the skies," exclaimed an American patriot; "you nnot outreach the loftiness of his character." No one can look at this soaring white shaft and t feel a surge of inspiration. Straight, tall, unadorned, it rises in the sky as a defender of all the high ideals George Washington gave to America.

Atlantic Ocean

Pacific Ocean

UNITED STATES

MEXICO
Vera Cruz
Mexico City
POPOCATEPETL
CHICHEN
KEY WEST
CUBA
Christobal's
GUATEMALA
HONDURAS
NICARAGUA
COSTA RICO
PANAMA

VENEZUELA
Caracas
COLOMBIA
Bogota
GUIANA BR. D.
ECUADOR
Quito
PERU
Lima
MACHU PICCHU
Cuzco
La Paz
BOLIVIA

B R A Z I L

Amazon
PARAGUAY River
PARAGUAY
Parana River
ARGENTINA
CHILE

RIO DE JANEIRO 16
IGUAZU FALLS 15
IGUAZU RIVER
URU

FORT JEFFERSON 9

CHICHEN 11

12

PANAMA 13

MAP showing location
of FORT JEFFERSON,
of Marvels in CENTRAL
and SOUTH AMERICA
and our route of travel
Chapter
9 Fort Jefferson
Chapter
10 Popocatepetl
Chapter
11 Chichen Itza
Chapter
12 Christophei Castle
Chapter
13 Panama Canal
Chapter
14 Machu Picchu
Chapter
15 Iguazu Falls
Chapter
16 Rio Harbor

CHAPTER IX

FORT JEFFERSON

On the night of April fourteenth, 1865—five days after General Lee's surrender to General Grant had brought an end to the Civil War—President Lincoln was attending the theater, in Washington. In the middle of the performance, a misguided Confederate sympathizer, an actor named John Wilkes Booth, seeking to avenge the defeat of the South, slipped into the presidential box and shot Lincoln, inflicting a wound from which he died a few hours later.

Having committed this monstrous crime, Booth leaped from the box to the stage, and fled.

But his dramatic leap was not altogether successful. His spur caught in the American flag that draped the President's box, and tripped him in such a manner that he broke his leg when he landed on the stage.

Even so, before anybody was able to stop him, he managed to limp out the back door, mounted a waiting horse, and with a fellow-conspirator disappeared into the night.

Five hours later (at four in the morning) Booth and his companion, looking for a doctor to set Booth's leg and relieve the torture he was suffering, were directed to the house of Samuel Mudd, a doctor living in southern Maryland. Doctor Mudd, knowing nothing of the assassination, and acting only as any doctor would to a stranger in such great distress, set the leg, bound it up, and persuaded the two travelers to remain in his house the rest of the night. Next morning Booth and his friend, using assumed names, paid the bill and departed.

Because of this merciful act Doctor Mudd was arrested, taken to Washington, and tried on the charge that he was a friend of Booth's and had helped plan the assassination.

Doctor Mudd insisted that he knew nothing of the plot. But the military courts, vengeful beyond all reason, sentenced the unfortunate doctor to life imprisonment.

The prison chosen was Fort Jefferson, and to this place Doctor Mudd was sent in chains. He had every reason to believe that he would not live long here, for Fort Jefferson had the most evil reputation of any prison in the country. That it was also one of the most extraordinary structures, not only in America but in all the world, probably concerned the doomed man very little.

In 1846 our government, desiring further to strengthen our coast line against foreign invasion, decided to build a fort on one of the Dry Tortugas, a group of tiny coral islets out in the Gulf of Mexico, 120 miles west of the southern tip of Florida. As it was intended that this fort should rule over all shipping entering the Gulf, the military authorities tried to make it the Gibraltar of America.

With nothing to build on but a waterless, wave-swept coral key, and with their source of supplies in Philadelphia, thirteen hundred miles away by sea, the army engineers erected the largest mass of unreinforced masonry ever raised by Americans— that is to say, masonry that is all brick and stone and not held together in any way by steel or concrete beams. Six-sided, it was built around an enormous court one thousand feet long and fifteen acres in extent—a plot of ground as big as twenty football fields. The walls were fifty feet high and dropped right down to the sea, so that the coral key was all *inside* the fort. To protect these walls from the waves, and to help keep out enemies, a water-filled moat was made by encircling the whole fort with a separate breakwater built out thirty feet from the walls. In the fort's construction fifty million bricks were used, all brought by sea from Philadelphia. To fortify it, four hundred guns were mounted behind the gun-ports and on the battlements. No other American military project ever demanded such staggering amounts of labor and material, or was ever built at such great cost—a dollar for every brick, some people said.

Fort Jefferson, built by the United States Government in 1846, on a coral islet in the Gulf of Mexico, was designed to be the Gibraltar of America. Its location is 120 miles west of the southern tip of Florida. In this Fort's construction, 50,000,000 bricks were used, and the cost is said to have been a dollar for every brick. Some four hundred monster-guns looked through the gun-ports. The parade ground inside the walls was as big as twenty football fields. But this enormous Fort never fired a shot at an enemy. It served chiefly as a Federal prison during the Civil War. The most celebrated prisoner was Dr. Samuel Mudd, sentenced to life imprisonment for having set the broken leg of John Wilkes Booth, who assassinated President Lincoln.

Nor did any other fort ever turn out to be such utter folly. The water about the fort, the engineers soon found out, was too shallow for enemy boats to approach within cannon range. And so, seeing that it was useless as a fort, the government, during the Civil War, turned it into a military prison. Then, about 1870, this huge and desolate building was abandoned, and given over to the ghosts of prisoners who had perished there by the hundreds, and to the sea birds that had come in to take possession of this vastest ruin in all America.

It was not foreign enemies or wars that caused the final abandonment of Fort Jefferson, but traitors from within—the mosquitoes. These tiny villains bred in swarms in the rain-water cisterns, and, unopposed, scattered their deadly yellow-fever germs. They attacked everyone who came to the little coral key—the soldiers, the prisoners, the guards, the officials. Several times epidemics of the fatal fever spread so rapidly that the afflicted died faster than they could be buried.

Into this sinister, fever-ridden fortress in the sea, Doctor Mudd was thrust. The guards chained him to the floor of his cell and singled out "that Lincoln murderer" for the harshest treatment. Before he had been there very long the terrible pestilence struck again. As usual everybody went down before it. The prison doctor died. Doctor Mudd volunteered his services and was accepted. Then he too caught the disease. But he *had* to live, for he was the only doctor left to treat a thousand fever cases. And live he did.

Meanwhile his wife, back in Washington, was working heroically in her husband's behalf. And after a four-year struggle she succeeded in getting him "pardoned"—pardoned for a crime he had never committed.

Soon after Doctor Mudd departed, the other prisoners and soldiers were likewise transferred elsewhere, and the mosquitoes were left in complete possession of Fort Jefferson.

Today, this grim and tragic structure, dead and almost forgotten, but intact, still stands on its coral key. Except that most

of the guns are missing—Cubans took them for scrap iron—Fort
Jefferson presents the same picture that Doctor Mudd beheld
when in 1869 he departed from this cursed place—free.

Let's go and see it for ourselves.

From Key West, a Florida town built on an island sixty
miles off the tip of the peninsula at a point half-way from the
mainland to the fort, we take a fishing boat. All night we travel
westward across the waters of the Gulf, and at dawn wake to find
the scowling walls of the fortress ahead of us, rising like a sea-
monster with a hundred eyes, right out of the waves.

We land at the crumbling dock where Doctor Mudd landed in
1865. There is not a human being in sight. A bridge takes us
across the thirty-foot moat and into the portal.

Inside the walls we come upon the enormous parade ground
—the twenty football fields. But it is strewn with weeds and
wreckage. From time to time tropical hurricanes have struck the
fort, and torn to pieces the abandoned barracks and wooden sheds
inside the court. These same storms have likewise smashed the
breakwater in several places, and through the breach tons of sand
have swept to fill the moat on two of the fort's six sides.

But the massive walls themselves seem to scorn every assault.
After all the raging battles with the sea and wind, scarcely one
of the fifty million bricks is out of place.

We wander down the long vaulted corridors. In these corridors rows and rows of cannon once stood, pointing their muzzles
through the cannon ports . . . all gone now. We pass the rows
of cells where the prisoners were kept. We enter one of the
darkest and dampest. It was Doctor Mudd's.

We climb to the top of the walls and look over the inside edge,
down upon the acres of devastation in the court. We see piles of
plaster and timbers where houses once stood, and thickets of cactus
that might once have been gardens. The wreckage is evidence of
the cruel power of the hurricanes.

Entirely around Fort Jefferson runs a moat thirty feet wide and ten feet deep. On the outs edge of the moat a breakwater keeps the waves from beating against the Fort's walls. But, as can see, on the left side of the Fort hurricanes have made a gap in the breakwater and filled moat with sand. These same storms have also wrecked the barracks on the parade ground. T

rible epidemics of yellow fever caused Fort Jefferson to be abandoned about 1870. No one lives on the island now, but the Fort is far from quiet. Overhead fly countless sea birds which, day and night, keep up a screaming that beats upon one's ears. They live on Bird Key, a bird preserve on the flat island in the background. Fort Jefferson was made a National Monument in 1934.

Photograph by Lieutenant Schildhauer of the Cuban Aerial Survey.

We look over the outside edge, down into the moat. Beyond, on all sides, is the open sea breaking against the low wall that protects the fort from the waves. In the moat itself, so an often-told story goes, the prison officials in the old days kept a school of hungry sharks. To escape from Fort Jefferson, prisoners had to swim this moat and brave the sharks. Few dared risk it . . . or so the legend claims.

Had *you* been a prisoner, which course would you have chosen? Would you have tried to escape and taken your chances with the hungry sharks, or would you have stayed on in this terrible place to be eaten by the yellow-fever mosquitoes? You would have stayed in the prison, of course, because nobody knew, in those days, that it was the mosquito that carried the deadly germ. In fact Doctor Mudd himself, when he was trying to control the epidemic, had the few soldiers who were able to stand, brick up the gun-ports "to keep out the yellow-fever poison that rises from the moat."

We are alone, but the fort is far from quiet. Overhead fly myriads of seabirds—terns and noddies—which, day and night, keep up a screaming that beats upon one's ears. Thousands and thousands of them live on a coral islet five hundred feet away. There they lay their eggs upon the sand and rear their young. A sudden sharp noise, or a fight among themselves, may cause the whole colony to spring into the air, and circle in such countless multitudes over the fort that they literally shut out the sun. At the time I visited their island I could not walk on the beach without stepping on their eggs, or make my voice heard above the uproar without shouting at the top of my lungs. When the hurricanes come, the great waves sweep completely over the flat island, and destroy every bush and blade of grass. But the birds keep coming back and building anew, seeming to feel they are safest when watched over by the grim walls and tumbled cannon of old Fort Jefferson.

We can visit Bird Key ourselves. It's a government refuge now for the terns and noddies, and as they are carefully protected

In the spring, Bird Key, the island close to Fort Jefferson, becomes the home of thousands and thousands of terns and noddies. These sea birds come from all over the Western Hemisphere. They build no nests but lay their eggs, and raise their young, on the sand. The eggs are so close together that it is impossible to walk on the beach without stepping on them. Hurricanes frequently drive great waves over the flat island and destroy the eggs. But the birds keep coming back.

they never have learned to be afraid of human beings. If you like, you can approach a mother noddie on her nest and stroke her head. And she will just sit there and purr like a kitten.

After my first visit to Fort Jefferson I wrote a story about it. A reader of this story sent me a letter, one of the most interesting and surprising letters I have ever received. And now that you've been with me to the fort, you'll take delight in this letter, too:

"NEWTON, MASS.

"Dear Richard Halliburton:

"In 1868, when Dr. Mudd was a prisoner in Fort Jefferson, *I lived there.* I was a little girl, thirteen years old, so you can see that I'm quite an old lady now. My father, an army lieutenant in the fort's garrison, had charge of the food supplies. A West Point graduate, he had been sent to the fort at the opening of the Civil War.

"For some reason he took my mother along with him, and my brother and sister and myself. We lived in the fort during most of the war. Just before the end of it, in 1865, when I was ten, my mother took us children to Key West to put us in school, as the only school in the fort was a tent, with one of the army sergeants as teacher. While we were in Key West, Lee surrendered to Grant; President Lincoln was assassinated by John Wilkes Booth; and Dr. Mudd was sent to our prison. Fortunately we were still in Key West in 1867 when the terrible yellow-fever epidemic of that year struck Fort Jefferson. My father was still on duty at the fort, but he had already lived through one attack of the fever and was immune. So he was able to help Dr. Mudd care for the stricken when the regular army doctor died. I believe my father helped nurse Dr. Mudd when *he* was taken sick.

"After the epidemic had passed, my father brought us back to the fort, and we stayed on there to the end of Dr. Mudd's imprisonment. I must have seen him among the hundreds of prisoners, though probably not very often as we were kept away from the prison quarters.

"The side of the fort in the picture that accompanies your story looks very familiar. Many times have my brother and I fished in the moat for crabs through the second row of portholes. In the picture I recognize the little house in the court where they condensed the sea water so that we could use it for drinking. But I cannot find the long, low wooden barracks for soldiers that used to stand near the entrance.

"I enjoyed your story about the sharks in the moat. But it is not true. There never was more than a single shark—one caught by two soldiers. They baited it with a piece of salt pork, and dragged it through the sluiceways into the moat. Then all the sluiceways were wired over so the shark could not get out. He was a sort of pet villain that we fed every day. I'm sure we could not have fed many sharks, as ham and canned meats were all the provisions we had, and too expensive for shark food.

"I do not believe there are any other people left alive who could tell you about Fort Jefferson as it was at that time.

"Forgive my writing at such length, but your story brought so many memories back to me I could not help sending this letter.

"Sincerely,

"Mary Wales Glover."

How pleased Mary Glover must have been when, in 1934, the government made Fort Jefferson a National Monument! For such a move assured her that this marvelous old sea-castle, her childhood home, standing in utter loneliness out there in the Gulf, would henceforth receive Federal attention and protection, as it fights its wild battles with the hurricanes, on through the years.

The moat around Fort Jefferson kept prisoners in, and enemies out.

CHAPTER X

POPOCATEPETL

Many people have asked me: "Which is the most beautiful country you have ever seen?"

And they are always surprised when I say Mexico.

But they would not be surprised if they had been there, for Mexico has beautiful people, beautiful flowers and forests, beautiful towns and villages. Above all, it has beautiful mountains. With Fujiyama and the Himalayas excepted, it is my opinion that Mexico's celebrated giant peaks, Orizaba (oh-ri-zah'-bah), Popocatepetl (poh-poh-kah-tay'-pet-l), and Ixtaccihuatl (iss-tok-see-wah'-tl), which means the Sleeping Woman, are the three most beautiful mountains in the world.

When the Spaniards came in 1519, Mexico was inhabited by a race of Indians called the Aztecs. We think of "Indians" as a naked, primitive people living in wigwams and hunting with bows and arrows. But not the Aztecs. *These* Indians were, in some respects, more civilized than the Spaniards themselves. They lived in splendid stone cities. Their great capital, Tenochtitlan (tee-noch-teet'-lan)—built where Mexico City now stands—had more inhabitants than Madrid at that time. Like the Egyptians, they built huge stone temples and pyramids. Their chief lived in a splendid palace. As stonemasons, goldsmiths, weavers, they were among the best in history. Even today the very ruins of their empire are among the first wonders of archeology.

But these highly cultured people had one custom that scored heavily against them—human sacrifice. Their gods were not kind and loving gods, but, with one or two exceptions, cruel and ferocious. Nothing except the gift of bleeding human hearts would persuade them to bless their worshipers.

In each Aztec city, on top a towering, mound-like temple called a *teocalli,* living victims were stretched before stone images of the gods, and their hearts cut out by the priests. (But don't you be afraid when we go to Mexico. These sacrifices took place long ago.)

96

Hugo Brehme.

Two of the most beautiful mountains in the world are in Mexico—Popocatepetl (the volcano on the left) and Ixtaccihuatl (The Sleeping Woman) on the right. This view was taken from the summit of a great pyramid built by the ancient Aztec Indians. On this summit, as the sun sank into Popo's crater, the Aztec priests used to sacrifice living human beings to their gods. A church stands on top of the pyramid now.

The great Sacred City of the Aztecs was called Cholula. Here, pilgrims from all Aztec-land flocked to worship and take part in the religious ceremonies. In this city, in honor of the supreme Aztec god, a stupendous *teocalli,* fourteen hundred feet on each side at the base, was reared. This *teocalli* is the largest monument ever built in the Americas. On top of its flat summit stood the holiest temple of the Aztecs, sheltering the image of the dreadful deity. And before this image hundreds of human hearts were offered up each year.

The pagan temple was long ago torn down from the top of the pyramid. In its place the Christian Mexicans built one of their first churches where they have continued to worship a better Deity in a gentler way than the Aztecs did. Unfortunately they have allowed the stone slopes of the pyramid to fall into ruin, and to be overgrown with bushes and small trees.

However, they may well continue to call such a spot holy! For surely nowhere else in the world is there a scene so likely to fill one with religious awe. To the west, in all their white majesty, rise Popocatepetl and the Sleeping Woman; and to the east, Orizaba. All three are poems of snow and far-off mystery. Popo, the smoking, the terrible volcano with a lilting, rolling name, soars 17,900 feet into the clouds, overtopping by 1000 feet its white-draped neighbor. Orizaba, 400 feet higher than Popo, is the highest and loveliest thing from Mount McKinley in Alaska to the Andes. Higher than the greatest Alps are these mountains. Half a mile and more Popo towers above Mont Blanc, and Popo's pale-veiled sister sleeps 2000 feet above the Matterhorn; while the peak of Orizaba would grace the very Himalayas with its unearthly beauty.

Of the three, Popo, to the Aztecs, was the most sacred and the most commanding, because it smoked and roared. Then, too, it played a grim rôle in their religious ceremonies. This volcano was directly west of the Cholula *teocalli,* so that the sun, if one watched it from the great pyramid, sank right into the smoking crater and was gobbled up. And when the last gleam disappeared —that was the signal for the priest to strike.

98

Popo is still there, still soaring above Cholula, still smoking, still crowned with clouds and snow. The brush-covered *teocalli* at its base is still there too.

And we are going to Mexico from Fort Jefferson, to see for ourselves this wonderful pyramid and this wonderful Popo.

We get off our boat at Vera Cruz, and travel inland. What glorious scenery—wild mountains and canyons, smothered in hanging moss and ferns and flowers! Arriving at Cholula we easily spot the *teocalli* because it is 180 feet high. Today it looks like one more forested hill, but its pyramidal shape has not changed.

In the late afternoon we reach the base and find the steps that zigzag up the face of the *teocalli*. Up these same steps, five hundred years ago, the Aztec sacrificial procession began its climb. We can imagine what such a procession was like—chanting priests in their barbaric feather headdress and feathered cloaks, escorting the victim and followed by many worshipers.

Higher and higher climb the Aztec multitude. The summit is reached. The sacrificial stone beside the image of the god is ready. There is no time to lose. The sun is all but touching Popo's snows.

Standing on the summit ourselves, and using our imagination, we see the victim·seized, his garments stripped away, his body stretched, chest up, on top of the stone block. We see five priests press down his limbs and head. A sixth is poised, knife in hand, above the waiting breast. . . .

A thousand people hold their breath.

Popo, in respect to the Aztec gods, is pouring forth a shaft of smoke into the high heavens. The sun has dipped into the crater crest . . . a half remains—a rim—a final signal gleam.

The knife descends. . . .

But let's stop thinking about such events, and enjoy the glorious picture of Popo, with its icy crown set on fire by the last rays of the sun. We mean to climb that mountain. It's too beautiful and too beckoning to resist.

99

Popo (on the right) and The Sleeping Woman (on the left) seen from a hilltop near Mexico C?
The outlines of the sleeping woman can be clearly traced in the snow. Popo is 17,900 feet h?
over 3000 feet higher than the highest mountain in the United States. Popo's sister, across
saddle, is one thousand feet lower. When Cortez, the Spanish conqueror, and his army of

Hugo Brehme.

nturers were invading Mexico in 1519, he marched between these two mountains. On our visit Popo we follow Cortez' trail through the gap, and are shaded by the same ancient pines that aded him. The first white man ever to climb Popo was one of Cortez' officers who explored the volcano's crater looking for sulphur which the army needed for gunpowder.

And the road we'll take there from Cholula is the same road Cortez followed in 1519, at the time of his conquest of Mexico.

Of course you know the story of Cortez. It is one of the immortal stories of history. With only four hundred men this great Spanish leader, coming to a strange land, the size and strength of which were all unknown, landed at Vera Cruz and burned his ships behind him. His followers, with no hope of escape, had to conquer or die. They were opposed by huge armies of well-trained and very brave Aztecs. But the Indians recoiled before the roar of Cortez' cannon and before the terrifying sight of men riding on *horses*. That made it possible for Cortez to defeat them time and time again, even when they outnumbered him a hundred to one.

The Spaniards' march led to Cholula; and then their route to Tenochtitlan wound on westward over the nine-thousand-foot saddle that connects Popo with the Sleeping Woman.

And we follow in their steps, climbing the trail that Cortez climbed, shaded by the same ancient pines that shaded him. We reach the summit of the saddle. Cortez could look down the other slope and see the Aztec capital. We can look down the same slope and see, on the same spot, the church spires of Mexico City.

Cortez himself did not stop to climb Popo, but he sent one of his officers into the crater to collect sulphur, which the army needed to make gunpowder. This officer was the first white man to ascend the mountain—perhaps the first person.

We must start our climb at three o'clock in the morning, and get as high up as we can before dawn, for the sun will burn our faces terribly at this high altitude, and melt the snow and make it slippery and treacherous.

Remember, we're going to climb almost eighteen thousand feet. Did you get tired climbing Half Dome in Yosemite? That was just half as high as this. No one but good climbers with stout hearts and lungs should challenge Popo. Everybody still wants to try? Very well then—don't forget your climbing staff and sun glasses. Here we go—to the peak—and no surrender!

Our trail, straight up the blunt cone, is deep in volcanic ash. Nearly two miles above, lighted by a million tropical stars, we see the icy summit flooded with luster. We sink ankle-deep in the cinders as we climb up the steep slope. Our progress is painfully slow. Our hearts pound furiously. More and more frequently we stop to rest and get our breath.

Struggling on, foot by foot, we reach thirteen thousand feet— higher than the summit of Fujiyama. On to fourteen thousand feet. Here the snow begins in earnest, and the wind and the dawn. We dig into the ever-steepening slope, noticing at the same time how the sky is growing red behind the peak of Orizaba, a hundred miles away, and how the Sleeping Woman, pale and snow-draped beyond the forested saddle, is beginning to awaken.

Up and up we crawl, higher than the summit of Mount Rainier —the horizon is bursting into flame; higher than Pike's Peak—the lights of Mexico City have faded; past the terrible Matterhorn— Popo's ice-armored pinnacle glitters in the sunrise; past fifteen thousand—past Mont Blanc—past sixteen thousand. We sink prostrate in the snow to rest and to relieve the cruel throbbing in our heads. The rising sun burns our eyes, despite the smoked glasses, and the icy blasts try to tear us from the slope.

But still we struggle on. Three steps in the snow, and three minutes' rest. We are gasping for breath. We reach seventeen thousand. Here, with only eight hundred feet more to go, a blast of extra-savage wind screeches down from above. We are completely blown over by it, and must dig our fingers in the slope to keep from being flung down the mountain side.

We recover, and grimly flounder toward the summit. This mountain *has* no summit. We are climbing to the moon up a ladder made of ice. The earth has floated far away. There is only wind, and light, and space, and a dull drowsiness in which we feel our mechanical legs sinking into the snow, and hear a violent knocking somewhere inside.

Now all at once the shimmering disappears and a black and ominous void drifts before us. . . .

103

Popo's beautiful snowy peak calls to all mountain climbers. We start our own climb at three o'clock in the morning. Our trail, straight up the blunt cone, is deep in volcanic ash. Nearly two miles above us we see the icy summit flooded with luster. Our progress is painfully slow

Through the snow we climb higher than Mount Rainier; higher than the Matterhorn; higher than Mont Blanc. When at last we reach the summit we are nearly 18,000 feet above the sea.

When we reach the pinnacle of Popo, a black and bottomless hole opens before us. Out of it pour roaring clouds of sulphurous smoke. It's the crater. We seem to be on the edge of the world. The wind rages about us, and the cold cuts to our very bones. We take a picture of the crater

The crater! We are on top and staring into the crater! On top!

One clear look about us, and we forget the conflict with the mountain. We seem to be on the roof of the world—nearly eighteen thousand feet. The wind rages about the crater crest, and the cold cuts through us, but we can stand it now, warmed by the joy of a battle won.

We must not stay too long, or we'll be frozen by the blasts. We take a picture of the smoking, snow-swirling crater, and fling ourselves down the iceberg slopes, fleeing from the pinnacle as if all the Aztec demons were after us.

Now that it's all over, are you half-dead? Is your face cooked? Is your nose frozen? Perhaps you won't be able even to walk tomorrow, your muscles will be so stiff. I couldn't, after *my* first Popo climb.

But we'll soon forget all about these miseries, and only remember, the rest of our lives, that we accepted the challenge, and climbed to the top of that glorious, gleaming Popo—one of the highest volcanoes in the world.

CHAPTER XI

THE RAIN GOD'S CITY

If you look at a map of the Gulf of Mexico, you'll see, jutting up into the middle of it from the southern side, a huge peninsula. This is the peninsula of Yucatan, and part of Mexico. Today it is a poor and, for the most part, uninhabited country. But five hundred years ago it was the home of a race of Indians called the Mayas (pronounced mah'-yahz), who had a culture even higher than the Aztecs.

Like the Aztecs these Mayas built fine stone cities, and had a marvelous capital. This capital, called Chichen Itza (chee-chen eat'-zah), has a fascinating history.

When the Mayas first moved into Yucatan, they found, near the center of the peninsula, a spot where the crust of the earth, in two places, had sunk to a depth of seventy feet, revealing, at this depth, two pools of deep water. These pools were a mile apart and each about seventy-five yards across. Assured of a water supply, they founded a city here. Chichen Itza means the City of the Itzas at the Mouth of the Wells.

One of these wells the citizens used for drinking, and for irrigating their fields of corn. The other was sacred. *This* pool held water sixty feet deep, and had seventy-foot sheer rock walls reaching down to where the water began. To the Mayas the whole appearance of this second pool seemed so gloomy and mysterious that they held it in great awe, and believed their god of rain, Yum-Chac, dwelt and held his court in its depths.

In honor of Yum-Chac, the priests built a marble altar at the brink of the well. Leading to the altar was a causeway—a raised stone road—fifteen feet broad and a quarter of a mile in length. Hundreds of sacred images in the form of feathered serpents, likewise of stone, reared up their heads along the two edges to form balustrades. And at the causeway's other end there arose a glorious temple—a white stone pyramid, one hundred feet high,

108

two hundred feet square at the base, and topped by a stone shrine.

This pool, this causeway, and this temple, played an important part in Mayan life. Together they served somewhat the same purpose the *teocallis* served in Mexico—a setting for human sacrifice.

When the rain would not fall and the corn began to wither, the Mayas felt that Yum-Chac was angry with them. To please him they believed they had to fling down to him, down into his deep pool, a beautiful fourteen-year-old maiden to be his bride.

The whole nation took a deep interest in this offering to Yum-Chac. Throughout the country all work stopped. Everyone who could, traveled to Chichen Itza to witness the sacrifice. Just before dawn on the morning of the Great Day the sacrificial procession gathered in the shrine at the summit of the pyramid-temple. Down the steep stone steps it moved. The King and his generals and his high priests led the way. Last of all came the covered chair enclosing the wretched little girl, dressed in her bridal gown and bridal veil.

Slowly this tragic procession, marching to the sound of drums and flutes, passed along the causeway—straight toward the altar —straight toward Yum-Chac's yawning pit.

But let's not just read about this wonderful city and its strange ceremonies. Let's go to Chichen Itza and see for ourselves where the sacrifice took place. Let's see the pyramids and palaces and temples and monuments—and even (though it may sadden us) the watery pit into which the little bride was flung.

Chichen Itza was abandoned by its people about five hundred years ago. No one knows why they went away. The entire population, over one hundred thousand strong, just disappeared, leaving their cooking pots on the hearth, their plows in the field. Did some terrible disease come and slay them all? Did the more powerful Aztecs capture the city and drag the people away into captivity? When the Spaniards came they found the beautiful white city uninhabited but unharmed. They found the buildings intact, but only snakes, bats and jaguars lived in them.

In Mexico, on the peninsula of Yucatan, are found the ruins of the wonderful city of Chichen Itza, built by the Maya Indians five hundred years ago. In this city stood stately temples, monuments, palaces, all made of white stone. The greatest of the monuments is this 100-foot pyramid, topped by a stone shrine. From this shrine and down these steps the little Bride of the Rain God

was carried to the Well of Death, accompanied by a solemn procession. To watch this ceremony, thousands of Maya Indians gathered on the steep slopes of the pyramid. Here they had a splendid view.

As Yucatan had no gold the Spaniards gave it scant attention. Not so the jungle. As the years passed, creepers, bushes and trees attacked the deserted buildings and slowly made wrecks of them. By the year 1900 the palaces were piles of jumbled stones, and the central pyramid merely a grass-covered mound in the forest. The overturned stones, however, were still unbroken so that archeologists were able, in recent times, to clear away the jungle growth and reconstruct the most important buildings. Today the temples and monuments stand, to a great extent, as they stood in 1400, to astonish everyone who passes by.

To get there we return to Vera Cruz from Cholula, cross the Gulf of Mexico by boat, and land on the north coast of Yucatan. A four-hour train trip and a short motor ride through the forests take us to Chichen Itza. We turn a corner, and behold!—the pyramid, crowned with the temple, rises before us in the distance. The automobile stops at its base, and we get out, eager to climb to the top. We scramble up the ninety ladder-like steps, reach the summit, and look back down the slope and over the silent jungle.

What a wonderful view! On one side we see a stone palace on top of a lofty terraced base. The roofless Temple of a Thousand Columns is just below it. In another direction we see the largest structure of all—the stone stadium where the athletic games were held. On another side appears the gracefully built observatory where the Mayan astronomers watched the stars and studied the heavens. And all about, scattered through the jungle, we see other public buildings, all white, all stone, suggesting to us a smaller Washington. (Do you suppose the time will come, centuries hence, when visitors—perhaps from another planet— will dig away the forests from the site of our own capital, and marvel at the ruins of the Lincoln Memorial and the White House and the Monument, and write stories about the wonderful civilization those ancient Americans developed back in the twentieth century?)

112

A Chichen Itza temple seen from the top of the great pyramid. The heavy black stone projecting from the wall is the head of a Feathered Serpent, the symbol of one of the Maya gods. In the distance the jungle presses upon the ruins.

This Maya temple is called The Temple of a Thousand Columns. You can easily see why. Up to a few years ago, this building, like all the others in Chichen Itza, was in complete ruins. But the Carnegie Institution carefully assembled all the fallen stones and rebuilt the structure in its orig-

We are standing on the very place, before the door of the temple atop the pyramid, where the brides of the Rain God began their tragic wedding march. We cross the threshold, past the carved feathered serpents that guard the entrance, to find ourselves in a windowless room of solid stone. The bats squeak about our heads—this has been their private property for five centuries.

Looking out in the direction of Yum-Chac's pit, we can see the Sacred Way. From this very room, as the hour of dawn broke over the land, the sacrificial processions moved toward the Sacred Well. Here the heaven-blessed maiden was brought, the loveliest of all the fourteen-year-old Maya maids, robed in riches, garlanded in flowers, to be sacrificed to the Rain God lest he withhold his blessings and parch the fields. Here the bravest young warrior in the nation, wearing a jeweled girdle and a plumed helmet, was waiting to escort the little victim on her last journey and attend her in the Rain King's court. Here, too, the priests, in their ceremonial dress, blared their conch-shell trumpets, announcing to the waiting thousands below that the fateful hour had come—that Yum-Chac was about to receive his bride.

From this room, down the sweeping stairs, on to the raised stone road, we see, in our mind's eye, the High Priest of the Feathered Serpent leading the glittering throng which follows him slowly toward the Well. The music, singing forth the glory of Yum-Chac, joins the vast procession—the conch-shells and the flutes, the muffled rumbling drums. Then, last of all, followed by the doomed young escort, the covered chair is carried forward on the shoulders of the bearers, who march with slow and measured tread. In this chair, curtained from the multitudes, the pitiful little bride rides forward to her destiny.

We follow the bride down the steps, along the Sacred Way. Feathered serpents, battered and time-worn, thrust their stone heads through the wall of bush and vine to look at us with stony eyes.

The quarter-mile of this causeway has stopped abruptly. The jungle crowds close on either side. A stone altar now blocks our path. Beyond that, and below, a dark, still, fearful chasm. . . .

We climb onto the ruined platform and peer over the brink. Down, down, full seventy feet the breakneck walls fall sheer, and at the bottom a dead sheet of water, two hundred feet across, lies motionless.

At this altar, as the sun breaks over the tree tops, the sacrificial procession halts. From this altar, the High Priest, amid a solemn stillness, raises his arms over the waters, and prays to the unseen deity, waiting in his submerged palace of wave and rock, to accept the sacrifice. A great hush comes over the worshipers. The drums begin to roll. Six priests take the girl from her chair and begin to swing her slowly back and forth over the brink of the pit. The priestly choir begins to chant. The escort is waiting at the edge. Louder beat the drums—the rhythm quickens—in a greater and greater arc the girl is swung—louder the chant—faster the drums—louder—faster—one swelling roar—the bride is hurled far out into the dark abyss; and like a streak of fire, sword aloft, the Maya warrior plunges after her. . . .

Falling, turning, the two victims lurch forward, the white wedding garments and the helmet's scarlet feathers fluttering for a moment side by side until man and maid strike the leaden waters, seventy feet below, with a dull and far-off boom that echoes from wall to wall across the pool. The ripples spend themselves against the rocks . . . a moment of hushed watchfulness . . . the sacrifices disappear . . . they have been received into the palace of their lord . . . the bride is safe in the Rain God's arms.

The last of these ceremonies took place five hundred years ago. Today, around the Well, all is still and desolate. The priests, the pomp, the drums have gone. The altar is in ruins, a little plot of grass and stones. The multitudes have vanished, and tangles of greenery displace them at the brink.

I'm sure you're going to ask: Did the victims ever try to swim? Did the fall of seventy feet (about the height of a six-story building) kill the bride and her escort? Were they knocked

see how it feels to be a human sacrifice, the author jumps from the Sacrificial Altar into the -foot Well of Death, at Chichen Itza. The stone altar from which the living sacrifices were ng can be seen just below the rim of the Well. Halliburton was able to swim to the rock wall d to climb up it by means of grape vines. But the Mayan sacrifices were dragged to the bottom of the pool by their heavy robes and jewels, and drowned.

unconscious before they drowned? Did their bodies ever come to the surface?

All these questions I can answer, because I dived into the Well myself—on two different occasions—just to see how it felt to be a human sacrifice. The first time I went head first. The second time feet first. Both times the shock of hitting the water from such a height gave me a terrible headache. Even so, I was able to swim over to the rock wall and climb the wild grapevines that now trail down from the altar.

So I am sure the bride and soldier-escort could have done the same thing had they not been so heavily laden with jewels and adornments. Dragged down by this weight they had no chance to swim, but quickly sank, side by side, straight to the bottom of the pool, sixty feet below. And here, in Yum-Chac's realm their young bodies lay, still imprisoned by the jewels, as the centuries rolled on, as their race died away, as their capital grew silent, as the jungles seized the temples and the palaces. And as they lay here the Rain God was changed into a storm cloud, in which form, to this day, he roars across the heavens, demanding that the Mayas bring him brides again.

But on moonlight nights, so the modern Yucatan Indians claim, the lonely spirits of the man and the maid, drifting through their watery tomb, rise from the depths of this Well of Death, to linger by the crumbling altar, listening to the misty music, the ghostly drums, and the chanting, thin and far away, of the Rain God's phantom worshipers.

Carnegie Institution.
The observatory at Chichen Itza where the Maya priests watched the stars.

CHAPTER XII

CHRISTOPHE'S CASTLE

The next wonder of the world we're going to visit is a castle—the castle of a king, of Henry Christophe, the Black King of Haiti.

From Chichen Itza we return to the coast of Yucatan, but there we can find no boats to take us where we wish to go. We must travel by air, and fly eight hundred miles straight east across the Caribbean Sea. After a six-hour flight we come to Haiti, the largest island, excepting Cuba, in the West Indies. On into the interior our airplane carries us, on over the mountains and canyons and jungles.

The north coast appears in the distance. Twenty miles back from it we see a bold peak over-topping all the others. From the summit of this peak, three thousand feet above the valley, soar the ruins of a spectacular castle—the Citadel of a giant, a tyrant, the most masterful Negro in history—Christophe.

Christophe has been dead more than a hundred years, but this marvelous Citadel still stands guard over what was once his kingdom. It stands there to remind the world that in this land a black man, through his own genius, rose to supreme power, and made his black nation rich and progressive, feared and respected.

Up to 1794 (George Washington was our President then) Haiti belonged to France. But in that year the half-million slaves, imported from Africa to work the fields of coffee and sugar cane, rebelled against the brutal treatment they suffered under the French planters. After years of bloodshed and the most terrible fighting between the rebellious slaves and the white planters, the slaves gained complete control of the country and drove the last remaining Frenchmen back to France.

A leader in this black rebellion was a young Negro named Henry Christophe. Born in the West Indies of slave parents, he had spent much of his boyhood as a dishwasher in a public bar.

119

But he was too tall, too strong, too capable, to remain long at such a job. When the revolution broke, he promptly joined the uprising slaves. When it ended he was a "General." By 1806 he had become dictator of a new nation, a nation one hundred per cent Negro. In 1812 he had himself crowned king.

And rarely in history has a king been so purposeful. He first put his slave subjects to work. He was determined to have obedience. He forced them with whip and bayonet to labor in the fields and on the roads. Anybody caught loafing was shot. No one could escape from his burning desire to rebuild the war-torn country, and to give it self-respect and security and pride.

As for pride, he set a grand example. He built for himself and his family a magnificent stone château, called Sans Souci (Without Care). In size and beauty it was not equaled this side of Europe.

Then he organized a court. He created a "nobility" with princes, and barons, and ladies-in-waiting for Marie-Louise, his Queen. There was a Duke of Marmalade and a Countess of Lemonade. To educate his dusky young daughters, Améthyste and Athénaire, he imported two American maiden ladies from Philadelphia. From them the little Princesses learned the graces of polite society, including poetry, the harp, and the straightening of kinky hair.

But for Christophe, industry and order in his country were not enough. His people had no patriotism, no heroes. He would give them a national symbol to respect. He would build a monster fortress on the summit of a near-by mountain called The Bishop's Bonnet, three thousand feet above his château. The fortress would lord it over the plain and the bay. It would be stronger than the French Army, or the voodoo enchantments of his primitive subjects—something without a rival in *any* land, something to make the world, and all the hated white men in it, stare with wonder and admiration.

So Christophe dreamed, and so his dream came to pass in brick and stone.

A path was built up to the summit of the mountain, and the work began. More than three thousand laborers were driven to work on the walls—women as well as men. Each woman carried eight ten-pound bricks on her head, every time she climbed up from the valley three thousand feet below. Barrels of lime and gunpowder, crude machinery, and cannon, cannon by the score, had to be dragged, amid groans and sweat and agony, to the summit. The ascending and descending slaves made two continuous lines each six miles long, an army of unwilling black ants. And all along the way were drivers with whips to speed the laggards. Christophe himself stormed up and down the trail shouting orders. It is said he shot to death numbers of his slaves to frighten those remaining into moving faster. He even went to work himself on the north corner of his fort, a vast wall 130 feet high built like the prow of a ship. He meant this bastion to be a monument to his own huge black fist.

And so the years succeeded one another, with the forced labor never ending on the peak. The walls rose to greater and greater —to unbelievable—heights, continuing the upward sweep of the mountain side—walls strong and cruel as Christophe's heart. By 1820 the King's tyranny had become almost an insanity. He took to beating his ministers with his riding whip. The slightest hint of rebellion brought down his wild wrath. Suspecting the loyalty of a company of guards at the Citadel, he lined them up, so one story goes, on the highest battlement of the great ship-like prow, and commanded them to march forward, right over the edge of the 130-foot wall. And so afraid were they of Christophe that they obeyed, to be dashed to pieces on the rocky mountain slope below.

Then at the height of his building mania, just before the last brick was in place, the King, now fifty-three years old, saw—or thought he saw—one day in church, the ghost of a priest he had executed. With a cry of terror Christophe fell to the floor—half his body paralyzed.

Christophe's Citadel, on the summit of a three-thousand-foot peak, twenty miles back from
north coast of the West Indian island of Haiti. Begun by the French in 1804, it was co
pleted by the Black King of Haiti who dreamed of making his Citadel the world's strong
fortress. He forced his black subjects to drag six hundred cannon and a million cannon b

Pan American Airways.

m the sea up to the fortress. The cannon and balls are still there. For nearly a hundred
rs after the black tyrant fell, the Citadel was given over to the jungle, but the U. S. Marines,
ing their occupation of Haiti, cleaned it of all jungle growth. Except for a few roofs missing it is in a nearly perfect state of preservation.

In a few hours the news had been spread by the beating of tom-tom drums. Before long, the army, learning that the tyrant was really helpless, mutinied. And on hearing of this mutiny the thousands of slave-laborers, struggling with their cannon up the trail to the Citadel, dropped their hateful burdens, and with shouts of joy rushed down the mountain, brandishing clubs and bricks and trowels, to take revenge upon their cruel King.

The yelling mob surged straight on toward the château, clamoring for Christophe's head. They were pounding on the doors. The King, knowing that if he were taken alive he would be tortured and torn to pieces, seized a pistol and fired a bullet into his heart.

To try to save the dead body from the rebels, Queen Marie-Louise, the two Princesses, and the young Crown Prince, wrapped it hurriedly in a blanket, fled out the back door, and, carrying the corpse, hastened up the path to the Citadel. The howling mob, unable to find Christophe in the palace, set fire to it. Then, suspecting where he might have gone, the rebels rushed up the mountain trail, close behind the fleeing family.

Desperate and spent, the Queen and her children, still bearing the King's body, reached the Citadel's courtyard, just ahead of the mob. There was no time to dig a grave . . . the rebels were running headlong through the lower gate. Then Marie-Louise noticed a huge vat of liquid lime, left there by the runaway plasterers. Into this white and all-consuming bath the black body of Christophe was dropped, and pushed downward until it disappeared.

The mob put the Crown Prince to death, but allowed the Queen and her two daughters to escape to Europe.

The bullet that killed Christophe killed his kingdom too. Freed from the grip of its brutal ruler, Haiti returned to its primitive African ways. The dukes and duchesses took off their shoes again and went back to work in the fields of sugar cane. The country soon forgot its once-proud place among the new nations of the Americas.

That great grim fortress, on the peak-top below our airplane, is Christophe's castle. And that white loaf-like mound in the courtyard is the vat of lime (now hard as stone) into which Marie-Louise flung the body of the King.

We land at Cape Haitien, the seaport for Christophe's kingdom—a hundred years ago the busiest port in the West Indies, now a sleepy little fishing village that doesn't see four ships a year.

We motor inland twenty miles and come to the ruins of Sans Souci, burned and gutted by the mob that overran the château on that fateful night. It is covered now with flowering jungle vines.

The trail to the Citadel leads upward from this point. We follow along it, as it tunnels through the jungle, trying to picture the plight of the Black Queen and her son and daughters as they hurried up this very path with the King's body.

After two hours we reach a clearing near the mountain top. And there, still farther above us, we see the Citadel's enormous prow rearing haughtily from the summit of the peak.

We reach the entrance. Fully 130 feet of wall rises sheer above us. The heavy gates, still on their hinges, allow us to pass inside. The steps are dark and damp. Bats fly about in the dimness. The walls and partitions are twenty feet thick. Christophe vowed they must outlast the ages; and outlast the ages we have no doubt they will.

And cannon! Surely such a collection of cannon is to be found nowhere else on earth. There must be six hundred rusty muzzle-loaders, some lined up on wooden carriages, some strewn about like wind-blown straws.

No less astonishing is the tremendous number of cannon balls. Tons upon tons of them lie piled up in metal hillocks everywhere, enough to feed the guns for weeks of continuous firing. The stores of gunpowder are there too, enough for the longest siege. Spilling out of the barrels stacked in dark stone cellars, the powder never has been disturbed; but the dampness of a century has taken the life out of it. Fortunately none of Christophe's enemies chose to touch a match to this dangerous store when it was still fresh, for the explosion would have blown the Citadel right off the mountain.

Rock steps lead us up to the courtyard. At one end, the barracks block out the sky. They are large enough to shelter five thousand men. And beneath these barracks are rows of dungeons which Christophe filled, as soon as they were completed, with victims for whom he thought shooting too merciful.

In the center of the courtyard we find the loaf-shaped mound of hardened plaster, twenty feet long and higher than a man—the vat of lime that received Christophe's body on the day of his death. Beside it is a small tomb inscribed in French: "Here lies King Henry Christophe—1767: 1820." But, of course, the tomb contains only a few chunks of plaster carved from the center of the mound—chunks in which were found the brass buttons on the King's uniform and the bullet in his heart, the only things that were not destroyed by the quicklime.

Climbing to the highest rampart, we look down at the world more than half a mile below. The bold skyrocketing walls of the Citadel fall one hundred feet or more on every side, and join the mountain top as gracefully as a tree rises from its roots. For the first time we can appreciate the giant size of the fortress—five hundred by three hundred feet—and grasp its full beauty. For beautiful it is, in a cruel, powerful way. The walls, once grimly gray, are now ablaze with bright orange moss, which has spread across the stones; and on this burning color the sunset falls with splendor.

Let me tell you of a wonderful sight I witnessed when, once before, I was standing on top this same gigantic prow and looking out upon King Henry's land.

It was about six o'clock, and the sun was just setting. All that day a storm had been threatening, and now, as night approached, I saw that a heavy black mist had gathered and filled the valleys

126

below with a black sea. Suddenly the thunder and lightning began to crash and echo within arm's reach, and wave after wave of black clouds, rolling in from the northern coast, now rapidly climbed up the mountain side. The clouds reached the lowest part of the walls and blotted out the realms beneath. Only the Citadel floated above this rising tide, its prow cleaving the oncoming billows so that a huge stone ship, beautiful, silent and alone, seemed to be sailing majestically forward into the darkness—on through the thunder—out across the sky—proud to bear the name of the great Black King who had launched it as a challenge to the world.

The courtyard of Christophe's Castle. The loaf-like mound in the center is solidified lime used in 1820 by Christophe's plasterers for mortar. Into this vast vat the corpse of the Black King was dropped by his wife and children to protect the body from the mob.

CHAPTER XIII

THE PANAMA CANAL

From Haiti we are going, on our quest for marvels, straight to Panama. For here we'll find another world-wonder—the Panama Canal.

For me this canal has always held a special charm. Long before I ever saw it I had read the story of the Isthmus it crosses; of the battles for gold, of the pirates and their plunder, that have crowded Panama with drama; of Columbus and Balboa who explored there; of all the colorful villains and heroes who have died there.

As a boy I followed with eager interest the construction of the Canal across this romantic country. What a thrill I felt when the first ship passed through!

As a young man I made a long-awaited trip to see it, and was so enchanted by the sight of this engineering miracle and by the history behind it, that I obeyed an impulse to swim it from end to end. I dived into its waters on the Atlantic side, and, by daily stages, swam to the Pacific—locks, lake and all—fifty miles.

So I like to think that I know the Panama Canal as well as anyone, and will make a good guide.

For four hundred years people had been thinking about a canal across the Isthmus, and about the ten-thousand-mile voyage around the tip of South America it would save. Soon after Balboa's discovery of the "South Sea" (as he called the Pacific), the Spanish conquerors proposed to the King of Spain that a canal be cut through Panama, to join the oceans. But the King thought the project too expensive, and dismissed it.

As the centuries passed, other schemes for a canal were born and faded. It was not until 1881 that a French company, headed by the famous French engineer, De Lesseps, began to dig.

Twelve years before, De Lesseps had successfully completed the hundred-mile Suez Canal from the Mediterranean to the Red

A flock of U. S. Army airplanes fly over the Gatun Locks of the Panama Canal. These three lock chambers lift a ship from the level of the Atlantic Ocean to Gatun Lake, ninety feet above. Each lock is 1000 feet long, 110 feet wide. The lake is artificial, made by damming up the Chagres River. The crescent-shaped dam can be seen near the upper center of the picture. Entering the second lock chamber is the American ocean liner, *California.*

Across Gatun Lake the procession of ships is never-ending. In this picture we can see six ships. (One is just coming around the corner in the distance.) Before the lake was made, this part of the Isthmus of Panama was dry land covered with jungle, and the islands seen here were hilltops. Now it's under deep water, and provides a waterway for half the Canal's fifty miles. The clear, blue water, the tropical skies, the jungled shores, all make the Panama Canal beautiful as well as wonderful.

Sea. But his attempt to repeat that success in Panama was one of the greatest tragedies of engineering history. The company had plenty of money, machinery, skill. However, they had not reckoned with the mosquito, or with the deadly fever germs this insect carries.

Hardly was the work begun before malaria and yellow fever descended upon the labor camps. Nobody knows exactly how many the fever killed, but the total was certainly not less than twenty thousand. The construction company dug more graves than canal. Unable to control the terrible scourge of fever, De Lesseps, after heroic but futile labor, had to abandon his dream. He left behind hundreds of railroad engines, thousands of derricks and dredges and freight-cars, to be engulfed by the jungle. The French company had spent $325,000,000. The total cost of the entire canal which the Americans built was $375,-000,000—only $50,000,000 more than the French spent. But for *their* vast outlay of money, the French gained nothing but jungle-covered graves and broken hearts.

In 1903 the Americans took over the work. They had learned by now of the mosquito's deadly character. So before a single spadeful of earth was turned, war was waged against the tiny pests. By 1906, the mosquito had been driven from the Canal Zone, and work could start.

Steam shovels began to dig from the Atlantic side and from the Pacific side at the same time. Across the pathway of the Canal stretched a ridge 660 feet high, called Gold Hill. This too the engineers attacked, and through its center they carved out Culebra Cut, the biggest ditch ever dug. A great artificial lake was dammed up to cover more than half the route with water, and huge locks were constructed to lift ships up to this lake and drop them down again.

As the man-made canyon deepened in Gold Hill, the lake rose to meet it. In January, 1914, the locks were finished, and a ship sailed through from ocean to ocean. That was one of the greatest days in the history of geography.

The Empress of Britain, the largest passenger ship ever to sail through the Panama Canal,
Gold Hill in the famous Culebra Cut. From 1906 to 1914 American engineers, with their
steam shovels and an army of workmen, dug away at this biggest man-made ditch in the w
It cuts through a ridge 660 feet high. Here, in years past, landslides from the walls of th
sometimes filled the channel and blocked traffic for several days at a time. But this no l

appens, as the walls have been dug safely back from the edge of the Canal. In the distance are he two sets of Pacific locks, a mile apart. The voyage through the Panama Canal takes nine ours. To sail around South America (which was necessary before the building of the Canal), the fastest ships took two weeks.

The author swims the fifty-mile length of the Panama Canal from the Atlantic to the Pacific. The Canal authorities allowed him to be locked through the locks like a ship. The swimmer's head is dimly seen (to the left of the rowboat) in one of the huge lock chambers

Aboard our own ship we reach the Atlantic entrance of the Canal. Ahead of us and behind are dozens of other ships that have collected here from a thousand ports and a hundred nations —battleships, tankers, tramps, long liners, sailboats, tugboats, freight boats—every flag, every color, an endless parade steaming up the channel through the tropical sunshine, on toward the magic water-steps—the most romantic journey granted the ships of the sea.

I remember this entrance to the Canal particularly well. As I swam across the outer harbor, everybody said I'd be eaten by sharks and barracudas. Because of these savage fish few people ever swam here. And likewise I remember the inner channel too, since the current from the emptying locks was so strong it took me seven hours to swim three miles.

But now, aboard our ship, neither sharks nor currents will endanger us.

We reach the first of the mighty locks. The double steel gates, as high as a seven-story building, fold back soundlessly. Each gate is seventy feet wide, and weighs four hundred tons. We are towed into the thousand-foot concrete chamber by electric "mules." The gates close behind, and the water-level in our lock begins to rise, as the water, flowing down from the lock above, rushes through the intake tubes. There are dozens of these tubes and each one is as large as a railroad tunnel. Our ship is lifted thirty feet. Now the gates ahead swing open, and we are towed on into the next lock—the second step in these giant stairs. Again the gates close after us. We are raised another thirty feet, as the water boils up beneath. Then through still another lock we climb, before we steam out into Gatun Lake, ninety feet above the level of the sea.

As a swimmer, I found it fun being locked through just as if I were a ship. I certainly looked and felt small—one lone wet head bobbing along barely above water in these enormous concrete pools. When I reached the end of the third lock the official in charge asked me how I intended to pay for the nine million cubic feet of water (as much water as it takes to lift the biggest ship in the world) that had been used to raise me the ninety feet from ocean level to Gatun Lake.

It took 9,000,000 cubic feet of water from Gatun Lake to send the *S.S. Richard Halliburton* through the Panama locks. Halliburton paid toll, like all other ships, according to his tonnage. He weighed one-thirteenth of a ton, and paid a charge of 36 cents.

The *U.S.S. Lexington*, one of the Navy's airplane carriers, steams past Gold Hill. This colossal battleship almost fills Culebra Cut. Ships the size of this one *do* fill the Canal's lock chambers. (Only a two-foot clearance is left on either side.) Several times the entire American battle fleet has been sent through the Canal at one time. Then the locks operate at a furious pace non-stop for two days and nights.

I answered that I was the *S.S. Richard Halliburton* and would pay toll just like all the other ships—according to my tonnage. So I was put on the scales and found to weigh one-thirteenth of one ton. The charge was thirty-six cents, the smallest toll ever paid by any ship in the history of the Canal.

Aboard our steamship we now see the big lake stretching before us, and we sail on across it. How surprisingly beautiful it is! We had expected to find the Canal a man-made thing, where Nature had been skinned and scarred and upturned and dug away. How different it proves to be! The years since 1914 have hidden every wound with vegetation. The entire Canal Zone is a garden that looks as if it might have been always a garden. Along the Atlantic channel leading to the locks, jungles drape the shore. Cranes and herons rise from the banks as our ship passes near. Parrots of a hundred hues screech overhead, and a colony of monkeys swing through the branches to watch us.

The lake itself is like a fairy lake, dotted with fairy isles. These isles are wild bowers where curious birds live among the blossoms. In the tree-tops cormorants roost by the thousand, waiting for unwary fish. Pelicans are everywhere, flamingoes, kingfishers, gulls. And all about is the deep-hued water; and above, the tropical sky banked with castled clouds.

For twenty-five miles we sail through an emerald and turquoise world. Ships pass us in a never-ending stream, coming from the Pacific. The lake shores now begin to close in. We are approaching the great cut. The channel has narrowed to five hundred feet. We can see both banks clearly. On one bank a group of logs seem to have been cast up by the waves. But look —the logs are moving. They are alligators! They are crawling back into the water. When I was swimming through this passage, I feared for my life every moment. A soldier with a rifle and a fine record for marksmanship accompanied me in a boat, to protect me from the alligators. But I always had the feeling that if an alligator seized my leg, the commotion would be so great that the soldier would probably shoot me in trying to shoot the enemy. Before I got safely through this dangerous stretch, my rifleman fired at a score of the ugly brutes lying on the banks just ahead of us. However, even when hit they always struggled back into the water, so that we never knew how many were actually killed.

Now, on our own journey, Gold Hill rises ahead. We are entering the world-famous Culebra Cut. Here the channel shrinks to three hundred feet, but the mountain walls soar nearly six hundred feet above. Sailing—or swimming—beneath these towering cliffs which have been torn apart by human hands, is as thrilling an adventure as the journey through the locks themselves. We stare in astonishment at the sight of this great void where once a mountain stood. Here, even more than with the locks, one has the feeling that this is the work of gods, not men.

During my swim, I was able to crawl ashore at the base of this cliff and climb to the summit. From there I could look down upon the toy ships steaming past. Just ahead were the Pacific locks, seen in miniature from these heights. Ten miles farther on lay Panama City—and, beyond that, the great western ocean.

The Pacific locks lower our ship. These locks are—they *must* be—even higher than on the Atlantic side, for the Pacific tide rises and falls twenty feet, compared with one foot on the Atlantic shore. What causes this great difference in tidal power, no one knows.

Another stretch of channel, deep-cut through the jungle, and we sail out once more upon the sea. This magic voyage has taken us nine hours. If you ever try to swim it, as I did, it may take you eight days, as it took me. But if there were no canal, and we had to go ten thousand miles around Cape Horn, the voyage would take us two weeks on the swiftest ship.

Now that you have seen this great engineering feat—with its vast locks, its glorious lake, its royal procession of ships—you are not likely to forget it. Some of you may even say, when our quest for marvels is over, that nothing you have seen in all the world can compare in wonder and in beauty with the Panama Canal.

138

This 660-foot ridge which ran straight across the line of the Panama Canal, was the greatest obstacle the engineers had to face. Millions of cubic yards of earth had to be removed in order to dig Culebra Cut through the ridge. The Cut here is 300 feet wide, and the water in it 50 feet deep. Here, even more than with the locks, one has the feeling that this was the work of gods, not men.

CHAPTER XIV

THE ANGEL ARCHITECTS

The strangest story I have ever heard took place four hundred years ago in South America.

On our visit to Mexico we learned about the highly cultured race of Indians called the Aztecs, who were at their peak about the time Columbus discovered America. At the same period, in South America, in what is now Peru, a similar Indian race known as the Incas had built up a nation that equaled Aztec-land in splendor.

The Incas numbered some eleven million people, gathered on the western slope of the mighty Andes. Their cities were constructed of immense stones—some of the biggest stone blocks ever laid by masons are still found in the walls of Cuzco, the Inca capital. Stone roads led from the sea to the mountain tops, crossing bottomless canyons on suspension bridges cunningly woven out of ropes. The Incas were skillful in many arts and crafts, especially in the mining and refining of gold. This metal was so plentiful in their country, and so commonplace, that they used it as we use copper or brass.

These people worshiped the sun. For this reason a great deal of shining gold went into their religious buildings. As a symbol of the Sun God, it gleamed from temple wall and altar. In the temple gardens at Cuzco, the flowers and trees were gold flowers and gold trees. Gold—gold—gold—it was beautiful—it remained bright—it gladdened the eye. That it had any special value, otherwise, never entered the Incas' heads.

But to the Spaniards, gold was everything. To them it was a sin against both heaven and earth that such treasures should remain in the hands of heathen Indians. And to correct this state of affairs, a Spanish soldier named Pizarro sailed south from Panama with an army of 165 adventurers, and assaulted a nation of eleven million people. That his conquest succeeded is one of history's military miracles—a miracle no less amazing than Cortez' conquest of Mexico.

One of the first things the Spaniards did was to capture, hold for ransom, and finally slay, the Inca King. Among his subjects, the King was considered a divine being, and when he perished beneath Spanish swords all the Inca armies felt that their gods had abandoned them, and fled before the invaders.

The road to Cuzco was thus opened, and the Spaniards hastened along it. On reaching the city they seized, first of all, the Convent of the Sun. In this Convent dwelt a hundred of the loveliest high-born maidens of the land, devoting their lives to the worship of the Sun God. The Spaniards intended to capture and enslave these beautiful priestesses.

But word of Pizarro's approach had raced ahead of him, and given the hundred maids time to escape. They were last seen hurrying over the crest of the Andes above Cuzco and down into the canyon of the Urubamba River, one of the great tropical gorges that descend the eastern slope of the mountains and lead on to Brazil.

For four hundred years the fate of these refugees remained a mystery. Then, in 1911, the mystery was solved—and the strangest story I have ever heard could be told.

About the year 800, while Europe was still sleeping through its Dark Ages, the Incas were a small but inspired tribe living on the Brazilian side of the Andes. At this period they built for themselves a granite city, a fantastic magic city, poised upon a pinnacle of rock, surrounded by the two-thousand-feet-deep canyon of the Urubamba River, and overshadowed by snow-clad mountain barriers reaching twenty thousand feet into the sky. No other city in the world ever had a setting so spectacular.

But I should not say *had* such a setting, as though this marvelous city no longer existed, for it is still there and we are going to visit it.

141

Machu Picchu, on a mountain top in Peru, was the capital city for the Inca Indians a thous[and] years ago. It contains four hundred hewn-stone houses, temples and palaces, most of which st[and] intact today. Yet so steep are the cliffs around it that the deserted city remained hidden from [the] world till 1911. In that year American explorers came by accident upon its sleeping sto[ne.] For four centuries, since the time of the Spanish conquest of Peru, Indians had been passing [and] repassing along the canyon at its base. But not one of them knew about the wonderful c[ity] buried in the jungle, 2000 feet above. The ancient Incas, looking for the most dramatic sett[ing] in the Andes for their city, chose the summit of this peak. Towering, snow-clad mountains [im]prison it. The Urubamba River roars around three sides of it, far below. To visit it, we climb [up] the cliff from the canyon floor, and come suddenly upon the white buildings—buildings "b[uilt]

Photograph by Richard Halliburton.

angels,'" the modern Indians say. There are dozens of these beautiful white structures, rising steps toward the pinnacle. We climb the stair-stepped streets, past the sacred plaza, past the anite temple, on up to the sundial on the tip-top of the mountain. And then we come to the ge of the terrifying chasm that falls two thousand feet below. From here we can see the gla-rs of the cloud-capped Andes, and hear the voice of the river thundering at the feet of these eak-neck cliffs. It was to this secret city that the one hundred Sun Maidens fled when Pizarro d his Spanish conquerors came to Peru. Here these high-born girls lived out their lives, lost m the world, in this granite eagle's-nest. At the height of its glory Machu Picchu contained no re than 9000 people. Yet, small though it was, no other ancient capital in the history of the world ever had the majesty of this pinnacled little Inca city in Peru.

The Indians living in the neighborhood today call this ancient Inca capital Machu Picchu (mah'-choo pee'-choo). Within its walls are some four hundred houses, all made of the purest granite blocks. And there are also temples, and palaces, and plazas, and monuments, of the same material. The altar in the Great Temple is a single granite block that weighs one hundred tons.

No mortar was used by the Inca masons to hold these blocks together. And yet, so skillfully were the blocks set in place, that the walls are still intact after all these centuries.

Strange to say, we shall find that the only quarry where the biggest stones could be obtained is at the *bottom* of the canyon, more than two thousand feet below. How the builders of this granite eagle's-nest ever moved such weights up to the towering top of the crag where the city stands, is a problem which baffles modern builders. The present-day Indians say that the ancient Incas had at their service angel architects, who understood the magic arts and could cause monstrous stones to drop from the granite cliff and take wing across the canyon to the temple walls. Even to us, this seems as good as any other explanation, for how the Incas could raise such structures, with only primitive tools and crude machinery, is more than we can understand.

For two centuries the Incas lived in Machu Picchu. Then, about the year 1000, the population outgrew the food supply. Looking for more space, the Incas abandoned their sky-scraping city and moved sixty miles across the Andes to Cuzco on the western slope of the mountains. Unable to write (though they were skilled in so many other arts), they kept no record of their former capital. As the centuries passed, Machu Picchu was all but forgotten.

But not *quite* forgotten. The Priests of the Sun secretly kept the place as a retreat in case their god failed them and such a refuge should prove necessary.

In 1531, when Pizarro came, such a refuge became *very* necessary. Under the guidance of a priest, the hundred terrified maidens from the Cuzco temple fled into the Urubamba Gorge.

144

Finding the hidden path to the deserted city, they struggled up it, to hide themselves away from the cruel white demons.

That they had escaped to Machu Picchu was unknown to Pizarro. It was not known even to the other Incas in Cuzco. The people there, puzzled by the total disappearance of the sacred maidens, invented a story that the Sun God had lifted them straight into the sky.

But in 1911 the American archeologist, Dr. Hiram Bingham, hunting for Inca ruins in the Urubamba country, was led by his Indian guides to the top of an especially steep and forbidding cliff, to look at "some old terraces." And there he came upon the angel-built city.

True, it did not look angel-built at first glance. Four centuries of tropical forest growth had covered everything. Scarcely a stone was visible under its blanket of moss and roots. But when this growth had been cleared away, Machu Picchu stood forth in all its shining granite glory, with all four hundred buildings intact, except for their missing roofs.

And in the sacred grave-yard, near the Central Temple, were found ninety-nine graves. All modern Peruvians believe these are the graves of the Sun Maidens who fled from the Spaniards.

But why only ninety-nine?

Because when the last priestess died, there was no one left to bury her.

I hope you'll be as keen as I was about visiting Machu Picchu. It's difficult to reach, but worth any journey.

This Andean peak overhangs Machu Picchu. It is not a volcano. The peak was first climbed by the American discoverers of the city. The climbers built a bonfire on reaching the top. This picture was made from below as the smoke curled up.

We sail down the west coast of South America to a Peruvian seaport, and then take a train that climbs fourteen thousand feet to reach Cuzco, now a modern city of thirty thousand people. Following the route of the escaping temple maidens, we cross the Andean ridge, descend for sixty miles into the Urubamba Gorge, reach the base of the ancient trail, and begin to climb on foot. Our zigzag path first leads upward through the dripping jungle, then scales a terrific precipice. We stumble over roots, clutch at vines. Enormous butterflies flit about us. Perhaps a fer-de-lance slithers across the way, for this deadly snake is found all too often upon Machu Picchu's peak.

We can look up now and see, a thousand feet above, a stone house or two. We hurry on, hot and breathless. We reach the first stone stairs, near the summit—go up them two at a time. Here is an Inca building—then another—and another—gleaming, sun-flooded, of flawless granite, rising tier on tier toward the peak of the ridge. On up through the dazzling maze we climb—across the sacred plaza—past the granite temple—up the winding granite stairs to the giant sun-dial which crowns the peak—on to the sun-dial—to the very edge of the appalling chasm which falls straight down two thousand feet beneath us. From this dizzy foothold we can see the copper sun sinking into the glaciers of a far-off cloud-capped world, and hear the voice of the Urubamba thundering at the foot of the precipice.

When twilight comes we leave the sun-dial and wander up and down the dim and spectral streets, trying to picture in our mind's eye the hundred last inhabitants, who lived out their lives amid these very scenes—doomed to life-long exile, cut off from the world.

We are alone on the mountain top, but perhaps we are not unnoticed. Perhaps the shades of the Maidens of the Sun are walking beside us—some young ghosts, some middle-aged ghosts, some very old ghosts, but all very lonely ghosts, still yearning for the temples of Cuzco.

What a strange life this holy band must have led! Guarding themselves from all contact with the outer world lest the secret of

146

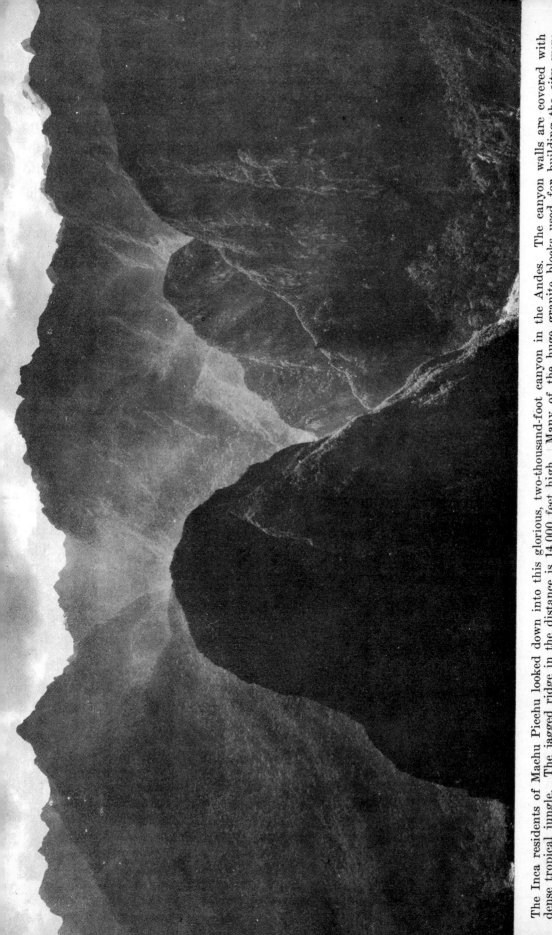

The Inca residents of Machu Picchu looked down into this glorious, two-thousand-foot canyon in the Andes. The canyon walls are covered with dense tropical jungle. The jagged ridge in the distance is 14,000 feet high. Many of the huge granite blocks used for building the city were quarried at the *bottom* of this canyon, and dragged up these terrific cliffs. Such a task today, with all our modern machinery, would be very difficult. How did the ancient Incas manage it? The present-day Indians say their ancestors had angel architects to help.

their escape reach the ears of Pizarro's soldiers, never descending from their high retreat, these well-born and beautiful women, perhaps without a single man to work for them or guard them, lived out their lives. They could have no cradles to rock, no children to sing to sleep, no sons in whom to take pride, no daughters to keep them company. We wonder if they were happy within their little realm; if they continued to hold sun worship in the temple of their refuge as they held it in Cuzco.

Pizarro and his men, though they remain in the capital a long time to strip the gold from the city, never learn of the mountain trail that leads to the lovely, lonely refugees. The seasons and the years drag past. The Priestesses of the Sun live on in Machu Picchu, unaware that the Spanish conquerors have left Cuzco in ruins, that the temples have been hurled down, that the people have been slaughtered and enslaved, that the Sun God is in exile.

The day comes—so runs the legend—when the beauty of these prisoners has faded. In their hidden city they grow old. The burial caves receive them, one by one. In time, only a few are left alive, very aged, very weary, forgotten by the world, forgetting it. These also pass, until but two remain. Then one buries the other—and one lives on amid the wonderful granite walls, the empty temples, with only ghosts for company. The merciless, hungry jungle is creeping up; the grass grows deep upon the stair-step streets, and the bamboo waves above the temple doors. The city's roofs have fallen in; the serpents sun themselves upon the granite dial, since no one ever comes to count the hours.

Alone, in the midst of all this ruin, the old, old woman, the last of the sacred Maidens of the Sun, sits listening to the far-away rumble of the river, and waiting—for the darkness.

CHAPTER XV

IGUAZU FALLS

In 1542, a year after Pizarro's death in Peru, a Spanish explorer named Alvar de Vaca, accompanied by a small band of soldiers, was on a journey of discovery down a river that now marks the boundary between Brazil and Argentina. Never had he seen a river so beautiful. It wound through a dense and flowering jungle. Orchids grew in the tree-tops, and at night jaguars crept through the tall ferns at the water's edge to drink.

One day, at a point where the river flowed especially deep and still, the explorers began to hear a strange and terrifying rumble some distance ahead. What could this be? Puzzled and afraid, they rounded a bend. Directly before them yawned a great chasm, over the brink of which the river fell with a roar.

Just in time to keep their boats from being swept into the abyss, the explorers gained the shore. They crept forward on the wet rocks to a point where they could look down into the churning cauldron below.

This was a day long to be remembered in the history of discovery. For De Vaca and his men had stumbled, quite unaware, upon what was then the greatest waterfall ever seen by white men —the Falls of the Iguazu.

And for seven score years (Niagara was not discovered till 1678), their find remained the unchallenged champion of all waterfalls. Do you remember that we mentioned these falls in our chapter on Niagara?

To see this amazing sight for ourselves, we must voyage from Peru on down the west coast of South America to Valparaiso in Chile, cross the Andes by train, and travel by river-boat six hundred miles up the broad Rio Paraná.

It is night-time when we disembark on the shore. There is a full moon. Horses take us some ten miles along a trail that winds deeper and deeper into the jungle. Halting at a clearing, our guide leads us on foot down a steep, rocky path, which we descend cautiously in the dimness.

In the jungles of South America. on the border line between Argentina and Brazil (See map on page 84.), is this marvelous Falls of the Iguazu River. Its rim is 10,000 feet wide—twice the width of Niagara. Its height is 220 feet, sixty feet more than Niagara. However, most of Iguazu is broken into two cataracts of 110 feet each. This picture shows only half the Falls It's impossible, except from the air, to get a view of the entire crest line. The volume of water flowing over Niagara is greater, most of the time, than the volume flowing over Iguazu. But during the annual spring floods, Iguazu's volume is twice as great as Niagara's. The depth of the Iguazu River plunging over the brink may then be sixty feet deep. Victoria Falls in South Africa, the third giant among waterfalls, has about the same amount of water as Iguazu. Victoria's

ight is 400 feet—180 feet higher than Iguazu, but Victoria's crest line is only little more than
lf as wide as the Falls pictured here. This wonder of the world was discovered in 1542 (136
ars before Niagara) by a Spanish explorer named Alvar de Vaca and a band of soldiers. When
come upon it we feel we have been enchanted and allowed a glimpse of the dream-realm of the
ants. And what a wild and beautiful dream-realm it is! Flowering jungles crowd the banks.
chids grow in the tree-tops. Monkeys and jaguars come down to the riverside to drink. Green
rrots and pink flamingoes fly across the tropical sky. And amid all this wonder and beauty,
there is no sign of man.

We are conscious now of a deep booming sound in the air, a booming which grows louder as we go on.

Then, abruptly, we reach the edge of a terrific mile-wide abyss, and stand before what seems, at the moment, to be all the beauty in the world changed into mist and moonlight, floating out from among the stars, and falling and fading into a bottomless fissure in the earth.

We are in the presence of the Iguazu.

At first the picture does not seem real. We feel as if we have been enchanted and allowed a glimpse of the dream-realm of the Giants. Then, clearly, the ceaseless rumbling drifts to us on the wind, and on the wind the mist, and we become aware that what we see is of this world.

Half a mile away a vast mass of water comes toward us from the dark horizon, to plunge downward into the great gorge at our feet. It is a river which, having wandered quietly through the forests of Brazil, here reaches the edge of the high plateau. Here, as though it knows that it is soon to die in the lowlands amid the mighty waters of the Rio Paraná, this upland river prepares itself for a grand climax to its career. And this climax is so dramatic that no one who sees it, ever forgets that the Iguazu surpasses all other rivers in the sublime beauty of its last hour, and becomes one of the wonders of the world.

In order to achieve this glory, the Iguazu moves with dignity toward destruction. It keeps its torrent in hand. There is no quick plunge, no single, mad, headlong dive. The river divides itself carefully and quietly into a thousand channels; and then, when every water-drop is ready, with one mighty charge along a front *ten thousand feet in length,* it hurls itself, cheering, over the brink, in superb cataracts of foam.

To come at midnight, in the midst of the wilderness, upon this moon-drenched vision, makes us stand and stare and marvel.

We recall the wonder we felt on seeing Niagara. But the rim of Iguazu is *twice as long,* and the drop, in places, sixty feet deeper. At flood season Iguazu has more water. This season,

152

however, lasts only a few weeks. At other times the volume is much less.

But strange to say, though Iguazu was discovered 136 years before the North American marvel, and 343 years before Victoria Falls, it is the least known of the three. For two centuries after De Vaca came upon it, the Jesuit priests who built missions in the neighborhood kept Europe aware of Iguazu. But about 1740, when the Jesuits were driven out and the missions burned, the very existence of this world-wonder was forgotten. Not until the beginning of the present century did advancing civilization bring Iguazu to light again.

Courtesy James Sawders.

Iguazu is broken up into hundreds and hundreds of spouts. They shoot over the brink between the many islets which line the crest, crash on the wide ledge and then form again in new groups and combinations.

The day following our moonlight arrival, an Indian guide—a descendant no doubt of the guide who led De Vaca—takes us to explore the Falls.

Standing at the point where the rim of the cataract joins the shore, we look over the edge into the chasm, named by the Spanish discoverers the "Garganta del Diablo"—the Devil's Throat. The crash of the falling river is frightening and fascinating. Its voice is even more deafening than Niagara's. But we notice that half-way down, the water, in many places, strikes on a ledge and divides into two 110-foot cascades, each 50 feet less than Niagara's single plunge.

Our guide offers to take us in a boat to the islands that stretch like stepping-stones along the crest-line. Such an adventure seems reckless indeed, with the river current driving everything, especially clumsy Indian dugouts, toward the brink. But the guide assures us he has often made the trip.

Each of us wielding a paddle, we push off into the stream several hundred feet above the Falls, praying that the power of our arms will be stronger than the current. It's an exciting, almost desperate contest. We bump against rocks, are scraped by floating logs. We paddle for dear life. We *have* to reach that first island—or else . . .

We make it!—and jump ashore. Wild ducks fly up from the thickets, alarmed at seeing visitors in such an unfrequented place. The Indian warns us that these jungle islands are favorite haunts for the boa-constrictors. We don't want to get tangled up with one of *them*.

From island to island we paddle, until we are in the middle of the cataract, with a mile of falling water—a whole Niagara—on either side. There is not a single evidence of man in sight. We see exactly what De Vaca saw, and we cannot believe he was more awed by this overpowering sight than we are.

Like Niagara, Iguazu is roughly horseshoe-shaped. But unlike Niagara, instead of concentrating its waters into two massive

154

falls, Iguazu is broken up into hundreds and hundreds of spouts. These shoot over the brink between the many islets which line the crest, crash on the ledge half-way down, and form again in new groups and combinations. Each individual spout has its own voice, but no two have the same note. Some shake the rock with booming bass notes; some, frail as spider's silk, chant a shy little melody. But all together they form a thousand-throated choir that roars out to this empty wilderness the same heroic music it sang at the beginning of history.

How fortunate we are to visit Iguazu while it still retains its unspoiled beauty. For soon the need of electric power to develop this forest domain will force Argentina and Brazil to build power-houses and power-lines where only the great trees, dripping with mist and moss, now stand. Some day there will be rows of cheap hotels where we now see showers of moon-flowers spangling the banks. The jaguars will be killed; the bright-winged life frightened away; the grandeur despoiled.

But when modern Progress has come down upon the Iguazu, we shall be able to remember the giant cataract as we first saw it falling in the moonlight—wild and glorious and free.

Among the great cities of the world, Rio de Janeiro, the glittering capital of Brazil, has no riv
for beauty. Its matchless harbor, surrounded by towering jungle-covered peaks and flooded i
tropical sunshine, makes one of the most glorious sights we shall see on our wonder-tour. Th
water of the bay is a deep and brilliant blue. The houses of the city are all painted in brigh

olors. Over all is an indigo sky. The dark Atlantic stretches to the east (at the right of the picture). Rio de Janeiro means the River of January. This name was given by explorers from Portugal who, spellbound by the beauty of the bay, anchored here in 1531. They arrived on New Year's Day, and, thinking the bay was the mouth of a river, named it the River of January.

CHAPTER XVI

THE RIVER OF JANUARY

If the cities of the world were to hold a beauty contest, which city do you think would be chosen Queen?

Paris would promptly demand the award, and scorn the claims of any other city. New York, Washington, San Francisco would receive votes from Americans. Austrians would name Vienna; Hungarians, Budapest; Australians, Sydney; Italians, Naples and Venice. But travelers who have visited them all, unite in choosing, for the rightful Queen, Rio de Janeiro, the glittering capital of Brazil. In their opinion—and in mine—Rio, for beauty, is without a rival. Our earth offers no more gorgeous sight than the picture of Rio's harbor and the luxurious metropolis that climbs from it up the mountain side.

Any collection of world marvels would be incomplete, I think, if it did not include the harbor of the City of the River of January.

A strange name for a city to have, isn't it? This name was given by the explorers from Portugal, who, spellbound by the matchless beauty of the bay, anchored there in 1531. They arrived on New Year's Day, and thinking the bay was the mouth of a river, named it Rio de Janeiro—the River of January.

It's a wonder these Portuguese navigators ever sailed away. Indeed, I'm not sure they did.

Almost at once the fame of Rio's bay began to spread across Europe. By 1620 a city had been founded on its shores. People came thronging from Spain and Portugal, eager to live in such a lovely place. By 1660 it was already a rich and proud seaport, the capital of Brazil. At the same time, New York was hardly more than a few dozen cabins, huddling, for protection against the Indians, behind wooden stockades.

On a peak-top, 2200 feet above Rio's harbor, stands this 100-foot white concrete statue of Christ, its arms extended wide to protect the happy and fortunate city below. From the statue one unbroken precipice falls all the way down to the shore of the bay.

Rio de Janeiro at night. Out of this shining sea of light the black peaks rise. The thousand of lamps lining the boulevard along the bay cast long reflections in the water. At the left, th Atlantic Ocean beats upon the white-hot shore. And over this glittering scene stands the statu of Christ, flooded with light, 2200 feet above the bay. (Look for it on right-hand page, in upper lef quarter of picture.) He holds out His arms to bless this paradise of beauty, this perfect unio of bay and mountain, of man and nature—this city of the River of January. This night pictur was taken from the top of Sugar Loaf, the 1300-foot rock spire guarding the entrance to th

Ewing Galloway.

harbor.   (See picture on page 157.)   Rio was more than three centuries old before anyone ever saw the city from this point, for, during all this time, no one had ever been able to
climb Sugar Loaf's steep, slick sides.   But a few years ago a sure-footed young Englishman
managed to reach the top.   There he planted a British flag, and no one could get it down except
himself.   Since then an observation platform has been built on the summit, which can be reached
by a cable-car.   Now, thousands of people every year visit the top of Sugar Loaf to behold—if
they go at night—the enchanting picture we see here.

To reach Rio from Iguazu Falls, we go back down the Parana River to Buenos Aires, the capital of Argentina, and there take an ocean steamer up the southern coast of Brazil. In the early morning our ship arrives at the mile-wide entrance to Rio's bay, and we see before us the world-famous harbor.

In this same harbor Magellan and his little fleet, on his celebrated first-voyage-around-the-world, anchored for two weeks. Just as he was dazzled by this vision of splendor, so are we. On three sides of us, steep peaks, drenched in jungle, tower a mile high out of the water. The water itself is a deep and brilliant blue. The forests on the jagged mountain wall behind are covered with a purple haze. Portuguese houses dot the slopes with red and white and orange. Over all is an indigo sky. The entire scene glows in the tropical sun that gives sparkle and splash to everything.

The buildings themselves, on close inspection, prove to be not so fine as in other great capitals. But that doesn't matter. You could build Rio of mud, and with its beautiful stage-setting it would still be the queen city of the world.

I first saw Rio in a manner in which few others have seen it. I arrived there during the time I was actively engaged in monkey-business—making my living with a hand-organ and a dancing, penny-grabbing monkey. Yes, that's true. I was an organ-grinder for a month. The monkey's name was Niño.

Looking for pennies, Niño and I roamed along Rio's palm-lined streets, playing *La Paloma* and *Valencia* at the top of my hand-organ's lungs. We paraded up and down the beautiful bathing beaches, followed by crowds of children in bathing suits. The Pied Piper of Hamelin never collected so many children as my monkey did. He loved the Brazilians and they loved him and gave him many pennies, which he brought to me.

One day Niño and I made an excursion by cable-car to the summit of Sugar Loaf, a thirteen-hundred-foot rock rising like a sentinel at the harbor entrance. It's as steep and smooth as

162

This gigantic statue of Christ, made of white concrete, and overlooking the harbor of Rio de Janeiro, is one of the biggest and most impressive statues in the world. It can be seen, day or night, from almost any point in the city below. The statue itself is 100 feet high. The pedestal adds another twenty feet.

Half Dome in Yosemite. Until some years ago, this peak, too, was supposed to be absolutely unclimbable. Then one morning the entire city was amazed to look up and see a British flag flying from the top of it. How had the flag got there? Who was the impudent person that had dared plant a foreign banner on top of Sugar Loaf?

A sure-footed young Englishman had done the trick. For days he kept in hiding while the whole angry city of Rio tried, by all known means, to get that flag down again. Then, at the height of the excitement, the flag suddenly disappeared. While nobody was looking, the Englishman had climbed up a second time and removed it.

Once conquered, the summit of Sugar Loaf soon became a favorite resort. Now there is a passenger car that carries you to the top on a cable. And from here, as from an airplane, you can look down at the painted harbor, the forested peaks, the three hundred jewel-like islands—and the Atlantic Ocean—that surround you.

But even more wonderful is the view from a much higher peak called Corcovado, which means the Hunchback. This peak is 2200 feet high, and from its summit one unbroken precipice falls all the way down to the harbor. Rising above this summit is a hundred-foot white figure of Christ, its extended arms protecting the happy and fortunate city below. From a thousand viewpoints in the streets and the harbor, the statue is visible. And at night, when the stone Christ is flooded with searchlights, His towering image seems to float among the stars.

On our own trip to Rio, we'll first explore the city and the bay, saving Corcovado for the last. We visit Sugar Loaf, the islands, the tree-lined avenues, and go swimming at the beaches where I once swam with Niño. Then, to visit Corcovado, we climb aboard a cog-railroad which takes us up the steep slopes. We mount through gardens and past villas, all bright with flowers and blossoming vines. On top, the giant statue towers straight above us. We walk around the base, come to the edge, and look over.

As at the Grand Canyon, we just stand silent under the spell of so much grandeur, certain that *this* is the most marvelous sight in the world. Peaks and pinnacles encircle the curving shores. Palaces and palms adorn the shining city. Sailboats fleck the intensely blue water, and scores of ships, entering or departing from this fairyland, leave their milk-white wakes across the bay. If we look to the east we see the Atlantic Ocean, and, in the far distance, the line where its waters meet the sky.

European Photos.

The hand and arm of the statue of Christ which stands on the mountaintop above Rio. The position of the statue is so high above the bay (two-fifths of a mile) that the clouds often gather in a vast white blanket below it and blot out the city. Then, to a visitor standing at the statue's feet, it seems to be floating across the sky, detached from the earth.

With the sunset comes a new beauty. The glittering bay mirrors the burning clouds, and then grows dark, while the topmost dome of Sugar Loaf still reflects the last gold rays.

Now the lights go on. This is the most enchanting moment of all. Countless numbers of twinkling lamps, almost half a mile below, dance and gleam and beckon. They outline the broad boulevards that skirt the harbor; they are clustered on the summit of every peak. They melt into one great blaze above the theaters and cafés. They rush before ten thousand motor cars, far out along the Atlantic beach. And over all the swimming sea of lights the glowing Christ, lifted above us, holds out His arms to bless and safeguard this paradise of beauty, this perfect union of bay and mountain, of man and nature—this city of the River of January.

CHAPTER XVII

GIBRALTAR

The Rock of Gibraltar! What a thrilling world-marvel we have in store for us here! It's the greatest fortress on earth, the almighty Lion of Rock, the Lord of the Mediterranean! To the ancient Greeks and Romans it was one of the Pillars of Hercules, towering fourteen hundred feet above the narrow straits where the Mediterranean joins the Atlantic. This was the point beyond which the early mariners dared not sail lest they come to the edge of the ocean and fall off. It has been, for two thousand years, the most famous of landmarks, the best-known symbol of power and defiance, its name known to every child in every civilized country in the world. We certainly mustn't miss *this* on our wonder-tour.

In my own childhood I saw pictures of this mighty Rock many times. I read how the Saracens, twelve hundred years ago, moving westward along the north coast of Africa, looked across the Straits of Gibraltar from the peaks on the African shore, and saw the great jutting Rock daring them to come and seize it if they could. To the Saracens of that time nothing seemed impossible. Under the leadership of their bold commander, Tarik, they accepted Gibraltar's challenge in the year 711, crossed the Straits, and took possession of the Rock. For himself, Tarik built a castle on the slope (Gebel-al-Tarik—the "Rock of Tarik"—became Gibr-al-tar). Then, using this castle as headquarters, he and his Moslem soldiers marched inland to conquer most of Spain.

And they held Spain and Gibraltar, as my history book told me, for seven hundred years. During these seven long centuries, all the ceaseless flow of Saracen commerce and people, the passage of their armies and fleets, used the Rock as an anchor and a stronghold.

But by 1462 the Spaniards were able to drive the Moslem invaders back to Africa. And when the last Saracens fled, they sailed from Gibraltar, from the very harbor where their ancestors had first set foot seven hundred years before.

Rid of her ancient enemy, Spain took possession of the Rock. Naturally, rival nations wanted it too, for whoever held Gibraltar controlled the entrance to all the Mediterranean. Attack after attack was made upon it. Spain lost it, and regained it, and lost it again. In 1704 Gibraltar fell into the hands of the English. In 1779 the French and Spanish together tried to wrest it away, but failed after a four-year siege. During this siege, over fifty battleships attacked the Rock by sea, and forty thousand soldiers by land. At times four hundred pieces of artillery were pounding away at the fort all at once. The defenders numbered only seven thousand. But *they* had the Rock to protect them, and plenty of red-hot cannon balls to fire back. These sizzling iron shot, called "hot potatoes" by the English defenders, set fire to the Spanish ships and caused their powder magazines to explode. The siege was in its fourth year when a treaty of peace ended the war, and left the English still in possession of the Rock.

Since then, as everybody knows, England has held on stubbornly to her prize, ignoring the fact that it is a natural part of Spain.

All this I learned as a boy in school. Gibraltar became one of my travel goals. When I saw it at last, there was no disappointment. It *did* look like a crouching lion, guarding the Straits. It *was* inspiring to behold. And I had several adventures on the Rock that will keep it bright in my memory for the rest of my life—adventures such as being arrested and tried as a spy because I had taken photographs of the view from the summit, a view that included a few cannon.

And because Gibraltar fascinated me, I want to be sure that you get to see this fortress too.

To reach it, we must cross the Atlantic from South America. As we approach the Straits, we see the famous landmark from afar. It looms high above everything. And directly opposite, eight miles away on the African shore, rises its twin, the other Pillar of Hercules.

We sail between these Pillars, into the Straits. Europe is on our left hand, Africa on our right. The Mediterranean stretches

e Rock of Gibraltar. Towering fourteen hundred feet above the narrow straits where the
diterranean meets the Atlantic, this great Lion of Rock for two thousand years has been the
t famous of landmarks. It is the world's best-known symbol of power and defiance. England has owned it since 1704.

Gibraltar is defended by more than 700 guns. We are allowed to enter the gun galleries. There we find long corridors dug out of the solid rock, and scores of cannon lined up in them. The cannon muzzles, looking through small openings in the face of the cliff, command the water of the Straits, far below.

ahead of us, the Atlantic behind. Closer and closer we approach the Rock. Higher and higher it grows. Is it as regal as you had hoped? Does it fill all your expectations?

From a distance, we cannot see a sign of the heavy cannon with which the fort bristles. But I can tell you for a fact that there are at least seven hundred monster guns (some people say a thousand) glowering down at us through round eyes in the Rock, or hidden in secret galleries, ready to spring out into the open at the press of an electric button.

As soon as we land we find the road which climbs to the summit. We follow it. About a third of the way up we pass the remains of Tarik's castle. I should know, because it's the local prison now, and I was held behind bars there until the military court found out that the "dangerous foreign spy" was only a young American student, out seeing the world and taking very bad photographs of all the interesting things he saw—cannon included—to send back to his family in Tennessee.

Climbing farther along the road, we come to an iron fence and a gate guarded by a sentry box. An English soldier now takes charge of us and guides us higher into the Rock's military zone. Special permission allows us to enter the gun galleries. Here we find long corridors dug out of the solid rock, and scores of cannon lined up in the hewn chambers. The cannon's muzzles, looking through small openings in the face of the cliff, command the water of the Straits, far below.

The cannon we are allowed to see are mostly old and useless, some of them dating back to the Napoleonic wars. But we know there are other galleries containing the newest and most deadly modern guns, which you may be sure no civilian is allowed to inspect. Gibraltar is the spearhead of the British Empire, and the War Office guards its secrets jealously.

Leaving the galleries behind we continue on up, higher and higher, right on to the pinnacle of Rockgun Point, fourteen hundred feet above the sea. Here, commanding two oceans and two continents, we find a nine-inch cannon. We climb onto it and look over the brink of the Rock, out upon the world.

And what a glorious world it is! Africa and Europe, the Atlantic and the Mediterranean! We can see the tiny ships far below, creeping east to Suez; turning, we see the sloping city on one side, and on the other a sheer precipice from the edge of which we could drop a stone into the waves a quarter of a mile below. Northward is Spain with its snowy Sierras; southward, the jagged crest of our wonderful Rock sags and rises once more to a point even higher than our own. The Straits glitter in the sun. The African Pillar of Hercules, so clear and so close, greets us from the other continent. Jupiter must have felt just as we feel, when he commanded the universe from the summit of Mount Olympus.

173

We climb to the pinnacle of the Rock of Gibraltar, fourteen hundred feet above the sea. We are in the presence of two oceans and two continents. The Mediterranean lies on the left of us, the Atlantic on the right. Across the Straits, only eight miles away, the peaks of Africa rise even higher than our Rock. Behind us tower the snowy mountain tops of Spain. We can see the tiny ships, far below, creeping east to India. On one side is the sloping city; on the other, a steep

recipice, from the edge of which we can drop a stone into the waves a quarter of a mile below.
upiter must have felt as we feel, when he commanded the universe from the summit of Mount
lympus. To the ancient Greeks and Romans, this huge Rock was one of the two Pillars of Her-
les. Its twin rose from the African shore opposite. This was the point beyond which the early
mariners dared not sail lest they come to the edge of the ocean and fall off.

The ridge of the Rock of Gibraltar, showing the signal station on the top. In the lower right corner we see a large white patch. This is a concrete rainwater-catch. Rain is the great Fortress' chief source of water. Gibraltar is a natural part of Spain, and for 200 years the Spaniards have been urging that England give it back to them. But since it guards the entrance to the Mediterranean, England has clung grimly to this all-important

Photograph by Richard Halliburton.

This moment, we are sure, is one of the great moments, one of the great adventures, of our lives. For my own part I can remember few that were greater. One of these was when I flew five thousand feet *above* the Rock of Gibraltar in my own airplane, the *Flying Carpet,* on my way to Timbuctoo, and looked down upon this pinnacle where we now stand.

The *Flying Carpet* made one wide circle, high in the air over Rockgun Point, saluted the mighty stone monarch, and then sped on to Tarik's country and beyond. As the fort faded away behind me, I thought, for the first time, of its future instead of its past. England has spent $250,000,000 fortifying the Rock against attack from land and sea. But I wondered, as I winged out over the indigo Straits, if the next war would find the greatest fortress in the world able to protect the city, and the docks, and the fleets of battleships in the harbor—and my jail—from being destroyed by bombs rained down from the *air.*

I realized one thing for a certainty: whatever becomes of this supreme fort—no matter who loses it or who seizes it, no matter to what purpose it may be put in the future—the Rock of Gibraltar, as long as the earth lasts, will remain one of its grandest monuments.

CHAPTER XVIII

CARCASSONNE

"I'm growing old, I've eighty years;
  I've labored all my life in vain.
In all that time of hopes and fears,
  I've failed my dearest wish to gain.
I see full well that here below
  Bliss unalloyed there is for none;
My prayer would else fulfillment know—
  Never have I seen Carcassonne!
Yet could I there two days have spent,
  While still the autumn sweetly shone,
Ah, me! I might have died content
  When I had looked on Carcassonne."

So crooned, one day, close by Limoux,*
  A peasant, double bent with age.
"Rise up, my friend," said I; "with you
  I'll go upon this pilgrimage."
We left, next morning, his abode.
  But (Heaven forgive him!) half-way on,
The old man died upon the road.
  He never gazed on Carcassonne.†

* Pronounced Lee-moo'.
† Quoted from a translation by John R. Thompson from the French of Gustave Nadaud.

There have been many, many people who have dreamed, as that French peasant dreamed, of visiting Carcassonne.

I was one. But I had better luck than that old man. I looked upon this City of Romance.

And if you'll go with me I'll take *you* there and show you why the old peasant wanted to see it, more than anything else on earth, before he died.

Like you, in his youth he had heard stories of the glamorous Middle Ages, of knights in armor, of damsels in distress, of cruel kings, and ogres and dragons. He had been told about castles on hilltops, about sieges where the attackers fought their way with swords across drawbridges, and where the defenders, shouting from the battlements, met the attack with showers of boiling oil and a hail of arrows. He liked to imagine himself bravely helping to defend a high-walled stronghold.

That was in his youth. Now, in his old age, he realized that such storied castles and citadels, with a few exceptions, were all gone—that in modern times, alas, most of them had been dragged down or had fallen into ruin.

But he knew that *one* such citadel, the very greatest of them, was still standing, every stone of it, as proud and towering as ever —Carcassonne. He knew that if he could go *there,* he would see the exact setting where his story-book battles had been fought, where the pageant of siege and conquest had reached its most terrible height. He would see the same moat and drawbridge, the same towers and walls and battlements, that had held back the Saracens and defied the bravest kings and captains of those far-off days. He would stand upon the walls that had echoed with the shouts of warriors and the clash of swords. He knew that all this exciting past was caught and preserved in Carcassonne. And he wanted, above all things, to gaze on this city which had filled his imagination ever since he first read tales of chivalry.

How sad it makes us to learn, in the poem, that he failed.

No such misfortune as his is going to happen to *us.* We've crossed Spain from Gibraltar, traveled over the Pyrenees, and are almost in sight of Carcassonne.

This city is in southwest France. It was an important center even before the birth of Christ. Often wrecked by enemies, but as often rebuilt, it saw the rise and fall of the Roman Empire. And for eight centuries afterward, it played a leading part in the affairs of this part of Europe.

A warlike race called the Visigoths made it their capital for three hundred years. The Saracens held it for fifty years. In the Middle Ages it stood long and terrible sieges. Its famous counts fought again and again against the kings of France for its possession.

Carcassonne—the City of Romance. In southwest France, this city, with its wonderful walls
the Middle Ages, has been the scene of battle and bloodshed for centuries. Of all the med
towns in France, this one was the most strongly fortified. Here the pageant of siege and
quest reached its most terrible height. Its walls and battlements, with their fifty towers,
back invasion after invasion, and defied the bravest kings and captains of those far-off days.
nobleman who held Carcassonne labored furiously to make it secure against any foe. By 1285 i

Courtesy Illustrated London News.

ged with two sets of walls, one inside and above the other. And from them, the peak-topped
vers rose to command every possible approach. If an enemy did break through the walls, the
stle would have been the hardest part of all to take. Carcassonne was as war-minded and as
ll defended as a battleship. In fact, after 1356, invading armies ceased even to threaten this
werful fortress. It was like threatening a stone mountain. What was the use? Carcassonne
is now a national monument, and houses only a few hundred people.

All the occupants of the citadel had one thing in common—a burning desire to strengthen the walls and fortifications. Each nobleman who held Carcassonne labored furiously to make it secure against any foe. By 1285, when it was definitely in the hands of the French King, the city was ringed with two sets of walls, one inside and above the other; and from them, fifty peak-topped towers rose to command every possible approach. If an enemy did break through the walls, the castle would have been the hardest part of all to take. Carcassonne was as war-minded and as well defended as a battleship. In fact, after the year 1356 when the Black Prince failed in the attempt, invading armies ceased even to threaten this unconquerable fortress. It was like threatening a stone mountain. What was the use?

But in the course of centuries, the city slowly lost power and importance. When cannon were invented, its vast walls and towers were no longer a defense. So the citizens moved down the hillside onto farms in the valley below, and left, almost deserted, what was one of the strongest walled cities in all Europe. But so skillfully and so solidly was it built, that it has since defied the centuries.

We see it first from afar, crowning a ridge above the Aude River. And between us and that hilltop, seven hundred years disappear. It's as if we've been given a magic eye that can whirl time back and see things exactly as they were at the time of the Crusades. Perhaps if we watch, besiegers will storm up the hill, with trumpets sounding, with armor flashing, to be met by spears and arrows from the walls.

But no besieging army appears, so we decide to climb the hill ourselves. We reach the moat, cross the drawbridge, enter the massively fortified gate, and pass through the double tiers of enormous walls, into a foreign world. Ancient houses lean crazily along the narrow, crooked streets. There is almost no one in sight. Where are the swordsmen and cross-bowmen who should have been guarding the gate? Where are the knights in armor who should be posted about the castle walls, and the noble ladies and banners and attendants that should be giving life to this deserted citadel?

182

We first see Carcassonne from afar, standing on the top of a ridge above the river. Between us and the hilltop, seven centuries disappear. Perhaps if we watch, besiegers will storm up the hill, with trumpets sounding, with arms flashing, to be met by stones and arrows from the walls. After we have climbed the hill ourselves, we reach the moat, enter the huge and heavy gates, and pass through the walls into a twelfth-century world. We climb to the ramparts, and here we can see the loop-holes through which the missiles were rained down upon the attackers. From here, too, we can look out across miles and miles of the rolling country of southern France.

Steps lead up the ramparts, and further up into a tower, where we can see the loop-holes through which arrows and stones were rained at the attackers. Ours is but one of the fifty towers—we can count the other forty-nine from where we stand. The castle itself has ten.

From this tower the defenders of the citadel must have seen many an enemy army approaching across the river. Here the Count of Carcassonne awaited the attack of his enemies, perhaps soldiers of the King of France. We can imagine the Royalists rushing the lower walls, placing their ladders, climbing up, falling back before the downpouring of arrows and flaming pitch.

The attackers retreat, only to come forward again with more ladders, more men, more determination. This time they reach the top of the lower wall and swarm over. But they now find themselves in a narrow corridor faced by a second and even stronger line of towers.

The defenders have retreated into the inner, shorter line, and are slaughtering their assailants who have been caught between the outer and the inner walls.

The King's army tries to rush the entrance gates. Here the shower from above is ten times as deadly. The bodies of Royalists are heaped up below the drawbridge, but the gates have scarcely been touched.

Encouraged, the Carcassonnians themselves open the inner gate, sally forth into the narrow space between the walls, and strike down every enemy found trapped there. Fired with success, they now lower the bridge, and charge across the moat surrounding the outer wall, straight into the ranks of the besiegers.

The crash of the two armies is shattering and frightful, but the Count's men have the dash, the confidence. They know this is their chance for victory.

Before such an onrush, the King's followers crumble, and turn, and flee.

And Carcassonne, smoking with the battle, surrounded by dead and dying, has proved once more its military strength.

All this is memory from the dim past now. No army has assaulted Carcassonne in many a long year. And today the proud citadel has very few inhabitants. But the ghosts are still there—the ghosts of Crusaders, Saracens, Visigoths, of Franks and French. And on each moonless night, any true native will assure us, these ghosts parade along the empty battlements and fight each other for possession of the silent walls. Then, with the approach of dawn, they march down the shafts of the ancient wells into the deep dungeons, to watch over the treasures which the people of Carcassonne believe are buried there.

As we depart from this romantic place, we glance back again to see the city's fifty towers still shining in the sky. We remember the poem, and the old peasant's desire—his one desire, and that not fulfilled. We are doubly sorry for him, and grateful for the privilege that a kinder fate has granted us. For we have seen the wonder-city from the days when knighthood was in flower. We have been to Carcassonne.

Mount St. Michael (often called by its French name, Mont St. Michel) is a strangely beautiful little island off the northern coast of France. Since the earliest times it has been a holy place. Over 1900 years ago French monks began to build the wonderful abbey on its summit. This mount

CHAPTER XIX

MOUNT ST. MICHAEL

On the northern coast of France, where the province of Normandy faces the English Channel, there rises a curious rocky islet, half a mile from shore, that is justly one of the most celebrated islets on earth. In any treasury of world-marvels it must always be one of the brightest jewels.

Like Carcassonne, the history of this isle goes back into the dim past. Long before the Roman era it was a pagan holy place—a bold, granite, tree-clad hillock rising 260 feet high in the midst of a great oak forest—not an island at all. On the summit stood a pagan shrine. Somewhere off in the distance, the English Channel washed the low, flat shore.

Then the Romans invaded northern Europe, pulled down the shrine, and set up a temple to Jupiter instead. With the arrival of Christianity, Jupiter, in turn, was overthrown. But the early Christians were no less impressed by this great natural altar in the forest. Where the Roman temple had stood they raised a rude chapel in which they could say their prayers. For almost two centuries, converts and pilgrims and gifts poured in upon this place of worship on the hilltop. Built in honor of St. Michael, the patron saint of France, it grew larger and richer. And still it looked out upon the green oak groves below.

Then, one day in the year 725, while the monks were kneeling in the church, the earth began to tremble, to heave, to sway back and forth violently. They rushed to the windows to learn what terrible misfortune had overtaken them. It was a great earthquake.

And there below their church they saw the ocean rushing inland with a horrible speed, high as the oak trees, an overwhelming wall of water which no man-made structure could resist.

But the Mount, while it shuddered with the shock, stood safe against the tidal wave. The water raged past, as far as the first line of hills—then began to recede, as swiftly as it came. And with

187

On our visit to Mount St. Michael, we reach the shore of Normandy. When we look out across flat tidelands, dreary and half-hidden in the mist, we can scarcely believe that the sight we see not a mirage. There it is, springing alone out of the English channel—a glorious high-tower islet, surrounded by medieval walls, clustered with quaint dwellings, all struggling reckles

uphill toward the abbey which crowns the top of the rock. Who could have told us that the abbey would make such a fairy-tale picture? The island is separated by half a mile of tide-washed beach. The shore itself—once an oak forest—is now flat pasture land where sheep and cattle graze. The abbey is a national monument now and uninhabited except for the guards.

it went all the houses, trees, cattle, and human beings, on the low-land. Horrified at the disaster, the monks watched helplessly as the whole rich plain below them was carried out to sea. When the flood at last departed, they found themselves surrounded on every side by water, water, water, where, so short a time before, there had been farms and forests. St. Michael's Mount had become, in the twinkling of an eye, the Island of St. Michael.

But it was still only a part-time island. Twice a day, a forty-foot tide went out—one of the highest tides found anywhere in the world—and left the hillock again standing high and dry on the tidal flats, linked to the shore by half a mile of beach.

Naturally the monks were grateful to God for their deliverance from the great tidal wave. So, instead of abandoning their tide-washed home, they turned from farming to fishing; and whatever riches the sea gave to them they gave freely to their Mount.

As the centuries passed, the modest chapel grew into a splendid abbey lifted up on the very pinnacle of the isle. For beauty and richness this abbey had no rival in Christendom. No other shrine in France drew so many pilgrims, or received so many gifts from kings.

On our own pilgrimage, we think we know what to expect, for Mount St. Michael, as it stands today, has been pictured perhaps more than any other abbey on earth. But when we reach the coast of Normandy, and look out across the flat marshlands along the shore, all dreary and half-hidden in mist, we can scarcely believe that the sight we behold is not a mirage.

There it is, springing all alone out of the sea—the glorious high-towering islet, surrounded by medieval walls, clustered with quaint dwellings, all struggling recklessly uphill toward the abbey which crowns the tip of the rock. Who could have told us that the abbey would make such a fairy-tale picture? Those great stone buttresses, strong and heavy though they are, seem scarcely able to prop up the buildings which soar higher and ever higher, one above the other. We see, piled up, the bishop's palace, the private chapels, the church itself, and the topmost tower of stone which

Publishers Photo Service.

When the great tidal wave, which struck Mount St. Michael 1200 years ago, had subsided, the monks living in the abbey found themselves surrounded on every side by water, where there had been farms and forests before. Since then, twice a day, a forty-foot tide goes out—one of the highest tides found anywhere in the world—and leaves the hillock standing high and dry on the tidal flats linked to the shore by half a mile of beach.

thrusts up one final gilded spire, half a thousand feet into the sky, as a pedestal for the shining statue of St. Michael.

Such an astonishing vision makes us hurry along the causeway (built in recent times between the shore and the Mount) to get a closer view. And the closer we come, the better we appreciate the beauty of this upsurging little island.

As we enter the frowning gates, we are reminded that the sea was not the only enemy St. Michael's monks had to fear. There was constant warfare in those days. So the bishops had their armies to command, as well as their prayers to say. They raised great walls around Mount St. Michael, and deep in the rock under the altar they dug dungeons and torture rooms to hold captive the enemies of the Church.

The walls needed to be high and strong. Against so rich an abbey, attacks were frequent and stubborn. English armies, during the Hundred Years' War (1340-1450), besieged the island several times, expecting it to fall easily into their hands. But it did not surrender even when the English had captured all the rest of northern France. Protected by St. Michael, it remained free, and French.

With all its wars and sieges, the abbey enjoyed periods of peace, too. And during these peaceful times, pilgrims continued to come in by the hundreds. To provide for them the monks built more houses and *more* houses until the tiny town (only two-thirds of a mile around at the water-line) filled every inch of space within the walls. But long before Columbus sailed for America, the town had stopped growing for lack of room, and had reached the same state we find it in today, huddled, clinging, and climbing.

To visit the abbey itself (now a national monument and unoccupied except for the caretakers), we clamber up steps and ramps, up steep alleys arched by flying bridges. We pass through deep doorways and dark corridors, up more steps. We enter carved stone halls where French knights feasted with the princes of the Church, halls empty and silent now. We move on through delicate chapels, across tiny gardens that are scarcely more than

192

unt St. Michael had to withstand many a siege, for it was very rich. For protection against acks, the monks built a strong belt of walls around the shore of the island. Between wars and ges pilgrims came by the thousand to worship here at St. Michael's shrine. On the tip-top of spire, half a thousand feet above the sea, stands the winged statue of St. Michael, the patron saint of France.

window boxes, and come at last to a high balcony which overlooks the town.

But still we have not reached the top. Up echoing spiral steps we go, into the supreme tower, into the very spire itself, where our view is almost as lofty as St. Michael's own. In sheer giddy swoops the walls fall away below us, straight to the base of the abbey's foundations. Below that, in steep terraces, the town scrambles down to the water's edge. And beyond, on all sides, is the shallow sea, for the tide is in. If we are patient and have the time to wait, we can watch the forty-foot tide flow out. It does not melt slowly, as on most shores, but rolls away in one great charging wave, leaving five miles of sand exposed; and then comes rushing back again, a relentless wall of water, with the speed of a racing horse.

How many times, from this high point, the monks looked out upon enemy armies battering at the sea-gate between the tides! How many times, from this same place, these monks watched the attackers flee, defeated, as the sea rolled in to defend the island it had made! And standing here, when the siege was over and peace had come again, the lookout, almost daily, shouted down to the garrison that a king or a baron, a knight or a bishop, accompanied by his followers, was riding across the flats toward Mount St. Michael; or that a multitude of pilgrims were assembling on the shore, waiting for the outgoing tide to leave them a bridge of sand.

Among the confusion of roofs and walls and stair-step streets, falling away below, one curious object catches our eye. It's an abandoned wooden track, three hundred feet long and three feet wide, which climbs at a steep angle straight toward us up the rocky slope. This track, supporting two parallel rails, begins at the sea-wall and ends at the abbey, at a point two hundred feet high. We ask our guide to explain its purpose.

In answer he tells us a strange story:

From the time the abbey was built, down to fairly recent days, this inclined track served as the abbey elevator. It was used mostly for the lifting and lowering of provisions and building materials. The car was only a huge wicker basket set on small iron wheels fitted to the track. A rope tied to the basket acted as elevator cable. Lifting power was supplied by two monks, at the upper end, turning a crank and windlass which wound up the rope. The basket very rarely carried passengers—only an occasional wounded soldier, or a monk who was too old and fat to climb the long steep steps.

When the English were first besieging Mount St. Michael, at the beginning of the Hundred Years' War, one of their officers, looking up at the abbey from the tidal flats, noticed this crude elevator, and the wicker car sliding up and down the track. The elevator gave him what he thought was a very clever idea . . . the car might be used (if somehow he could get possession of it) to hoist his soldiers right into the abbey itself, high above the defenders on the lower walls.

First of all, in secret, he tried to make friends with several of the defenders inside the town, and fortune favored him. By bribery he was able to win the aid of four disloyal French monks who were willing, for money, to betray their abbey.

Two of these monks, under cover of darkness, helped a picked band of twenty English soldiers over the wall, planning to place them, one at a time, in the elevator basket. Then the other two traitors, seizing the crank, at the upper end of the track, were supposed to wind in the rope that pulled up the basket. Twenty men, each armed with a sword, stood ready to make this daring journey.

Then, just as the first soldier was being lifted to the summit, the commander of the abbey-garrison discovered the plot. Quickly and quietly he seized and killed the two traitor-monks working the windlass. Then he himself continued to wind up the car.

Down below, the other two monks, unaware of what was happening above, continued to help the invaders over the wall and into the basket. One by one the soldiers, cautioned not to speak or to make any noise until all twenty were united in the abbey, disappeared as the basket was hauled up the track into the darkness. Up with a soldier—down empty—up with a soldier—down empty—silently and stealthily, twenty times.

The forty-foot tide rushes in from the sea and past Mount St. Michael with the speed of a gallo-
ing horse. This terrible tide has been the Mount's chief protection, for every attacking army h
had to flee before it or drown. During the Hundred Years' War between France and Engla
the English attacked the Mount again and again, but the tides prevented them from taking it.

ccasion they tried (with tragic results) to enter the abbey by means of the abbey-elevator
slid up and down an inclined wooden track. Part of this track is still preserved and can be
seen on the right hand page slightly to the right of the crease in the picture. It runs between
vo white houses half way up the hillside and enters the abbey just below a large black window.

Outside on the starlit beach, the English waited impatiently for the gate to be flung open from within by their fellow-country-men.

But violent and terrible things were taking place at the basket-elevator's upper station. As the English soldiers, one by one, reached the top, they were swiftly dragged out of the basket by the abbey guards and beheaded with one blow of an ax. Then, over and over, the basket made another trip down for another unsuspecting victim. . . .

Presently the English commander received word that all twenty of his men had disappeared into the heights above. Eagerly he peered up toward the black summit of the Mount, watching for the signal torch which would tell him that the abbey had been seized and the defenders killed.

Ten minutes he waited. No torch appeared. No clashing sound of battle came down to him from the peak top—only silence. Twenty minutes—half an hour—two hours—four. Dawn came . . . still no signal from his men. And then the tide swept in, and he and his army had to flee for their lives.

Why, thought the commander, had his twenty bold soldiers not given him the signal? Why had they failed to open the gates? Standing on the shore, and looking out across the insurging tide at the proud, unconquerable Mount soaring triumphant in the sunrise—he knew the tragic answer.

CHAPTER XX

THE ORNAMENT AND THE HONOR OF FRANCE

This is a story about a great cathedral. But let us delay a moment, so that we may first approach it at the side of a young girl who played a heroic part in its history. . . .

In the year 1412, in the little town of Domremy, in France, a baby, destined to become her country's most famous girl, was born.

She died at nineteen, but so inspired had her short life been and so tragic was her death, that from that time to this she has been the national heroine of France.

Of course you know whom I mean—Joan of Arc.

As a child, Joan was different from the other village children. She had a more serious nature, and a deep feeling for religion. She liked to listen to stories about the saints. When the other girls were dancing in the village square, Joan would be found in church.

When she was thirteen, just a barefooted little peasant still unable to read, she happened to be sitting one day in her father's garden. Someone spoke to her—or so Joan always thought. She looked up to answer. There was no one in sight. But before her there shone a great light, and from this light came a voice, sweet and gentle as an angel's. Strange to say, Joan was not afraid, for it was the voice of St. Catherine speaking to her, and giving her spiritual counsel.

And this vision, Joan said, came again and again to her. Some times St. Margaret accompanied St. Catherine. Joan saw these two saints dressed as queens, very beautiful and radiant. Sometimes they were accompanied by St. Michael. These heavenly visions appeared and talked to Joan two or three times a week for five years.

All during these years France and England were at war. By the time Joan was seventeen, the English had overrun half of

France, and were about to besiege Orleans, one of the most important cities in the country.

The news of Orleans' distress was carried even to the village of Domremy. And Joan's voices, turning from spiritual to national things, told this innocent and unlettered country maid, who had probably never been a day's journey from her village in all her life, that she must rescue Orleans and save France. They also said she must help place Charles, the timid Dauphin (a title given the Crown Prince), on the throne which had been denied him by the English and his own French rivals.

Was any other seventeen-year-old girl in history ever given such an astounding order?

The order was no more astounding than the fact that Joan prepared to carry it out. Her family thought she had lost her mind . . . a simple barefooted peasant girl going off like this to rescue besieged cities and show the Dauphin of France how to win his crown! Why didn't she stay home, tend her cows, and mind her own business?

But Joan was determined. She felt that her voices had commanded her, and that they were voices straight from God.

Overcoming every difficulty, she reached the nearest French army-post. There, at a time when the fortunes of France were at their lowest point, Joan's faith in herself—in her voices—so impressed one of the officers that he agreed to help her. We may as well try farm-girls-who-hear-voices, he thought—everything else has failed to stop the English.

She kept insisting that she must see the Dauphin; that if he would only follow her advice she would make him King.

Not believing such fantastic promises, but moved by Joan's eagerness, the friendly officer persuaded the Dauphin actually to receive her.

At the castle of Chinon, where the Dauphin was holding court, Joan was brought into the royal presence. The Dauphin hid himself among his courtiers. One of them, just to make fun of what they all thought was only a half-mad child, pretended *he* was the Dauphin.

200

But some power guided Joan, to the amazement of everyone, straight to the real Prince.

She kneeled at his feet, and in her peasant speech said, "Most noble Dauphin, I have come from God to help you and your kingdom."

The Dauphin no longer took her earnestness lightly. There was something very forceful about this girl. He talked to her in private. Again she assured him, "I am God's messenger, sent to tell you that you are the King's son and the true heir of France."

At length, moved by the clamor of the people who believed Joan was truly sent from Heaven, the Dauphin agreed to give her whatever she wanted for her plan to save France. First she asked for a suit of armor. She got it. Next she asked for permission to rescue Orleans. She got that too. Then off she went to the besieged city, carrying a white banner and accompanied by a band of armed followers.

And so inspired was her leadership, and such a fighting fury did she arouse in the French soldiers, that they not only rescued Orleans from the English, but drove the invaders back in a dozen other battles.

In triumph Joan returned to the Dauphin. She insisted that nothing now stood in the way of his coronation; that he must go to the city of Reims and be crowned there, where for generations the kings of France had been crowned before him. And after long hesitation Charles agreed.

At the head of their army, Joan and the Prince marched toward Reims. As they drew near the city, Joan saw ahead, lifted high above the houses, the towers of an enormous and sublimely beautiful cathedral. Solid stone though it was, it seemed made rather of lace, so carved with sculpture were its walls, so gracefully and delicately wrought its towers, so countless its statues and spires and pinnacles.

On July 16, 1429, Joan and her companions gathered in the plaza in front of the church. The full glory of the structure, with its wealth of sculptured stone, its gorgeousness of ornament, looked down upon her. For over two hundred years the people of Reims

Before the great portals of Reims Cathedral stands the statue of Joan of Arc on horseback and clad in armor. Joan first saw this wonderful cathedral in 1429. This heroic maid was then just seventeen years old. The full glory of the church looked down upon her. For two centuries th

of Reims had been building this marvel of marvels. When Joan, with shining eyes, looked on it for the first time, she knew she beheld "the ornament and the honor of France."

had been building this marvel of marvels. Into its construction had gone not only the fortunes of its builders, but their hearts and souls as well. Each workman had been proud to give, without pay, his labor and his skill, since the church was a holy monument to the glory of God.

And more: it was also to be, from its very beginning, the royal, the national church of France. On this spot the country's first Christian king, Clovis, had been baptized in 496. And from that day until Joan's own time—over nine hundred years—Reims had been the sacred city, its cathedral chosen for the coronation of French kings.

All this history made *this* church blessed above all others. When Joan, with shining eyes, looked at it for the first time, she knew she stood before "the ornament and the honor of France."

Right beside the Dauphin, who was followed by a vast and glittering train of nobles, Joan entered the great portals. High up over the doors she saw the rows of stone kings who had reigned before *her* King. Inside, she found the very scene about which she had been dreaming for months—the pageant of the coronation. The Bishop and his priests were dressed in priceless robes, the Dauphin in gold cloth. Amid incense and blazing candles and the music of trumpets he walked to the altar. There in a flood of rose light streaming down from the great jeweled windows, the Bishop of Reims put the crown upon the head of the Dauphin and named him Charles VII, King of France.

Through all the pomp and ceremony, Joan stood beside her Prince, holding a cross in her hands. And then, when the Bishop had spoken, this inspired girl—she was still only seventeen years old—who alone had brought this historic moment to pass, fell at the new King's feet. "Gentle King," she said, "now is fulfilled the will of God that I should raise the siege of Orleans, and lead you to the city of Reims to receive the holy coronation, and show that you are indeed King and the rightful lord of the realm of France."

204

Ewing Galloway.

From 1429 to 1914 Reims Cathedral continued to receive the homage of all the world. All French kings up to 1824 were crowned here. It was called "noble among the churches of France," and the centuries rolling over it seemed to make it only more noble, more beautiful.

But less than two years later, this heroic maid, deserted by Charles, betrayed by those she had saved, hated by the princes of the Church—this heroic maid, in her nineteenth year, was taken prisoner and tried on the charge of being a witch. Judged guilty by a court of bishops, she was given over to the English, and in May, 1431, in the public square of Rouen, was burned to death at the stake.

Joan of Arc's tragic end took place more than five hundred years ago. Many of the scenes with which she was familiar have disappeared. But the scene of Charles VII's coronation—Reims Cathedral—still stands.

From 1429 to 1914 the Cathedral continued to receive the homage of all the world. French kings up until 1824 were crowned there. It was called "noble among the churches of France." It was called "the most beautiful structure produced by the Middle Ages." The centuries rolling over it seemed to make it only more noble, more beautiful.

In 1896 a grateful French nation erected a statue of Joan of Arc, in armor, on horseback, sword aloft, in the plaza before the great doors—the plaza where she had first stood and looked with wonder on the Cathedral of Kings.

Then came 1914 and the Cathedral's years of agony. Early in the War a German shell set on fire the repair-scaffolding around the front portal, and the flames cracked and defaced the statues of the kings and saints. And this was but the beginning of Reims's ruin.

Altogether some three hundred heavy shells struck the church. The interior caught fire. The roof crashed in upon the altar where Joan of Arc had stood at the coronation of her King. In the windows the ancient and glorious jeweled glass that had shed its light upon her head was smashed to bits. The stone angels were left wingless, the saints headless. The lace towers were gashed and torn. In the aisles, fragments of broken statues lay in heaps. Fortunately, French soldiers rescued the beloved statue of Joan, in the midst of a bombardment.

During the Great War, between 1914 and 1918, Reims Cathedral suffered terrible injuries. It was torn by German shells and blasted by flames. The delicate statues and stone carvings were shattered; the ancient glass windows smashed to bits. The flaming roof crashed in upon the altar where Joan of Arc had stood at the coronation of her King. French soldiers are here parading before the war-ravaged church. They have removed Joan's statue, and piled up sand bags around the door.

In the city outside, a thousand houses were completely destroyed. Nearly two thousand civilians lost their lives.

As a youth in school, I had the sad experience of seeing Reims Cathedral less than a year after the War was over. Nothing had been done to repair its terrible injuries. Sand bags were still piled high against the doors. Gaunt and blackened it rose—a corpse of a church, roofless and desolate. Nothing I saw along the battle front gave me such a heartache, or brought home to me the brutality of war so strongly as the sight of this Cathedral's shattered glory.

The sculptured front face, and the towers overhead—scarred and blasted though they were—had not collapsed. I thanked God for that much. Even in this broken state, the Cathedral was still magnificent. War itself and all its fiendish weapons seemed unable to destroy the nobility and beauty of this divine structure.

I have written overlong about this world-marvel, its history and its tragedy, because I want you to sense the majesty of this heroic and time-worn building; to feel, as you enter its doors, the reverence that I felt.

As Joan first saw it, we see it too, from the distant plain, towering above the city. Beginning in 1920, it enjoyed a long period of careful and loving reconstruction. The roof has been rebuilt—thanks to American donations—so that from afar the church makes much the same appearance as before the War.

We reach the city. Almost every house we see is new. We emerge from one of the narrow streets and find ourselves in a public square. . . . Before us towers the Cathedral.

We knew it was going to be impressive, but we were not prepared to be so overwhelmed. True, the windows are refitted with modern stained glass; new heads and arms have been put upon the saints; new sculpture placed upon the shattered walls; the towers bolstered up again; the whole church streaked and spotted with new stones which stand out sharply from those that have been weathering through the centuries. But despite all these sad patches on its beauty, the Cathedral, seen from the public square, presents as inspiring a picture to us as it did to Joan of Arc when she stood on this same spot five hundred years and more ago.

To our delight we find the statue of Joan herself—still lifting high her sword, still courageous—back in its place before the great portal. And it seems to us that the Cathedral has caught from Joan her own unconquerable spirit.

We enter the doors. When we have become accustomed to the indoor gloom we see, where there used to be a magnificent array of medieval art, only a vast barrenness. It is roofed and walled, yes. But gone is the wealth of carving—the statues, the stone tapestries. The archbishop's throne, the stalls, the pulpit, the choir, the altar where Joan watched Charles VII crowned, are no more, consumed in a furnace of fire when the flaming roof crashed down. While substitutes have been put back, they can not compare with the beautiful originals.

But the modern rebuilding has not shaken the spirit of the great structure. With all its injuries and repair, it is still noble among churches—still the ornament and the honor of France.

Otto Bettmann.

Reims Cathedral in flames, fired by German shells in 1914.

CHAPTER XXI

THE TIGER OF THE ALPS

The Alps! Since the days of ancient Rome, the very name of these mountains has carried with it a thrill and a challenge. For more than twenty centuries, this glorious group of dazzling peaks and glaciers, of deep-set mountain lakes and tumbling streams, of pine forests and flowering glades, has stirred the imagination of the world.

The Alps are not remarkable for height (with two or three exceptions they are no taller than our Rockies), but as a group they are intensely dramatic—close together, commanding in form, wrapped in glittering snow. Even as a boy I was drawn toward them. Over my desk in school there hung a poster showing one of their highest peaks—the Matterhorn. My picture was titled, "The Tiger of the Alps." Every time I looked up at its snowy pinnacle, I had a new urge to rush away to Switzerland and try to climb this very Alp.

When, just after leaving college, I stood at last in its shadow, the Matterhorn did not disappoint me. I had not realized, from the picture, how proud it was, how all alone it stood, how straight-up its walls rose. It was far more dangerous looking than I had expected. How did anybody *ever* climb to the top!

But I knew that if it were the last thing on earth I did, I was going to try just that.

The fact that the Matterhorn had an evil reputation did not discourage me. I knew there was a special graveyard where the Matterhorn's victims were buried; and a museum where their climbing gear is preserved as a memorial. But its bad name only lent added interest. Who wants to climb a mountain that *isn't* dangerous?

Up to 1865, the Matterhorn was considered hopelessly unclimbable. The other great peaks of the Alps—Mont Blanc, Monte Rosa, the Jungfrau, the Dom—had long since been conquered. *This* mountain, however, defied the world. It had already killed several

210

reckless adventurers who dared approach too near its top, and it promised the same fate to any who followed them.

Then in 1865 four skillful English mountaineers, led by a famous climber named Whymper, came to Switzerland to try the impossible—to scale the Matterhorn. With three Swiss guides the party started up from Zermatt, the village at the mountain's base. The villagers said good-bye to them with heavy hearts . . . the climbers were surely headed for their doom.

Steadily these seven bold sportsmen mounted upward, tied by a single stout rope to one another. The route they chose to the summit lay along a ridge where two of the steep pyramid's three sides meet. They clambered to a point within six hundred feet of the top. There they faced the obstacle that had turned back or killed all previous climbers—the "hang-over," a place where the ridge was worse than straight up-and-down. It actually leaned out over the valley.

These climbers, however, were not to be stopped. They clung to the rock even here. They crawled over it, plowed through the summit's snows, and attained the topmost height.

The tyrant had been mastered.

But on the way down, disaster overtook the party. Just at the hang-over, the youngest member of the group, a Cambridge student, slipped on the ice, plunged over the edge of the precipice, and, as all seven were roped together, pulled one after another into the abyss until only Whymper and two of the guides were left. They braced their bodies in desperation against the drag of their falling comrades; and the rush was checked, with the three Englishmen and one guide dangling four thousand feet above the glacier. For a moment the rope remained taut; then, unable to bear the strain, it broke, and let four of the seven fall to a tragic death.

My own climb was one of the grand events of my life. To be sure, it was a struggle every inch of the way, both for my climbing

The Tiger of the Alps—the Matterhorn. Few mountains in the world are as proud and beaut
as this wonderful peak. It is only 14,780 feet high (slightly higher than Mount Whitney,
highest mountain in the United States), but so straight-up are its rock walls that no one
able to climb it till 1865, many years after all the other peaks had been conquered. Of the se

who first reached the top, four were killed on the way down. They crawled up the edge of
sharp ridge facing "this way" in the picture. On our climb we follow the same route. The
p out-jutting elbow, one quarter of the distance below the summit, is the "hangover"—the
cially dangerous point where the cliff leans out over the valley. Fixed ropes are now used
to help climbers past this difficulty.

Ewing Galloway.

companion and for myself. I found here a much steeper, more difficult and more exhausting climb than Popo, though not as high by three thousand feet. Without the assistance of our two able and tireless Swiss guides, who roped themselves to us and dragged us back every time we started slithering toward the graveyard in Zermatt, we could never have reached the top. When we finally got down, and safely home to our hotel, I ached so painfully from head to foot I swore I'd never do battle with this mountain again.

But that was several years ago. The Matterhorn's hardships have faded somewhat in my memory, and I recall far more vividly the thrills. In fact, if you are willing to take a chance and attempt the climb, I'll go too.

Oh, so you were waiting for the invitation?

All right—but don't blame me if you're sorry!

From Reims we go by train south to Switzerland, along the shores of Lake Geneva, then travel up the narrow canyon of the Visp River, and reach Zermatt. We find this charming little mountain village shrinking deep into the valley as if frightened by the terrible frozen pinnacles hanging over it.

In the morning sunshine we see the boldest of the pinnacles rearing up before us, scorning the earth and holding itself apart from other Alps. It's our Matterhorn.

We secure guides, one for each of us, and cleated shoes, and ice-axes, and sweaters—it will be cold on top. If we *get* on top!

The first stretch is easy, a zigzag path up the lower slopes, through groves of pines. All day we continue to twist up this trail. At nine thousand feet we begin to suffer from the thinness of the air. At eleven thousand, in the later afternoon, we come to the log hut where climbers pass the night. Breathless and spent, we wonder how much higher our lungs and legs will let us go tomorrow.

And then we glance down into the valley from which we have climbed, and forget how tired we are. Our cabin overlooks a field of glaciers far below. A semi-circle of snow-sparkling crags looms before us, while four thousand feet above, the Matterhorn's white crest catches the rays of the waning sun, and warns us to stop where we are.

After resting in our bunks until three o'clock in the morning, we start again. This early departure is wise, for we should complete as much of the climb as possible before the sun rises to melt the ice and make it doubly dangerous. Each of us roped to a guide, we brave the freezing air, and by starlight begin to ascend the cliff.

We are now following the same ridge up which the Whymper party blazed their trail. It grows steeper and steeper, and increasingly difficult. We crawl upward with great caution. Our ridge of rock is only twenty inches wide, with two thousand feet to fall on either side, in case we slip. Snow and ice have filled every crack. The guides ahead of us swing their axes to chop a foothold. We have to use elbows and knees and toes and teeth, as well as hands and feet, to gain each yard.

We come to one especially dangerous point which I have good reason to remember. On my previous climb, I lost my footing here and began to slide down the west wall of the Matterhorn. But my guide was used to amateur climbers like me. In a flash he leaned his weight on the rope connecting us, and I stopped with a jerk.

Every few minutes now, we halt to get our breath. Our heads are spinning; we are suffering from mountain sickness, and trembling from weariness. You say this is much worse than Popo? Well, I warned you it would be.

And our troubles have just begun. We're coming to the hang-over, the place where four of the Whymper party lost their lives. To add to the difficulties, an icy wind, thick with snow from the cliffs, tears at us, freezes our faces, stiffens our fingers. In order to stand against this blast, we cling like glue to the rock-face, not daring to look down.

Since Whymper's day, the hang-over is not quite the terrifying place it used to be. An iron spike has been driven into the rock above the bulge, and twenty-five-foot cables dangle from it. We

215

clutch these cables, but we are too cold, too exhausted, to pull ourselves up those twenty-five feet. The guides expected this; so going ahead, they heave away at our safety-ropes, and help us to drag ourselves up and over.

The last few hundred yards are steepest of all, and deep in snow. We hope we'll reach the top soon—we can't hold out much longer.

Our guides yell at us above the howling wind to keep going, keep going. With half-closed eyes, we struggle desperately on.

"You're there!" shout the guides. "Look!"

We look. Was there ever in the world such a sight! We are 14,780 feet high—three-fifths of a mile lower than the rim of Popo, true; but the view here is even more glorious. We're on the point of what seems a towering spire of ice. On all sides of us falls the abyss. Switzerland's peaks and valleys, pitched and tumbled, lie below. We can see every mountain in the Alps— Mont Blanc, huge and white to the west, rising several hundred feet higher than our own peak; the Jungfrau, lovely and pale and snow-blanketed, ruling the north. Down Monte Rosa's slopes, to the east, the great Gorner Glacier moves its shining sea of ice. To the south fade the plains of Italy. Flocks of clouds roll along far down in the valley. Overhead the sky is almost black.

We are more tired than we have ever been in our lives, but oh, so proud. This crystal air, this sky, this snow and space, send a surge of rejoicing through our hearts. We have achieved the first ambition in the life of every mountaineer. We've climbed the Tiger of the Alps.

But this perch is perilous. We must escape from it while we can. Straining and struggling to get safely back down the four-thousand-foot ladder, we rest at the shelter, and then limp on home to Zermatt. As we enter the peaceful little town, we look behind us, up at the soaring frozen monster we have conquered. We still can't quite understand how we ever got up it, or having got up, how we ever got down.

At this moment the sunset is turning this huge iceberg to one vast orange flame. A crown of angry clouds has gathered about its pinnacle, and they too seem set on fire. We know a storm is brewing on the summit, that up there the wind is screeching across the black sky and lashing the snow in fury from the rocks.

But down here in this serene and gentle world, the children come to welcome us back, with flowers in their hands; and the soft tinkle of cowbells floats across the valley as the herds wander home in the twilight.

As for ourselves, we can think only of bed, and of rest for our aching limbs. But tomorrow—how proud we'll be! For we have won our diplomas as mountain-climbers—we've scaled the Matter-horn.

At the top of the Great St. Bernard Pass, leading across the Alps from Switzerland into Italy, one finds the grim and heavy buildings of the St. Bernard Monastery. It is the most famous and most romantic monastery in the world. Situated at an elevation of 8100 feet, the buildings are half-

CHAPTER XXII

THE MONASTERY OF ST. BERNARD

As every schoolboy knows, Switzerland is separated from Italy by a towering wall of Alps. The Matterhorn itself is set squarely on the border line. Upon its summit there are two crosses—one in Swiss territory, one in Italian.

Winding up and over this mighty range, several highroads lead from one country into the other. Naturally, these roads seek the passes.

At the summit of the loftiest of these highways, right beside the Swiss-Italian border, there stands on the Swiss side of the line, at a point 8100 feet high, a huge and gloomy building, box-shaped and unadorned. It looks just like a prison. This building has been inhabited continually for nearly five hundred years, but there is not a tree or a garden in sight—only a vast expanse of ice and rock, overshadowed by the highest peaks in the Alps. During five months of the year, this building is half-buried in snow. The drifts are so deep from December until May that no outsider can come to it except on skis, and without them no one who dwells there can escape.

Then *why,* I am sure you're asking, do I include such a grim, frozen and unbeautiful place in a Book of Marvels?

I include it because this building is the Monastery of St. Bernard, the most famous, most romantic monastery in the world.

It is natural that this place should be well known in Europe, located as it is at the top of the pass through which runs one of the most frequented motor roads on the continent. But its fame is not limited to Europe. Who in America, or South Africa, or Australia, has not heard of this monastery? Yet it is not because such famous military leaders as Hannibal and Cæsar and Napoleon led their armies past its site, that the monastery is so celebrated abroad. Nor is it because of the long history of the Bernardine Brotherhood, which has its headquarters here. It is because of the wonderful *dogs* who live here and rescue travelers from the snow.

219

The world-famous St. Bernard dogs accompany their master on a visit to the statue of St. Bernard, the monk who founded the monastery at the top of the Alpine pass named for him. These huge and intelligent dogs have been trained to seek out travelers lost in the snow and to lead the monks to the rescue. The monastery building can be seen in the background.

It is likely that every boy or girl who reads this page has seen, at some time, a picture of a St. Bernard dog, with a flask of brandy attached to its collar, bringing aid to a snow-bound wayfarer. The details may vary; the dog may be dragging the unconscious traveler out of a drift, or barking over his fallen form to attract the attention of the monks. But whatever the illustration, the idea has struck the imagination of us all and made the St. Bernard dog loved and respected throughout the world.

The history of the home of these dogs goes back nearly one thousand years:

As soon as northern Europe was converted to Christianity, the Holy City of Rome became one of the favorite goals of pilgrims. To get from England and France to Italy, they had to cross the Alps; and the pass they usually chose was the shortest—but the highest and steepest and coldest of all. Such a large number of pilgrims perished on this pass, from cold and exposure, that a young Italian monk named Bernard, in the year 950, founded a monastery at the summit to provide a refuge for travelers in distress.

The moment Bernard's shelter was finished, the number of pilgrims using this pass increased four-fold, since it then became the safest pass over the mountain barrier.

The monastery housed only thirty monks, yet hundreds more applied for admission—a strange fact, since in no other monastery was life so hard. During the spring, winter, and fall the monks had to be constantly out in the snow, searching for exhausted travelers. Then, in summer, they were flooded with visitors, twenty thousand a season, whom they had to feed and lodge.

At the same time, while the summer weather permitted, they had to drag up to their eight-thousand-foot home all the provisions and equipment required during their long winter imprisonment, when the snow piled thirty feet deep around them.

In 1560 the demands upon St. Bernard's original building became so great that it had to be torn down to make way for a larger one. The "new" building, as bare as its surroundings, with no more grace or ornament than a big stone barn, contained one hundred rooms and four hundred beds. Its walls were six feet thick, to keep out the cold.

This is the building you see today, when, having struggled up the pass, you reach the top.

And it is in this building that the celebrated St. Bernard dogs wait to greet you.

In Zermatt we are not far from the road that climbs to the famous monastery. I am well acquainted with this road, and will make you a good guide. I climbed it once on the back of an elephant.

221

An *elephant?*

Yes—and this is why:

You've heard about Hannibal. He was the great general from Carthage (an ancient city, long since destroyed, that used to stand on the north coast of Africa near the modern city of Tunis). Hannibal, at war with Rome, led his army from Africa to Europe, then across Spain and France, on over the Alps, and down upon the plains of northern Italy. With him went a herd of war elephants, on the backs of which the Carthaginian officers rode.

I thought it would be a sporting adventure to retrace Hannibal's march over this same mountain trail, riding, as he rode, on an elephant. And to this end, I set my plans. But in place of the herd of three dozen huge beasts which figured in Hannibal's military march, I could boast of only one. That one, it soon turned out, was quite enough elephant for me.

Historians differ as to which of the Alpine passes Hannibal used. But the St. Bernard monks insist he used *their* pass. True, it was the highest, snowiest and most dangerous way to cross. But for this very reason, they argue, it was the one pass left unguarded by the Romans—the best reason in the world for the Carthaginians to choose it.

With much satisfaction I agreed with the monks that the pass Hannibal most probably used was the great St. Bernard, for on that route I could stop over at the renowned monastery. And I felt sure that both the monks and the dogs would be pleased by a visit from an elephant.

I will tell you more about my elephant jaunt as we go along.

On our own trip, you and I had better ride up in an automobile. After all, Hannibal would certainly use trucks today—they're quicker, as I found out.

From the base of the mountain range, on the Swiss side, the road starts to climb, twisting and zigzagging beside a roaring torrent. As we mount higher, we pass through heavy showers of rain and through bursts of summer sunshine. The ice-armed peaks above and ahead glitter for a moment against the blue, and then are swept from sight by a wave of clouds.

Associated Press Photo.

he year 218 B.C., Hannibal, the great general from Carthage, in northern Africa, led his army
the Alps, by way of the St. Bernard Pass, for an attack on Rome. With him marched a herd
hirty-seven war elephants. These were used to carry Hannibal's officers and to frighten the
es of the Roman cavalry. Retraveling Hannibal's Alpine march, the author rode an elephant
is own over the Great St. Bernard Pass from Switzerland into Italy. The elephant, named
sabethe Dalrymple, came from the Paris zoo. Crowds of Swiss and Italian children followed
he heels of the huge beast as she climbed and descended the famous pass, for she was the first
hant to cross the Alps since Hannibal's herd marched by, twenty-one hundred years before.

We pass neat little farmhouses perched on the slopes. The natives, busy in their gardens, pay no attention to the motor-cars that roar by. But you should have seen them when my elephant hove in sight! The peasants looked up to find an enormous, unearthly beast lumbering along—the first elephant most of them ever had beheld. Some of the women and children screamed and ran. Some of the men stood in their tracks too surprised to move or speak. No elephant had come this way since Hannibal's herd of thirty-seven marched up this same road more than 2100 years ago.

But Dally (that was the elephant's pet name—her full name was Mademoiselle Elysabethe Dalrymple) just kept ambling gaily forward, ignoring the excitement she was causing among the mountaineers. Nor did the automobiles and auto-busses disturb her in the least. Only one difficulty arose—horses. Every horse that caught sight of the elephant shook with terror, reared and fled. As a precaution, I kept a big cloth sack handy, and each time a horse approached, my elephant-trainer ran ahead to put the sack over the horse's eyes until we could get past. Livy, the Roman historian, describing Hannibal's first big battle in northern Italy, tells a similar story: "Hannibal's elephants, looming large in the front ranks of his army, gave rise to such fright among the horses of the Romans, not only by their strange appearance, but also by their unfamiliar smell, as to bring about a general panic."

In our motor-car, we come presently to a village high up on the mountain-side, called St. Pierre. Julius Cæsar stopped here several times on his journeys back and forth between Rome and Gaul. And in 1800, Napoleon, leading his French soldiers into Italy, rested for a while in a little hotel called, to this day, "The Hotel of Napoleon's Lunch." The moment he departed, a rope was drawn across the door of his room, and from then until now, nothing in that room has been changed. We can look in at the door, as Dally and I did, and see the chair Napoleon sat in, and the knife and fork he used, and the plates he ate from.

224

From a painting by J. Girardet.

In the year 1800, Napoleon, in the tracks of Hannibal, led an army of French soldiers over the Great St. Bernard into Italy. He crossed the pass in May, before the deep snows had melted. His soldiers, forced to drag cannon in sleds up the long steep road, suffered terribly. In this painting, Napoleon is shown receiving the welcome of the St. Bernard monks and dogs before the doors of the monastery.

The author and his elephant and her trainer reach the 8100-foot summit of the Great St. Bernard. The elephant, during her visit to the monastery,

About a mile farther up the pass we turn a corner, and Mont Blanc towers ahead. Another corner, and we come to a tunnel cut in solid ice, a tunnel through which the road runs for six hundred feet. This tunnel never melts except toward the end of the longest, hottest summers. When Dally reached this same shimmering cylinder, I feared trouble, for the icy ceiling was very low. But she was just able to squeeze through.

As our automobile emerges from the tunnel, we see three monks, each with a huge and beautiful dog, waiting to greet us. At this point Dally had *her* first sight of the big St. Bernards. And the dogs had *their* first sight of an elephant. Never in their lives had they been so astonished. At first, growling and mystified, they refused to venture near the curious trunk-swinging monster that confronted them. By coaxing and lugging, we finally persuaded one of the biggest dogs to meet the lady. He sniffed cautiously at Dally's feet, but remained taut and ready to spring away if she made an unfriendly move.

Dally, on the other hand, took no more notice of the dog than she would have taken of a turtle. She plodded on around the last switchback, and up the last steep grade that led to the door of the monastery. The arrival of an elephant brought the monks rushing into the road. They stood about wide-eyed; and all their dogs, barking furiously, ran around in circles trying to decide which end of Dally was which. Over two thousand visitors, who had gathered from far and wide to be on hand at the top of the pass when Dally arrived, climbed on the roof and hung out the windows.

That night, after the crowds had departed, the monks declared that Miss Dalrymple's visit had brought to their monastery more visitors and more excitement than they had known since they entertained Napoleon. I went out to the garage where she was stabled, and repeated the message to her. But she just went on happily eating hay.

When you and I reach the summit, our engine is boiling and grinding from the strain. My old friend, the prior, greets us in the friendliest fashion, and leads us to comfortable quarters in the great bleak building.

As soon as we have rested, we are taken on a tour of the monastery, which now includes the century-old hotel across the road. We look into the museum and the library, the chapel and the sleeping cells. How surprised we are to see what modern comforts the monks enjoy in their old stone barrack! Today, though the monastery was built during the reign of Queen Elizabeth, one finds there a central heating plant (greatly needed with the temperature at zero and below, five months of the year), electricity, telephones and a radio.

Where once there were thirty monks, one now finds only fifteen, since the motor age and the railroad tunnels under the mountains have simplified trans-Alpine travel. More people than ever visit the monastery, but nine out of ten come by automobile, so that the chief assistance the monks render during the summer is to run a filling station! In the snowy months, most travelers take the train *under* the Alps, and complete in two hours a journey that used to take two weeks.

We are eager, of course, to know all about the famous dogs, and the prior, who is very proud of them, is happy to enlighten us.

The St. Bernard is a cross between a bulldog and a sheep dog. Its face and head and chest have a decided bulldog quality. It has also the bulldog's strength, character and toughness, but the intelligence of a sheep dog.

For generations the St. Bernards have been accustomed to cold weather, and are now as much at home in the snow as Arctic huskies. They have their kennels outdoors, and only in the bitterest winter storms do they like to come inside.

Before the days of telephones, the monks made it a practice, once the snow season had begun, to start out each morning on skis, accompanied by their dogs, to look for lost or injured people. And many and many a half-dead traveler, caught in a blizzard or buried by an avalanche, would have been overlooked but for these keen-scented, intelligent dogs. In snow storms, when all sense of direction is lost, a St. Bernard leads the way. And stranger still, the monks insist that when unexpected travelers, approaching the

The St. Bernard dogs are a cross between a bulldog and a sheep dog. When full grown they sometimes weigh as much as two hundred pounds. For generations they have lived in cold weather and at high altitude, and are perfectly at home in the snow. Through the centuries they have saved the lives of hundreds of people who have been lost in blizzards or buried under avalanches.

monastery, are overwhelmed by cold and snow, and in desperate need of help, the dogs sense the fact, bark to be released, push through the drifts to find their man, and rush back to guide the monks to the rescue.

One dog is always called "Barry," in memory of an especially clever and courageous St. Bernard which, toward the end of the nineteenth century, saved so many lives that he became famous all over Europe. His body is now preserved in a museum at Berne. His son, "Barry, Junior," had a career only a little less heroic. The son's body, also carefully mounted, is on display at the monastery.

The first St. Bernard Monastery was built in the year 950. Six hundred years later, during the reign of Queen Elizabeth of England, the original building was torn down and the present building put up. Its walls are six feet thick, to keep out the cold. Inside are four hundred beds for travelers. Each year, during the seven months when the road is open, some twenty thousand people visit the Monastery. During the five snow-bound months the drifts are so deep that no outsider can climb the pass except on skis, and without them no one who dwells there can escape. Thus an

Despite the monks' splendid efforts to safeguard the pass, lives still are lost—two in 1934, three in 1926, five in 1917. During the past century a dozen monks themselves, and many of the dogs, have perished in their efforts to save others, or died as a result of exposure and exhaustion.

We are sad to leave these hospitable monks and friendly dogs, but Rome itself still lies ahead of us, and we must push on down the pass.

Dally, descending this same road, had one very alarming adventure. By accident I rode her into the mountain war games of the Italian Alpine Army. Without warning, a battery of big guns fired real shells across the valley ahead of us—shells which exploded all too close for Dally's peace of mind. Terrified, she wheeled about and charged in wild panic right through a company of Italian soldiers—just as Hannibal's herd must have charged the Romans. The soldiers retreated helter-skelter up the side of the mountain, believing, no doubt, that Italy was being invaded again by the Carthaginians.

With Dally under control once more, we descended the twisting road to a plain eight thousand feet below, and marched on a hundred miles south to Turin, where Hannibal fought his first great battle against Rome's legions. At this point Dally began to limp. So I brought my elephant expedition to an end.

But we, in our automobile, continue through Turin to Genoa, then to Pisa for a look at the Leaning Tower, and on to Rome. With us we carry a souvenir of the St. Bernard Monastery which will keep us reminded of that extraordinary place for years to come. Beside us in the motor-car is a big ball of light brown fur—a month-old puppy, one of the sturdy and courageous St. Bernards—which the prior gave us when, with his blessings he sent us down the snow-banked mountain highroad into sunny Italy. We call the puppy, "Barry III."

231

CHAPTER XXIII

ST. PETER'S

Twenty-one years after the crucifixion of Jesus, an evil young prince named Nero became Emperor of Rome. To win for himself the good will of the people, he built a huge amphitheater in which popular spectacles of all kinds were held. Here wild animals fought with men, gladiators battled with each other, convicts were thrown to the lions. Here, too, when the followers of Christ, having deserted the old pagan gods, began to cry out against the horrors that took place in Nero's theater, they themselves were butchered in the cruelest fashions the Emperor could invent.

In the center of this amphitheater stood an ancient red granite obelisk, brought from Egypt. Rising on its base to a height of 120 feet, it formed a great hub around which the deadly games and chariot races were held.

Into the shadow of this obelisk was brought, one day in the year 67 (so says sacred tradition), an elderly man who in his younger years had been a fisherman on the Sea of Galilee. He had been seized by the Romans for his stubborn preaching of Christianity, and was condemned to crucifixion like the Master about whom he talked so much.

Feeling himself unworthy to die in the same manner as Christ, the old man asked to be crucified head down. This last favor, according to legend, was granted him.

This Christian martyr was Peter, one of Jesus' Twelve Disciples, the man who, along with St. Paul, established the Christian religion in Rome.

Just outside Nero's theater was a graveyard where the burned and butchered bodies of Christians were buried. Into this cemetery the body of Peter, like the others, was cast.

But Peter did not die in vain. His death only won more followers to Christianity. Two hundred and fifty years later, the Roman Emperor himself, Constantine the Great, was converted. Constantine began at once to build a church over Peter's grave. In

Peter's, in Rome, is the largest church in the world, and the greatest monument to the Chris-
n religion. Soaring over it is the tallest and widest dome ever built. The church took 120
ars to complete—1506 to 1626. It stands over the spot where St. Peter, one of Jesus' Twelve
sciples, was buried in the year 67. The tall obelisk in the center of the plaza was brought from
ypt in Roman times and first set up in an amphitheater. Close beside this obelisk St. Peter
was crucified. It was later moved to its present position, and topped with a cross.

doing this he destroyed Nero's bloody theater, and used part of the foundations for the new memorial to Nero's victim.

Constantine's church was called St. Peter's. It stood for 1100 years and became the burial place for the dead Popes. Here, also, kings and emperors from all over Europe came to be crowned before St. Peter's tomb.

Then, about the year 1450, this historic structure showed signs of collapse and was torn down, the tombs of the Popes being preserved. In 1506 (the year Columbus died) the reigning Pope, Julian II, began to build, on the same sacred spot, a new church. He resolved to make *this* church twice as large and a hundred times grander than the original. The new St. Peter's was to be the most magnificent place of worship in the world. It must be large enough to hold the entire population of Rome (at that time 80,000 people). It must be the supreme, awe-inspiring monument to the Christian religion, for all time to come.

The greatest architects in Italy were invited to assist in this vast work. The drawings of one named Bramante seemed the best—certainly they promised the *biggest* church—so he was put to work. It was understood, of course, that he would respect the tombs of all the Popes, who were still buried on the spot, and would build the central dome over the grave of St. Peter.

As the walls rose, people began to say that Bramante's church seemed designed for the use of giants rather than human beings. Everything was planned on a scale more ambitious than even Imperial Rome had dreamed of. The new church was to be 450 feet wide and 700 feet long. The ceiling of Reims Cathedral, one of the loftiest in the world, was 125 feet above the floor—so St. Peter's ceiling (apart from the dome) was made to overtop it by another 25 feet. As for the dome of Bramante's church, it was so huge that the entire dome of the Capitol at Washington, including the statue of Freedom, could be placed inside it with 65 feet to spare.

This same scale of bigness guided the builders in everything. St. Peter's was given 44 altars. The piers supporting the dome were 60 feet around. Some 750 columns were necessary to hold up the roof. Instead of just a few holy images, 390 statues adorned the church. Nearly all of them were of great size. The cherubs, whether marble or mosaic, were not fat little babies to hold in your arms—they were enormous infants seven feet tall; and the figures of doves which flew around them were as big as roosters.

St. Peter's grew and grew. Such an undertaking could not be completed in one year, or in one generation. Popes came, ruled, and died—and still the work went on. Some twelve architects, one after the other, spent a good part of their lives building it. Raphael, one of the greatest artists in history, was in charge of construction for a time. To the immortal Michelangelo, when he was over seventy years old, was entrusted the raising of the dome. He refused all payment for his work. He, in turn, died before he could see his dome completed.

But nothing seemed to halt the progress of the church. Rome itself was seized and sacked by outside enemies; the Pope was forced to flee; the State was torn by rebellions and civil war. Yet the work went on.

The builders did all they could to make St. Peter's impressive. Their eyes fell upon the red granite obelisk which since pagan times had continued to stand on the site of Nero's ruined theater. In 1586, when the church was half finished, the obelisk was moved to its present position in front of the new structure's entrance, and a cross placed on top of it. In no better way (said the architects) can we illustrate the victory of Christianity over paganism, than to have this very obelisk, which witnessed the death of Peter, stand before the doors of his church and hold aloft the cross!

Not until 1626—120 years after the corner-stone was laid—did the new church receive its finishing touches. And even after that, another 40 years passed before work on the noble 650-foot piazza in front, with its fountains and encircling rows of columns, was brought to an end.

The completed building defies description. To comprehend its magnitude and magnificence, we must see it for ourselves. And see it we shall, soon, for we are hurrying down the Italian peninsula from the Alps toward Rome.

Only from the air can one grasp the full size of St. Peter's. It is seven hundred feet long and four hundred and fifty feet wide. It builders made it large enough to hold the entire population of Rome at that time—80,000 people. The dome is so big that the entire dome of the Capitol Washington, including the Statue of Freedom on top, could be placed *inside* it with sixty-five to spare. We climb to the top of it. To reach this high point we must mount forty flights

irs, for the great gilded ball on the summit is as high above us as a forty-story building. From
ball we can see all of Rome at our feet. We can see the plaza and the obelisk, far below. No
er church in the world can compare with this one for sheer splendor. Nor has any other
rch such a magnificent approach. On the right hand page we see the group of buildings
called the Vatican. In these buildings the Pope lives.

While still several miles away, our road takes us over the brow of a hill—and Rome appears in the distance. Towering above the other buildings like a giant over pigmies, the dome of St. Peter's commands our eye.

We ride on to the wide entrance of the piazza. No building we have ever seen has such an approach. From both sides, wide half-circles of stone columns reach out to gather us in.

Within the piazza two marble fountains are tossing a river of water into the air; and in the center, topped by the shining cross, is the obelisk.

Straight before us now rises the huge front face of the church. We approach the massive portals. Above us is the balcony where the Pope appears on special occasions to give his blessing to the multitudes who gather in the piazza below.

The outside of St. Peter's is wonderful enough. But wait till you see the inside!

We enter the great doors and, under the spreading sky of gilded stone, wander more deeply into this huge church. There are no pews, no chairs, only the expanse of smooth-worn floor. But all around us are statues and monuments of marble and bronze.

Farther down the long vista of the church we come to the most famous of the statues. It is of St. Peter. It had the place of honor in the original church, and was reverently enthroned in the new one.

Close by this statue the high altar soars heavenward. It stands free from the walls, directly beneath the dome. Over it, supported by four twisted columns, spreads a bronze canopy, one hundred feet above the floor. At the foot of this altar is an open sunken room, reached by broad marble stairs. We look down into it. Our eyes rest upon a tomb lighted by golden lamps. It is the tomb of St. Peter—on the spot where his body was brought for burial after his crucifixion.

Wide World.

The best time to see St. Peter's is during a church festival. *Then* the pomp and glory of the ages are poured out in long processions and solemn ceremonies, and St. Peter's, bright with light and banners and scarlet robes, presents a dazzling picture. In the distance the hundred-foot altar rises above the grave of St. Peter. Soaring over the altar is the vast dome.

Then we look up. The dome skyrockets above this sacred spot. The ceiling of the dome is 360 feet high. Imagine a 30-story skyscraper. Now imagine a dome *entirely enclosing,* and hovering over, such a skyscraper—with an 80-foot lantern and cross on top of *that*—and you can get some idea of the great size of this canopy. If Michelangelo had never done anything else in his life but dare to build this dome, he still would go down in history as one of the giants of architecture.

I know you've been waiting to ask me: "Can we climb the dome?"

Yes, it is climbed every day. But remember, to reach it, we must mount forty flights of stairs, for the cross on the summit is as high above us as the top of a forty-story building.

An easy winding ramp carries us up the first two hundred feet. On the walls we note bronze tablets recording the visits of kings and queens and generals through the centuries. We reach the roof of the church and walk across to the outside of the dome. It looks as big as a hill. More iron steps bring us to a door in the enormous shell. We step inside and glance down—270 feet to the stone floor —right into the sunken room where St. Peter lies buried. Down there we can see tiny figures, made only of heads and arms, sliding slowly across the floor. To think that a race of such specks lifted this mountainous dome above us!

Up more steps we climb, now inside the dome, now outside. At last, laboring for breath, we reach the lantern. On top of the lantern is a great gilded ball, and on top of the ball a cross. There's a ladder above us leading to the cross. And a ladder, naturally, is meant to be climbed.

Pushing on, we reach a little door that opens into the ball, and crawl inside. It is ten feet in diameter, big enough to hold eighteen people—if they don't mind crowding. But they also mustn't mind roasting. The heat of the sun is concentrated in this hollow sphere of bronze until, on a bright day, one minute inside is almost enough to cook you alive.

Up and over the ball goes the ladder. This ascent now is really dangerous. But we'll be satisfied with nothing less than the very top. Hold fast and don't look down—your head may swim. And it's a long way to fall. We are beginning to think this is a better place for eagles than for us.

We finally get there, stand on top of the ball, and grasp the base of the cross as a support against the wind.

We have a clear view all about. The full immensity of the church spreads below us, and the full magnificence of the dome. We can see the piazza and the obelisk, far away and far below. We can see all of Rome, for that matter—its churches, its palaces, its dark and distant ruins. We can see the winding Tiber, and can follow it right down to the blue Mediterranean.

We are certain, as we clamber down from the peak and return to the interior, that no other church can compare with this one for sheer splendor. And yet, grand as it is, we are still not seeing St. Peter's at its best—but only in its everyday attire. We must come back again during a Holy Year, and attend one of the great festivals. *Then* the pomp and glory of the ages are poured out in long processions and solemn ceremonies, and St. Peter's, bright with candles and banners and scarlet robes, presents one of the most dazzling pictures one can hope to see.

CHAPTER XXIV

AUGUST 24th, IN THE YEAR 79

On the morning of the 24th of August, in the year 79, the city of Pompeii, some 125 miles south of Rome, awoke to face another hot summer day.

Along the flag-stoned streets the heavy-wheeled wagons began to rumble, bringing in loads of grain from the farms, and fish from the harbor on the Bay of Naples.

Soon a good part of the city's twenty-five thousand people were on their way to work, or occupied with breakfast and house-cleaning. From behind the walls of the flowering courts and gardens came singing and laughter, and the sound of running water.

With a clatter of wooden blinds the grocers threw open their markets and placed their trays of fruit and vegetables on the sidewalks. From across the way came the fresh odor of baking bread. A wine shop occupied the corner, and before it the teamsters stopped their horses, and paid a few pennies for a glass of wine and a plate of fried octopus.

By eight o'clock the streets were swarming with traffic. Among the pedestrians were numbers of boys and girls carrying their slates, and strolling, none to hastily, toward the neighboring school. Passing a blank wall, one little boy (who should have known better) took a piece of charcoal and scribbled upon it the Greek alphabet which he was just learning from his Greek teacher. Nearly every person in Pompeii had a dog, and numbers of these were following at the heels of the school children.

An hour later the Forum, too, had come to life. A crowd of people stood before the new political placards that had been pasted on the walls during the night (the annual election of magistrates was drawing near), and argued about the candidates.

Pompeii on that August morning was a happy, busy, noisy town, just like your town or mine, and filled with people who, except for a different mode of dress, were just like you and me. They went to school; they worked hard; they fell in love; they married and raised families; they were fond of the theater and

242

athletic sport. They had their little joys and sorrows and prides and jealousies and heartaches—the same kind of heartaches we have today.

We know all this, we know every detail of the lives of the Pompeians—exactly how they lived, and what they wore, and what they ate, because Pompeii on that day was suddenly entombed alive beneath a deluge of volcanic ashes, and remained sealed up for eighteen centuries. Then archeologists uncovered it about one hundred years ago—and there was Pompeii, much as it had been at one o'clock on that final, fatal afternoon.

This city, because it is the one city in the world that gives us a perfect picture of life in Roman times, well deserves a place in our Book of Marvels.

All during the lifetime of Christ, and up until twelve years after the crucifixion of St. Peter, Pompeii had been one of the most prosperous towns in that part of Italy. Many Roman noblemen, attracted to the loveliness of the town's position close by the Bay of Naples, had built villas there.

Sweeping up from the Bay and hanging over the town was the beautiful four-thousand-foot mountain called Vesuvius. Vineyards grew right to the summit. On the summit itself lay a wide, flat, grassy hollow walled in by rocks. In this hollow place the boys of Pompeii used to pasture their goats. At that time Vesuvius had no more resemblance to a volcano than one of the Blue Ridge Mountains of Virginia.

Then in the year 63 this tranquil peak began to be disturbed by a series of earthquakes all around the base. One such quake severely damaged several of the public buildings in Pompeii. The same shock wrecked the theater in Naples where our friend Nero (who fancied himself as a musician) was conducting an orchestra at a public concert. Nero escaped, but the concert was upset completely.

Then came the 24th of August, 79.

At one o'clock on the afternoon of that day, Vesuvius exploded.

Fortunately for history there was an eye-witness who survived the disaster and reported exactly what happened. And that report has been preserved through the centuries even until now.

On the shore of the Bay of Naples, at that date, dwelt one of Rome's most distinguished authors, named Pliny. He was also an Admiral in the fleet. With him lived his brilliant sixteen-year-old nephew, Pliny the Younger, who likewise hoped to be a writer. The elder Pliny perished in the disaster, but the younger Pliny escaped and reported in detail what he had seen, in a letter to a great friend of his uncle's, Tacitus the historian, in Rome. I quote the letter in shortened form:

"You ask that I send you an account of my uncle's death.

"We were living at that time at Misenum, twenty-two miles from Pompeii on the opposite side of the Bay, where my uncle was stationed with the fleet under his command. On the 24th of August, about one in the afternoon, my mother asked him to observe a cloud of very unusual size and appearance rising above Vesuvius. The cloud shot up to a great height, at one moment white, at another dark and spotted as if it carried earth and ashes.

"My uncle, desiring a nearer view, ordered a light vessel to be got ready. Then hastening to the place whence others were fleeing, he steered his direct course across the Bay to the point of most danger.

"And now cinders, which grew thicker and hotter the nearer he approached Vesuvius, fell upon the ship. After debating a moment whether he should retreat, he said to the captain who was urging that course, 'Fortune favors the brave—carry me to the shore.' And so about sunset he was landed at Strabiæ, three miles the other side of Pompeii, and went straight to the house of a friend.

"Mount Vesuvius was now blazing in several places with spreading and towering flames, and their brightness was intensified by the darkness of the night. But my uncle, hoping to soothe the fears of his host and prevent a panic, sat down to supper with great cheerfulness, or at least (what is equally heroic) with all the appearance of it.

"Meanwhile the courtyard of the house was being buried under a mixture of pumice-stone and ashes at such a rapid rate that escape would soon have been impossible. My uncle and his friends consulted together as to whether they should hold out in the house, or wander about in the open. The house now tottered under repeated and violent earthquakes, and seemed to rock to and fro as if torn from its foundations. In the open air, on the other hand, they dreaded the falling pumice-stones; yet this by comparison seemed the lesser danger of the two. They tied

---

Vesuvius in eruption. Flaming lava, rocks, gas, and ashes, are flung hundreds of feet into the air to fall back on the country for miles around. From a hole in the mountain side a river of white-hot lava runs down the slopes. *Ewing Galloway.*

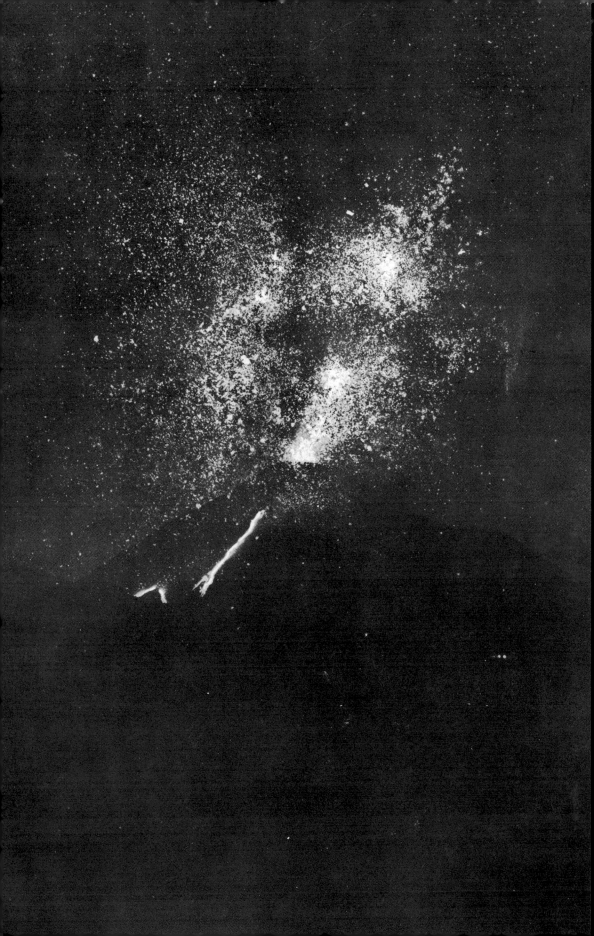

pillows upon their heads with napkins, and this was their whole defense against the showers that fell around them all night long.

"The hour of dawn arrived, but at Strabiæ a deeper darkness prevailed than in the darkest night. My uncle and his party thought proper to go down upon the shore to observe from close at hand if they could possibly put out to sea again, but they found the waves running extremely high.

"Soon after, a strong smell of sulphur descended on the beach. My uncle, who was fat and suffering from an affliction of the throat, sank down upon a sail, some poisonous vapor having blocked his breathing. His friends, too stricken themselves to carry him, had to flee for their own lives and leave him behind. When the light finally broke through (two days and two nights later) his dead body was found beneath the ashes.

"Meanwhile my mother and I were still at Misenum. All during the night of my uncle's absence the earth shook violently. About the sunrise hour my mother, terrified, burst into my bedroom, and we decided to leave the city at once as all the houses were ready to fall down. Our example was followed by the whole of the panic-stricken population, who pushed hurriedly past us as we set out.

"There were extraordinary things to see. Carriages were rocked by the heaving ground until they threatened to overturn. The sea appeared to retire, leaving the shore extended, and many creatures belonging to the sea stranded on the sand. From behind rolled down a threatening black cloud, pierced by glittering lightning and flames. When my mother saw this she begged me to abandon her and take to flight alone, that I might at least save my own life. I on the other hand seized her arm and compelled her to go on.

"Soon dark night fell around us as it does in closed rooms when the light is put out. There were heard lamentations of women, cries of children, shouts of men. Some called to their parents, others to their children, others to husband or wife; some bemoaned their own fate, others that of their dear ones, some even prayed for death. Many raised their hands to the gods, still more cried that the gods no longer existed, that the last eternal night had come.

"Meanwhile the ashes continued to pour down. Had we not often stood up to shake ourselves we should have been covered by them and overwhelmed by their weight. But at last, the thick cloud little by little melted away until the sun came forth again. Everything seemed changed, and covered with ashes as if with snow."

Young Pliny and his mother then returned to their wrecked home in Misenum and waited there till they heard the tragic news

Before Vesuvius' terrible eruption in the year 79 (the eruption that buried Pompeii at its feet), the mountain in no way looked like a volcano. Forests and vineyards grew to the summit. And on top was a big grassy hole where the boys of Pompeii pastured their goats. Then, unexpectedly, the mountain exploded in 79, and has been an active volcano ever since. It never stops smoking, and at night the red glow over its peak can be seen a great distance.

of the Admiral's death—from one of his officers who had been with him to the last, but who had managed to escape.

This letter of young Pliny's (of which I've given only part) is perhaps the most famous schoolboy composition in all history.

But back to Pompeii.

If at Misenum, eighteen miles from Vesuvius, things were as bad as Pliny tells, how much more frightful must the scenes have been in Pompeii itself, right at the mountain's base!

There twenty-five thousand people, tossed about by the earthquakes, hearing the explosions and seeing the black blanket spreading right above them, were filled with terror. Everywhere was wild confusion. Children fled home from school. In quest of them their parents struggled through the streets. In the darkness no one knew which way to turn. Frantic, everybody tried to escape at once along the road that led south, away from the volcano.

And a large majority of the citizens *did* escape. But some two thousand waited overlong, desperately trying to find their loved ones, or hoping to collect their money and treasure. A number of these, staggering and gasping, retreated into cellars to wait until the storm blew over. Most of them were still there eighteen hundred years later.

For two days and nights the deadly shower of stone and ashes fell upon the suffocated, quake-rocked city. The upper stories of all the houses, being of wood, were crushed and burned, and then pitched into the streets by the quakes. Upon this wreckage the ashes piled twenty feet deep. Succeeding eruptions of Vesuvius piled another fifteen feet on top of these. Trees and bushes took root on the new surface; vineyards were planted there. In time the very name of Pompeii became little more than a myth.

Not till 1748—almost seventeen hundred years later—did people again take an interest in Pompeii. During the next century a few treasure-hunters dug pits here and there in the ruins. Then in 1860 the clearance of the ashes began in earnest, and has gone on until this day. Pompeii is now completely free of its mantle, a Roman city risen from its grave.

And I'll show you through it if you'll come with me.

CHAPTER XXV

THE CITY THAT ROSE FROM THE DEAD

To reach Pompeii we travel from Rome south to Naples, and a few miles on beyond, following the coast, and skirting the sweeping slopes of Vesuvius. Right above us the volcano soars gracefully into the sky. From its summit a long plume of sulphurous smoke trails out over the beautiful Bay.

We come to the dead city, enter the gates of the city walls, and walk down the paved streets. The flagstones are exactly as they were in 79, cut deep with ruts made by chariot wheels and by farm carts such as were bringing grain into town on the day of the destruction.

On either side are rows of stone shops, their upper wooden stories missing but their lower stories all intact. We pass the wineshop where the teamsters stopped for a drink. The great wine jars are still in place, as is the counter behind which the proprietor stood. On one counter was found a circular stain where a customer had dropped his glass at lunch-time on that fatal day—to flee.

Next door we come to the fruit and vegetable market. Here the excavators found (and sent to the museum) rows of charred turnips, beans, peas, and baskets of figs, grapes, plums. On another shelf a box of chestnuts came to light. In the back yard were discovered skeletons of pigs and sheep. We can imagine their pitiful squealings and bleatings when the earth began to shake and the deluge of ashes to come down. But their owner did not listen. His only thought was to save himself.

In the bakery, across the street, row after row of loaves of bread, in the ovens when the bakers ran away, have been unearthed —bread over eighteen centuries old, baked by Vesuvius. From the carpenter's shop hammers and nails have been recovered; from the sculptor's studio, several half-carved statues; from the restaurant on the corner, the dishes and pots and pans. All these things we can see in the museum at Naples.

249

On the morning of August 24th, in the year 79, the Roman city of Pompeii, resting in the shadow of Vesuvius, was a happy and busy little city of 25,000 people. By night, earthquakes had shaken it to pieces, fires had destroyed all the wooden buildings, and volcanic ash, pouring down from Vesuvius had buried the ruins under fifteen feet of ashes. Over two thousand people perished in the disaster. For seventeen hundred years the

The next place we visit is the ruined Temple of Isis. In this temple took place a typical Pompeian tragedy—a case of delaying too long to escape:

When the ashes began to fall, the priests of Isis collected the temple treasures, the gold coin and silver vessels, and retreated into an inner room. But soon the poisonous gases reached them and they began to choke. One priest, refusing to die in this trap without a struggle, seized a bag of gold coins, and made a dash for the street.

He reached the porch of the temple, and through the ash-filled darkness, started down the marble stairs. At that moment another quake of the earth knocked the temple's columns from their bases. One column crashed upon the half-suffocated priest. His body was recovered eighteen hundred years later, still grasping the temple's gold. When the excavators broke into the inner room the skeletons of his fellow-priests came to light in the anguished positions in which they had died.

I spoke earlier of the school children stopping on their way to school the morning of that dreadful day, to scratch their A B C's upon the walls. After these many years this scribbling can be read almost as clearly as when it was written.

All the people of Pompeii, adults as well as children, seemed to have been guilty of this bad-mannered wall-writing. We find their scrawl in scores of places on the blank stones. The "John loves Mary" type of composition is a favorite. An inscription that makes us all smile, reads: "Good health to anybody who invites me to dinner."

The walls around the Forum served as more than a writing-board for the scribblers. These walls were used as signboards, too. The gladiatorial fights were announced here, and the new plays. One poster on display the day of the disaster, and recovered by the excavators, reads: "Thirty pairs of gladiators will contend tomorrow at the amphitheater." A political poster urged the citizens of Pompeii to "vote for Valerius for magistrate. He is a good fellow, an upright official, and will look after the people's money."

251

Another notice offered to pay "$10 reward for return of lost wolf-hound. Brown coat. Answers to name of Rex."

As I have mentioned already, Pompeians were very fond of dogs. Over the door of one house we are shown the picture of a canine, and the sign, *"Cave Canem"*—beware the dog. And one of the most touching things we see in the museum is the mummy of a dog, lying on its back, and twisted in its last death agony. What was his story? Had he refused to leave his master who had fallen in the street? Was he caught by the poisonous gases as he looked frantically through the wreckage for a child? Knowing the fidelity of dogs, we can be reasonably sure he died serving the household in which he lived.

Like most cities, Pompeii was made up of a few costly homes and many modest ones. The houses of the rich, being the more solidly built, were the best preserved. On their walls, painted a brilliant red, we see some of the loveliest pictures in all ancient art—pictures from Greek mythology showing the gods in human form. There are also pictures of the Bay of Naples, and one of Vesuvius as it looked before the eruption.

Inside the courtyards stood beautiful statues of marble and bronze, many of which have been left in place by the excavators. We enter such a courtyard. How bright the colors are after all the centuries of burial, how clear the pictures!

One of the finest and most tragic of the houses we visit is the villa of Diomedes. This Pompeian citizen was a nobleman of wealth and position, and his household one of the largest in the city.

But alas!—when the storm broke, instead of trying to escape along with the frenzied mobs struggling through the streets, he led his entire family and all his servants into the basement—a terrified group of sixteen people. Diomedes' young daughter took along her dog and pet goat. The family also carried a supply of food and water.

Then, all too soon, Diomedes realized what a fatal mistake he

Like most cities, Pompeii was made up of a few costly homes and many modest ones. The costly houses, made of stone, are best preserved. In them we find carved marble columns, pictures painted on the walls, and bronze statues in the courtyards. Thousands of these beautiful art objects were found by the diggers.

had made . . . the gases were creeping slowly into the underground refuge . . . his family was beginning to suffocate. Driven into action, the despairing Diomedes, accompanied by one slave carrying the house key, stumbled up the stairs into the ash-buried court. They reached the gate and unlocked it, and turned to fetch the half-dead family. But just then a wave of flame and sulphur smoke swooped down, and both men perished in their tracks.

The excavators found Diomedes, with his gold still in his money belt; the key to the house lay near the slave. In the basement all fourteen skeletons were recovered, with their heads still wrapped in tunics, their only defense against the gas. The skeletons of the dog and little goat lay close beside Diomedes' daughter. The food and drink had not been touched.

With sad hearts we look into the basement room where this whole family died.

In our tour of the world we have already seen, and shall see later, ruins of ancient cities that reveal to us wonders from past ages. But in no other case can we feel so close to the people who lived in these cities, as in Pompeii. The Pompeians were so *human,* like people we know. Pompeii might have been our own home town suddenly buried by some disaster, and unearthed again.

While Pompeii slept for eighteen hundred years beneath its tomb of ashes, Vesuvius continued to be an active volcano, and is roaring and smoking right down to today. From time to time through the centuries it has burst forth with special fury and destroyed everybody living on its slopes. In 1631 an eruption killed eighteen thousand—several times as many as in 79. Perhaps tomorrow, or next month, or two hundred years hence, it will explode again and bury nearby Naples as it buried Pompeii. How would you like to be there when it does?

We certainly must not leave this remarkable part of the world without a visit to Vesuvius.

A cog-railroad takes us up the steep slope to the top—four thousand feet. All the lower slopes are covered with vineyards still making wine just as in 79. But the upper slopes, where the

Pompeian boys used to pasture their goats, are now a burned wilderness of volcanic ash.

We reach the crest and look down into the booming, steaming crater. Fountains of cinders are shot up and fall back again. We stand on a hard mass of lava at the crater's rim. It's so hot we feel the heat through our thick-soled shoes. We thrust a stick into a smoking crack, and the stick quickly bursts into flames. The horrible boiling deep down in that great hole in the earth is more frightening than at Popo, for the crater of Vesuvius is much more active and we are closer to it.

We look behind us, down toward the sea, and locate Pompeii less than five miles away. From this very crater, here beside us, burst the fire and ashes that overwhelmed that happy city, there

Ewing Galloway.

No matter where we walk amid the ruins of Pompeii, Vesuvius, sending forth its never-ending plume of smoke, always looms in the distance.

at the bottom of the mountain. Farther along the coast we see the beach where Pliny the Elder perished. And on the other side of the Bay of Naples we locate Misenum, from which his young nephew escaped when the storm broke.

In the late evening we return to Naples. From the window of our hotel we look toward Vesuvius. Flashes of red light are shooting up from the summit, inflaming the sky; and the sight sends over us a chill of anxiety. The people of Naples, however, are used to this fiery menace hanging above them, and never even notice the volcano's tantrums.

But as we go to bed we wonder if Vesuvius is going to explode again *tonight* and if it does shall we be buried in ashes like the Pompeians. . . . We wonder if the excavators, eighteen hundred years from now, will find our camera and toothbrush and wrist watch and our "quaint clothes"; and if they'll be interested in the story we've written in our diary about our ascent of Vesuvius the *very afternoon* of the disaster. We are sure, if the excavators do unearth us, they'll say: "How human those people were! They must have been just like us."

CHAPTER XXVI

THE MAGIC GROTTO

Do you believe in magic enchantments? Did you ever see a fairy princess? Have you ever been bewitched?

You say, "No!" And you add to yourself: "Just imagine anybody asking us such foolish questions!"

But don't you scoff at my questions too soon. I can take you to a really truly enchanted place and show you magic rocks and magic water and magic light, all in a magic sea-cavern. Any boy or any girl who swims in the water of this grotto is turned into a fairy-like being. And if you are not actually bewitched, you *think* you are, which is just as interesting.

And if I fail to make good my promise—money back!

From Naples we can look out across the Bay toward the open Mediterranean. About eighteen miles away we see, through the haze, a rock-bound island with towering walls rising straight up from the waves.

This is the island of Capri, famous throughout the world because of its enchanted cave.

The Romans who lived on Capri knew about the cave. They used it as a refuge for small boats in rough weather. It made a little haven 160 feet long, and 100 feet wide, with a roof arched high overhead. Inside, the Romans cut steps that climbed up from the water to a broad ledge; and from this ledge they cut a rock tunnel which led on upward to a villa built over the cavern's entrance.

The entrance itself was from the sea through an arch perhaps fifty feet high. Through this opening the waves flowed back and forth. When Vesuvius erupted in 79, and buried Pompeii, tons of ashes fell on Capri too, and the family living in the villa above the sea-grotto no doubt sought refuge inside it. But in those days the cave was in no way unusual. There were dozens of others up and down the Italian coast just like it. Then about the year 500, an earthquake rocked the ocean floor all around the island, and Capri sank almost fifty feet deeper into the sea.

The arched entrance of the grotto also sank, nearly out of sight. Only three feet of clearance remained above the water. The same earthquake caused the rock-tunnel to fall in. With one entrance blocked completely, and the other one almost, the very existence of the grotto was forgotten—for thirteen hundred years.

Sometime during these long centuries, the cave became enchanted.

The people of Capri first learned about the enchantment in 1815, the year of Napoleon's downfall at the battle of Waterloo. One day, an old fisherman, passing the spot, saw a school of what he took to be huge fish swimming out from the recess in the rock. One of the fish came up close to his boat. The fisherman threw a harpoon into it. At once (so he later declared) the sea was stained with blood; and there rose to the surface not a fish but a bleeding sea-monster with the head and arms of a human being. This monster shook its fist at the fisherman, and then disappeared beneath the waves.

The fisherman fainted, and was washed ashore in his boat. He lived only a few hours afterward, and died raving about the terrifying creature he had harpooned outside the little cave in the cliff.

Straightway ominous legends about the cave began to spread. Everybody agreed it must lead inward to a great sea-cavern filled with evil spirits.

One man said he had observed smoke and fire issuing from the entrance.

Another insisted he had seen creatures like crocodiles creeping in and out.

Another declared *he* had seen the entrance open and close seven times a day.

A story everybody repeated was that at night the Sirens sang sweetly in the grotto, but that in the day one heard moans and groans.

Young fishermen refused to venture near, believing that the Sirens swam out and dragged youths into the cave.

Two priests, at length, resolved to brave this devilish cavern, and drive out the demons who dwelt in it. They actually swam through the entrance—only to turn about and come racing out again in terror. They swore the cave was filled with human bones.

For several years after that, nobody dared approach it.

Then in 1826, two adventurous Austrian artists decided to explore that sinister hole in the rocks, come what might. They built a fire in a flat tin bucket, pushed the bucket ahead of them through the cavern's entrance, and swam in . . . to find . . .

But I shall not tell you what they found. I'm going to take you there instead.

From Naples in the early morning, a small steamer brings us to Capri. At the little port of Marina Grande, skiffs await us, and in these we are rowed along the rocky coast for a mile or two. Our grotto's entrance is so small that we should have gone right by it without a guide.

We approach the hole in the rock. It doesn't look big enough for our skiff to enter. Nor is it big enough unless we all lie flat on the bottom, and pull in the oars.

Our hearts are beating a little faster. This is the spot out of which the sea-monster swam — the monster that shook its bloody fist at the fisherman. In this cave once dwelt the Sirens who used to seize young sailors and stack their bones around the walls.

Gendreau.

The entrance to the Blue Grotto, on the island of Capri. This hole in the rock wall leads from the sea into the grotto. The hole is only four feet high. To get through it, in our boat, we must lie flat on the bottom and pull in our oars.

An inrushing wave sweeps up through the low entrance to the Blue Grotto. We look abou
—and gasp. The water, the walls, the arched dome overhead, are aflame with blue-burning
Magic seems to have been worked on everything. The water has been turned to bottomless
shot full of unearthly blue light. A shimmering, fairy blue dances on the walls and ceiling.

Keystone.

our hands through the water. Instantly they are covered with a mesh of diamonds, and ripples of fire in their wake. We put on our bathing suits, and dive into this quivering cloud. We become fiery comets leaving behind a trail of sparks. At last we have seen something that makes us believe in fairy-tale enchantments.

But it's too late to turn back now. Our boatman has grasped the guide-cable strung along the tunnel. He commands us to close our eyes tight and not to raise our heads.

In a few seconds an inrushing wave strikes us; the boatman gives the fixed cable a mighty pull. With a wild lurch and a shower of spray we are shot through the keyhole . . . and suddenly the skiff is quiet again.

"Now," shouts the boatman, *"sit up and look!"*

We open our eyes—and gasp. There's been a miracle! The cave *is* enchanted; we *are* bewitched! There are no monsters, no Sirens, no human bones; but the water, the walls, the arched dome overhead, are aflame with blue-burning fire.

Magic has been worked on everything. About us hang the draperies of an azure fairyland. The rock of the cavern walls has been changed to a curtain of soft sapphires ashine with silver spangles. And the water we float on is no longer water. It's a bottomless sky shot full of unearthly blue light. Blue—blue—blue—silvery, shimmering, fairy blue dances on the ceiling, electrifies the quivering lake and touches the very air with supernatural radiance, overwhelming us with its blue beauty.

We've gone to heaven, but we are still alive. We dip an oar into the enchanted blue cloud supporting our boat. The oar turns to flaming silver. We drag our hand through what, on the outside of the entrance, is water. Instantly our hand is covered with a mesh of diamonds, and leaves ripples of fire in its wake.

Nothing we have seen on our wonder-tour was ever so divinely beautiful as this water, these walls, this light.

The impulse comes to swim in this phantom blue.

Our skiff pulls over to the ancient rock steps, cut by the Romans from the water to the ledge, now only three feet above. On the ledge, and in the blockaded rock-tunnel that led in Roman times upward to the villa, we put on our bathing suits.

Then comes the most wonderful sight of all. We dive from the ledge into the quivering blue cloud. Each of us, plunging downward, becomes a fiery comet leaving behind a trail of glit-

262

tering sparks. From our path ten thousand burning bubbles rise to the surface. The agitated water casts bright reflections all about us, and the whole grotto gleams and dances.

As we swim back and forth on the surface, over this liquid light, we are transformed into great silvery fish that stir the sapphire sky we swim upon with sapphire flames. As we have the grotto all to ourselves there is no one to object to our splashing and shouting and reveling in this airy, fairy world.

Will you believe in magic *now*? Will you believe there is enchantment on earth even today? Do you still think I ask foolish questions?

You apologize?

Good!

Just for that I'll tell you a secret. It wasn't really the fairies or the Sirens that cast a spell over this cavern, but the sunshine and the sea outside. You remember I told you that the original entrance sank deep into the sea at the time of the earthquake? Well, the sunlight penetrating the ocean outside flows into the cavern by way of this submerged opening, and then up through the water inside, to shine upon the walls. You have seen sunlight shining through colored windows in churches, and casting beams of the same shade on the floor. The Blue Grotto is colored almost the same way. The beams pass through the vividly blue and gloriously clear water of the Bay of Naples, and then, penetrating the interior of the cave, tinge everything with the Mediterranean's pure azure hue.

But I still am sure, despite this explanation of the cavern's supernatural beauty, that the fairies at their best could never have created such loveliness as this. Nor could Oberon himself, the fairy king, ever have bewitched us with his magic wand as completely as we were bewitched by the sight of the blue-burning walls and the blue-burning water of this wondrous cave.

Above us rises the Acropolis, the crown of glory set upon the brow of Athens, the queen city
ancient times. And on top of this great rock one of the first wonders of the world awaits us—
the Parthenon. This Acropolis was the fortress of ancient Athens. On its flat summit the Ath
nians built a group of marble temples that have given us a standard of beauty and perfecti

Boissonnas.

ever since. These glorious temples were built over four hundred years before the birth of Christ. But even today, though shattered and blasted by time and .nan, the ruins of these 2300-year-old marble buildings make one of the most beautiful and inspiring sights in the world.

CHAPTER XXVII

ATHENA'S TEMPLE

Our ship, bringing us from Italy eastward through the Ægean Sea to Greece, enters the harbor of Piræus.

Looking shoreward, we see the land rising gently toward a large white city some five miles inland. Out of the center of this city there springs a high altar-like rock.

This rock is the Acropolis, the crown of glory set upon the brow of Athens, the queen-city of ancient times. And on top of this rock one of the first wonders of the world awaits us.

By motor car we travel the distance between the harbor and the city, following the curving road that leads up to the Acropolis. We reach the entrance, climb the flight of broken marble steps, and find ourselves face to face with—the Parthenon.

The time-worn marble columns (those that still stand) of this most glorious and most famous of all temples rise above us. We reach out and touch one of them, to be sure that this marvel is real, and no longer just the beautiful picture we've seen all our lives.

A feeling of awe comes over us . . . we are standing before something more than just a famous ruin—it is the ruin of the finest monument of the world's Golden Age, when men worshiped beauty. We know we tread on sacred ground. The greatest geniuses of ancient Greece have moved across this same pavement —sculptors, artists, teachers, writers, warriors.

We wander down the tall row of columns. How worn they are by twenty-three centuries of wind and rain, how scarred by battle! But now in the late afternoon sun they glow with life. We look out between the columns toward the shining Ægean Sea, and find that the very light has turned to a lilac color which bathes every stone about us with the same lovely shade. "Violet-crowned Athens," watched over by this sublime marble temple, was held

266

We reach the entrance to the Acropolis, climb the broken marble steps, and have our first glimpse of the Parthenon. . . .

For twenty-one hundred years the Parthenon stood in all its glory. Then about two hundred and fifty years ago the Turks, who were at that time the rulers of Athens, stored their gunpowder in this Greek temple. The Venetians, at war with the Turks, attacked the Acropolis, and fired a by the Greeks to be the most wonderful sight granted to them by their gods.

And who can say, standing today beneath this gleaming colonnade, and looking out at sunset across the lilac-hued city, that our modern world can offer us a finer sight?

If you will sit down here on this marble step, and lean back against a column—here where we can see the Ægean—I'll tell you more about this Parthenon:

The Parthenon was finished 438 years before the birth of Christ. It was built in honor of Athena, the goddess who watched over the city. To help in the construction the most inspired sculptors and artists of the time were called together.

Entirely around the building, on the outside wall of the central hall—up there where I'm pointing—once ran a broad marble band of stone pictures. This marble band was carved by Phidias, perhaps the greatest sculptor who ever lived. It is considered the finest sculptural work to come from the hand of man.

Phidias and his fellow artists turned the Parthenon into a treasure-house of beauty. All around us, here on top the Acropolis, they also built these other smaller buildings you see. Gold and ivory were used in great quantities for ornament. On every side stood marble statues of the gods and heroes. Almost every day, when the Parthenon was young, a procession with flowers and banners marched up the same steps we climbed, and into this Great Temple to worship Athena. Her statue stood just over there. What scenes of fresh and glittering beauty the Athenians beheld in those days!

But now *we* behold only the ruins of all this glory. Roman conquerors were the first to rob the Acropolis of its treasures. From it whole shiploads of marble gods were sent to Rome. What the Romans left, later invaders gathered up to adorn their cities back home. Yet, through it all, the Parthenon itself (stripped of its gold and ivory) escaped serious injury—thanks to the great size of its building blocks and to the great weight of its columns. Still standing, it had to watch the glory of Greece slowly die; had

269

A rainbow adorns the Acropolis. The picture of Athens, watched over by the beautiful Pa
non, was held by the ancient Greeks to be the most wonderful sight granted to them by their

d when we look out through the Parthenon's mellow-gold columns, upon this same shining city,
we wonder if, even in our modern world, there is another sight as fine.

to watch Athens, the center of art and learning in the ancient world, sink back until it became a poor and half-forgotten village.

For a thousand years—up to 1456—the Parthenon was used by the Greeks as a Christian church. Then the Turks captured Athens. *They* made of it, for the next four hundred years, a Moslem city. They turned the Acropolis into a fort. Over there by the Porch of the Marble Maidens, they raised a minaret which stood for two hundred years. Here, inside the Parthenon, the Turks stored their gunpowder.

And so it came to pass, in 1687, that the Venetians, at war with the Turks, attacked the Acropolis and shot a cannon ball through the roof into the powder kegs. Flames burst forth and caused a terrible explosion. The roof was blown into the air, half the walls hurled down, many of the columns smashed. Look there on the other side—you can see some of the pieces still lying on the ground.

This was one of the most tragic art losses the world has ever suffered. After it had stood in all its beauty for 2100 years, after it had survived a dozen invasions by the Romans and the barbarians, this matchless temple had to meet destruction from a single cannon ball at so recent a date as 1687.

This heart-breaking misfortune was the signal for another long period of robbery. The sculpture was hacked and stolen by everybody. Peasants used Phidias' statues to build goat-pens. The Turkish army crushed marble gods to make gravel for their roads. At the end of a hundred years of such treatment, it seemed that soon there would not be even a fragment of the Parthenon's sculpture left.

Realizing this, Lord Elgin, an English nobleman, managed in 1816, to remove the few portions which still remained of Phidias' work. He shipped them to London, where they were placed in the British Museum. There one can see them today. These "Elgin Marbles," though they are only broken pieces, are all we have of the beautiful sculpture that once adorned this magnificent structure.

Not until Greece won her independence from Turkey, in 1833, was the ruin of the Parthenon given any protection. It is safe now, for the modern Greeks, as well as the lovers of art in every country, do all they can to guard it from further harm.

As you can see too well, the Parthenon is only a ruin, but it still has the highest place of honor in all architecture. It has given to mankind, on down the ages, a model of beauty and perfection which we still do our best to copy to this day. Whenever you see, anywhere in the world, a row of noble columns (like these) forming a porch—the "Greek temple" style of building—you may be sure that the Parthenon furnished the inspiration. For example, the architecture of almost every public building in the city of Washington comes from ancient Athens. Our Lincoln Memorial, our Supreme Court Building, our Capitol, are echoes of the Parthenon. There is hardly a state-house in America, or a post-office, or a Colonial dwelling, that is not in some degree a child of Athena's Temple.

But as we sit here among its ruined walls and columns, we agree that no modern copy of the Parthenon is half so beautiful as the ruin of the Parthenon itself.

CHAPTER XXVIII

NO WOMAN'S LAND

Will all the boys on our wonder-tour please assemble *here*.
And all the girls please assemble *there*.

For the boys I have railroad tickets to Salonika in northern Greece. The girls must stay in Athens for a few days, and amuse themselves. There will be plenty to see. They'll join us later on.

Please don't everybody ask at once why! The reason is perfectly simple. The next wonder of the world on our list is a curious little country where *nothing female is allowed*. Boys can go, but no girls; bulls can go, but no cows; rams, but no ewes; roosters, but no hens; cats, but they must be tom-cats; dogs, but they must be males. Only winged creatures like birds and butterflies can bring their wives and daughters across the border.

The border is patrolled by police whose sole duty is to keep out wolves and women.

So, you see why girls can't go.

You say you don't believe such a silly country exists?

But I assure you it really does. It's nearly a thousand years old, and considers itself an independent and separate country, though it is in Greek territory and under Greek protection. It has four thousand inhabitants, and every inhabitant is a male, as all the inhabitants have been since the state was founded.

No child has ever been born within this country's boundaries, not for a thousand years.

The citizens occupy the same ancient buildings, read the same ancient books, wear the same style of clothes, lead the same kind of lives, as their country's founders who lived in the year 900. All the inhabitants wear long beards. Hair-cutting is not allowed. Instead, the men's tresses are gathered into a big knot at the back of the neck and secured with hairpins.

In this weird country all games and sports are forbidden; singing and dancing are strictly banned; there is a law against bathing and fighting.

Ewing Galloway.

On a rocky peninsula, called Mount Athos, in northern Greece, monks of the Orthodox Greek Church several centuries ago built twenty enormous monasteries. Of these twenty, this one, named Simopetra, is the most amazing.

The capital is called Karyes, which, in English, means Nuts.

I tell you I'm *not* making this up. These are all solemn facts—about the Holy Communities of Mount Athos.

I can show you exactly where Athos is.

If you will look at a map of Greece, you will find on the northern coast of the Ægean Sea the port of Salonika. Then if you will look eighty miles east of Salonika you will find three narrow peninsulas extending like crooked fingers into the Ægean. Of these, Athos is the most eastern—thirty miles long and five wide. Rising above the southern tip is a beautiful peak six thousand feet high, of pure white marble. This is the famous Mount.

On the rugged sea-slopes of this peninsula, placed from one to three miles apart, are twenty lonely monasteries all devoted to the Greek Orthodox Church (once the state church of Russia). Each is enclosed within a huge and ancient stone building, heavily walled, and built around a court. Several of them were founded between the years 900 and 1000. The youngest was already a hundred years old when the Pilgrims came to America. Fortress, castle, college, church—they were all four things in one.

It is in these crag-crowning monasteries overlooking the sea that the entire population of Athos has been living for ten centuries, dressed in long black gowns, never shaving, piously idle when they are not in church, and concerned only with the salvation of their masculine souls.

Now if you're convinced that such a place as Mount Athos exists, we'll be on our way. Will the boys please say good-bye, politely, to the girls? This separation won't last long—only a few days.

Soon after our coastal steamer leaves Salonika, we see Mount Athos far in the distance, rising out of the Ægean. The mountain's white marble summit is barren of vegetation so that it seems to be always snow-clad, and serves as a great white beacon for mariners.

Nearer and nearer we approach. After several hours' sailing we are close enough to see several of the monasteries perched on

277

In this flying fortress-monastery of Simopetra a hundred monks dwell today. From the time it was built, over seven hundred years ago, no woman or girl has ever set foot in it. And no female animal. Roosters are allowed but no hens; bulls but no cows. It's a very masculine heaven these monks live in.

crags along the shore. Presently we drop anchor before the little port of Daphne, where, for a thousand years, men fleeing from the wicked world have entered this land of refuge.

On the beach, long-bearded and long-haired monks in black gowns look at our passports and examine our baggage. They tell us we must go inland over the mountain ridge to Karyes, five miles away, to get permission to visit the monasteries. There is no road, only a mule trail; but as there is no wheeled vehicle on the peninsula, such trails are good enough.

We find that Karyes is a town like no other place on earth. From all outward appearances it might be any other town in Greece. Orchards and gardens surround it. Pack animals and their drivers move along its crooked streets. Church bells ring at all hours; the cocks crow at dawn; and in the spring birds build their nests in the village trees. Karyes has shops, inns, dwellings, a bank and post-office.

But for a thousand years no woman, no girl, has ever set foot in Karyes.

A single day in this strange town and we begin to have the "jitters." We come upon a barnyard containing half a hundred chickens—all roosters; and a dozen head of cattle—all bulls. Shepherded for the day into a courtyard is a flock of sheep—all rams. Caravans of pack-horses and mules pass down the street— every one a male.

We enter the shops to look at the goods on sale and get acquainted. We see only monks—monks—monks. There is a little department store; the "salesgirls" are graybeard monks. They do not sell one article of female clothing. The village laundress is an old monk; the servants are young monks. We begin to wonder if we are dreaming and having a nightmare—if we have stumbled upon a place enchanted by some evil magician, where only one sex exists, where no woman's sympathy would ever comfort us . . . a world without a mother or a child.

We are more than willing to leave Karyes behind. In such an

empty-hearted town we feel sure there can be very little that is worth while.

We haven't time to visit all the monasteries, and it isn't necessary, as life is much the same in each one. If we see everything thoroughly in a single monastery, we can rest content.

I've been in most of them and suggest we choose Simopetra—the Rock of Simon. It is the most boldly placed, and the most difficult to reach, for it is lifted up on a pinnacle of rock twelve hundred feet above the shore.

We come to it from the sea by means of a big rowboat. We round a promontory, and there it is, shining, far up on the face of the cliff. It seems to climb on wings, soaring into the sky as if it were trying, like the Tower of Babel, to reach the gates of Heaven. For the first 150 feet of its base—the height of a twelve-story office building—there is not a single opening. Then

Artists-monks in their monastery studio paint pictures which decorate Orthodox Greek Churches all over the world.

in circles around the top are four wooden galleries jutting out from the surface of the wall.

We follow the zigzag trail up the cliff. We reach the base of the wall. But we have to continue climbing another two hundred feet, up endless tunneled stairs and passages, to reach the entrance.

Then from the topmost gallery we look back down the breathtaking cliff and out upon the sea, twleve hundred feet below.

Our interpreter tells us how Simopetra came to be built on such an outlandish point.

Several hundred years ago, a hermit living on the spire of rock had a vision, and saw a monastery rising from this very place. He persuaded one of the church architects to examine the rock and see if a monastery *could* be built here. The architect, as he climbed to the top to make his survey, had with him a water boy. The boy, struggling upward with his water pitcher, slipped and fell eight hundred feet . . . only to be seen a few minutes later climbing back again with his pitcher still unbroken and water-filled. It seems an angel, dressed in a monk's black gown and hat, had caught the boy as he fell and placed him like thistle-down upon the path below. This, the architect decided, was a sign from Heaven that the site had divine approval. And so Simopetra rose.

About one hundred monks now live in this flying fortress, detached from the earth in fact as well as in spirit.

Yet they welcome us cordially. The guest-monk (the special monk who takes care of all visitors), fat and dirty and good natured, leads us through courts and corridors and up rickety stairs. These stairs were worn thin long before Columbus discovered America. Our bare, cell-like rooms have sheltered guests like ourselves for seven centuries. The beds, too, we soon decide, are just as old.

We eat a supper of octopus, a dish that tastes like boiled automobile tire and is less easily digested. As we chew away on the octopus' long feelers, half the monastery stands around to watch. They are mostly old men with white beards, for few Greek youths of today care to become monks.

Simopetra stands 1200 feet above the sea, on the summit of a steep cliff. In this monastery we visit the monks for several days. We live on octopus, bread and wine. Our cell-like rooms have sheltered guests like ourselves for seven centuries. Our beds are likewise seven centuries old. We go to religious services at two o'clock in the morning. The services last three hours.

The author was once imprisoned for a week in Simopetra by a January blizzard. He became a monk (for the time being), wore the black gown, let his beard grow, and went to church four times a day.

When night comes we find it hard to sleep on our eleventh-century beds, for we are constantly awakened by wooden gongs sounding, and by monks tramping into the chapel for endless services. Their chanting comes thin and far away through the sighing of the wind, as it blows across the wooden galleries leaning out twelve hundred feet above the sea.

I once spent an entire week in this very monastery. A January blizzard struck the peninsula while I was there, and I couldn't escape, for snow blocked the trails, and the sea raged so violently no boat could approach the shore to take me away. I put on the regulation black gown and lived exactly as the monks lived. The hardest work I did was getting up in the January weather every morning at two o'clock and going to religious services for three hours. Sometimes I fell asleep again in my wooden stall.

However, I'll make a good guide as I know my way about.

The library is always the most interesting place in the monasteries. It often contains beautiful books copied out by hand long before printing was invented. During the Middle Ages the greatest scholars in Europe came to Mount Athos and, for the libraries there, wrote books on sheets of sheepskin, books dealing with medicine, music and history. We may hold these same marvelous books in our hands and look at the colored pictures which were painted on the sheepskin pages, sometimes as long as thirteen hundred years ago.

From the library we visit the chapel. We gasp at the magnificence of the decoration. Into this church, and the nineteen others

282

like it on the Mount, the emperors of old Byzantium (Constantinople) poured the gold and silver and jewels which they, as masters of the Western world for nine centuries, had seized from a hundred conquered nations. Not pounds but wagon loads of gold were spread across the altars. Huge gold chandeliers were hung from the domes; gold candlesticks, high as a man, lighted the chapels. Much of this glory remains intact for us to see today. At special times, such as Christmas and Easter, this sea of gold reflects the gleam of countless candles, and the monks appear in gorgeous vestments handed down from the time of Byzantine kings.

But alas, since all the old monks are dying off, and since no new young monks are coming to take their places, the monasteries on Mount Athos must soon close their doors. Deserted, they will become romantic ruins like the castles on the Rhine. We are fortunate to have seen one of the finest of them while it was still open and its chapel filled with light and life. When our children return to Mount Athos they may find all the wonderful treasures and priceless books removed to museums in Athens, London and New York; they may find the buildings tumbled down, even our own skyscraping Simopetra, and overgrown with forests and inhabited only by birds and foxes. *Then,* when Mount Athos has become public property again, say in twenty-five years, any girl who wishes may visit it, for there will no longer be any guards left at the border to keep out the wolves and the women.

Most of the monks on Mount Athos are old men, for, in modern times, very few young men in Greece care to live on this lonely peninsula.

CHAPTER XXIX

THE HEART OF RUSSIA

In the summer of 1812 the largest army ever gathered together under one general, up to that time, was marching across Europe. Napoleon, the French Emperor, had declared war on Russia and was leading 600,000 soldiers into that vast country—straight toward Moscow.

The Russians were no match for Napoleon. They fought bravely but were always defeated and had to retreat time and time again. As they retreated they burned the crops behind them and destroyed all supplies that might help the invaders.

The French, deprived of food, died by the thousands. And yet, despite the great number of men lost each day from sickness and hunger, Napoleon pushed on grimly, deeper and deeper into the stripped and barren country. As the endless miles rolled behind him, his army dwindled from 600,000 to 300,000, and finally to 150,000.

Then at last, when Napoleon had marched eastward from Paris sixteen hundred miles—as far as from Denver to New York—he came to a hilltop and saw Moscow spread below him.

He saw a city such as his eyes had never beheld before, a city out of Asia rather than out of Europe. Bright-colored spires and shining domes seemed to float above the houses. Turning his gaze toward the center of the city, Napoleon caught sight of the world-famous Kremlin, an enormous fortress surrounded by walls from which tall towers rose. These walls enclosed a cluster of palaces and churches topped with bulb-like Tartar domes, all agleam with gold.

Just outside the Kremlin, Napoleon's gaze fell upon St. Basil's Church, the strangest building in Russia. This church had been built by Ivan the Terrible 250 years before in honor of a half-mad monk who, alone among Ivan's subjects, dared denounce the Tsar for his cruelty. From its towers bulged rainbow-hued domes

284

t. Basil's Church is one of the strangest buildings in the world. Its dozen oriental domes, all bright with color and gold, make it look like a building from India or Turkestan.

that looked like giant turbans from India. Napoleon thought to himself: The architect who built that church must have been a madman, but a madman with a love of exciting and fantastic beauty . . . and surely *this* must have been his wildest fancy. I wish he were alive today. I'd send him to Paris and have him build a church for me just like St. Basil's.

That evening, Napoleon, and what was left of his army, marched into Moscow. The army assembled on Red Square, a huge open plaza right beside the Kremlin. (The Square was called "Red" because of the blood spilled there during previous revolts and executions.) St. Basil's stood at one end of this plaza. Despite Napoleon's admiration for the church, the French turned it into barracks for soldiers. The Emperor himself moved into one of the Kremlin palaces.

Napoleon's capture of Moscow by no means brought an end to his troubles, for he found the city completely deserted. The only citizens who had not fled were the invalids, and the Russian soldiers who were too badly wounded to be moved. Many of the art treasures, all the money, food, horses, vehicles, had disappeared along with the 300,000 inhabitants.

Hardly had Napoleon begun to make himself at home when word was brought to him that Moscow was on fire, not in just one place but in a dozen places. The fire had been set by the Russians themselves, who were determined to destroy their city with everybody and everything left in it, rather than allow it to remain in possession of the hated French.

Every effort was made to put out the flames, but without success; for a high wind arose and spread the fires with frightful speed.

Toward the Kremlin itself the fire swept. Napoleon climbed to a tower-room in the palace he was occupying, and from the window looked out over the walls upon the sea of roaring flames. The houses of 300,000 people seemed to be on fire all at once. Flames were leaping a hundred feet into the sky. From time to time the ground shook as a great building collapsed with a terrifying crash.

As the Emperor gazed upon this scene of destruction, the glass in the window became so hot that he had to retreat to a lower floor. And there his generals told him that the four hundred ammunition wagons and forty thousand pounds of gunpowder, collected in the courtyards below, were in danger of being fired by the rain of sparks. If *that* happened, the Emperor, along with his guards, and the glorious gold-domed Kremlin churches, and the palaces of the Tsars, would all be blown to bits. Everybody must move out of the Kremlin at once.

Realizing how great was the peril, Napoleon made his exit from the fortress through the gate leading to the river bank. From here on horseback he galloped down the flaming streets and sought safety in another palace several miles outside the town.

For three days and nights Moscow burned. When, on the fourth day, heavy rains put a stop to the fire, two-thirds of the city had been reduced to ashes.

Napoleon then returned to inspect the smoking wreckage. He found that the Kremlin, thanks to the fact that it was set apart from the crowded city and surrounded by its stout stone walls, had escaped the flames and had not been seriously damaged. Heroic efforts on the part of the French soldiers had saved the ammunition and powder from explosion. Viewing the wreckage around Red Square, Napoleon was happy to find that St. Basil's Church, the church whose colored domes had so enchanted him when first he looked down upon Moscow, still stood unharmed.

The French clung to the ruins for another month, hoping the Russian Tsar would beg for peace. But the Tsar knew that the invaders' army, now cut off from France, was starving and rapidly melting away. So he refused to talk peace with Napoleon. The French Emperor, with only one-sixth of his once great force left to him, and with only Moscow's ruins to shelter even these few remaining troops, realized there was no longer any hope of conquering Russia. In fact, he now thought only of escape.

The story of Napoleon's retreat back to France is one of the most horrible stories of history. Attacked on all sides by the re-

In the center of Moscow is a walled inner city called the Kremlin. Here, for centuries, up
1700, the Tsars lived. And here were the buildings that housed the government of Russia.
1700 the government was moved to St. Petersburg (now Leningrad). But since the Bolsh
Revolution in 1917, the Russian capital has been moved back to the Kremlin. From its w
on all four sides, rise tall towers. Within the walls are the holiest churches in Russia, topped

g gold domes. On our visit to the Kremlin we see the rooms where Napoleon lived in 1812,
he and his French army had seized Moscow. We see the cathedral where all the Tsars of Rus-
re crowned, from Ivan the Terrible down to Nicholas II, the last. When the Russians them-
set fire to Moscow in 1812, to prevent its sheltering Napoleon's army, the Kremlin and St.
Basil's Church were almost the only parts of the city that escaped destruction.

vengeful Russians, unable to obtain food, overtaken by a severe winter, the ragged, hungry wreck of an army which had left Moscow, was almost destroyed before it reached the Russian border. Napoleon, himself, and a handful of his guards, got home to Paris—all that were left of the 600,000.

Moscow, during the years since the fire of 1812, has been completely rebuilt. It is now, under the Soviet Government, a great and modern city of four million people, and the capital of Russia. Napoleon would not recognize it today. But the Kremlin, with its domed churches, its vast palaces and towered walls, is just the same as when the French invaders marched away from it. Red Square, too, with the addition of Lenin's tomb, looks almost as it did in 1812. And St. Basil's Church, which escaped the flames, still stands in all its glory, as bright-colored as when Napoleon first looked down upon it from the hilltop.

This Kremlin, this Red Square, this St. Basil's, we must see on our wonder tour.

From Mount Athos we take a boat back to Salonika. And from here, reunited with the girls in our party, we travel by train across Bulgaria and Rumania. Then another train ride of eight hundred miles across Russia (see map, page 168) brings us to Moscow —and Red Square.

We had not dreamed the Square was so big and so splendid. The Kremlin walls, painted white and adorned with towers, extend along one side. We see the spires of the churches and palaces rising above the walls, within the fortress. On the Kremlin side of the great Square stands the black-marble tomb of Lenin.

We look toward the Square's far end. There looms that strange cluster of colored domes—St. Basil's Church.

We stare at this church in wonderment. It simply can't be real. But it *is* real. We walk up to it. The closer we approach, the wilder and crazier it seems; and yet we find it strangely beautiful. Delighted that it escaped the flames when Moscow burned, we go inside. There is no one large room, but only a series of little chapels—chapels once used as barracks for Napoleon's men, but now turned into a museum.

Back in the Square we visit Lenin's tomb. Lenin, the father of the Bolshevik revolution, died in 1924. To enshrine his body, the Bolsheviks built the black-marble monument in the shape of a pyramid. Inside, Lenin's body, wonderfully preserved, rests in a glass case for all the world to see, and crowds of communists pass before it as respectfully as we would pass before the body of Washington.

We join the long line of patriots waiting for their turn to enter the tomb. Moving slowly, our hats in our hands, we pass through the open marble doors. Here before us is Lenin's body, looking very life-like, and seeming to be asleep. He is fully clothed. Over him is spread a Persian shawl. His hair and beard have a reddish color; his mouth looks tired but determined. At each corner of the platform on which the body rests, a soldier stands rigid. We have to look twice at these guards to be sure they're alive.

From the tomb we next walk beneath one of the Kremlin tower-gates, and find ourselves within the walls. Up to the year 1700, at which date the capital was moved from Moscow to St. Petersburg, the Kremlin had been the home of the Russian Tsars, and the headquarters of the government. And now again, since 1917, the Russian government is back in the Kremlin.

We are shown all the interesting features of this famous fortress. Here, in one palace, Napoleon lived during those tragic days in Moscow. From this high window the French Emperor looked out upon the burning city. We visit the museums and see ancient and beautiful things that belonged to the Tsars. In the gold-domed churches we see the heavy silver chandeliers that Napoleon carted off when he began his retreat—treasures quickly recovered by the Russians when the French dropped every burden in their headlong flight. In the Assumption Cathedral, the most richly decorated of all, we are shown the spot where all the Tsars of Russia were crowned, from Ivan the Terrible down to Nicholas II, the last.

On one side of the Kremlin lies Moscow's famous Red Square. At the far end rises St. Bas
Church. The black marble pyramid, beside the Kremlin's white wall, is the tomb of Lenin,
father of the Russian Revolution. Every November seventh, the anniversary of the day when
Bolsheviks seized control of the government in 1917 (It's the Bolshevik Fourth of July.), a v

Sovfoto.

..ry parade is held in Red Square. A hundred thousand soldiers march past Lenin's tomb,
..y a brass band of nine hundred pieces. The soldiers are followed by a parade of 2,500,000
..workers. Along with forty thousand other visitors we watch from the grandstand.

In another part of the Kremlin we see the biggest bell in the world. It is rightly called the King of Bells. Cast in 1734, it weighs two hundred tons, is twenty feet high and sixty-eight feet around the base. It took twenty four men to swing the clapper. Broken in a fall, after it had been in place only three years, it has not since been rung, but rests on the ground. We go inside the bell, through a broken hole in the shell. Another fifty people could go along with us and we would not be crowded.

Nearby is the biggest cannon ever made. We think the sixteen-inch guns on our battleships are monsters. But *this* gun has a bore of *thirty-six inches*. Of course it was too big ever to be used in warfare. Alongside it is a row of 875 French cannon captured from the fleeing Napoleon.

We have timed our visit to Russia so as to be in Moscow on the seventh of November. This is the great national holiday in Soviet Russia—its Christmas, Thanksgiving, and Fourth of July, all rolled into one. On this day, every year, the government fills Red Square with a vast military and patriotic parade. There are forty thousand people in the grandstand, and a million more standing in the streets outside the Square. We have the good fortune to be seated near Lenin's tomb. At one corner of the tomb is the box occupied by the highest Bolshevik officials. They are so close to us we could take pictures of them if we were allowed.

Before us a hundred thousand soldiers march —across the same ground where Napoleon reviewed his troops in 1812. A military band of nine hundred pieces plays marching music.

Sovfoto.

The biggest bell in the world —broken by a fall—is on display within the Kremlin. It weighs two hundred tons.

Military tanks play a big part in the Soviets' November celebration. In this picture we can count one hundred and four of these rumbling monsters crossing Red Square. Napoleon reviewed his troops on this same plaza in 1812. How his eyes would stare if he could see a parade of tanks, like these, roaring across the Square he knew so well.

Then the cavalrymen gallop by. And tanks! The Bolsheviks boast that they have more tanks than any other country. These iron monsters thunder before us, a hundred at a time.

Overhead the sky is black with war planes, a thousand flying all at once.

Then when this bewildering array of fighting men has marched, ridden, rolled and flown before us, the workers' parade begins.

Over 2,500,000 workers march through Red Square, a river, a tidal-wave, of humanity. Here we see more people than the total population of any city in America except New York and Chicago. Every factory, every school, turns out on this day, with all its members, with floats, banners, music, of a thousand sorts.

More and more astonished, we stand for eight hours watching this endless parade go by. These marching, cheering regiments, the tanks, the thundering swarms of planes, framed in this magnificent Square, all make a picture that will always rank high among the marvelous sights we have seen on our tour of the wonders of the world.

Sovfoto.

A giant Soviet airplane flies over a Kremlin tower.

CHAPTER XXX

THE MOTHER OF CHURCHES

Over the dark waters of a great inland sea our steamer sails. We have left Moscow behind, traveled south to the city of Odessa, and are now crossing the Black Sea. As we approach the southern shore, we notice, just ahead, opening to receive us, the entrance to a narrow channel winding between hills. This channel is called the Bosporus. Through it the Black Sea flows south into the Hellespont, and on to the Ægean. (See map, page 168.)

The Bosporus divides two continents. As we sail down it, we see Asia on the left bank, and Europe on the right.

For twenty miles our steamer races along with the current. Then, suddenly, a vision from the *Arabian Nights* rises up ahead on the European shore . . . a forest of ghostly minarets, tall and slender, springing from a hilltop and shining in the sun.

We have come to Istanbul, once called Constantinople—before that, Byzantium.

Closer and closer our steamer moves—closer to the mosques, the domes, the towers. From this dream city, one huge structure stands forth, topped by the tallest dome of all and adorned at the four corners by four slim minarets.

This is Santa Sophia, the Mother of Churches.

Some three hundred years after the birth of Christ, the Roman Emperor named Constantine became a Christian—the first Roman ruler to be baptized. It was he, you remember, who built the first St. Peter's Church over the grave of the martyred disciple. Later, wishing to free his empire entirely from the old pagan religion, he moved his capital from Rome eastward to Byzantium. There, where Europe and Asia are separated only by the Bosporus, Constantine built a new city which he hoped would become the heart of the Christian world.

About two hundred years later, Justinian, the greatest of the rulers who followed Constantine, came to the throne. *This* Em-

Aboard our steamer we sail through the Bosporus (the dark channel of water across the cent
of this picture). Asia is on the far shore, Europe on the near. Suddenly, on the Europea
side, a forest of minarets, tall and slender and shining in the sun, springs from the hilltop. W
have come to Istanbul, once called Constantinople—before that, Byzantium. From this drea
city three great mosques stand forth. The largest of the three—the one on the left-hand page-

Gendreau.

anta Sophia, the Mother of Churches, and one of the wonders of the world. Earthquakes have
ral times shaken the city to pieces. But this marvelous building, with its soaring dome, has
ays endured. At the extreme right, the mosque with the six minarets (only five showing) is
the Blue Mosque. The domed buildings in the lower right-hand corner are the city bazaars.

peror's ambition over-topped that of all other Byzantine kings. Justinian dreamed of raising, to the glory of the Christian God, a church that would be the marvel of the age, a church bigger and more beautiful than any temple ever built for the pagan gods.

And so this giant-spirited Emperor commanded his architects to build just such a church. With a lordly gesture, about the year 530, he swept away the acres of houses standing where he wished his great structure to stand. He stopped all other public works in order to assemble sixteen thousand builders. He searched the empire, both in Asia and Europe, for the finest materials, and forced Athens and Rome to send him shiploads of riches.

The building costs left the royal treasury empty. But Justinian was not the man to be dismayed. He merely seized the salaries of all the state officials, closed the schools, and made the army serve without pay. With the money saved, he bought forty thousand pounds of silver and half a million pearls just for the altar.

Over his church Justinian spread a dome that is one of the wonders of architecture—a dome not so high nor so wide as St. Peter's, but much flatter.

At last, in 537, Justinian's temple stood complete, faced inside with marble from a hundred lands, roofed by the great dome.

This was the Emperor's proudest hour. Surrounded by his attendants, accompanied by a thousand priests and a great orchestra and choir, Justinian mounted to the silver altar and cried out for all the multitudes to hear, "Oh Solomon, I have surpassed thee! My temple is greater than thine!"

For 916 years Justinian's temple served as a Christian church —about three times as long a period as has passed since the Pilgrims landed in America. Thousands upon thousands of people came from every corner of the civilized world to behold it. Other churches rose by hundreds, but not one of them could compare with Santa Sophia in size and magnificence. (The present St. Peter's, itself, was not begun until 1506—nearly a thousand years after Santa Sophia.)

Santa Sophia was built by the Christian emperor, Justinian, and completed in the year 537. Thereafter for more than nine hundred years it served as a Christian church. For magnificence it had no rival in the world. (St. Peter's was built eleven hundred years after Santa Sophia.) But the Turks, on capturing Byzantium in 1453, turned the great church into a great mosque. They built the four minarets at the four corners. From these, up until recent times, a Mohammedan crier, called a muezzin, has called a Mohammedan city to prayer. Santa Sophia today is a museum, and its minarets are used no longer.

The outside of Santa Sophia might be mistaken for a fort. But wait till you have a look at
inside. Its enormous size takes your breath away. The most astonishing part of the mosque i
huge dome. This dome is not as high or as wide as St. Peter's, but much flatter. It's so flat, a
tects wonder how it stands, and why it doesn't fall down. When Justinian had compl

is church, fourteen hundred years ago, he boasted that *his* temple was greater than Solomon's.
Today all the Turkish symbols have been removed in order to allow artists to restore the interior
to its original appearance. Now, for the first time in its long life, this famous building is open
to visitors from all countries and of all religions.

A French historian, passing through Byzantium with the Crusaders, exclaimed about this church,—after it had already been standing six hundred years: "It is a paradise of beauty, the throne of the glory of God. It rises to the heavens. It is the marvel of the earth."

That was in 1130 when Byzantium was the largest and most civilized city west of China.

But doom was on the way. From Asia, armies of Turks and Arabs, inspired by the teachings of the Prophet Mohammed, were moving, slowly but surely, towards Byzantium. These Mohammedans hated Byzantium because it was Christian, and were determined to conquer it.

Unable to stop this invasion, Constantine XIII, the last Christian emperor of Byzantium, saw his empire falling to pieces. In 1453 the end came.

Knowing his city was lost and he about to die, he made his way into Santa Sophia to say farewell to it. He looked up at the huge figures on the ceiling of the marvelous dome—Christ and the Apostles and the Saints. He knew they soon would reign no more in their high places—places they had graced nine hundred years.

And so it came to pass. Over the bodies of ten thousand Christian dead, Sultan Mohammed (named after the Prophet) rode into the great church. The interior was packed with terrified citizens praying for rescue, but no rescue came. Mohammed mounted to the silver altar, knelt toward Mecca (the Moslem Holy City) and gave thanks to Allah for the victory.

Everyone supposed the Sultan would destroy the Christian church at once. But the Sultan did no such senseless thing. He saw that the glorious temple might be just as much the pride of *his* city as it had been of Constantine's—if it were turned into a mosque.

And turned into a mosque it was. The Sultan stripped it of every Christian symbol. Over the pictures of the Saints he spread verses from the Koran (the Mohammedan Bible). The silver altar and the pearls he gave to his officers. At each of the four corners, outside, he erected a minaret from which his priests might call a Mohammedan Byzantium to prayer.

This historical event took place thirty-nine years before Columbus discovered America. But Santa Sophia still stands as unshaken today as it was then.

This is the famous building we behold from our ship as we sail down the Bosporus. And toward it we find our way the moment we land at the dock. Climbing a hill, we come to a great open square before the mosque. Santa Sophia rises above us, a huge mass of hewn stone, adorned at the corners by Sultan Mohammed's minarets.

At first glance Santa Sophia is disappointing. One might mistake it for a fort.

But, oh—the inside!

I first saw the inside in 1919, during the month of Ramadan, the month most sacred to the Mohammedans. Then, as at our Christmas and Easter seasons, thousands of worshipers were pouring into the great mosque.

And on the Night of Power, the last night of Ramadan, I followed the crowd through the bronze doors. The interior, brightly lighted, soared about me and above me, vast and magnificent beyond belief. The acres of floor space below were densely packed with worshipers—so densely, in fact, that they could not kneel, but had to stand, hands held up to their faces, and merely bow toward Mecca. A High Priest led this throng of twenty thousand faithful. Each prayer, chanted from twenty thousand voices, echoed and re-echoed across the immense dome above. I wondered as I stood spellbound in the midst of all this splendor, if Justinian himself, in this same building, had ever beheld any sight as wonderful as this Night of Power.

Twelve years passed before I came again to Istanbul. But what changes had taken place! The Sultan's government had been overturned, the mosque's priests driven away. Though outwardly the same, Santa Sophia was almost empty.

But again I went back to pay my respects to this ancient and storied church.

305

Alone, about nine o'clock at night, I entered the courtyard before the mosque and found it deserted. All the glitter of twelve years before had gone. There was almost no light but the crescent moon—just two or three small lamps. I took my shoes in my hand, plunged into the dark emptiness, and felt my way down a corridor that led to the dim interior.

This Temple of Divine Wisdom—that's what *Santa Sophia* means—had been wonderful enough the first time I saw it, with its dazzling lights and praying thousands. But now in the darkness and the silence, with the moonbeams streaming down through the windows of that wide-spread dome, I felt, even more than on the first visit, that I beheld a temple too mighty, too soaring, to have been built by man.

Presently a guard came in to clear the mosque of visitors, put out the lamps, and lock up for the night. I retreated into the shadow of a column and was not seen. The guard departed, leaving me all alone in this haunted temple.

For three enchanted hours I roamed about my wonderful church, touching, through the shadow veil, the columns and the walls. I leaned back against a column and looked up at the fearless dome, and watched the moonlight streaming down from the openings in this stone canopy two hundred feet above.

How still the great mosque had become at this midnight hour; how peaceful its dark gloom! My lodging was far away and the carpets in my corner deep and very soft. I made a pillow of my coat, and stretched upon a carpet bed. The moon continued to ride in the heavens, wheeling around the circle of windows upon which the great dome spread its wings. And as it wheeled, the shafts of light that fell upon the carpets at my feet wheeled too. I lay quite still and watched the slow procession of these beams, wondering if they were the ghosts of the emperors who once ruled Byzantium—the Christian kings who had worshiped here—the Sultans of the Mohammedans. . . .

Hour after hour these shadow figures moved, slowly pacing their path across the temple floor . . . and then the moonlight

306

waned, and one by one the specters faded back into their crumbling tombs.

Next morning, soon after the doors were opened, I walked out unnoticed by the guards.

Now, again, I am about to visit this Mother of Churches—and this time I'm taking you with me.

We enter the great doors—through these same doors Justinian passed fourteen hundred years ago. And there we stand and stare. . . . "The paradise of beauty, the throne of the glory of God. It rises to the heavens. It is the marvel of the earth!"

We know just how that Crusader-historian felt when *he* stood here in the twelfth century.

"But," you say, "where are the carpets and the altars? Where are the priests, and the verses from the Koran on the ceiling? They are missing. Santa Sophia is certainly enormous enough—but how empty it seems!"

Publishers Photo Service.

It is true—the carpets, the altars, Mohammed's decorations that I saw, are not here. For the giant mosque is no longer, after fourteen hundred years of service, a place of worship. It has been turned into a museum by the new and unreligious Turkish government. English and American archeologists—Christians—have taken possession and removed all the ancient rugs and scraped off all the Koran scriptures. But now, instead, we can see the superb Christian decorations, in clear view again, and as fresh as on the day when Justinian first unveiled them to the Byzantines.

Otherwise the church-mosque is unchanged. The marble walls, the columns, the dome, have been untouched by the centuries. We look up at them in admiration and amazement, and understand why the Byzantine Emperor felt certain he had built a temple greater even than Solomon's.

The last time I visited Santa Sophia I was able to climb one of the minarets at dawn and stand beside the public crier, the "muezzin," as he greeted the sunrise and called all Istanbul to early-morning prayer.

We, too, can climb the minaret, but as the building is no longer a mosque, there is no muezzin. However, just across the great square from Santa Sophia there is another mosque (one of the few left open by the government) that is still used for religious services—the beautiful Blue Mosque. Tomorrow morning we may be able to accompany the muezzin to his balcony near the top of the minaret, in *that* mosque, and watch the sun rise upon Santa Sophia—and hear the call to prayer.

When morning comes we are out of bed before five o'clock. Hurriedly we dress and hasten to the courtyard of the Blue Mosque just as a pale light is breaking in the east. We wait for the muezzin. He arrives presently, wearing a flowing silk robe. We explain, through our interpreter, that it is our ambition to climb the minaret with him and listen to his call, close at hand.

308

European Pictures.

The Blue Mosque stands at the opposite end of a great public square from Santa Sophia. It is not as old as Santa Sophia by nearly a thousand years, nor nearly as large. By climbing with the muezzin to the top balcony of a minaret of this Blue Mosque we are able to stand beside him as he calls all Istanbul to prayer, and to watch the sun rise on the Mother of Churches, across the way.

He looks about. At this hour there is no other mosque official awake to object. He tells us we may follow him.

Behind him, in the blackness, we feel our way up the winding stairs. We emerge on the high balcony, with the sun just ready to spring out of Asia, across the Bosporus; and all Istanbul, gray and misty, sleeping at our feet. Some two hundred yards across the Square, Santa Sophia, huge and shapeless in the early shadows, swells and soars against the glowing horizon.

Allāhu akbar—Allāhu akbar. The muezzin leans out to the east, out to the sun, and chants in that high-pitched voice always used, which sounds like mournful wolves howling. *Allāhu akbar— God is great.*

Ashadu anna lā ilāha illallāh—I testify there is no god but God. There is no god but God.

The chanting priest now leans to the north and looks beyond Santa Sophia, and on up the channel of the swirling, awakening Bosporus toward the dim Black Sea—*I testify that Mohammed is the Prophet of God—Come to Prayer—Come to Prayer.*

The muezzin turns to face the west where most of the city lies, with its forest of domes and minarets, all tinted brightly with the first colors of the sunrise—*Hajju 'ala's-salāt—salaaaaaaaaat— Come to salvation—salvaaaaaaaaashun.*

His morning call to prayer over, the muezzin signals to us that he is ready to descend from the minaret, and that we must follow him. We take one last look at Santa Sophia, now washed in golden light from the early sun. We know that in another hour the doors of the Mother of Churches will be open for the day, to welcome the throngs of visitors—visitors from all countries and of all religions—who may now come to her freely, as in ancient times. And we know that they will rejoice to see her, despite her great age, standing as firmly as on the day her doors first opened, and ready to continue standing, more proud and beautiful than ever, for another fourteen centuries.

Dear reader:

I hope you have enjoyed our travels together. I've had a happy time, myself. You remember, when we first met, I said I wanted you to *live* geography as well as study it? Well, we *have* lived it, haven't we? Now we know how really wonderful our world is—or rather, the Occident-half of it—because we have seen its wonders with our own eyes, and touched them with our own hands.

Asia and Africa we have not yet visited, and these two continents contain temples and mountains and cities and waterfalls as marvelous as those of the Occident. We can go and see these, too, if you like, on another world-wonder tour.

So let's hope we can meet again, some day soon, where we have parted company this time—and sail on.

Your friend,

Richard Halliburton

PROPER NAMES PRONOUNCED

Acropolis	a-krop'-o-lis	Coronado	koh-roh-nah'-do
Ægean	ĕ-jee'-an		
Alvar de Vaca	ahl'-var day vah'kah	Cortez	kor'-tez
		Culebra	koo-lay'-brah
Améthyste	ah-may-teest'	Cuzco	koos'-ko
Alpine	al'-pine		
Andean	an-dee'-an	Daphne	daf'-nee
Andes	an'-deez	Dauphin	daw'-fin
Argentina	ar-jen-tee'-na	De Lesseps	duh less-eps'
Athénaire	ah-tay-nair'	Diomedes	dy-oh-mee'-deez
Athens	ath'-enz		
Athos	ath'-os	Dom	dŏm
Aude	ode	Domremy	dong-re-mee' (dong nasal)
Bagdad	bag'-dad	Don López de Cárdenas	don loh'-payz day kar-day'-nahs
Balboa	bol-boh'-ah		
Bernardine	bur-nahr'-deen		
Blondin	blon-dan' (nasal ending)	El Capitan	el kah-pi-tahn'
		Fujiyama	foo'-jee-yah'-mah
Bolshevik	bol'-she-vik		
Bramante	brah-mahn'-tay	Garganta del Diablo	gar-gahn'-tah del dee-ah'-bloh
Brazil	brah-zil'		
Budapest	boo'-da-pest		
Buenos Aires	bway'-nos ī'-rayz	Gatun	gah-toon'
Byzantine	bi-zan'-teen	Genoa	jen'-oh-a
Byzantium	bi-zan'-ti-um	Gibraltar	ji-brahl'-ter
		Gorner	gōr'-ner
Cæsar, Julius	see'-zar, joo'-lee-us		
		Haiti	hay'-ti
Capri	kah'-pree	Haitien	hāy'-tı-ĕn
Carcassonne	kar-ka-sawn'	Hannibal	han'-i-bal
Caribbean	kar-i-bee'-an	Hellespont	hel'-es-pont
Carthaginian	kar-tha-jin'-ee-an	Hennepin	hen'-nĕ-pin
		Hercules	her'-kew-leez
Caspian	kas'-pee-un	Himalayas	hi-mah-lay'-yahz
Chagres	chah'-gress		
Cheops	kee'-ops		
Chichen Itza	chee-chen eat'-zah	Iguazu	ee-gwa-soo'
		Inca	in'-kah
Chile	chil'-i	Istanbul	ees-tahn-bool'
Chinon	shee-nong (nasal ending)	Ivan	ī'-van
		Ixtaccihuatl	iss-tok-see-wah'-tl
Cholula	choh-loo'-lah	Jerusalem	je-roo'-sah-lem
Christophe	krees-toff'	Jungfrau	yoong'-frow
Cibola	si'-boh-lah	Jupiter	jew'-pi-ter
Clovis	kloh'-vis	Justinian	jus-tin'-i-an
Constantine	kon'-stan-tyne		
Corcovado	kor-koh-vah'-doh	Karyes	kar'-yes
		Koran	koh'-ran

La Paloma	lah pah-loh'-mah	Rainier	ray-neer'
L'Enfant	long-fong' (nasal ending)	Ramadan	ram-a-dahn'
		Raphael	raf'-ay-el
		Reims	rance (nasal ending)
Lenin	len'-in	Rio de Janeiro	ree-oh day zhahn-ay'-roh
Leningrad	lĕn'-ın-grăd		
Limoux	lee-moo'	Rouen	roo-ong' (nasal ending)
Livy̆	lıv'-ı		
Machu Picchu	mah'-choo pee'-choo	Saint Basil	saint bă'-zil
		Saint Bernard	saint ber-nard'
Madrid	mah-drid'	Saint Pierre	saint pee-yair'
Magellan	mah-jel'-an	Salonika	sah-lah-nee'-ka
Marmora	mahr'-mo-ra	Sans Souci	song soo-see' (song nasal)
Matterhorn	maht'-er-horn		
Mayas	mah'-yahz	Saracen	sar'-a-sen
Mediterranean	med-i-ter-ay'-nee-an	Sequoia	see-kwoi'-ya
		Sestos	ses'-tos
Michael	my'-kel	Simopetra	see-moh-pay'-trah
Michelangelo	mee-kel-an'-je-loh		
		Seville	se-vil'
Misenum	me-zay'-num	Sierra Nevada	si-air'-a ne-vah'-da
Mohammed	moh-ham'-ed		
Mont Blanc	mong blong' (nasal endings)	Suez	soo-ez'
		Tacitus	tas'-i-tus
Monte Rosa	mon'-tey roh'-zah	Tarik	tar'-ik
		Tenochtitlan	tee-noch-teet'-lan
Mont Saint Michel	mong san (nasals) mee-shel'		
		Thessaly	thes'-a-lee
		Tibet	ti-bet'
Moscow	mos'-koh	Timbuctoo	tim-buk'-too
Moslem	moz'-lem	Tortugas	tor-too'-gahz
		Turin	too'-rin
Naples	nay'-p'lz	Turkestan	tur-kess-tan'
Napoleon	na-poh'-lee-on		
Niño	neen'yo	Ulysses	u-lis'-eez
		Urubamba	oo'-roo-bahm'-bah
Odessa	o-dess'-a		
Orizaba	oh-ri-zah'-bah	Valencia	vah-len'-sya
Orleans	or-leenz'	Valparaiso	val-pah-ry'-zoh
		Vera Cruz	vay-rah krooz'
Panama	pan-a-mah'	Vesuvius	ve-soo'-vee-us
Parana	pah-rah-nah'		
Parthenon	par'-the-non	Waterloo	wah-ter-loo'
Peru	pee-roo'	Whymper	whim'-per
Peruvian	pee-roo'-vee-an	Xerxes	zerk'-zeez
Pisa	pee'-zah	Yerba Buena	yair'-bah bway'-nah
Pizarro	pi-zahr'-roh		
Pliny	plın'-ı	Yosemite	yoh-sem'-i-tee
Pompeii	pom-pay'-yee	Yucatan	yoo-kah-tahn'
Popocatepetl	poh-poh-kah-tay'-pet-l	Yum-Chac	yoom'-chok
		Zermatt	tser-maht'

The Orient

RICHARD HALLIBURTON'S

Complete

BOOK OF MARVELS

THE BOBBS-MERRILL COMPANY
Indianapolis PUBLISHERS *New York*

CONTENTS OF THE ORIENT

ROUMANIA

YUGOSLAVIA

Danube River

BULGARIA

Black Sea

AND THE FIRST BOOK OF MARVELS

ITALY

ALBANIA

GREECE

SALONICA

ISTANBUL

TURKEY

FROM ISTANBUL

ATHENS

SMYRNA

1 EPHESUS

OLYMPIA

HALICARNASSUS

2

3 RHODES

KNOSSOS

7

CRETE

SYR

CYPRUS

Mediterranean Sea

4

ALEXANDRIA

JERUSALEM

SUEZ CANAL

TRANS JORDA

5.6 CAIRO

PYRAMIDS

MT. SINAI

HEJ

Red Sea

LIBYA

To Timbuctoo

EGYPT

Nile River

MAP *showing location of Marvels in the Mediterranean Basin*

Chapters

1. Ephesus
2. Halicarnassus
3. Rhodes
4. Alexandria
5 and 6. The Pyramids
7. Knossos

FRENCH EQUATORIAL AFRICA

ANGLO-EGYPTIAN SUDAN

THE ORIENT

CHAPTER I

THE TRAVELS OF DEMETRIUS

One fine spring morning, 250 years before the birth of Christ, a twelve-year-old Greek boy named Demetrius, living in ancient Athens, stood before an open window in his father's house and looked eastward toward the Ægean Sea. All about him climbed the white houses of the beautiful city. Close at hand rose the rocky Acropolis, crowned by a gleaming temple—the Parthenon. And beyond, five miles away, his eyes rested on a cluster of buildings which marked Piræus, the seaport of Athens. Out from Piræus he knew that the ships, with their tiers of oars and their great white wings, were sailing off that very morning to the far corners of the world—off to Sicily, to the Hellespont, to the islands of Crete and Rhodes, to Tyre and Sidon and Carthage, even to Egypt and the Nile.

And the thought of these winged ships and these foreign lands brought to little Demetrius a joy that made him want to shout aloud, for within another hour he, Demetrius, was to leave Athens with his father, Diomede, and travel to Piræus and board a ship, and set out to see these very lands and all the wonders they contained. This "grand tour," as it was called, was his reward for the good record he had made during the past term in his school.

The year before, Demetrius had traveled with Diomede to the city of Olympia, in western Greece. There he had seen the Olympic Games and met a number of the athletes. There, too, he had visited the world-famous gold-and-ivory statue of Zeus in the great temple. His teachers had all told him that this statue, many times bigger than life-size, was one of the foremost wonders of the world. When Demetrius looked upon it, in the mysterious gloom of the temple's halls, he scarcely dared breathe, for he felt he was looking upon the father of the gods himself.

3

The gold-and-ivory statue of Zeus, the father of the gods, at Olympia, in western Greece. Built about the year 450 B.C., it was 200 years old when Demetrius and Diomede traveled from Athens to see it. This statue was considered one of the Seven Wonders of the ancient world.

That had been the summer before. Now Demetrius was setting out for a ten-times finer vacation. Diomede had promised him that on *this* journey they would visit Ephesus and the Temple of Diana, about which such glowing stories were told. And they would go to Halicarnassus and the tomb of King Mausolus, the most wonderful burial monument in the Greek world.

And Rhodes, with its Colossus!—that amazing statue which everyone said must have been built with the help of the gods.

They were going to Alexandria, too, the great Egyptian seaport, just to visit its world-renowned lighthouse.

Then, after Alexandria, the Pyramids! All his life Demetrius had seen drawings and read descriptions of the Pyramids. *Nearly three thousand years old!* It was difficult for the boy to understand how anything could be that old and still endure. His geography teacher had explained to him that all the houses in Athens, with Corinth and Sparta thrown in, would not supply enough stone to build one of these enormous tombs. The very thought of seeing them, and the famous Sphinx resting in their shadow, made his heart leap up.

Diomede at last was ready. Demetrius embraced his mother, said good-by to the household, and jumped in beside his father in the family chariot. Dioméde cracked his whip. The horses bounded forward, and away they sped down the road that led to the harbor.

Having left the chariot with servants at Piræus, they boarded their ship, a ship with fifty oarsmen and a huge purple sail. A strong breeze from the land made starting easy. Swiftly and gracefully the craft glided out of the bay. Demetrius looked back at the receding shores of Greece and saw, five miles inland, the Acropolis lifting up its holy temple; and in his young heart he bade farewell to the goddess Athena, the protector of Athens and the goddess he loved most of all.

Then he looked toward the east, straight across the Ægean . . . there was where adventure lay and all the marvels he was going to behold.

I think I know just how that Greek boy felt. I can understand his excitement, because when I was twelve I dreamed, as he dreamed, of visiting the lands beyond my little neighborhood.

Sometimes I drew maps of the United States, of Europe and Asia, on the blank pages of my schoolbooks, and traced a line of travel from one famous city to another. This led me to wonder-

5

ing where people traveled before there *was* a Paris or a London, when the Alps and Venice were unknown, when America lay somewhere far off in space beyond the edge of the earth.

I wondered, for example, where I would have gone 250 years before the birth of Christ. I chose this date because it was a time in history when people, especially the ancient Greeks, were more civilized, in some ways, than we are today. To what countries and cities did *they* go when they wanted to visit the marvelous works of man and nature? What were the great sights of *their* world?

As I grew older I was able to find out more about those ancient days, to learn where the great cities were and what made them great. I even went to those very cities myself, and saw, with my own eyes, what was left, after all these centuries, of the wonders that astonished people then.

In this book—in the first six chapters—I'm going back again to those scenes of ancient glory, and I want to take with me every boy and girl who likes to travel. Demetrius and his father will be our guides and lead the way. We will learn, first, where they went and what they saw. Then we'll follow in their tracks—tracks made 2200 years ago.

We left Demetrius and Diomede in their boat sailing eastward across the Ægean Sea. Toward what harbor did the pilot turn?

Diomede had promised his son that the very first place they would visit would be the celebrated city of Ephesus. Ephesus lay on the eastern shore of the Ægean, on the Asiatic side, two hundred miles straight across the sea from Athens. To this city the oars and the sail were driving their ship.

In 250 B.C. Ephesus was a large and proud city, built mostly of marble. It had 200,000 people, and walls eight miles around. Its harbor was filled with Greek and Phœnician merchant ships bringing crowds of travelers from all the foreign lands. They

6·

From "The Book of Knowledge" by permission of the Grolier Society, publishers.
The Temple of Diana at Ephesus in Asia Minor (now Turkey) was the largest and richest temple in the ancient Greek world. (The smaller Parthenon, in Athens, was more beautiful and had finer sculpture.) In ancient times thousands upon thousands of pilgrims and travelers came here to worship. To all the Greeks of Demetrius' day, this was the Great Temple.

Courtesy "Wonders of the Past."

In 250 B.C. when Demetrius and Diomede came to visit Diana's Temple at Ephesus, this beautiful building was at the height of its glory. Though made of the purest white marble, it glittered with color, for the marble was painted bright hues, and great quantities of gold shone from the roof and walls.

came to trade, but more especially to worship at Ephesus' wonder-temple, a temple known everywhere for its great size and splendor, the Temple of Diana of the Ephesians.

This marvelous structure had been built about one hundred years before. It was half finished when Alexander the Great (the young Greek general who conquered all the known world) marched by, during his conquest of this part of Asia. He was so amazed at its vastness and beauty that he offered to complete it at his own expense if only the people of Ephesus would carve his name upon it as the builder. They refused, saying: "It is not fitting that one god should build a temple for another god." Alexander felt flattered and departed peacefully.

The Ephesians, a people famous for their ambition, were determined that their temple should be the most magnificent ever built. They wanted it to outshine the Parthenon in Athens as the sun outshines the moon. The Parthenon was 230 feet long and 100 feet wide and surrounded by 58 marble columns, each 34 feet high. So the Ephesians designed their temple to be 400 feet long and 200 feet wide, and gave it 127 columns, each 60 feet high. Nothing went into it but the purest and whitest marble. Raised upon a broad platform, it could be reached from all sides by sweeping marble steps. To the Greeks of that age, this was the Great Temple. Indeed, it has been claimed that Diana's shrine attracted more travelers than any other building in ancient history. (Even so, artists and architects all claim that the Parthenon, though smaller and simpler, was the finer and more beautiful of the two. Today, the Parthenon is far more famous.)

Demetrius and his father reached Ephesus two generations after the temple was completed. Hurrying down the city's crowded central avenue, they came upon it. Demetrius' eyes grew big before such mighty grandeur. Together Diomede and the boy climbed the steps, stared up at the giant columns, and entered the vast and somber interior. At the far end they beheld the huge statue of Diana glowing faintly in the deep shadows. There in this half-light the two pilgrims from Athens, father and son, bowed their heads with reverence and wonder before the sacred image, and asked the goddess to grant them her blessings.

9

Diana's Wonder-Temple stood for 500 years. Then, in the year 260, barbarians from Europe destroyed it and carried away the priceless treasures. The very site of the temple was lost for centuries. Only a hole in the ground now marks the spot where this ancient Marvel was built.

Diana's temple stood in all its glory for 500 years after the date of Demetrius' visit—until the year 260 A.D. At that time it was robbed and burned by the Goths, barbarians from Europe who had invaded Asia. These invaders left no stone of the temple standing. The ruin was so complete that, before many years had passed, sand and grass had covered over the fragments until even the site was lost. The Crusaders, on their way to Jerusalem, came along in 1100 and asked to see the wonderful temple about which they had heard so much. The Ephesians themselves asked, "*What temple?*" They no longer remembered that there had been one.

In 1869 an Englishman set out to find and excavate the ruins. There *must* have been a temple . . . so many ancient historians had written about it. But he spent twelve months digging here and digging there before he discovered the location—in the middle of what had become a swamp. The foundations were not injured, but were buried under thirty feet of mud and water. Fortunately there were enough building-stones and broken columns recovered to help artists to give us a perfect picture of this marble masterpiece.

And now we, too, are on our way to Ephesus. Our ship, steaming across the deep-blue Ægean Sea, winds its way through the isles of Greece. We land a few miles north of Ephesus, at modern Smyrna on the Turkish coast.

Then we come to the once-glorious city.

Is it possible, you ask, that we have the wrong place? Where is the great harbor? Where are the marble walls and towers?

Alas, none of these things exist today. The harbor where Demetrius landed was filled with silt centuries ago. Forests of trees grow over it. Turkish farmhouses rise where fleets of ships, in from Tyre and Carthage, once rested at the docks. Present-day Ephesus is only a miserable little town completely cut off from the sea. Of the great paved highways that led to it, of the marble forums and palaces and theaters, only scattered bits remain.

A Turkish youth takes us to the marsh. Splashing through

10

mud, we come to a big excavated hole in the ground, half-filled with water. There, in the middle of this excavation, we can see a few pieces of shining stone, almost covered over by the muddy pool.

"This," the youth tells us, "is the temple of Diana."

Only by closing our eyes, by shutting out the mud, the swamp, the wreckage, can we see what once stood here, can we see what Demetrius saw . . . the throngs of awe-struck worshipers from a hundred lands—the marble columns, carved and gleaming—the marble steps—the gold and ivory statues—Diana's marvelous temple, the glory of Ephesus, one of the Seven Wonders of the World.

Lucky, lucky Demetrius!

In ancient times the city of Ephesus was a great seaport. The Temple of Diana overlooked the harbor. Silt filled in the harbor centuries ago. Today forests grow where ships once dropped anchor and unloaded their cargoes.

CHAPTER II

HALICARNASSUS

Aboard another cargo boat, Diomede and his son left Ephesus and sailed on down the coast of Asia Minor. (See map on page two.) They were headed toward more world-wonders.

"Are Halicarnassus and the Colossus of Rhodes going to be as interesting as Diana's temple?" Demetrius asked his father.

"As for Halicarnassus," said Diomede, "the great sight there is only a tomb, but it is considered the most beautiful tomb ever built. We mustn't miss it, especially as we pass right by it on our way to Rhodes. We're going to find that Halicarnassus is a much smaller city than Ephesus, though impressive in its own way.

"A hundred years ago the city was more famous than it is now. Then it had an unusually good and wise king named Mausolus. He governed so well that when he died he left his people free from war and misery—and very rich.

"His queen was named Artemisia. She continued to rule the country after his death. She knew her husband had been a great man and a great king, and she wanted his name and glory to endure through the ages. So she decided to build for him a tomb that would be the most magnificent monument Greek genius could fashion.

"She sent to Athens for gifted artists, sculptors, and architects. A great square was cleared in the middle of the city, and there the tomb of Mausolus began to rise. And just as Artemisia wished, it outshone all other monuments of its kind in beauty of design and in richness of materials. We *still* call any splendid and imposing tomb a mausoleum.

"The monument's over a hundred years old now, but even today it's so fresh and radiant you might think it was built just yesterday. I've seen it several times. There's a square marble base. Above this, on each side of the square is a row of columns. Above that is a tall, steep pyramid. And on top of the pyramid is the most *wonderful* marble chariot, drawn by four enormous marble horses. In the chariot stand the marble figures of the King and

12

From "The Book of Knowledge" by permission of the Grolier Society, publishers.

The third Wonder of the World—the marble tomb of King Mausolus at Halicarnassus, just south of Ephesus. The tomb was 140 feet high and topped with a huge marble chariot drawn by marble horses, and driven by the marble figures of King Mausolus and his Queen. This wonderful tomb stood for 1000 years.

Queen, one-and-a-half times life-size. I should guess that the chariot is about 140 feet above the ground.

"I know you've been told in school that artists have a reverence for this tomb that is almost worshipful. They include it in the Seven Wonders of the World."

Late in the afternoon Demetrius' ship, having sailed eighty miles southward from Ephesus, entered Halicarnassus Bay. And there on the shore, a half-mile away, rising above the marble city and glittering in the sunset, stood the world-famous Mausoleum.

Demetrius and Diomede landed at the dock and walked up the winding streets to the plateau where the monument stood. Never had Demetrius dreamed that sculptured stone could be so beautiful. And he was happy, too, that all this beauty had been created by artists from his own Athens. Entering the tomb beside his father, he stood silently before the carved gold casket that held Mausolus' body.

Together they climbed to the open gallery supported by the columns, and then on up the steps through the center of the pyramid. Breathless, they reached the top, and crawled out right beside the marble chariot. Demetrius looked above him and saw Mausolus and Artemisia driving their huge prancing steeds. The Greek boy caught hold of the horses' marble tails. He stroked their strong legs. He even climbed into the chariot and stood, beaming with delight, between the eight-foot statues of the royal pair.

And standing in this mighty chariot and helping the marble king hold back his marble horses, little Demetrius, with his eyes shining, looked down upon the stately city below, down upon the crowded streets, out over the blue bay surrounded by mountains— a bay sprinkled with white sails of brave Greek ships bringing more travelers like himself to behold Mausolus' tomb. And he felt certain that in all the long history of the world, the world had never been as wonderful as *now*.

Unlike the temple at Ephesus, this famous Mausoleum lasted for a long, long time, for the citizens of Halicarnassus were proud of their monument and protected it with jealous care for a thousand years.

But against earthquakes they had no power, and, little by little, earthquakes shook it down, until by 1404 it was in ruins. At that time the city was attacked by Turks. The Christian defenders seized the tumbled blocks of the Mausoleum to make a fort, and broke up the overturned statues to make lime.

Finally, nothing at all remained above the ground to show the location of the famous monument. But in 1859, after digging deep into the rubbish covering the plateau, archeologists were able to find pieces of the tomb's columns and statues. And only these fragments (now carefully guarded in the British Museum) give us any real idea of what Demetrius and Diomede saw in 250 B.C.

In our own sailboat we leave Ephesus behind and again follow the sea tracks of the two Athenian travelers, southward along the coast of Asia Minor. What gorgeous scenery! The mountains, capped in clouds, come right down to the water.

Then we turn the corner of a headland, and enter Halicarnassus Bay, and catch sight of the modern town rising sharply from the shore.

I'm glad we saw the ruins of Ephesus first. It prepares us for the even greater fall from glory in Halicarnassus. Today the marble city of Mausolus is only a dirty little fishing village.

On shore nobody can tell us where the Mausoleum stood. The fishermen don't even know what we are talking about. Unguided, and followed by curious stares, we wander up the single narrow street to a little plateau. We know the wonder-monument was built on a plateau. Perhaps this is it. But we cannot be sure. There are grass-grown excavations everywhere.

We stand upon this grave of a once-proud city, and again feel a little envious of Demetrius, envious of the poetic world he lived in. How sad, how cruel, that this world should have been so completely destroyed; for was it not, perhaps, a better world than ours? We have radios and airplanes and motorcars, but Demetrius and Diomede, like most Greeks of that Golden Age in history, had the time and the desire to love beauty, and to understand beauty, and to live for beauty. If Demetrius should return to earth today, would he be happy to remain here, or would he want to go back to the ghosts of ancient Greece as fast as he could?

What do *you* think?

CHAPTER III

THE COLOSSUS

Once more Demetrius and his father put out to sea. For sixty miles they sailed eastward along the coast of Asia Minor. After a full day's voyage, they saw a large and mountainous island looming on the starboard side some ten miles from the mainland. This was the island of Rhodes. With boundless interest Demetrius watched it approach, for he knew that on the island's northern tip was the city of Rhodes, and that over the entrance of the harbor there towered a bronze statue which was the biggest and most wonderful metal image ever created by man—the far-famed Colossus.

While the ship was still some four miles away, the statue came into sight.

"Look! There it is!" exclaimed Demetrius, standing on the deck beside Diomede. "Tell me—why was it built? How old is it? How tall is it? Can we climb to the top?"

"As for its age," answered Diomede, "I think it was finished about thirty years ago. I know it took twelve years to build. It's an image of Helios, the sun-god. There's a wonderful story about that statue."

"What is the story, Father?" asked the boy.

"Well, about forty years before you were born—and ten years before *I* was born—an army of 40,000 Macedonian soldiers from northern Greece attacked Rhodes. To batter down the walls these invaders brought along huge bronze siege machines. Rhodes was in a terrible plight, for the number of attackers was greater than the total number of men, women and children inside the city. But the defenders were brave. They beat off every assault and held out for more than a year.

"Fortunately for the Rhodians, the King of Egypt was their friend. And he finally sent a great fleet to rescue the city. When the Macedonians saw the size of the approaching fleet, they hurriedly retreated from the walls and fled to the mainland.

16

The Colossus of Rhodes—the fourth Wonder of the World—was a statue of Helios, the sun-god. This giant statue (without pedestal) measured 110 feet high. The pedestal added another 50 feet, making 160 feet in all. It was made entirely of bronze. Behind the giant's open eye-sockets beacon fires gleamed at night. The statue was shaken down by an earthquake only twenty-three years after Demetrius' visit. *Courtesy "Wonders of the Past."*

"You can imagine that when the people of Rhodes saw their enemies departing, and their friends arriving, they nearly went wild with joy. They poured out through the gates and collected all the heavy bronze war machines that the Macedonians had left behind. One of the Rhodian councilmen suggested that these tons and tons of machines be melted up and the metal recast into a gigantic image of Helios, their sun-god. This would be a fine monument to their heroic defense. And it would help them—and the world—to remember forever that they had won a great victory with the help of this god.

"Then another councilman suggested that they might make the statue serve a useful purpose, too . . . why not put a beacon light in its head to guide sailors into the port at night?

"The Rhodians all agreed to this statue idea. A famous sculptor named Chares undertook the smelting of the metal machines and the casting of the image. He chose as a proper site for the monument the tip of a small peninsula that forms a breakwater between the harbor and the open sea.

"Now look carefully. There's the big stone pedestal the statue is standing on. This pedestal itself is fifty feet high. On this foundation Chares planted the enormous bronze feet, and from them built up the legs, then the body, then the arms, and last of all the head. The hollow feet and legs were filled with blocks of stone to steady them. The body was braced by a framework of iron rods. . . . I'll show you all this when we get there.

"Twelve years Chares worked on his statue. It stood 110 feet high when it was finished. The 110 feet plus the 50-foot pedestal made 160 in all. Chares was very proud of the Colossus. In fact he was *so* proud that when someone showed him something wrong with the construction he killed himself. That happened less than thirty years ago. I remember hearing about it when I was a child."

The four miles to the harbor had been cut down to one.

"Demetrius," called his father, "come to the prow of the ship now, and you can see the crown of sun-rays around Helios' head—

and his outstretched arm. He is welcoming us to his city. If it were dark, we could see the beacon fires shining from his eyes. You asked about climbing to the top. Yes, you can. There's a spiral stairway inside the body from feet to eyes. I've climbed it myself."

Closer and closer Demetrius and Diomede sailed toward the towering bronze god, until they passed right below his pedestal and could look straight up at his head, 160 feet above. (Centuries later a foolish story grew up that the Colossus straddled the entrance to the port and that ships sailed beneath his widespread legs. But this is fiction. No Greek sculptor would have designed any statue of a god in such an undignified pose. Helios' feet, we can be sure, stood firmly together on the stone pedestal.)

Demetrius could hardly wait to land. The moment the ship docked, Diomede took his son straightway to call on Helios. At close range the statue seemed to the boy more astonishing than ever. His only thought was to get to the top.

Just as Diomede had said, there were spiral steps inside that led up through one leg, through the hips, the torso, the shoulder, the neck, the head, and finally to a small platform, right behind the open eyes, where the fires were kindled at night. Demetrius, close behind his father, climbed and climbed all these steps with increasing eagerness.

Reaching the statue's eyes, the climbers looked out—and what a glorious picture they beheld! There was the harbor below, and the snow-capped mountain range on the mainland, and the ten miles of blue water between the island and Asia Minor. Looking through a small window in the back of Helios' head, they could see, on the inland side, the white city twisting up the green hills behind the harbor, a city surrounded by the stout stone walls that had defied the famous siege fifty-three years before. In the harbor Demetrius counted some three hundred boats loading and unloading cargoes; and every few minutes, with oars creaking and sails spread, another ship, moving into the port, or departing, swept across the shadow of the sun-god.

Here is a remarkable drawing showing the Colossus straddling the narrow entrance to the inner harbor at Rhodes. But this is only a fanciful picture. Centuries after the statue fell, a foolish legend grew up that the Colossus stood in this manner, and that ships sailed beneath his widespread legs. We know this is fiction. No ancient Greek sculptor would have dared make a statue of a god in such an undignified pose. Helios' feet, we can be sure, stood firmly together.

stone pedestal. When the statue was overthrown in 227 B.C., the broken pieces, fortu-
fell along the breakwater, and not into the harbor. There they lay for 800 years. One
traveler, after examining the fallen giant, wrote that few men could clasp their arms around
mb; that its fingers were taller than most statues; and that wide caverns gaped within its
broken limbs.

That night Demetrius wrote a letter home to his mother.

Dear Mother:
   I am having a wonderful time. I wish you were here.
Today Father and I climbed up to the head of the Colossus.
We were 160 feet above the harbor. After we had seen everything, Father said he wanted to go back to the inn and take
a nap. But I asked to stay and he let me. As soon as he
left I crawled out on Helios' outstretched arm, right to the
hand. But the guards yelled at me to come back. I wasn't
a bit scared. I like the Colossus best of the things we've seen
so far. I'm sending you a picture I drew of it. X marks
the spot on the outstretched hand where I was sitting when
the guards yelled at me. I am well. I hope you are the same.

                    Love,

                               DEMETRIUS.

This marvelous and awe-inspiring statue, upon which so much
labor and treasure had been spent, stood for hardly more than half
a century. In 227 B.C., just twenty-three years after Demetrius
and Diomede had visited the island, a terrible earthquake threw
down the city walls, and caused the Colossus to break off at the
knees and fall. Fortunately, it fell along the peninsula and not
into the water. There the enormous fragments lay for over 800
years. One of the Egyptian rulers offered the Rhodians a sum
equal to $3,000,000 in our money to pay all expenses if they would
build it up again. But the people of Rhodes had decided that the
god was displeased by the whole idea, so they refused Egypt's
offer.

   Descriptions of the Colossus have come down to us from travelers who saw it after the fall. These reports tell us that the
statue, even when it lay flat on the ground and in pieces, still excited the greatest wonder. One Roman historian, after examining
the fallen giant, wrote that few men could clasp their arms around
its thumb; that its fingers were taller than most statues; and that
wide caverns gaped within its broken limbs.

   In the year 672 the Arabs occupied Rhodes, and the Colossus
came to a sad end. The tumbled pieces—some 300 tons of them—
were sold to a junk dealer, shipped to the mainland, and "carried
away on 900 camels"—to what new destiny no one knows.

With Halicarnassus behind us and Rhodes ahead, you and I are again following Demetrius. We have a good wind for our sailboat, and the waves race beneath us. We left the Mausoleum city at dawn. Toward sunset, Rhodes draws near—a splendid, clean little town, now an Italian colony.

We reach the two breakwaters extending like encircling arms across the harbor. There is a 200-foot gap between the points. The tip of the left-hand jetty (so the people of Rhodes insist) was the site of the Colossus. We look intently at the spot as we slide by, and try to picture the shining Helios who once stood guard there, extending his right arm to welcome the world to Rhodes.

This mental picture of the Colossus makes us think of our own Statue of Liberty in New York. They might have been twins. Like the Statue of Liberty, the Colossus stood overlooking a harbor. They were both made of metal—one copper, one bronze. Again like the Statue of Liberty, Helios had a crown of sun-rays encircling his head. Liberty holds a beacon light in her hand; Helios' beacon shone from his eyes. Of the two images themselves (without their pedestals), Liberty, because of her uplifted arm, has a greater height by forty feet.

This mental picture of the Colossus makes us think of our own never fallen into decay. It is still a thriving port. The enormous walls, rebuilt several hundred years ago with fanciful gates and towers, give the city a fairy-tale air that charms everyone who visits it.

We climb the towers facing the harbor. Close at hand is the busy little port bright with colored sails of the Greek fishing boats. There, on the mainland, ten miles away, the great snow-blanketed mountain range shoots up. I'm sure the Colossus never grew tired of looking at this romantic scene.

How sad, with so much loveliness and life about him, and with so many worshipers to honor him, that this magnificent giant, at the height of his world-wide renown, had to perish when only fifty-six years old!

CHAPTER IV

THE PHAROS

About the time Demetrius and Diomede were ready to leave Rhodes and continue their tour, a large galley from Carthage came along, headed for Alexandria, the great seaport of Egypt, to pick up a cargo of grain. This was exactly where Diomede wanted to go with his son next. So they took passage, headed southward across the open Mediterranean, and soon left the Colossus far behind.

On the second day stormy weather set in, and the clouds hid the sun and the stars, so that the captain had to steer almost by guesswork. But around midnight of the fourth day the lookout shouted that the ship was exactly on its course, with the coast of Egypt only thirty miles away. From his high perch on the mast, he had seen the flashing light of the greatest lighthouse ever built by any nation in any age, ancient or modern—the Pharos at Alexandria.

Demetrius was weary from the long stormy voyage, but he had refused to go to bed on that last night. He wanted to be awake in order to see the very first gleam from the famous Pharos; for, like the Colossus and the Mausoleum and the Temple of Diana, the sea-shining beacon was always counted as one of the world's Seven Wonders.

Some twenty-five years before the time of our story, the rulers of Alexandria, then one of the largest and most powerful cities in the world, had built this monster lighthouse at the entrance to their harbor. Immediately it became the talk of all seafaring men from India to Gibraltar. And with good reason, for it rose *six hundred feet*—a height nearly four times that of the Colossus at Rhodes—and sent such fiery beams into the night that they could be seen many leagues away. Built entirely of marble (for steel girders were unknown), this marvelous building today would overtop any structure in the world, except the Eiffel Tower in Paris, the towers of the Golden Gate and Hudson River bridges, and a few of the tallest skyscrapers in New York.

24

The fourth Wonder of the ancient World—the towering lighthouse at Alexandria, the great seaport of Egypt. It stood 600 feet high—higher than any lighthouse today. Inclining ramps, inside the walls, led to the beacon. Demetrius and Diomede rode up these ramps on donkeys. At night the light could be seen for thirty miles at sea. *Courtesy "Wonders of the Past"*

The Pharos was not designed in the slim, tapering style usual for lighthouses, but rather in the shape of a modern skyscraper. The base of it was a square block-like structure, 400 feet high, filled with military barracks and offices. This was topped by a smaller tower which raised the lighthouse another 100 feet higher. Above this tower gleamed the round fire-chamber itself. Whether the lamp was fueled by wood or oil is not known. But it *is* known that the lamp was backed by an enormous mirror that cast an extremely powerful beam.

Demetrius, having caught sight of this welcome beam, at last went to sleep. When he woke he found his ship tied snugly to a dock—and the marble Pharos soaring 600 feet above.

As 'at Rhodes, Demetrius wanted to lose no time in seeking out the city's first wonder. He soon saw that the lighthouse stood on an island 200 yards out from the mainland. Leading to it from the shore was a stone bridge built by the harbor engineers, and over this bridge Demetrius and Diomede made their way through the throngs of traffic.

They came to the Pharos. Speechless with wonder, Demetrius looked up at its size and height. Not having seen the Pyramids, he was sure *this* must be the biggest—as it was indeed the tallest—structure built up to that time. Even Diana's Temple, which he had admired so much, seemed small compared to this cloud-crowned lighthouse.

It would have been well, in a tower of such great height, to have had electric express elevators. But for the ancient Greeks and Egyptians electricity was still only a bolt of lightning in the sky. Nor were there any stairs. Stairs would have prevented the caravans of donkeys from climbing to the summit with the daily supply of fuel for the beacon-fires. So the ascent was made by broad ramps, or inclines, that climbed at an easy grade inside the walls from story to story. Consequently it was possible to hire donkeys and ride all the way to the beacon.

Demetrius and Diomede did just this, and started up the first ramp with the donkey-boys trotting close behind.

Imagine riding to the top of a 600-foot office building on a donkey!

The Alexandria lighthouse stood on an island at the entrance to the harbor. The gap between the island and the mainland is now filled in. On the site of the lighthouse, a modern fort has been built. This wonderful beacon, made all of marble, was just finished when Demetrius saw it. It continued to serve mariners for 1100 years. The broken stump stood for five centuries longer.

At the first "set-back," the 400-foot level, they found a broad terrace. Here tradesmen had established a small market where one could buy lemonade, fruit, and morsels of roast lamb on sticks. Diomede bought Demetrius a cup of lemonade and two huge red pomegranates from the gardens along the Nile.

At 500 feet they came to the immense stone lamp itself. Around its base was the observation platform where tourists could rest and enjoy the sensational view.

Demetrius, leaning over the parapet, could see thirty miles or more of the Mediterranean on one side, and just as far inland on the other. Directly below him spread the beautiful city, and a harbor that was the busiest in the world. How small the ships and buildings appeared to be from this great height! People on the docks looked just like little bugs scurrying about.

Demetrius persuaded his father to remain here on top long enough to watch the sun go down, and after that to wait till the lighthouse attendants fired the beacon.

About half-past six a giant flame suddenly leaped from the lantern. Its blaze lighted up the entire top of the tower, and on the upper platform turned twilight to noontime.

Satisfied with having seen this dazzling beacon at such close range, Demetrius was willing now to descend the tower with his father and return to their lodging. That night the Greek boy went straight to sleep, weary from his climb up and down the mountainous lighthouse; but delighted, too, for he had seen another of the world's wonders; his hunger for adventure was being gratified; his dreams were coming true.

The Pharos stood for over 1600 years. It shed its light for the ships of Cæsar and Cleopatra. Its light was shining brightly on the first Christmas Eve. Around it grew up the largest city in the ancient world except for Rome.

About the year 850 the first of a series of disasters befell the Pharos—after more than 1000 years of service. At that time Egypt was occupied by Mohammedans from Arabia, and the Pharos was a great help to their fleets in their wars with the Christians. Fortunately for the Christians, the Caliph ruling in Alexandria had an overwhelming greed for wealth. A Christian spy, plotting against the Arabs, managed to whisper into his ear that a vast treasure was "known" to be buried beneath the lighthouse. So the foolish Caliph began to tear down the great tower in quest of these riches.

And before he realized he was being duped he had destroyed the two upper stories. Then he tried to build the tower back again, but he did not have the skill. Also he had let the wonderful mirror crash to the ground, and he did not know how to make another. So for centuries only the stump of the Pharos stood, dark and useless.

In 1375 an earthquake—the enemy of all stone structures in this part of the world—threw the stump to the ground. So enormous was the mass of ruins that 100 years passed before all the broken blocks had been hauled away.

Our own ship—a modern liner—is guided to Alexandria at night by a lighthouse beacon; but its tower, a slender concrete cylinder, is scarcely more than one-tenth as lofty as the Pharos.

In the morning, after we've landed, we stroll along the modern stone docks. The swarming confusion of ships is still there, just as it was 250 years before Christ. Alexandria is still a great port, and the second largest city in Africa (Cairo is the first), but it is no longer supreme in the eastern world as it used to be. The island on which the Pharos stood is part of the mainland now (the gap between the lighthouse and the mainland having been filled with sand many years ago). Upon the exact site of the lighthouse, right beside the sea, the Egyptians have built a fort.

When we reach the walls of this fort, I ask you to close your eyes and turn on your imagination. "Above you," I say, "that white marble tower rises, high as the Tower of Babel. It shines faintly in the starlight. From its soaring pinnacle fiery flames are leaping forth, burning the very heavens. They beckon across the stormy seas to the ships of all the nations, inviting them to this safe harbor to find shelter for their cargoes and their passengers in Alexander's glorious city."

You say this isn't a very satisfactory way to go sightseeing?

You're right, I know. Well, the next world-wonder on our schedule we'll be able to see and touch and *photograph* . . . no more dreams!

29

CHAPTER V

THE FIRST WONDER OF THE WORLD

Demetrius stood before the Pyramids, the greatest, the oldest, the first, of all man-made wonders.

From Alexandria, he had traveled with his father by sailboat through the canal that joined the port city to the Nile, and then up the river a hundred miles in the direction of Memphis, one of the chief cities of Egypt.

Some twelve miles below Memphis their boat stopped at a magnificent stone dock, the landing-place for visitors to the Pyramids. The river here was four miles wide, for this happened to be the flood season, at which time small boats could approach within a mile of the great tombs. Leaving their boat, Demetrius and Diomede looked inland—and there the Pyramids were, the three of them, built on a rock plateau one hundred feet higher than the river, and right at the edge of the desert.

To Demetrius the Pyramids looked just like the drawings he had seen of them at school in Athens. But, though they were old friends, he was still not prepared to find them so monstrously big. They blocked out whole sections of sky with their mountainous mass of stone.

Nor had he realized they were so beautiful. They were so white and smooth and splendid, so proud of being the hugest and solidest mass of masonry ever raised in the history of the world. (The Great Wall of China had not yet been built.)

The Pyramids were then—250 years before the birth of Christ —almost 3000 years old.

King Kheops' Pyramid, the largest of the three, measured 750 feet square and 480 feet high. It was of solid stone. To build this tomb the King worked 100,000 slaves for 20 years. The building blocks averaged 2½ tons apiece, and most of them had to be quarried on the far side of the Nile, ferried across, pulled up a long incline, and lifted, as construction approached the cap, 480 feet. And this process had to be repeated 2,300,000 times. Every day for twenty years an average of 300 blocks, each weighing 5000 pounds, made this journey, and were laid in place by the stone-

Keystone.

ve thousand years ago the Sphinx was carved out of solid rock, close by the Pyramids, in Egypt.
ne head is that of King Kephren who built the Second Pyramid, the body that of a lion. The
ne tablet shown here, covered with Egyptian picture writing, tells the story of the building of
the great monument 3000 years before the birth of Christ.

The Pyramids as they looked to Demetrius and Diomede in 250 B.C. The larger one at the r
was built by King Kheops for his own tomb; the one at the left by King Kephren. In fron
Kheops' Pyramid are smaller tombs for his family. In front of Kephren's Pyramid is a ra
stone causeway leading down toward the Nile valley, past the Sphinx, and ending at a valley ten
In the lower left corner is a smaller Pyramid under construction. It shows how inclines allc
the slaves to drag the stones from one level to another. From 3000 B.C., when the Pyra

After Hölscher.

re built, to about 650 A.D., the sides of the tombs were covered with smooth white limestone.
body could climb the Pyramids in those days. Then the Arabs conquered Egypt, and, to build
ir own cities, they removed this smooth, white, outer casing. This left the great steps of brown
ne we see today. The Pyramids stand about one hundred feet above the level of the Nile, on
a table-land at the edge of the Sahara Desert.

masons—25 blocks every hour of daylight, or one 5000-pound block every 2½ minutes—for 20 years. And all this terrific labor was provided by the straining, sweating muscles of slaves, for steam and electric engines were unknown.

Demetrius and Diomede walked along the causeway that led from the valley to the Second Pyramid. For 3000 years people had been traveling this raised stone road—travelers, priests, kings and humble folk. Alexander the Great and his invincible little army had trod here only 82 years before. About 120 years before that, Herodotus, the great Greek historian, had been here, and had written the description of the Pyramids which all Athenian schoolboys, including Demetrius, loved to read in their history classes.

Excited as never before on his world tour, Demetrius walked beside Diomede up the causeway. At its far end, this raised stone road opened into a beautiful temple right at the foot of the Second Pyramid. Here Demetrius watched the priests holding services and praying for the soul of the dead Pharaoh buried in the marvelous tomb soaring above.

Leaving the temple, the two travelers hastened over to the Great Pyramid, built by King Kheops. *This* was the amazing monument Demetrius had been most eager to see ever since he could remember. And it was far more wonderful than he had expected. Slowly, so as to miss nothing, he and his father walked around the towering pile, admiring its immense bulk and gazing up at its peak. Having climbed to the head of the Colossus, and to the lantern in the Pharos, Demetrius would have liked to climb to the apex of the Pyramids, too. But this, of course was impossible, for the four sides were perfectly smooth. The great steps we see today, made by set-backs in the tiers of brown stones, did not exist then. These angles were all filled with white triangular limestone blocks which turned the Pyramid's sides into steep, sloping, perfectly flat surfaces. The thought came to Demetrius that it might be fine sport if, having reached the top by some means, he could slide all the way down. He wondered how fast he would be moving when he hit the rock plateau at the bottom, and whether he would be badly squashed.

34

All day Demetrius and his father remained in the neighborhood of the Pyramids, examining, with increasing wonder, the details of each. In the late afternoon they strolled over to the Sphinx, which crouched near the stone road. They had passed the Sphinx that morning on their way up the causeway, but in their eagerness to see the Pyramids they had not given the famous statue much attention.

The Sphinx was a curious and gigantic monument cut mostly out of the solid rock nearly 3000 years before—at about the same time the Pyramids were built. It had the form of a crouching lion with the head of a man, the face being a likeness of King Khephren, the successor to Kheops. From its front paws, the only part made of brick, to the tip of its tail the figure measured 240 feet. The head, nearly 70 feet high, was crowned with the King's royal headdress. The 13-foot face, stony and calm, looked toward the Nile. Demetrius walked in between the Sphinx's paws and, though he stood on tiptoe and reached up as high as possible, he could not touch the tops of them.

Along with all the other sightseers who had come to visit this monument, Demetrius and his father were pounced upon by swarms of native Egyptians who insisted on being hired as guides. Diomede had to use his walking stick to beat them off. And, as pests, the donkey-boys were worse. They trotted at Demetrius' heels begging for pennies until he gave them all his purse contained.

Demetrius had never ridden on a camel (nor had he even seen one till he came to Alexandria). These humpbacked beasts fascinated him, and now was his chance to get acquainted with them, for lined up before the Sphinx were several camels for hire. They were fitted with bright-colored trappings and silver-studded saddles. Silver bells hung from their halters. To please Demetrius, Diomede hired one. The driver made the camel kneel, and the boy climbed aboard. Groaning, the big beast lurched to its feet and lifted the lad high off the ground. Demetrius shouted with delight. Then, proud as a young king, he rode his mount, led by the driver, out around the two largest Pyramids and back to the

e Sphinx from the air. The head and body are carved from rock. The forelegs and paws are
de of brick. For the past few centuries sand covered the entire body—with only the head show-
g above the ground. The stone nose, and stone beard, unprotected, were destroyed. But the body,
ried under sand and not dug clear until recently, today looks just as Demetrius saw it in 250
. The body is 240 feet long, the top of the head 70 feet above the ground, the face 13 feet high.

starting-point. Before the little Athenian dismounted, a Greek artist, using an ink brush and a small square of papyrus paper, made a quick sketch of him, perched high on the humped camel, with the Sphinx and the sunset in the background. Diomede bought the sketch for Demetrius to take to his mother.

There was a glorious full moon that night. It rose pale and mysterious out of the hills on the far side of the flooded river. Under its light the groves of palm trees stood black against the shining waters of the Nile. The desert, out beyond the plateau, melted into a moonlit sea of dreams. The three Pyramids glowed with a weird unearthly beauty, and tried to outdo the huge pale moon in splendor.

The two travelers looked back at Kheops' tomb. One side of it was radiant, one side plunged in shadow. Diomede was so deeply stirred by the sight that he took his son by the hand. "Demetrius," he said, "you're looking at the oldest man-made thing on earth. The *age* of the Pyramids—3000 years—is as wonderful to me as their size. Do you suppose they'll still be standing here 3000 years from *now*? I don't see why not. I think it's quite likely—when Diana's Temple is a hole in the ground, and Athens itself only a memory—that people will be coming from all over the world to visit the Pyramids. And I feel sure that these tombs will amaze people then, just as much as they've amazed you and me tonight."

As the hour grew later and the moon rose higher, a cold wind began to blow from the desert. Diomede saw to it that Demetrius wrapped his Greek cape closer about him. They climbed to the causeway and walked once more down to the Nile. A river boat was ready to carry them back downstream to Alexandria on their way home to Athens. . . . Demetrius' road to romance was drawing to a close. On the deck of the Nile boat the little Greek boy sat clutching the rail and looking one last time toward the Pyramids. His father sat beside him, but they did not speak. They were both moved to silence by the fading sight of these mighty tombs—so disdainful of man, so unconcerned with time—standing there pale and ghostly in the moonlight.

40

CHAPTER VI

THE PYRAMIDS TODAY

And now some 2200 years have passed since that lovely night. Diomede's prophecy—that the Pyramids would be standing many centuries after he and his son visited them—has come true. For we, on our own wonder-tour, have followed Demetrius from Alexandria on up the Nile, and are now in the presence of these same gigantic tombs that Demetrius saw.

But how changed they are! Demetrius would rub his eyes in bewilderment if he came back. The Nile has moved some distance toward the east, away from the Pyramids. The causeway is only a dimly traceable ridge in the sand. The temples that stood in front of the Pyramids are no more. The Pyramids themselves, though as solid and unshaken as when Diomede brought his son to see them, have been stripped of their smooth white casing, revealing, beneath, the receding tiers of huge brown weather-beaten blocks up which we can climb to the top.

What has happened to the white casing? Who went to all the trouble of removing it?

The Arabs, who invaded Egypt about the year 650, were the offenders. They needed stone to build mosques and palaces in their new city, Cairo, which they had founded on the Nile just opposite the Pyramids. Naturally it was easier to drag down the old blocks of stone from Kheops' and Khephren's tombs than to cut new ones from the quarries.

So they seized, first, all the triangular blocks that fitted the angles in the climbing steps. But when they tried to remove the two-ton blocks beneath, they found these too heavy, the task too great. They gave up, after taking thirty feet off the peak. On the Second Pyramid, they left the topmost hundred feet of the casing itself in place. We can see it there ourselves.

And yet, though the Pyramids have so greatly changed in appearance, they amaze us just as much as they amazed Demetrius. For, think of it!—they are nearly 2200 years older than they were in 250 B.C.

41

The Pyramids as we see them now. The Great Pyramid, built by Kheops, is the last on the rig
When built, it measured 480 feet high, and 750 feet square. One hundred thousand slaves worl
twenty years to put its 2,300,000 enormous blocks of stone in place. When the Arabs remov
the outer casings from the Pyramids to get building stones, they took about thirty feet off the p
of the Great Pyramid, leaving the flat space shown in this picture. For some reason, the Ar

the casing on the peak of the Second Pyramid. Because of this smooth peak, the Second amid is still extremely difficult to climb. The Third Pyramid, at the left, is much the llest of the three. Though greatly changed in outward appearance since Demetrius' time, the yramids have much the same shape today as when the Greek travelers came to visit them.

Pictures Inc.

Seen from an airplane, the Pyramids in modern times still offer us an amazing sight. Compare this picture with the one on page 33. More than 2000 years separate these two pictures. Note that the surfaces of the Pyramids are different in the two views. Only a trace of the smaller tombs can be seen in front of Kheops' Pyramid. The stone causeway, though clearly visible, is in complete ruin, likewise the valley temple. The Sphinx has

Following the example of Demetrius, we walk completely around Kheops' tomb, wondering how the Egyptians, with all their 100,000 slaves, were able to pile up such a vast mountain of stone. Indeed we wonder how they ever got *one* of these enormous blocks in place.

On the north side our Arab guide leads us into the three-foot entrance of a tunnel that has been cut straight into the heart of the Pyramid. Here awaits us an adventure such as the Athenian travelers never dreamed possible. For once we can turn the tables on Demetrius by having an experience that would make *him* envy *us*—a visit into the very center of the tomb.

In building his Pyramid, Kheops left open, near the middle of it, a stone room thirty-five feet long and half as wide, in which he planned for his mummy to rest as long as the world endured. To reach this burial vault the masons left a narrow tunnel through the stones. After his death the tunnel was plugged with blocks of granite, to prevent grave robbers from ever getting inside.

When Demetrius and his father saw the Pyramids, this tunnel was still closed and the entrance still walled over. In fact it was not until 4000 years after Kheops' death, and 1000 years after Demetrius' visit, that anyone succeeded in reaching the central chamber.

In the year 818 an Arab ruler named Al Mamoum, the son of Haroun-al-Raschid of *Arabian Nights* fame, was Sultan of Egypt. Lured by the belief that in the heart of Kheops' Pyramid vast riches had been buried with the King, Al Mamoum resolved to mine his way in and take possession of the treasure.

But by that time the location of the original tunnel had been so completely lost that the Arabs started cutting twenty-five feet below the entrance. With terrific labor they hewed their way through the solid blocks for over one hundred feet. The stone was so hard, their tools so poor, that the workmen were about to give up, when their chisels, entirely by accident, broke into the original tunnel.

This gave them fresh courage. Shouting with excitement, they raced along the passage with torches blazing—but only for a few yards. The tunnel suddenly turned uphill, and at this elbow

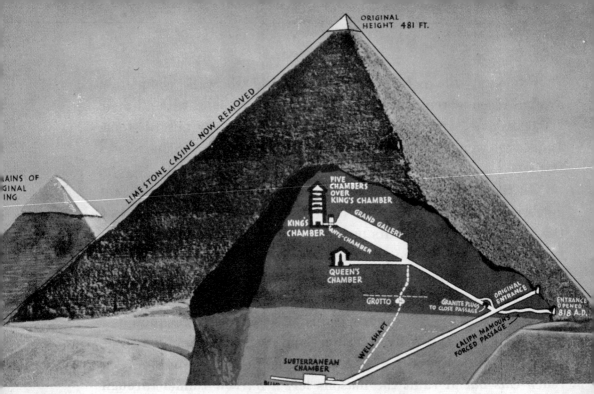

This picture helps you see how the inside of the Great Pyramid looks. The builders left an inclin[ed] passage from the outside, to the center of the tomb, where King Kheops' body was to be burie[d]. This passage was later plugged. The Arabs, in the year 818, unable to find the original openin[g], dug a tunnel of their own, and got inside. They found the burial chamber empty.

Wide Wo[rld]

In this picture the upper hole, in the side of the Great Pyramid, shows the original entrance to t[he] passage leading to the King's burial chamber. The lower hole, where the two soldiers stand, w[as] the one dug by the Arabs. We use the upper entrance to visit the interior of the Pyramid.

enormous blocks of granite barred the way. Against this granite, Al Mamoun's cutting tools made no impression. So he ordered a passage cut *around* the granite plug, through the softer limestone, and thus entered the ascending tunnel. Hurrying on ahead of his workmen, he came to a great inclining hall. This hall was only 7 feet wide, but 155 feet long and 30 feet high. (See chart on opposite page.)

At the upper end, at a point about 200 feet above the base of the Pyramid, the Arabs reached the burial chamber. It was walled and roofed with unbelievably huge blocks of red granite, blocks weighing not two tons but thirty. With fast-beating heart Al Mamoum held high his torch, and with staring eyes peered about the solemn granite-walled room . . . looking for the piles of jewels, the gold, the treasure, he had come to find. . . .

But all about him he found only granite emptiness—no gold, no treasure. To one side, on the floor, rested an enormous red-granite sarcophagus—open and lidless. The mummy of the King was not there. *Nothing* was there but the empty granite coffin. Knowing that not even granite plugs could resist human greed and treasure-mad invaders, the family of King Kheops had only pretended to bury his body in the tomb. As a further deception they had carefully filled up part of the lower tunnel with stone blocks. The mummy itself had been buried, secretly, somewhere else—just where, no one has ever known.

Poor Al Mamoum had gone through all this terrible toil in vain. But he at least opened a path which all visitors to the Pyramids have been able to follow to this day.

Through the tunnel-entrance we ourselves climb into the echoing passageway. Watch your head—the entrance is only three feet high. Guided by electric lights, we descend to reach the uphill elbow. Kheops' granite plugs are still in place. We go around them through Al Mamoum's by-pass. Still climbing and climbing, with low-bent necks, we come to the sloping Great Hall, the one thirty feet high. Up this we move until the King's Chamber opens before us . . . and there is the same solemn emptiness Al Mamoum found in the year 818—more than 1100 years ago. Overhead are the thirty-ton granite slabs which the Arabs

47

blackened with their torches. On one side rests the huge granite coffer, as empty as ever—a coffer that has rested here in this black stillness for nearly 5000 years.

Back in the open air again, we find that the afternoon is far gone. If we are to watch the sun set from the top of the Great Pyramid we've no time to lose. Up the northeast corner there is a trail worn smooth by the thousands of visitors who have climbed before us. We find it easily. The block-steps are from three to four feet high, so we must use our arms as well as our legs to make the ascent.

Never in our lives have we climbed such giant stairs as these. Arab guides help push and pull us up each block. Every few minutes we stop to get our breath, and look back down at the steep-stepped slope. And as we climb, struggling and straining to lift *ourselves* from one block to another, we think of the tragic fate of the 100,000 slaves who, naked in the sun and lashed by whips, had to drag up to these heights each of these monstrous stones.

With a final effort we reach the little platform on top, and, gasping, sit down to rest. We've climbed 450 feet—high as a forty-story office building. The sun has touched the horizon, and is setting on fire the desert behind us, the same desert into which Demetrius watched the sun sink 2200 years ago. Five miles to the east, across the green and fertile valley, we see the main channel of the Nile. Reflecting all the scarlet of the sky, the river rolls on, the giver of life in this rainless land today as it was in King Kheops' time.

As we stand upon the supreme point of our great stone pile, watching the sun burn itself out in the west, a full moon rises with oriental splendor out of the eastern hills, as pale and mysterious as on the night it rose to shine on little Demetrius. As the moon-light falls on desert and river we ask ourselves where, in all our quest for marvels, have we ever seen a picture as marvelous as this.

Gendreau.

this corner of the Great Pyramid are the giant steps to the top. The blocks are from three to feet high, so we must use our arms as well as our legs to make the ascent. Once on top, we 450 feet above the desert—as high as a forty-story office building. The view from the summit of the Sahara Desert and Nile River is one of the most wonderful sights a traveler can find.

Once before, on my first trip to Egypt, I climbed this Pyramid alone, and watched the moon sail overhead. And at dawn I saw the Cairo minarets pierce the eastern sky. But I almost froze to death. And so, since we have left our fur coats behind, I do not suggest any such adventure for us now.

And anyway we have not seen the Sphinx.

In the moonlight we climb down the Pyramid, block after block, and walk over to greet one of the oldest and most famous statues in the world. How immense it is, this crouching lion with King Khephren's head! For the last eighteen or twenty centuries, and up to quite recent times, the Sphinx's body was buried

50

A group of American sailors visit the Sphinx. When Demetrius came here, the Sphinx had a nose and a fine beard. But these were shot off by Egyptian artillerymen who turned their cannon on the Sphinx and used it as a target. *Acme.*

in sand, with only the head showing. This was fortunate, for the buried part was protected from sand storms and vandals. Since the day when Demetrius had his picture drawn before the Sphinx, many a misfortune has befallen the great statue. Age and weather have damaged it. The foolish Moslems, thinking it the image of some heathen god, have sadly disfigured it. One Egyptian general, teaching his soldiers to handle artillery, had them use the statue for a target, and showered it with exploding shells.

Consequently, as we walk up to the Sphinx, we find that the King's six-foot nose and eight-foot beard are missing, that part of the royal headdress is blasted away, that his stony face is hacked and broken. But despite all this, that face, in the night shadows, seems still powerful and majestic. Archeologists recently rescued the buried part of the statue from its tomb of sand, and thus revealed to us the same ancient lion-body, perfectly intact, before which two Greek travelers, father and son, once stood so wonderingly in the moonlight.

We turn toward home and leave behind this vast graveyard with its mighty monuments to the mighty dead. As Diomede moved away he had spoken to Demetrius, saying he believed the Pyramids would be standing for another 3000 years. This was nearly 2200 years ago. But we can be sure they will be standing another 5000 years from *now*, when New York and London are holes in a marsh, or fragments in a museum. In the year 7000 they will still be here, proud and solid as ever—still disdainful of man, still unconcerned with time—when some wise Diomede, perhaps flying in from another planet, brings his twelve-year-old boy to Egypt to show him, on their road to romance from star to star, the supreme achievement of the men from Earth.

(The Statue of Zeus at Olympia, the Temple of Diana at Ephesus, the Tomb of King Mausolus, the Colossus of Rhodes, the Lighthouse at Alexandria, and the Pyramids, were the first six of the Seven Wonders of the ancient world. The seventh Wonder, the Hanging Gardens of Babylon, we shall describe later in this book.)

51

CHAPTER VII

THE LABYRINTH

During my boyhood days in Memphis, Tennessee (a city named after the Memphis in Egypt), the school I attended paid special attention to public speaking. Every Friday was "speech-day," and every student had to "speak a piece."

I never could memorize anything, but if I was allowed to tell a story after my own fashion I could sail away with the greatest of ease and put in all the gestures without thinking. One Friday I became so absorbed in my story and made so many gestures that I fell off the platform.

I remember that story well. I'll remember it as long as I live. Made partly of truth and partly of dreams, it's one of the undying stories of the world. It's been told for thirty centuries by schoolboys. Demetrius no doubt recited it in Athens on speech-days. It was perhaps his favorite story. May I tell it to you now?

Halfway between Greece and Egypt, where the Mediterranean meets the Ægean Sea, lies the island of Crete. Today, even as in Demetrius' time, Crete is of small importance. But this was not always the case. Back in the earliest pages of history, the island was the center of a marvelous civilization. Under the leadership of Minos, its greatest king, Crete conquered all the neighboring states and ruled the Mediterranean with a mighty fleet; Knossos, the capital, was the greatest city in the western world, and the royal palace the wonder of the age.

When Minos came to the throne of Crete there had been great rejoicing throughout the land, for he was noble, wise and brave. And no woman in the country could compare in beauty with his wife, Queen Pasiphaë (pronounced Pa-SIF-a-ee). Not many years after their coronation two children were born to them—Androgeos (An-DRO-jee-us), a boy, and Ariadne (Ar-ee-AD-ne), a girl. The boy, as he grew to manhood, became the most famous athlete in the empire. His proud countrymen even sent him to Greece (in that early day still an out-of-the-way and half-civilized place) to compete with the Athenians in their athletic sports. In Athens he easily defeated all the local champions in every contest

52

The Athenian king, named Ægeus, happened to be of a proud and selfish nature. Ægeus could not endure the fact that the princely young foreigner had won all the honors. Filled with jealousy and hate, he set assassins upon Androgeos and had him slain.

Quickly the news of this terrible deed sped back to Crete. At once King Minos, brokenhearted over the murder of his son and vowing vengeance, swept down upon Athens with his great war fleet, burned the city, and forced the citizens to pay him, every nine years, a tribute of seven youths and seven maidens. These young captives, in chains, were delivered to King Minos in Knossos, and there given over to a most tragic fate.

Some years before the death of Prince Androgeos, his mother, the Queen, had given birth to a horrible monster, called the Minotaur, which was but half human. It had the body of a man, but the head of a bull. Naturally the King was deeply ashamed of this disgrace in the royal family. To prevent the people of Knossos from learning about it, he ordered his famous engineer and architect, named Dædalus, to build a labyrinth to imprison the monster. Dædalus obeyed, and filled the labyrinth with so many confusing passages that once the Minotaur had been driven inside there was no chance of escape.

The Minotaur had a ferocious appetite. It especially liked to feed on human beings. Athenian youths and maidens were just the thing! And so into the labyrinth King Minos, still vengeful over Androgeos' death, thrust his miserable young captives, on each year of tribute. And there they were eaten by the Minotaur.

Twice this ghastly tribute had been paid. A third group was being selected in Athens when young Theseus, the son of the guilty King Ægeus, offered himself as one of the victims. It was his hope that he might be able to kill the Minotaur and put an end to the misery being suffered by his countrymen.

Ægeus was loath to see his only son so sacrifice himself. But Theseus refused to yield. He asked his father to watch for the return of the tribute ship. If it came back to Athens still carrying the black sails of mourning, this would be a sign that the desperate plan had failed and that Theseus was dead. If the ship returned white-sailed, Ægeus would know that his son had conquered the monster, that the Athenians had escaped and that all was well.

Once more the shipful of unhappy youths and maids set out for Crete. There the Minoans seized them and led them to Knossos. Straightway they were dragged before the King in his throne room. Beside him stood his daughter Ariadne. When she looked upon young Theseus—tall, handsome, and bearing himself like the young nobleman he was—Ariadne promptly fell in love with him. The thought of Theseus' being devoured by the Minotaur caused her such anguish that she resolved to help him escape.

Into Theseus' prison-cell the Princess managed to smuggle a ball of finest thread, and a sword. The sword Theseus hid in his tunic, and the thread he unwound behind him as he and the other thirteen young sacrifices were driven into the labyrinth.

Far away, through the twisting corridors, they heard the hungry Minotaur bellowing, and they shook with terror. And soon the monster, seeing his new victims, rushed upon them. But Theseus was ready. He plunged his sword into the Minotaur's neck and stabbed him to death.

The Greeks, rejoicing at their deliverance from a dreadful death, now turned and followed the thread back through the twisting maze of passages. Coming to the entrance, Theseus and all his companions made their escape. And he took with him not only his own Athenians but Ariadne as well. She feared that if she did not flee with the Greeks she herself would be punished with death by her father.

Theseus embarked at once for Athens. But in his impatience to be home again, he forgot to change the sails from black to white . . . and King Ægeus, half-crazed with anxiety, was keeping watch, day after day, from a cliff above the sea. . . .

The ship at last appeared—black-sailed. Frantic with grief and remorse, Ægeus flung himself into the waves and was drowned. And from that day to this the sea has been known as the Ægean.

Theseus kills the Minotaur. This picture was drawn on a vase in Athens, several hundred years before the birth of Christ. This subject was always popular with ancient Greek artists. All boys of Demetrius' time knew the story well.

In Knossos, King Minos' own heart was heavy too. His own son dead, and now his daughter gone off with the Athenians! Such crushing events turned Minos into a tyrant. Bitter over the whole Minoan tragedy and hating everyone connected with it, he locked up Dædalus and his sixteen-year-old son Icarus in the labyrinth, just because Dædalus had not built it well enough to hold the Greeks.

But this prison was not able to hold Dædalus, either. Besides being an engineer and architect, he was also the greatest mechanical genius of the age. And now he turned his ability to planning some means of escape.

55

Wings! That was what he and his son needed to bring them release from the labyrinth's high-walled but roofless passages. Wings of feathers and wax! Secretly he labored on this daring idea, and in time he was able to make wings that worked. He fixed a pair of them first to Icarus' young shoulders, and then to his own. Together they flew out of the labyrinth and away from Crete, high above the fleets of the tyrant King.

Icarus, excited by his ability to fly, tried to see how far above the clouds he could go. His recklessness brought him too close to the sun. The wax that held his wings melted, and the boy fell into the sea—called the Icarian Sea ever since. The father, having seen his son die so needlessly, flew on and on, cursing King Minos as bitterly as Minos had cursed Ægeus.

Dædalus was many hours in the air before he reached the friendly shores of Sicily. But even here poor Dædalus was not safe, for King Minos had come rushing after him, determined to recapture the cunning fugitive. Fortunately the King of Sicily was just as determined that his winged guest should not be taken. He received Minos with a show of good will (though really hating him) and promised to surrender the famous runaway. Pleased with his welcome, Minos, weary from his long sea voyage, asked for a hot bath. A huge tub of boiling water was prepared. Then the Sicilian King's three daughters, waiting for their chance, rushed upon their royal guest, flung him into the boiling tub, and scalded him to death.

If this story is full of bloodshed and savagery, that is because it comes down to us from the earliest times, when life was wild and cruel. But again I say that it is one of the immortal stories of the world. Theseus, in later times, became the foremost hero of the Athenians, who never grew tired of telling the story in poetry, in song, in marble and bronze. That's how I know that Demetrius knew it well.

When the buried city of Knossos, on the island of Crete, was uncovered, fragments of beautiful plaster pictures, like the one here, were found in the ruins. This one shows a young priest-king walking in his garden and followed by butterflies. He is probably leading a sacred bull.

But why, you may ask, are we being told this old story—a story we've heard all our lives?

I've told it because we're on our way to Crete, to Knossos, to *see* the labyrinth and the throne room of King Minos.

Had we been traveling across the world in quest of its marvels before the year 1900, we would not have thought to visit Crete. For up to that time the story of Minos and Theseus and Dædalus was supposed to be just a romantic legend. No sign of a great Cretan city had come to light. King Minos was remembered only as a character in a wonderful myth.

And then, in 1900, Sir Arthur Evans, the English archeologist, came upon a huge mound near the present city of Candia, in Crete. It was covered by trees and small farms. Even so, to Dr. Evans, it looked man-made. He dug into it with a hundred laborers, cleared off twenty feet of rubbish—and behold!—the foundations and walls of an enormous palace, such as only a great and powerful king could have built and occupied, were revealed.

As Sir Arthur dug deeper, the size and richness of the palace unfolded; corridors and courts at various levels, secret passages, blind galleries, a bewildering system of small chambers . . . the labyrinth!

He next found that a city large enough to shelter a hundred thousand people surrounded the palace. But nowhere could he find any city walls. Then, indeed, he was certain this was Knossos, for it is known that King Minos depended for security on his "wooden walls"—his warships.

For centuries these warships gave the city protection. But this protection ended when a storm destroyed the fleet about 1400 B.C. Enemies poured in upon a defenseless Knossos and pulled the mighty palace to the ground. Sand and rubbish slowly covered the site, buried the galleries, courts, statues, the theaters, the throne room, and preserved them all for 3300 years, until Dr. Evans unveiled them again for us to see.

And see them we must. With Egypt and the Pyramids behind us, we land at the Cretan port of Candia—the port for ancient Knossos.

author examines two of the enormous jars that stored olive oil in ancient Knossos. There are 200 of these jars still to be found in the storehouses of the once-buried palace of King Minos.

King Minos' city is four miles inland. To reach it we follow a road used 1400 years before the founding of Rome, the road along which Theseus was led from Candia harbor, and along which he fled with Ariadne. When unearthed, the flagstone pavement was found in perfect condition. It measured only four feet wide. This narrowness surprised Dr. Evans until he realized that horses were unknown on King Minos' island. Everybody walked, so a four-foot pavement was wide enough.

On reaching the palace we find that much of it has been rebuilt. Dozens of Minoan columns, rooms, terraces, now stand in place again. On every side there are bulls' horns or pictures of bulls to remind us of the Minotaur.

We are shown King Minos' storehouse for olive oil. It consisted of a cellar holding two hundred earthenware jars, some of them nine feet high. Many of these giant jars are still intact.

On the walls and in the museum we see beautiful pictures painted on plaster—princes walking in a garden, toreadors vaulting over bulls, portraits of girls adorned with jewels and flowers. And the colors of these pictures are still as bright as they were in the year 2000 B.C.

Last of all we find the throne room—and there before us is the very throne of King Minos himself. This is probably the oldest throne in the world. It was hewn out of one block of stone 4000 years ago. For 700 years it seated the kings of Crete. Then the palace fell and buried it—for 3300 years. Now the throne is back in place, in the same room where it stood 40 centuries before.

Since the throne is made of solid stone, there is no harm in our sitting upon it, one at a time, and trying to picture, in our mind's eye, the events that have taken place here. What marvelous scenes this room has known, what heroes have stood an arm's length away!

Seated on this throne, King Minos ruled his people and made his empire a great power in the world. Seated on this throne, he heard that his wife had given birth to a monster, half man and half beast.

Here, too, word had come that his son was slain by the jealous King of Athens. And from here he had ordered his captains to punish Athens in revenge.

60

King Minos' throne—the oldest throne in the world. It was hewn out of one piece of stone 4000 years ago. For 700 years it seated the kings of Crete. On the walls are pictures of griffins—unreal animals with heads of birds and bodies of lions.

In this room he had received three shipments of the fourteen youths and maidens, and ordered them fed to the hungry Minotaur. Here, perhaps, Ariadne first saw Theseus.

While seated on this throne King Minos heard that Theseus had killed the Minotaur and escaped, carrying off the faithless Princess. Here, in that moment, the King's soul turned to vinegar, his kindly reign turned to cruelty.

And when he learned that his famous architect had flown away on wings, it was from this very throne that the King rose up in wrath, swearing that he would drag Dædalus back—and from here he set out for Sicily, never to come home again.

ROME

Mediterranean Sea

GIBRALTAR   ALGIERS   KNOSSOS   To
                    TUNISIA   Isfa
FEZ   JERUSALEM
MOROCCO   ALGERIA   ALEXANDRIA
                                CAIRO   GULF
RIO DE ORO   OF AKABA
                    From Knossos   LIBYA   EGYPT   JEDDA

                              AFRICA

                    FRENCH   ANGLO-
TIMBUCTOO   8   WEST AFRICA   EGYPTIAN
                                         SUDAN
            Niger River
                         NIGERIA   FRENCH
LIBERIA   ASHANTI   EQUATORIAL
                              AFRICA   ET

Atlantic Ocean   CAMEROONS

                                        BELGIAN   Lake
                         Congo River   CONGO   Victoria   KEN

                                                TANGANYIKA
                                                TERRITORY

                    ANGOLA
                              VICTORIA   Zambezi River
                              FALLS 9   RHODESIA

MAP *showing location*
of Marvels in Africa   SOUTH
                              WEST   BECHUANA   MOZAMBIQU
Chapters   AFRICA   LAND
  8. Timbuctoo
  9. Victoria Falls   India
 10. Mecca
                              UNION
                              OF
                              SOUTH AFRICA

                                        CAPETOWN
                    CAPE OF GOOD HOPE

CHAPTER VIII

THE SLAVE CITY

We're in an airplane now, roaring along at 200 miles an hour. We're crossing a great desert. For half a day we have seen little but a sandy, stony, lifeless waste. Twice we have flown over lost oases, circling the tops of the palms to allow the astonished desert dwellers to behold an airplane. At another time, we climbed to 10,000 feet to pass safely over a barren mountain range. This desert seems without end.

And no wonder! For it is the Sahara, the vastest, hottest, cruelest desert on earth. But we must cross it just the same— 1600 miles, the distance from New York to Mexico—to reach the next world-wonder I want you to see.

But please don't be alarmed. I know where we're going.

Back in Candia, the story of Dædalus' flying from Crete to Sicily gave me an idea. The next marvel on our list lay deep in the heart of Africa. Why not fly, like Dædalus? . . . We'd *never* get there overland. I had no anxiety about finding the way. I had found it once before, in my own airplane.

It's now four o'clock in the afternoon . . . and the pilot is gazing intently ahead watching for something to appear. There —he sees it. He shouts to us above the roar of the engine: "Look! It's the Niger River." All day this river, flowing right through the middle of the sand-sea, has been our goal, for near its bank is the wonder-city we have come to visit.

And soon we catch sight of the city itself, a great cluster of mud houses, crisscrossed by narrow streets. In the center is a market square crowded with people. Here and there mud minarets rise above the flat mud roofs.

Has this city a name?—you ask.

Indeed it has a name, a very famous name.

It's Timbuctoo.

Timbuctoo has no undying legends to give it a place on our list of marvels. It has no age-old tombs or once-beautiful marble monuments. But it's a wonder-city just the same.

63

In a moment you'll see why—I hope. At least *I* saw why, the other time I came here by plane.

We have, by now, descended to 1000 feet, trying to find the cleared stretch of desert used for a landing field. At 500 feet a truly wonderful thing happens—just what I *wanted* to happen.

Right before our eyes Timbuctoo begins to disappear—to be blanketed over, blotted out, by a vast dark cloud that rises up magically from the chimneys and housetops. The cloud seems alive. It is made of thousands and thousands of distinct and separate particles, each particle moving free of its neighbors. We rub our eyes in bewilderment. One minute Timbuctoo lies below us, clearly seen in the desert sunshine. The next minute it disappears beneath a cloud poured forth from the chimneys. We can well understand why Timbuctoo is considered such a weird, mysterious town.

Then a small part of the cloud floats close—almost *too* close—to our propeller, and the mystery is explained.

The cloud is not smoke.

It is not locusts.

It is not sand.

It's storks!—storks in countless multitudes, wheeling and

In Timbuctoo, at nesting time, one sees hundreds of thousands of storks. They roost on every wall and roof. When they take to the air all at once, they make a vast cloud. *Publishers Photo Service.*

A child of Timbuctoo rides his "Shetland pony." Children living in towns in the Sahara Desert perhaps never travel ten miles from home. But they play the same games as other children the world over. And they always seem happy.

flapping in pairs, in flocks, in waves, over the housetops of Timbuctoo . . . storks, alarmed and amazed by this roaring dragon that has come shooting out of nowhere into their midst. A hundred thousand storks have risen from their nests to form this panic-stricken mass, this tossing sea, below us.

We land. Most of the city's 10,000 people hasten to meet us. We see that they are nearly all Negroes, along with a few

Two Tuareg sheiks from Timbuctoo. This fine race of Arabs rules over the Negro population of the town. Among the Tuaregs the men—not the women—all wear veils, and think it very bad form to show their faces. They own wonderful riding camels, capable of traveling 100 miles across the desert in a day.

Arabs. The aristocrats of the town are a tribe of fierce desert fighters called Tuaregs. From the backs of their beautiful camels they look down at us with scorn. They have a very curious custom. The men of the tribe wear heavy veils which hide all of their faces except the eyes. They start wearing these veils at fourteen years old and never appear without them till they die. For a Tuareg man to show his face to his fellows is to be disgraced. The women of the tribe never wear veils. Frequently, if they have work to do, they wear no clothes at all above their waists.

Our arrival, by airplane, has caused no end of excitement. Crowds of laughing, shrieking little Negro boys, stark naked, run at our heels and follow us along the city's crooked lanes. Above us, on each ledge and wall and roof, roost our friends the storks, returning to their nests and noisily clapping their beaks as if quarreling with us for disturbing them.

We exclaim about the great cloud of these birds we have just seen. A French official (Timbuctoo is a French colony) says the storks are nothing . . . we should see the bats! Wait till night! For every stork in Timbuctoo there are one hundred bats. He explains that they live in vast colonies in the mat ceilings of almost every house in town, squeaking and squirming all day, flying in and out the windows all night. They are a pest, a plague, a curse, but nobody ever does anything about it. Bats inside and storks outside. To the natives of Timbuctoo this is one of Nature's unchanging laws.

The "rest-house" is shown to us. It's just a barren shack where travelers can sleep (if they bring their own beds). The entire roof is covered with storks' nests. And our "bedrooms" seem to be the head-office for all the bats in Africa.

The very first day, about sunset, this army of evil-smelling little beasts swarm down upon us. We are suffocated with bats. They get into our beds, our hair, our soup, as they swirl around the rooms and out the open windows. We flee to the roof to escape. There the storks, forming a united front, again clap their beaks and threaten us if we dare set foot on their private roof. We don't know *where* to go.

On my previous visit to Timbuctoo I tried to solve this stork-and-bat problem. With me was my pilot named Moye Stephens. He and I spent our first three days at this same rest-house fighting bats. At last, to help us in this warfare, we resorted to a means used by most of the other thirteen white residents in Timbuctoo—slaves.

The buying and selling of Negro slaves has occupied the Arab overlords of Timbuctoo for centuries. Thousands of slaves brought to America before the Civil War started from this far-away desert city on their long sad journey.

But in recent years, since this part of Africa became French territory, the number of slaves for sale has greatly decreased. However, if one is in need of servants it is still possible to buy them from the Arab chiefs. And so, following the local custom, Stephens and I, with a friend who could speak both French and Arabic, went to a dealer and explained to him our need for two good bat-bashers.

All he had to offer us at short notice were a boy and a girl, each about ten years old. We had planned to buy grown-up slaves, but on second thought we didn't see why children couldn't fight bats as well as grownups could. The two shown to us were goat-herds, and seemed about as tough as the goats. They had pretty, smiling faces, and the whitest teeth I've ever seen. Their skin, of course, was black as ink—and all of it was showing.

Their price was five dollars each.

The girl we named Little Eva, and the boy we called Monkey.

Back in the rest-house we turned Monkey loose on the bats. But we soon found out that he *loved* bats. He felt toward them as we feel toward kittens and puppies. If he did catch a bat he'd play with it the rest of the day.

Little Eva was supposed to fetch water. Again we had bad luck, for every time she went with her bucket to the well she'd stay away two or three hours, playing in the puddles. Stephens would then stride out in the streets looking everywhere for Little Eva, resolved to give her a good spanking. But she always saw him first, and would come running up and throw her muddy arms around Stephens' neck—*so* glad to see him! She adored Stephens. So what could he do? We never could make her understand that she was a *slave*.

Every day new problems in slave-training confronted us. We bought our two little savages a cot apiece, but, as they had never before in their lives seen a cot, they didn't know whether to sleep on it or under it. Remembering the books I'd read on the care and feeding of children, I also bought for them enough fruit and canned milk and spinach to balance their diet—lots of vitamins. They ate the canned milk, but gave the fruit and spinach to the goats.

The desert city of Timbuctoo was once—before the end of slavery in America—a great slave-trading center, with a population of 100,000. Now it's a crumbling town of only 10,000 people. But the bats and storks, in vast swarms, have taken over the deserted houses. There is no sound of traffic in Timbuctoo, as the streets are all covered with deep sand. In the distance rises a mud minaret beside a mosque, for Timbuctoo is a Mohammedan town.

And then there was the bathing problem. They had never bathed before in all their ten years . . . which was good reason for them to begin now. Stephens and I took them to the river and taught them how to lather their bodies with cheap, perfumed, pink soap, and then wash it off. At once they fell in love with bathing. In fact whenever we missed them from their bat-bashing they were sure to be down at the river taking a bath.

But they always bathed very badly. They'd smear their bodies with lather, and then play around in the mud and sand—and then come home!

The clothes problem, too, had to be faced. True, ten-year-old Negro children in Timbuctoo do not wear any clothes. But just the same, since they were our children, and trotted at our heels when we went to call on the French Colonel, we felt they should at least wear pants.

So I bought red pants for each of them, and a red turban, and red beads for their black and shining chests. They were proud as peacocks in their beautiful costumes, and strutted around among their playmates. Unfortunately neither of our slaves ever understood the reason for clothes. After a great effort Monkey finally learned to wear his costume with some grace. But Little Eva was utterly shameless. In the most public possible places—before the Colonel's house, or in the market square—she was sure to take off her pants.

One evening when Stephens and I were busy, as usual, feeding Little Eva and Monkey their supper and tucking them in bed, Stephens said to me: "Dick, I'm just realizing who the two slaves are. They are you and I!"

And it was true. Every time we had an invitation to dine out we had to reply: "Thanks very much, we'd like to accept, but we can't leave the children."

When the great French national holiday came around—July 14th—the Colonel refused to accept any excuses. He ordered that every white resident in Timbuctoo gather at his house at six o'clock to drink a toast to France. As there was no escaping this command, I gave the children an early supper and got them to bed before Stephens and I went off to the party.

Nearly all the houses in Timbuctoo are made like this—mud walls and flat roofs. It almost never rains in this desert city, so the houses stand for many years. But one good rain would wash them away.   *Black Star.*

Never before having left the children alone, I was somewhat worried about them all evening. And on returning home, just before dark, I found my worst fears justified. Monkey's bed was empty . . . and on the top of the house I heard a most alarming uproar. I climbed to the roof. There was Monkey, freed from his cruel masters (and also freed from his pants), having the time of his life. He was pushing the storks, one after another, off their nests, just because their rage at such treatment amused him. The storks, the most sacred of birds, naturally fought back against their small black-skinned tormentor, and came swooping down to attack him with their wings. And to defend himself against them, he was reaching inside the nests, and seizing the eggs, and *throwing the storks' eggs at the storks!*

71

My patience burst. I turned him across my knees, and, for the first and only time in my life, gave a child a sound spanking.

But, as usual, I got much the worst of it. The roof still sizzled from the day's heat, so that after one minute of spanking-exercise my party collar was a wilted rag, my fresh linen clothes soaking wet, my hair in my teeth, and I myself hot and red and angry. Only Monkey kept cool, and waited patiently for all the commotion to subside.

Next day Stephens and I took the slaves back to their original owner, since it was easy to see that as slave-trainers we were no good. At the Arab camp we had to pay the dealer ten dollars each —twice as much as we had paid *to get* the children—to bribe him to take them off our hands.

But to us it was worth almost anything to know that we were out of bondage at last, that we were slaves no more.

You say you'd like to meet Little Eva and Monkey before we go? I'd like to see them again too, but I'm afraid there's no use trying. Several years have passed since I said good-by to them. They are almost grown now, and I have no doubt that they've been sold long ago by their Arab owner to other Arabs somewhere in the vast Sahara. Wherever they are, I hope they have kind masters—and lots of pink soap, and vitamins, and the reddest pants in Africa.

The Negro citizens of Timbuctoo believe that the spirits of the dead come back to earth in the form of crows. To give the crows a place to perch, the building-timbers of this old mud minaret are allowed to stick out from the walls.

CHAPTER IX

THE SMOKE THAT SOUNDS

Up to the middle of the past century the interior of Africa, south of the Sahara and the Nile, was as unknown to civilization as the interior of the moon. For three hundred years before this time ships had visited the coast ports to trade, or to capture slaves, but what lay inland no one knew.

Then about 1840 there came along a determined Scotch missionary, who, far more than anyone else, brought light into this great realm of darkness and revealed to the world what lay there. His name was David Livingstone.

Thirty years of his life Livingstone devoted to exploring Africa. Through trackless jungles, across deserts, up and down unknown and unnamed rivers, he pushed his way. One-third of the continent—from the Cape of Good Hope to the equator and from the Atlantic to the Indian Ocean—was covered by his travels. This is an area larger than the United States. What had been a blank map of vast extent, he filled with mountains and valleys, with enormous lakes and countless villages, with fertile and barren lands, with swarms of strange birds and animals, with new races of human beings. He was the first white man ever seen by many of the Negro tribes he visited. But so great were his courage, wisdom and kindness, and so wonderful his medical skill, that everywhere he went he was treated as a superior being—a white god. Inspired by him, waves of other pioneers followed in his tracks to carry on his work. Thanks to David Livingstone, Africa ceased to be the Dark Continent.

In 1855 this most famous of African explorers was descending a river called by the natives the Zambezi. No other European had ever ventured into this part of the wilderness. Along the way he kept hearing stories from his black guides about a fearsome place, farther downstream, that was the home of monsters and devils. This place the guides called Mosi-oa-Tunga—the Smoke that Sounds.

With difficulty Dr. Livingstone persuaded his black friends to approach it. In small boats his party moved with the current, cautiously, closer and closer to the terrifying mystery.

73

The Smoke that Sounds—in southern Africa. This is the native African name for Victoria Falls and its curtain of mist that rises 1000 feet above the booming, plunging cataract. The Zambezi River (barely visible through a rift in the mist) is a mile wide above the Falls. Below, it is squeezed

Presently, some three miles ahead, he saw an amazing sight. Stretched straight across the river before him, from bank to bank, there rose a great curtain of towering mist-columns. The curtain surged upward like a long row of gigantic fountains. The tops of the columns seemed to mingle with the clouds. And from the direction of the curtain there came a deep, roaring sound such as volcanoes make in time of eruption.

Creeping forward, Dr. Livingstone soon approached near enough to see that the river—here a mile wide—appeared to end abruptly at this roaring vapor wall, for on looking through gaps in the curtain he could see nothing beyond it but jungle.

Landing at the upstream end of an island in the middle of the river (the island's farther end was still hidden in mist), he pushed ahead through the underbrush.

Suddenly the ground at his feet dropped dizzily away.

Peering through the mist, he found himself looking down upon an enormous half-concealed waterfall which stretched for half a mile on either side of the island.

He saw that the river plunged headlong, with a shattering roar, *three hundred and forty feet*, and sent its storm of spray a thousand feet into the air.

Livingstone had discovered one of the three greatest waterfalls on earth.

But the discoverer *still* could not see where this mile-wide river went after it leaped over the edge. It just disappeared— "into a hole in the ground," the natives said. Indeed it did seem to lose itself in the yawning crack into which it fell. This crack, while long enough to engulf the river broadside, was only 250 feet wide—so narrow that the vapor filled it and completely veiled over the river's next adventure. Another day of exploration had to pass before Dr. Livingstone learned that the canyon wall, opposite the falls, was split in the middle by a gash barely 100 feet across, and that through this slit the boiling river made its tortured escape. In other words, the chasm was T-shaped; the river rushed over the top of the T and emptied through the stem.

Imagine it—a mile-wide river falling 340 feet, and then being funneled into a gorge no wider than a city street!

Listening to the roar of rage which the Zambezi gave forth in protest against this shattering plunge and violent crushing, the explorer understood why the natives feared to venture near the falls. For its voice was one of the most terrifying sounds made by the forces of nature.

Livingstone named this display of savage power after the quiet and gentle Victoria, his Queen.

Victoria Falls is over 3000 miles from Timbuctoo. But we have our airplane and need not be discouraged by the distance. The sight will be well worth the long trip. Leaving the city of the storks behind, we fly on southward down the Niger River. At length we reach the Atlantic coast and, still flying southward, follow the shore for another 1000 miles. We cross the equator. Then we turn sharply inland and fly toward the east for five hours.

Our pilot sees it first—the mile-wide, forest-lined Zambezi. In a moment more we catch sight of the towering curtain of vapor rising high above the water. Beyond this vapor-wall we see not a trace of the river—only the jungle, rolling on.

What a strange sight—Victoria Falls from the air! It seems to fall *up,* not down.

Safely landed, we move on foot back toward the Smoke that Sounds. We can hear the roaring. Through the tree tops we see the towers of mist rising to the skies. But still we see no river, no down-rushing water.

Our path leads us nearer and nearer the battle, nearer the smoke. We have never heard the ear-splitting sound of an artillery duel, but we believe we are hearing one now. And we are marching on, right into the teeth of it. Has this path no sense? It's leading us straight to destruction!

Then it stops, right at the edge of doom. Before us and below us screams a hurricane of bursting water. We are on the downstream rim of the chasm, the rim which faces the falls. The curtain of water, opposite, is only 250 feet away, but we can not see it. For in this narrow abyss in front of us, and for half a mile on either side, the Zambezi seems rather to explode than fall. The violent blasts of wind shoot the clouds of smoke far

e Zambezi River, at Victoria Falls, tumbles 340 feet into this amazing slit in the rocks. The
is a mile long, but only 250 feet wide. Except in the summertime, when the river is very low,
gorge is so filled with clashing spray and vapor that the Falls itself is completely hidden.
is picture was taken during the low-water season. The big island in the center of the river is
point from which Dr. Livingstone first saw the Falls.

up into the sky. These clouds condense and fall again and rise again, in perpetual motion and never-ending fury. They beat upon us and blind us. The shock of so much power dashing downward at our feet is physically painful. We are half-drowned in spray.

Somewhere on the invisible brink opposite is the island where Livingstone first beheld this monster waterfall. Fully 340 feet below, hidden in the foam and clouds, we know the raging waters are rushing from the two ends of the trough, to meet and clash in the middle. And we know that where they meet the conflict has gouged out a 100-foot breach in the imprisoning rock.

We cling to the ledge called Danger Point that overhangs this narrow alley of escape. Somewhere beneath us the tortured river is writhing out of the pit, racing on down the gorge toward freedom.

Close about us is the Rain Forest—a jungle warmed by hot tropical sun, and drenched every moment of the day and night in clouds of spray. Eternal rain drips from every leaf and petal. Everything here grows as big as Jack's Beanstalk. The trees, the vines, the flowers, in a wild riot of growth, drive one another over the brink as they struggle for more room in this hot, wet world.

And high over the forest, and low in the gorge, the rainbows shine. One great glowing arch bends over the falls itself. And wherever the mist drifts in the wind we find another.

We are having the good fortune—or is it ill fortune?—to visit Victoria Falls at flood season. We have witnessed the height of its power. We have heard its voice at the loudest, and been a little paralyzed by its savage tantrums. But, because of the blankets of spray, we've seen almost nothing of the actual falls. At this time the sheet of water crashing downward is perhaps fifty feet thick. Four months later, our guide tells us, it may be less than three feet thick. Then the mists and the buffeting winds subside. The marvelous canyon is revealed, right to its lowest depths. We could then safely take a boat on the upper river, follow Dr. Livingstone's course down to his island, look over the edge, and see a very subdued Victoria Falls sliding gracefully and none too noisily down the stone chutes to the gorge.

But with the present Battle of the Marne going on before us

y from the air can we get a general view of Victoria Falls. Here we see the full sweep of the
hty curtain of falling water—and the narrow canyon through which the raging river escapes.
 picture shows the river at flood season, when the water was fifty feet deep. A fortunate
wind, for the moment, has blown away most of the mist. *Galloway.*

in this smoke-filled abyss, with the shattering bursts of the cannon echoing about us, and the columns of seething smoke blotting
out the sun, we have a hard time believing the guide's story about
the falls' summertime peacefulness. However, since Dr. Livingstone, who first described the cataract's behavior, tells the same
story, we know it must be true.

A rare view of Victoria Falls taken (at the dry season) from the downstream brink of the gor
The Falls drops 340 feet, but only 200 feet can be seen here, and only about a third of the mi
long crest line. Wherever we look, across this roaring chasm, we see rainbows shining in the tro
cal sun. Along this lower brink on which we stand, the sun and drenching mist give so much h
and moisture to the vegetation that a dense jungle, called the Rain Forest, has sprung up. Eve
tree and vine grows big as Jack's Beanstalk. Standing here we are bathed in spray and deafen
by the Falls' roar. No artillery battle could make more noise. The natives who live in this part
Africa are frightened by the Falls. They say the gorge is the home of evil spirits, and they will
go near it. The white people of South Africa insist that Victoria is the biggest waterfall on ear
North Americans say Niagara is the biggest. The people of Brazil and Argentina say Iguazu is
biggest. Certainly these three giants stand in a class by themselves, far above all other riv

Gendreau.

d each has a good claim to being king of waterfalls. Victoria is much the highest—340 feet,
inst 220 for Iguazu, and 160 for Niagara. Niagara has the most water most of the time, but
h Victoria and Iguazu have more water than Niagara during the brief flood season. Iguazu's
st line is two miles long—longer than Niagara and Victoria put together. Niagara is the most
ible. Iguazu has the wildest and most beautiful surroundings. Victoria roars the loudest.
azu was discovered by Spanish explorers in 1542; Niagara by Father Hennepin in 1678; Vic-
ia by Dr. Livingstone, a Scotch missionary, in 1855. Two million people a year see Niagara.
haps ten thousand a year see Victoria (a railway goes right to it). But only a few hundred a
r can make the long difficult journey to Iguazu. (For stories about Niagara and Iguazu, see
First Book of Marvels.) Each of these three waterfalls ranks high among the natural wonders
of the world.

Standing face to face with this mighty spectacle, we naturally ask ourselves how it compares in size and power with other great waterfalls of the world. Our guide assures us that Victoria is the "biggest." But what about Niagara? What about Iguazu, in South America? Those of you who traveled with me to visit the Marvels of the Occident will remember how wonderful we found these other two giants—Niagara, over which plunges the discharge from four of the five Great Lakes—Iguazu, with a crest-line two miles long, and a drop of more than 220 feet. . . .

Of these three, which together leave all rivals far behind, it is difficult to choose the greatest. Victoria, with its 340-foot drop, is highest. (Niagara's drop is 160 feet). But Iguazu is broadest —almost as broad as Victoria and Niagara put together. Niagara has the most water, most of the time, though not as much as Victoria or Iguazu in flood season.

So you see it *is* difficult to choose. In fact I can think of only one way to settle the rival claims: We'll dismiss all three claimants and give first place to a great cascade which you'll find on none but the oldest maps—in the region due west of the Straits of Gibraltar. Here (according to the most reliable early sea-captains) the entire Atlantic Ocean comes to the edge of the world and falls off.

Not one of our waterfalls can compete with *that!*

CHAPTER X

ALLAH'S CHILDREN

Are you a Christian?

Or a Jew?

Or a Buddhist?

Or a Hindu?

If you are you can't visit our next world-wonder. It's reserved for Mohammedans—and reserved so strictly that anyone found there who is *not* a Mohammedan is killed.

You say you'd rather skip it?

Right-o! But I insist on taking you as near as is possible without having anybody murdered. For this is a truly wonderful place, a place you should know more about. It's just a small city in the desert of Arabia, yet it is the hub of the universe for 200,000,000 people. To see it is the supreme hope of their lives. Merely to go there purifies their sins. If they die there they are sure their souls will be received in Paradise.

It's Mecca.

I've been within eight miles of this world-famous town (as close as any non-Moslem is allowed to go), so I'll be a good guide that far.

The way there, from Victoria Falls, is hard. In our airplane again, we fly north for hours over dense jungle. We re-cross the equator and speed high over Lake Victoria. There we strike the headwaters of the Nile, and follow it, still going northward, for 1400 miles. Then, turning sharply to the east, we cross 300 miles of desert, so desolate that we pity the caravans crawling slowly beneath us.

Next comes the Red Sea, but we fly straight on over it. Soon the flat eastern shore comes in sight and we spiral down to the seaport of Jedda.

We *have* to land here, for Mecca lies just forty-five miles beyond, and no airplane carrying "infidels" like ourselves is allowed to fly any closer.

Exclusive News Agency.

The city of Mecca—sunk in a rocky valley in the Arabian desert—has been a holy city since earliest history. For centuries before. Mohammed was born here in the year 570, people came from all over Arabia to worship idols in the great square. Against this idol-worship Mohammed preached

Jedda is overflowing with pilgrims, for we have come at the pilgrim season. The narrow streets, the markets and the waterfront all swarm with shouting, struggling throngs of visitors on their way to the Holy City. They pour in by the shipload—and pour out, on camels, on foot, in buses, through the eastern gate where the road leads on to Mecca.

Some of the pilgrims have come from the Philippines, some from India, Persia, Syria, Turkey, Egypt, from Timbuctoo, from Algeria and Morocco, even from Russia and the East Indies. We see coal-black faces from central Africa; fair faces, with blue eyes and blond beards, from Istanbul; brown faces from Tunis, yellow faces from the Far East. They are speaking twenty languages. Some are rich men traveling with many servants; some are so poor that they must beg their bread along the way.

But they all have two things in common: First, a burning desire to reach Mecca and to honor the same Prophet and the same God at the Great Mosque, thus washing clean the sins of a lifetime; and, second, their pilgrim garb.

They are all dressed in exactly the same costume. It consists of two huge white Turkish towels, one wrapped around the waist, and one around the shoulders. This humble costume makes all the pilgrims look alike. King and beggar, saint and sinner, are put on the same common level. Everyone is welcome—except unbelievers like us.

In one day, during the holy season, as many as 50,000 of these white-toweled pilgrims may enter Mecca. But they must all expect hardships; they must all risk death. There have been times when plagues of cholera and smallpox struck these great mobs of worshipers, killing half of them. Yet each year, in the face of such risks, there come pilgrims who, to reach the Holy City, have *walked* from farthest Asia, spending perhaps three years on the journey.

What *is* it, I'm sure you're asking, that brings Moslems to Mecca from such distances? Why is it so holy? Why can't we go there too?

I can answer these questions.

In the year 570, Mohammed, who founded the religion named after him, was born in Mecca. Even then, Mecca was a sacred city. Its chief glory was a cube-shaped granite temple called the Kaaba, supposed to have been built by Abraham, the father of Isaac, centuries before the birth of Christ. This very holy place was being defiled by the worship of idols. Against this worship Mohammed, when he was forty-two years old, began to preach. Believing he was God's messenger, he told his followers what he thought were Allah's rules for the true way of life. These rules, written down by his disciples, finally became the Mohammedan Bible, known as the Koran.

This new prophet soon won many followers in Mecca. But he also aroused the hatred of the idol-worshipers. In 622 they rose up against him and sought to kill him. Mohammed fled from Mecca to another Arabian city called Medina, where he was sheltered by a large band of his converts.

With this flight from Mecca, Mohammed's teachings began to spread on across Arabia, and then to the East and to the West, across the world. So this flight is of great importance in Mohammed's far-flung realm. In fact, the Moslems count time from that event, just as we count time from the birth of Christ. For them, this is not the twentieth century—it's the fourteenth.

From the year 622 until today, Mohammedans from every Moslem country in the world have made a pilgrimage to the Holy City to worship at the sacred shrines upon the date of the departure of the Prophet from Mecca. And once this pilgrimage—this *Hadj*—has been made, the pilgrim has the right to carry the title *Hadji* before his name—a title that gives him great honor the rest of his life. And in order that even strangers may know of this honor, he is allowed to wear a green turban on his head.

But let non-Moslems beware! Sacred Mecca is strictly for Mohammed's followers. On pain of death no infidel is allowed to enter the walls. Fanatical soldiers guard the way. In Mecca itself every man, woman, and child is a spy eager to point out anyone he thinks might be an unbeliever—to stone him to death if this is proved to be true.

From time to time a Christian comes along who has lived so many years with Moslems that he is able to make the pilgrimage disguised *as* a Moslem. But so far as anyone knows, there has never been a single case of a non-Moslem who, without language or training, has just walked into Mecca because he wanted to see the sights.

Which is bad news for *us*.

However, let's go as close as we can and see as much as possible.

First of all we must dress like the other pilgrims. We buy the regulation Turkish towels and put them on. Hats are not allowed, but we can carry umbrellas.

Wearing this uniform we must follow the strict code of behavior that goes with it. Above all we must not quarrel. We must not use violent language. We must not take any form of life; and this includes mosquitoes, lice, and flees. We must not even scratch ourselves—we might disturb some of Allah's little creatures. There is no law, however, against sprinkling one's body with insect-powder and allowing the flees to die of indigestion.

Along with thousands of other white-toweled pilgrims we push our way through the crowded narrow streets of Jedda to the gate where the Mecca road begins. Just outside this gate we find a scene of wildest confusion. All the world seems to be going to the Holy City. Several hundred camels, resenting their heavy loads, groan and snarl. Countless donkeys bray. Motorbuses, bursting with passengers, honk frantically for their right-of-way through the confusion of men and beasts.

In the late afternoon we are ready to start. We choose camels to transport us. Each camel carries two passengers, in a double wicker basket slung across the hump. The two passengers must get into the two sides of the basket at exactly the same time. Hold tight, or we may be pitched violently to the ground if the camel stumbles! Better make yourself as comfortable as possible, for we must ride all night. It is too hot to travel by day.

87

In the center of the Sacred Square, at Mecca, stands a cubical stone temple, always kept veiled i
camel's-hair cloth. Around this temple, the pilgrims, at sunset and sunrise, range themselve
prepared to pray. Then, from the top of the tall white minaret (rising from the far corner of th

urt), the call to prayer rings out: *Allahu akbar—God is great.* The pilgrims—perhaps as many 50,000—bow low in unison, stand up, bow down, their Turkish-towel uniforms making waves of white that rise and fall in time with the murmur of their voices.

Lurching, we start off. The string of pilgrims reaches along the desert road as far as we can see. The population of Mecca has suddenly swelled from 20,000 to 100,000, and all these new-comers, along with the tons of supplies they need, seem to be moving at once along this road to Mecca.

Just at sunset the road reaches the top of a ridge. We look back. There are the minarets of Jedda, and the Red Sea. Then we descend the ridge and move onward through the gathering darkness.

Hour after hour, guided by the stars, we swing along at a slow pace. The desert, now that the sun is gone, has turned very cold. We wrap blankets about us to keep warm. Of course there is no sleep—not in our cramped Pullmans. We do not see a single tree, for the country between Jedda and Mecca is a sandy waste.

Dawn finds us stiff and weary, but our first rest-stop is at hand —a roadside village halfway to Mecca. At an Arab "hotel" we are given bread and tea, and go to bed on a crude canvas cot. The flies and the dust and the noise of the passing caravans would keep us awake were we not so tired.

The second night we start off again. Just at sunup on the second morning we are stopped by guards. There is no village in sight, only a fort and a crumbling tomb in which Mohammed's mother is buried. The Arab guards look at our passports. As we expected, they turn us back—with the Holy City only eight miles beyond. We cannot see even its rooftops, for the city is hidden in a deep valley. But we realize we must be close. Our fellow pilgrims are hurrying past us with shining eyes and rising excitement. Just eight miles more, and their faith will be rewarded. . . .

And had *we* been able to go on, what would we have seen?

We would have seen a city walled in by mountains, and filled with seven-story wooden "skyscrapers." In the center is an enormous court, 600 feet square, into which the pilgrims push their way to say their prayers. In the middle of this court stands the granite Kaaba—the cubical temple built by Abraham. This Kaaba, 50 feet square and 70 feet high, is kept completely covered over with black cloth made of camel's hair. The cloth is changed once each year, just before the pilgrim season.

Underneath this black cloth cover is the Kaaba, the cube-shaped temple built by Abraham. This Kaaba is 50 feet square and 70 feet high. The camel's-hair veil is changed each year, just before the pilgrim season. One of the sacred duties required of each pilgrim is to walk three times around the Kaaba. In this picture we see an Arab (dressed in white pilgrim garb), and three children, performing this duty.

Exclusive News Agency.

The high point of the pilgrim season lasts only three days. Then the population of Mecca, usually about 20,000 people, swells to more than 100,000. Perhaps half of these, dressed mostly in white pilgrim garb, may gather at one time in the Holy Square at the hour of prayer. The pilgrims come all the way from the Philippines in the East and from Bulgaria and Timbuctoo in the West. A pilgrimage to Mecca brings each pilgrim great honor

Around this veiled granite block, the pilgrims, at sunset and sunrise, range themselves. From the minaret the call to prayer rings out: *Allāhu akbar—God is great*. The pilgrims—perhaps as many as a hundred thousand—bow low in unison, their towel-uniforms making waves of white that rise and fall in time with the murmur of their voices.

After the prayer each pilgrim must march seven times around the Kaaba, chanting special holy words. Next he must drink from a sacred spring called Zemzem. Its water is the holiest in the world. One drink of it purifies one's sins—if one is Mohammedan.

These and other ceremonies hold the pilgrims in Mecca three days. Then the white-robed multitudes depart, and Mecca becomes a quiet, half-deserted desert town again.

Though I got no closer than eight miles to the Kaaba on my first "pilgrimage," and did not drink from the Zemzem spring, I had an adventure which few Moslems, and no other Christians, have ever enjoyed. At the eight-mile post where you and I were turned back, the King of Arabia set up a "royal court" in a beautiful tent for my special benefit, and there graciously told me all I wished to learn about Mecca.

His name is Ibn Saud, and he is the greatest and most celebrated Arab in the world today.

Born a prince, he has carved an empire out of central Arabia with his sword, and made his name a symbol for honor, courage, and piety through all Mohammedan lands. He is six feet, six inches tall, and strongly built. He has been married 156 times (Mohammed allows each man to have four wives at once, and to divorce them, and marry four more, as often as he wishes). He has 56 living children. Besides being King of Arabia, he is also Guardian of the Holy Cities, and Allah's chief spokesman on earth—the Moslem Pope.

Eager to interview such a commanding and romantic figure, I brashly begged his secretary to telephone him, long-distance from Jedda to Mecca, to ask if he would grant me this honor. To my astonished delight, he agreed. And, since I could not enter Mecca to meet him, he offered to meet me at the eight-mile post.

When I reached the spot I found that a tent of brilliantly striped camel's hair had already been set up. Soon Ibn Saud arrived in a limousine and a cloud of dust, followed by a long caravan of cars all loaded down with his guards and servants. Some 500 slaves and soldiers accompanied His Majesty. On the running board of his car stood four black giants, dressed in scarlet uniforms and carrying bright curved swords. In the back seat, alone, sat the King, his enormous frame enfolded in a plain, unadorned white Arab gown.

When the car stopped before the tent, he stepped out and greeted me with slow dignity. He stood straight and tall, a great proud bear of a man, a figure right out of the mythical age of gods and heroes.

At the entrance to the tent he took off his sandals . . . the barefoot King, scornful of all foreign customs.

As he sat down in an armchair, his five oldest sons marched before him, and stood until their lordly father bade them be seated too.

Outside, the 500 Arab tribesmen, wild and lean, ranged themselves in a great circle, and walled us in with a fence of rifles and daggers.

Then for an hour Ibn Saud patiently answered my questions, through a friend who spoke Arabic and English—questions about his empire, his hopes, his fifty-six children, himself.

The King began to talk with me at four o'clock. He was still talking when he noticed that the shadows before our tent were very long. He knew that in a moment more the sun would be sinking beneath the hills. He knew that in Mecca and Medina the temple-criers, the "muezzins," would soon be chanting from the minarets, announcing that the day was done, that night was at hand, that the time had come to pray.

King Ibn Saud, King of Arabia and the Mohammedan Pope, poses for a photograph with the author. This picture was taken just eight miles outside the walls of Mecca.

We walked to the front of the tent, and I stood aside. Then the barefoot giant, the great King, knelt down, facing the Holy City, and bowed his forehead to the earth, and three times stood and knelt and bowed. Behind him his five sons took the same praying positions as their father, and bowed when he bowed, and stood when he stood. Behind them, row after row, the warlike tribesmen laid aside their daggers, and knelt humbly in the sand.

And the King, with his face lifted up toward the burning western sky, quoted aloud from the Koran:

"In the name of Allah, the Merciful,
   Praise is due to Allah, the Lord of the Worlds.
   Thee do we worship and Thee do we beseech for help.
   Guide us, O Allah, in the right path. Amen."

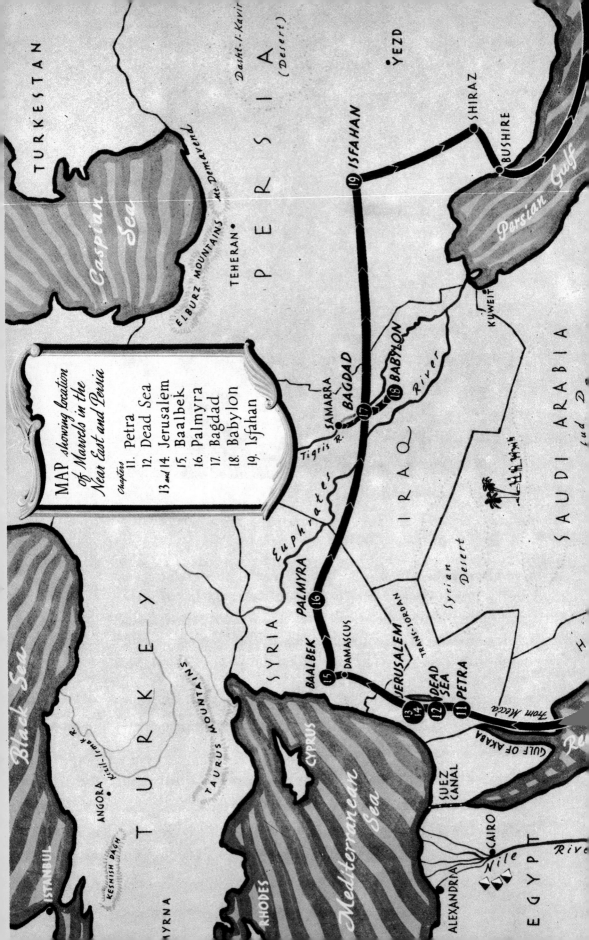

CHAPTER XI

THE ENCHANTED TEMPLE

What was the most exciting adventure you ever had—the adventure you'll longest remember? Was it your first airplane ride, when the pilot looped-the-loop? Was it the time your automobile stalled in a snowdrift, and you had to spend the night in a deserted cabin? Or the time you walked to the summit of Pike's Peak? Or the day you met the President?

My own adventure which I'll longest remember was a visit to an enchanted city.

The city of which I speak is hidden in the mountain fastnesses of Arabia. And now that we have reached Arabia on our tour of the wonders of the Orient, I look forward with delight to visiting this enchanted place again. And *this* time I shall take you with me.

But before we set out, let me tell you an Arabian fairy tale. The tale is about the secret city and its magic spell:

Once upon a time, in the far-off ancient days, there lived in Arabia a king who wore upon his finger a magic ring. Whoever wore it (and knew the secret words that gave the ring its power) could hold enslaved the jinns who, in those days, dwelt in the land.

With the aid of these jinns the King built for himself a capital that became one of the wonders of the Arab world. He called it Petra, which means "stone."

Now in no way was Petra like other cities. It was located in the wildest mountains in the middle of a barren wilderness south of the Dead Sea. A traveler looking for Petra would not have found it, unless he knew the country well, for the chief gateway was just a crack in the mountain wall. This crack led into a deep and sunless canyon, a thousand feet deep, and this canyon led into the city.

But once the traveler had reached Petra itself, no sight could have been more wonderful. All about were beautiful palaces and noble tombs, all carved with hammer and chisel right out of the solid stone cliffs that rose on every side.

97

The King did not spend *all* his time building these great rock monuments. Besides being the Lord of the jinns, he was also the most dreaded robber in Arabia. Riding forth from the canyon in the rock, his robber bands would drive the passing caravans into the hidden fortress. Nor could any vengeful army pursue the robbers, for so narrow was the canyon-corridor that four men could block it against 4000. Petra became a huge fortified storehouse where dazzling piles of stolen gold and pearls and silk were guarded by the citizens.

With so much wealth and power in their hands, the people of Petra were able to conquer all the neighboring nations. To the city they dragged captive artists and sculptors from Athens. Grander and grander grew their palaces, marvelously carved by the gifted Greeks . . . all in the sandstone cliffs.

Proud as they were in life, the Petrans became prouder still in death. They spent fortunes on their own tombs. Each noble tried to plan one grander than his neighbor's. It took the strength of the jinns to hew the great rooms in the solid rock, but only the graceful hands of the Greeks could carve the columns and statues.

Soon the very gods themselves grew jealous of the splendid temple-tombs being built at Petra to bury mere mortals. They thought of a plan to subdue these bold builders . . . they would fill the soul of the King (who held the key to Petra's power) with the poison of vanity and pride. This, surely, would bring about his downfall.

And, just as the gods planned, this poison *did* destroy him. Burning with envy, he saw the tombs of his nobles rising higher and more splendid every day . . . and there was not even a *little* tomb for the King—the King whose magic ring made all these wonders possible. More and more jealous he became, until, in a violent mood, he commanded his enslaved jinns and his Greek artists to carve for him a temple-tomb such as the world had never seen—a temple that must overshadow the temples of the nobles as the moon outshines the stars.

a wilderness of sand and rock, 100 miles south of the Dead Sea, is found the amazing city of
tra. During the lifetime of Christ it was a rich and powerful capital of a tribe of caravan-
bers. From out of the solid rock, the great nobles of the country had magnificent tombs carved
themselves. This tomb is nearly 200 feet high; the door 40 feet high. Notice the four tiny
res of men in the foreground. With their hands stretched overhead they can not reach even the
bottom sill of the great door. No one has lived in Petra for centuries.

So the King commanded, and at once he was obeyed. Roaring in anger at their hated enslavement, the jinns fell to work, hacking out tons upon tons of sandstone from the cliffs. Then the captive Greeks took their hammers and chisels and began to carve the rough rock into a sculptured temple. Slowly it took form, in one marvelous piece, massive and yet delicate, a poem in rose-red stone.

The King looked at this glowing masterpiece—and worshiped its beauty. Then, fearful lest a rival try to build a fairer monument than this, he commanded that the architect who built it be blinded.

All the people of the surrounding nations flocked to Petra to see the royal mausoleum. It became the city's crowning glory. But, just as the gods had planned, it soon proved to be the downfall of the King. The nobles, jealous, in turn, of their ruler's overtowering monument, plotted against him, and murdered him.

What madness was in this act! With the King, the power of the Petrans over the jinns departed. He alone had known how to use the ring he wore—the power that kept the jinns enslaved.

When his last heart-beat had ceased, the jinns found themselves free. No longer slaves, these terrible spirits burst the bonds that held them to their hated masters, and with a single magic word they enchanted the whole of the glorious rock city they had helped to build.

That was centuries ago. But Petra is enchanted still, unchanged in all this time. Its tombs, its monuments, the proud and lovely burial palace of the jealous King, are all still standing as on the day when the jinns, seeking revenge, cast their magic spell.

The Arab shepherds who tend their flocks in the neighborhood of Petra insist that this is a true story. And I half-believe it is, because I've seen Petra with my own eyes. . . .

The masterpiece of Petra's rock-carved temple-tombs is this tomb of a king. It is hewn right out of the rock cliff in one marvelous piece. A local legend tells that the King had command over the jinns and forced them to hack out the tons of sandstone from the canyon walls. Then Greek artists carved the rough rock into this delicate temple. The color of the carved rock is rose-red. The figure of the Arab guard gives a good idea of the enormous size of the tomb.

From Mecca, Petra is not far away—not for our airplane.

Our Mecca "pilgrimage" over, we ride our lurching camels back to Jedda, and once more climb aboard the plane. Our route this time is right up the eastern shore of the Red Sea—500 miles.

If you'll look at the map on page 62, you'll note that the northern end of the Red Sea is forked. The left fork makes the Gulf of Suez (and leads to the Suez Canal). The right fork makes the Gulf of Akaba. We fly up the Akaba-fork to the very end, and fifty miles on inland.

This fifty-mile stretch seems, from above, to be only a wilderness of barren mountains and rocky canyons.

But in the middle of this wilderness we'll find the magic city.

We see, presently, far below, a little oasis, surrounded by grim hills. This is our goal, for Petra lies close by. No use to hunt for Petra from our plane. Nothing can be seen of it from the air. We must go on foot.

Two Bedouins, who say they have no fear of jinns, offer themselves as guides. At dawn next morning we stand before the hidden entrance of the secret canyon-corridor. Without our guides we could have passed by the canyon and never noticed it.

Following the Bedouins into the corridor, we find ourselves at the bottom of a tremendous split in the rock, overhung on either side by black precipices, hundreds of feet high, that shut out the sky and the sun. These fearsome cliffs seem only to be waiting for a human being to pass below in order to close in upon the ribbon of space and grind to bits their helpless victim.

More and more uneasy, we move deeper into this dimly lighted crack. We can stretch forth our arms and touch both walls. Bats fly about our heads. At times the daylight almost disappears. We expect, any moment, to meet demons from the lower realms, for this is a corridor not for the passage of humans but for the goblins who hide from the sunshine. We seem to be walking in a world deserted by all living things ages and ages ago.

The first wonder of Petra's many wonders, is the narrow canyon that offers the only entrance to the city. This slit in the rock is so narrow that in places we can stretch forth our arms and touch both walls. Petra was safe from the attack of enemies, for four soldiers, in this canyon, could defend the city against 4000.
Notice the tiny figure on canyon floor. *Orient and Occident.*

But you can see for yourselves that it has not always been like this, for, here and there, the canyon-floor is still paved with well-worn blocks of quarried stone. Along this corridor the wealth of Arabia once ebbed and flowed. Here the caravans, laden with silk and ivory, passed, musical with bells, in never-ending streams. And the followers of a king, returning from Jerusalem, once filled this living canyon with the clatter of their cavalry.

But that was before the days of the enchantment.

We creep on, for over a mile, along the bottom of the gorge. Gloomier and gloomier it grows, more overhanging, darker and more fearful.

And then we turn a corner of the canyon, and suddenly, out of the gloom, a glorious vision springs from a cliff straight ahead of us. The cliff is carved into a gleaming, rose-colored temple, towering but delicately made. And down upon the temple's face, the sun, in a blaze of light, is pouring from an opening in the rocks above.

For the first few minutes we make no effort to understand this wondrous sight. And then we realize that this great jewel must be the temple-tomb built by the Greek artists, aided by the power of the jinns, at the order of the King of ancient Petra . . . "a temple-tomb that was to overshadow the finest monuments of the nobles, a temple such as the world had never seen before." So the King had commanded, and the artists and the jinns had obeyed. . . .

If we are not too bedazzled, some of us may also judge the temple by workaday standards. It's as tall as a ten-story building, and a hundred feet broad. Inside we find a great rock hall, forty feet square and forty high. Across the front there is a row of graceful columns. And spread over everything is the most delicate and wonderful carving—garlands and flowers and goddesses—all, all in the solid rock. And in this same lovely, gleaming form, this temple has stood for nearly 2000 years—ever since the day when the jinns cast their magic spell.

104

We creep for over a mile along the bottom of the knife-slit canyon. The rock walls almost close together overhead, shutting out the light. Then we turn a corner, and suddenly this sun-flooded temple rises up in front of us.

We move on past the temple-tomb, and soon emerge into the great basin in which the city itself was built. The walls, all around, rise up more than a thousand feet, and are so steep that no enemy could possibly climb down. And these cliffs are lined with temples, treasuries, tombs, in endless procession, all cut from the solid rock, all huge in size and beautifully carved. The finest ones, we can be sure, are the tombs of the nobles. No wonder the King needed all his riches and power to surpass them!

There is no corner of the city we do not explore. But all the time the *supreme* tomb is in our thoughts. And so, when night comes and the desert stars shine down upon this stone wonderland, we wander back to visit again the temple of the King.

How changed it is!—yet not less beautiful. We had thought that nothing could be lovelier than its coral color glowing in the sun. We now see that there *is* something lovelier—its coral color softened by the starlight. We lean against the cliff wall opposite. Standing there in the silver shadows, before this vision of beauty, we find it easy to believe, almost, the shepherd's fairy tale of jinns and magic spells. It *must* be true—for, otherwise, what would have kept this carved stone poem from crumbling into dust a thousand years ago?

Yes, I'm sure, now that I'm here again, with you, in Petra, that the adventure I'll longest remember was my first visit to this very place. And it may be that you, too, in the years to come, when the memory of the other wonders you have seen has grown dim—that you, too, will still recall, clearly, as one of the truly magic moments of your life, the sight of the starlit temple—eternal, silent, beautiful, and alone—guarding the enchanted city.

CHAPTER XII

THE DEAD SEA

Soon after we leave Petra, our pilot, flying on north over more arid wilderness, points ahead to a large lake. We all agree it's the bluest lake we have ever seen—the bluest and the most brilliant. Melted sapphires could not shine with a richer, deeper blue. It's set deep in a barren valley, and looks to be about ten miles wide and fifty miles long. Enclosing it, the valley walls, dull-gold, lonely, and lifeless, soar upward more than 4000 feet.

We are quite close to the lake now, and our pilot begins to glide our plane downward toward the dazzling water. Lower and lower we drift.

Then the pilot says, Look at the altimeter. We notice that the needle points to *zero*—to sea-level—and we are still high in the sky . . . the lake is hundreds of feet beneath us. We keep going down. The altimeter now says we are 500 feet *below* the level of the sea . . . 800 feet . . . 1000 feet . . . down, down we go . . . 1200 feet . . . is the pilot going to land on the water? . . . 1300 feet. . . . Then the plane straightens out, just in time, and we skim along only a yard or two above the dancing waves. At this same moment, a few miles to the east, great ships are sailing over the surface of the Mediterranean, one quarter of a mile above our heads.

But of course you know the explanation. This is the Dead Sea.

This sea—the lowest point on the surface of the earth—we must certainly include among the wonders of the Orient.

This famous body of water is wonderful in many ways. First of all it has an in-flow but no out-flow. The in-flow is the Jordan River. (We can see it quite clearly now, emptying into the blue lake from the north). For thousands and thousands of years this river has been pouring *6,000,000 tons of water every day* into the vast sink. Naturally there can be no outlet, for how, indeed, can water flow 1300 feet uphill to reach the ocean?

107

Then why, you ask, doesn't the Sea fill up and flood the whole valley? This very thing would happen, were it not for the fact that this valley is one of the dryest spots in the world—so dry that 6,000,000 tons of Dead Sea water *evaporate* every day. This evaporation keeps the surface at the same level all the time. If the Jordan were blocked off, and its flow stopped, the Sea, in time, would dry up completely, and leave a great hole fifty miles long, ten miles wide, and 1100 feet deeper than it is now. The bottom of this hole would then be 2400 feet below the surface of the Mediterranean.

But why is this curious lake called Dead?

I'll explain. The Jordan River has a tiny fraction of salt in it. (So has all other river water, though you can't possibly taste the salt.) As the river pours into the lake, the desert sun and heat evaporate the water, but do not evaporate the salt, which has no way of escaping. For this reason, the water that remains has become saltier and saltier, until it is the saltiest water in the world. The ocean is five per cent salt—one gallon to every twenty gallons of water. The Dead Sea is *twenty-five* per cent salt—one gallon to every four gallons of water. The Dead Sea, therefore, is five times saltier than the ocean. This, of course, makes it much heavier. If you try to swim in it—well, you'll see for yourselves, before long, what happens.

Because of the salt no form of life can live in this strange lake. Fish, snails, water weeds, washed down with the river, all die the moment they strike the blue and beautiful—but deadly— brine. This deadliness, centuries ago, gave rise to legends which told that even the air above the Sea was so poisonous that birds fell stricken and lifeless when they tried to fly across. Such a story was invented by some fanciful traveler, but it was believed until modern times.

It is legends like this that have given the lake a bad name. One always expects to find it dismal and depressing. What a surprise it is then for us to find that the Dead Sea has a wild and glorious beauty, and a color brighter than any body of fresh water we ever saw.

Such a wonderful Sea, you say, must have a wonderful history.

Indeed it has. We flew over a part of the water, near the southern shore, beneath which lie the ruined cities of Sodom and Gomorrah, of Bible fame. ·At least scientists believe that the ruins are still there, sunk below the briny waves. Up which of those steep barren mountain-walls, we wonder, did Lot climb, fleeing from the fire and brimstone that rained down? We know that Lot escaped. But his wife, failing to obey the Lord's commands, looked back at the flaming city, and was turned to a pillar of salt. We wonder which of those rocky spires below is Lot's wife?

I've asked the pilot to circle over that stump of a hill rising close beside the western shore. On top this hill once stood the fortress of Masada. Here, seventy years after the birth of Christ, some 4000 Hebrews, surrounded by the Romans and seeing no hope of escape, slew themselves rather than submit to slavery.

Look there, at the bottom of the hill. Do you see what seem to be streets without houses? That's the Roman military camp built at the time of the siege of Masada. This camp has been preserved nearly nineteen hundred years by the extreme dryness of the air.

Two more "sights" and I'll let the pilot land. Yonder, to the north, up the Jordan Valley, you'll notice another lake, smaller than the Dead Sea. That's the Sea of Galilee. Close by this lake, at Nazareth, Jesus spent His boyhood. He often preached along its shores, and sailed upon its waters. Since the Sea of Galilee has an outlet—the Jordan—*its* water is fresh.

Now, one last look. . . . To the west, on that low ridge—there's a city with domes and towers, and gray walls all around it.

That's Jerusalem.

Early next morning, having stored our plane at an airport in the neighborhood, we're back beside the Dead Sea. And we're in our bathing suits, ready for a swim. But please take warning. You will float like a cork. Unless you watch sharp you'll float *upside down.* Your head is the heaviest part of your body, and it will want to topple over and go down and send your feet up. You can drown with the greatest ease. It will help if you'll tie a rock to one ankle with a handkerchief.

From an airplane, flying at 10,000 feet, the Holy Land looks like this. The Dead Sea, sunk 1300 feet below the level of the Mediterranean, is about fifty miles long and ten wide. It has no outlet, and so grows saltier all the time. It is now five times saltier than the ocean. Herod's Castle, where Salome danced for the head of John the Baptist, hangs dramatically over the brink of the Dead Sea pit, at the top of a 4000-foot wall of rock. From here Herod could look across the dark chasm and see the towers of Jerusalem, 25 miles away. The Sea of Galilee, to the north, is fresh water. It has an outlet—the Jordan River.

SEA

ACRE

HAIFA

MEDITERRANEAN

JAFFA

JERUSALEM

BETHLEHEM

GAZA

MOUNTAINS
OF JUDA

HEBRON

And remember not to get any water in your mouth. The taste is simply *awful,* and will certainly make you sick. And if you get this brine in your hair, it's as hard to wash out as furniture glue. Of course no diving is allowed. In this dense water you would quite likely break your neck.

So we're all set for a jolly swim.

We wade out till the lukewarm water is up to our knees— our waists. When it reaches our chests we go floating merrily away, with our shoulders, arms and necks high and dry.

Try floating on your back—but watch that head. With a little practice you can learn to keep right side up. Then, when you become a really expert floater you can just relax in the water and read the newspaper, eat lunch, or take a nap.

We can't do any of these things now, though, because we haven't time. I want you to go on a special trip with me this morning, and it will take all day.

American Colony Photographs.

The water of the Dead Sea is twenty-five per cent salt. To every four gallons of water there is one gallon of salt. This makes the water very heavy. If you try to swim in it you float like a cork. Some swimmers can keep their feet down only by tying rocks to them.

You say you don't *want* to go on a trip? You say you would rather keep on floating around in the Dead Sea? All right—the lazy ones can stay behind. But *I'm* going—to the top of that mountain-wall farther down the eastern shore. On top there's something that I think is vastly interesting. I shan't tell you what's there. You'll just have to trust me. The climb is 4000 feet—and *very* hard. The weak sisters can't make it . . . we may get hungry and thirsty and cold and—

Oh—you *all* want to go?

Very well. Let's get this glue washed off us first at the bath-house. I've already hired a motorboat to take us down the lake to our mountain.

We find the climb difficult indeed. Leaving the boat, we follow, first, a narrow ravine, and then start up a rocky path on a side of the mountain hidden from the Dead Sea.

We climb and climb all day. Our shoes are ripped to shreds. Our hands are torn by thorns. I know you're wondering what on earth can be at the summit of this wild mountain. But there's no use asking me—yet.

Toward sunset we reach a level spot near the top, and find ourselves clambering over the ruins of an ancient palace. Broken building-stones lie about. Fallen columns are half-hidden by grass and sand. Just beyond is the summit itself. And right on the tiptop we find more ruins—ruins of a fort or citadel, this time.

I lead you (since I've been here before) to what was once a terrace of the fort—and you gasp at the sudden picture that unfolds. We are looking into the dark pit of the Dead Sea, 4000 feet below. In Arabic this spot is called *El Mashnaka*. It means the Hanging Place. This name fits perfectly, for our terrace is poised on the edge of a chasm almost as deep, and fully as awesome, as the Grand Canyon.

The entire map of the Holy Land is unrolled. The towers of Jerusalem, twenty-five miles away on a ridge beyond the chasm, rise up black and sharp against the sunset sky. To the north, the

River Jordan winds down from the Sea of Galilee. The great sink, far below, is paved in that matchless blue—a blue that changes to black as the twilight deepens and fills the chasm with darkness.

When the last red rays of the sunset have faded behind Jerusalem's towers, a cold and biting wind springs up. To escape it, we seek shelter in a cavern beneath the ruins of the citadel. This cavern has been cut out of the solid rock. It's sometimes used as a shelter for sheep, nowadays. But you can see that once it must have been a kind of dungeon. For why else, except to chain prisoners, would these crumbling iron rings have been set into the rock?

We build a fire in the cavern, and eat a supper of cheese and unleavened bread given to us by the shepherds.

Now, at last, I tell you why we've come to visit this ruined citadel on this wild mountain-top, and why we're sitting in this prison in the rock.

Do you remember, from the Bible, the name of Herod? It was Herod who ordered all the babies in Bethlehem killed, in his effort to destroy the newborn Christ. This infamous King had a son named Herod Antipas. The son, during the years when Christ was growing into manhood, was King of Moab, the country we're in now. Having many enemies, he looked about for a site where he could build a fortress, and live secure from all attack. He finally chose the peak-top of the highest and steepest mountain he could find along the Dead Sea's eastern wall. He chose El Mashnaka—the Hanging Place—*this* place. And then he built his citadel, with towers 200 feet high. We stood on the citadel's terrace at sunset. The rest of the fortress is gone. In the rock foundation, he hewed a big dungeon for his prisoners—*this* dungeon. Not far away he built a palace. We climbed over the ruins of Herod's palace this afternoon.

Herod loved his grim citadel. From its terrace he could look across the blue void that fell away from him—on across the ridge-top on the other side—and at sunset see the domes and towers of Jerusalem, just as we saw them an hour ago. And no matter how many enemies he might have there, *here* he felt safe.

114

To this stronghold Herod brought, in time, a wife named Herodias. She had been the wife of Herod's half-brother, Philip, and deserted him to marry Herod. While she was Philip's wife, she had a beautiful young daughter named Salome. And Salome came with her mother to Herod's mountain-top.

But no sooner was Herod home with his new bride than a holy hermit, called John the Baptist, came from his cave in the wilderness to cry out against Herod's marriage. It was unlawful and sinful, John said, to marry the wife of one's half-brother. Among the people of Moab, John stirred up so much feeling against both Herod and Herodias that the King had John seized and thrust into this very dungeon. Of course we can't be *certain* it was this dungeon, but historians think it is. It was used, as we can see, for a prison, and it's the only dungeon dug underneath Herod's citadel.

This was the state of things here at El Mashnaka when, in the year A.D. 29, Herod, to celebrate his birthday, gave a banquet for his ministers and army officers. The banquet was probably held in one of the great halls of the ruined palace just below us.

All evening Herod's guests had been feasting and drinking. Outside, the stars—the same stars that shine now, on us—formed a bright covering over the mountain-top. Down from the walls of this Hanging Place the world fell away into bottomless darkness, into the black depths of the Dead Sea chasm—just as the world falls tonight into the same black depths.

About midnight, the feasting over, the musicians come in bringing their harps and drums. With them comes Herodias' daughter, Salome, to dance for the King in honor of his birthday. In rhythm with the music, this beautiful girl glides and whirls around the center of the hall. And when the music ends with a crash of all the instruments, Salome falls to her knees at the King's feet.

Herod is dazzled by her beauty and her dancing. He bids Salome stand beside him, and he offers, on his oath, before all his guests, to give her whatever present she may ask for. "Ask of me," he said, "whatsoever thou wilt, unto the half of my kingdom, and I will give it thee."

115

The beheading of John the Baptist, from a painting by Puvis de Chavannes. The dungeon where this execution took place is still to be seen beneath Herod's Castle.

Salome did not know what to ask for, so "she went," the Bible tells, "and said unto her mother, What shall I ask?" and Herodias said, "The head of John the Baptist."

The Queen has been waiting for just such a chance as this to get rid of the trouble-making hermit!

And Salome returns to the hall to ask Herod to give her, on a silver tray, the head of John the Baptist.

Herod is "exceeding sorry"—he does not hate John *that* much —and he is also a little afraid of the wild preacher, because the people all say John is a man of God. But Herod has no choice . . . all his guests have heard him promise, on his oath. . . .

He calls for his executioner, and gives the fatal order.

116

Holding a torch, the swordsman leaves the palace and follows the short winding path up to our citadel here on top the Hanging Place. The guards unlock the dungeon door. John, unafraid, kneels—perhaps here where the fire is burning—and the sword falls.

Back in the banquet hall, Herod, troubled and silent, sits slumped in his chair. Salome, unhappy too, and trembling, waits by his side.

Then the swordsman returns and hands to Salome the present she has asked for.

It has become very dark in our cavern, and very cold, for the fire is low and a cold wind is blowing across our dungeon door. To keep warm, we must wrap up in blankets the shepherds have lent us.

Did I hear somebody ask me what happened to Salome? No one knows. After that one famous evening on this mountain-top —an evening men have talked about for almost two thousand years—Salome disappears from the pages of history.

Herod? Well, all the time and treasure he spent to build his palace and fortress were wasted. He was not allowed to live here very long after the death of John. He lost the friendship of the Roman emperor, and was sent away—along with Herodias—to far-off Gaul.

But please don't ask me any more questions. Our fire is nearly out and there's no more wood. I'd like to go to sleep—I'm nearly dead from that climb. Tomorrow morning you'll probably have to *carry* me home.

You say you're glad you cut short your Dead Sea swim to make this pilgrimage?

I thought you'd be. . . . Good night.

CHAPTER XIII

THE ROCK OF ABRAHAM

Jerusalem! We saw it first from high in the air while flying above the Dead Sea. It was then some twenty miles away. Before we landed, that morning, we flew right over the city, and could look down straight upon its domes and towers and crooked streets below. We noticed a great open space taking up one-sixth of all the room within the walls. Near the center of this cleared space we saw a broad platform paved with white stones . . . and on this platform a curious eight-sided building with a dome.

I asked you to pay special attention to this court because more chapters in history have been written about it than about any other place on earth.

And now that we have returned safely from El Mashnaka, we are ready to explore Jerusalem on foot.

Entering the city at the Jaffa Gate, we walk down David Street. Soon we come upon the Church of the Holy Sepulcher. Legend tells that this is the spot upon which Christ was crucified. For hundreds of years a church has stood here. It encloses the place where the cross was raised, and the rock-sepulcher where His body lay three days. All about us we see pilgrims who have come from every Christian country to pray at this sacred shrine.

Not far beyond this church we arrive at an enormous gate which leads us into the great open court we had noticed from the air.

Before us, in the center of the court, rises the eight-sided building with the dome. This building is called the Dome of the Rock. It's a Moslem mosque, and almost as sacred a place to all Moslems as the Church of the Holy Sepulcher is to all Christians.

We walk inside. What loveliness lies about us! It is hard to believe that so delicate and well-preserved a building can be so old. The Moslems built it in 698 A.D.

he most famous and most wonderful building in Jerusalem is the Dome of the Rock. It was built
Mohammedans as a mosque in the year 698. For them it is almost as sacred as the Kaaba in
ecca. It stands on the spot where the Temple of Solomon once stood—in the center of a great
square that covers one-sixth of the entire area of Jerusalem.

Nearly a hundred feet above soars the dome, supported by a circle of marble columns. On the floor directly below the dome we see, growing out of the bare ground, a rough outcropping of rock, sixty feet long, forty feet across, and four to seven feet high. To shelter this rough granite rock, this beautiful mosque was built.

In the hushed shadows we see a few Moslems kneeling on the thick carpets and saying their prayers. Let's find a quiet corner for ourselves, where we'll not disturb the worshipers. I want to tell you about this rock.

You remember Abraham who built the Kaaba in Mecca? This was the same Abraham who was commanded by Jehovah to sacrifice his young son Isaac. Jehovah told him—in the first book of the Bible: "Get thee into the land of Moriah, and offer Isaac there for a burnt offering upon one of the mountains which I will tell thee of."

Abraham came to this very rock here before us. This rock is on the top of the hill still called Mount Moriah.

Following the Lord's commands, Abraham bound little Isaac, and was about to make a sacrifice of him when the angel of the Lord called to Abraham out of heaven, commanding him not to slay the lad, saying, "for now I know thou fearest God, seeing thou hast not withheld thine only son from me."

Many years later, when Solomon had become king of Israel, he filled in the slopes of Mount Moriah in order to build his famous temple here. Over the Rock itself Solomon placed the Altar for Burnt Offerings. Into the Holy of Holies he moved the Ark of the Covenant, and surrounded it with his greatest treasures.

Let's go outside now, and look at the ground where the temple stood. But before we go, notice the hollow places in the Rock— hollows that look like the footprint of a huge horse. I'll want to tell you about these later.

We walk across the court to the outer wall. We climb to the top of it. From here we can look down on the other side. Sharply below drops a valley, called the Valley of Kedron.

The Dome of the Rock was built to protect the Rock pictured here. Upon this rough granite slab Abraham prepared to sacrifice little Isaac. Also the Mohammedans believe that Mohammed was brought to this Rock on a winged horse from Mecca. They point out the hollows in the Rock and say these are the huge footprints left by the winged horse.   *Galloway.*

Now, if you'll turn, you'll see the entire court spread before you. How enormous Solomon's temple must have been to cover all this space! How splendid it was, too! It was made of shining white limestone; and vast quantities of gold were used to gild the roof.

This marvelous building stood for 400 years. Then the Babylonians captured Jerusalem, destroyed the temple, burned the city to the ground, and dragged the Jewish population to Babylon as captives.

Later the Jews were allowed to return. In time, under King Herod, they raised here another temple—larger even than Solomon's. *This* temple was standing all during Jesus' lifetime. Here Mary, His mother, found Him when He was twelve years old, talking to the wise men.

But forty years after the crucifixion this temple, too, was destroyed—by the Romans.

More centuries passed. First one conqueror and then another held possession of the Rock of Abraham. And then, about the year 650, the Mohammedans, inspired by their new religion, swept down upon Palestine. The Mohammedans felt they should rule Jerusalem, since their Prophet Mohammed, himself, always thought of Jerusalem as the holiest place on earth—even holier than Mecca, his own home town. One Moslem legend tells how Mohammed, in a single night, was swiftly carried by the Angel Gabriel on a winged steed from Mecca here to Abraham's Rock. He dismounted on the Rock . . . and there is the footprint of the winged horse still showing—I pointed it out to you before we left the mosque.

When the Moslems had seized the entire Holy Land for themselves, they at once began to build, over the sacred Rock, the beautiful building we just visited. More than 1200 years ago they placed their Crescent at the summit of the dome, to show that the religion taught by Mohammed ruled in Jerusalem.

Today, as you see, that Crescent is still there.

122

Before we climb down from this wall, let me tell you a story about the Rock of Abraham—a modern story, and, I think, an amazing story:

You remember my saying that King Solomon placed the Ark of the Covenant and other sacred treasures inside his wonderful temple—the temple built over the Rock?

These things remained safe until the Babylonians captured Jerusalem, destroyed the temple, and dragged the people into captivity. At that time the Ark and the treasures mysteriously disappeared. Many guesses have been made as to what happened to them. The most popular guess is that the Ark is *still* underneath the Rock of Abraham, buried there by the temple-priests just before the city fell.

And it is true that there are caverns beneath the Rock. You can strike the Rock itself, and a hollow booming sound comes from somewhere below. Is it possible that the Ark and all of Solomon's treasures are buried in these caverns—buried there for 2500 years? Is it possible that the building of the later temples did not disturb the secret caves? If these treasures *are* there, and if they could be recovered, it would be one of the most exciting and important finds in the history of archeology.

Knowing this, a group of English adventurers, some years ago when the Holy Land was still a part of Turkey, came to Jerusalem with a daring idea. It was their plan to dig for the treasure, in secret, right under the noses of the Moslem priests. To help them escape with the treasure (in case they found it) they had a yacht anchored in the harbor of Jaffa, the port of Jerusalem— and the yacht was kept ready to flee at a moment's notice.

Then one dark night the leader of the band went to the Turkish night-watchman who stood guard over the Dome of the Rock. A large sum of money was offered him if he would let the "archeologists" enter the mosque at two o'clock in the morning, every night for the next month, and dig there till dawn. The leader explained their plan: It was to remove a big flagstone from the

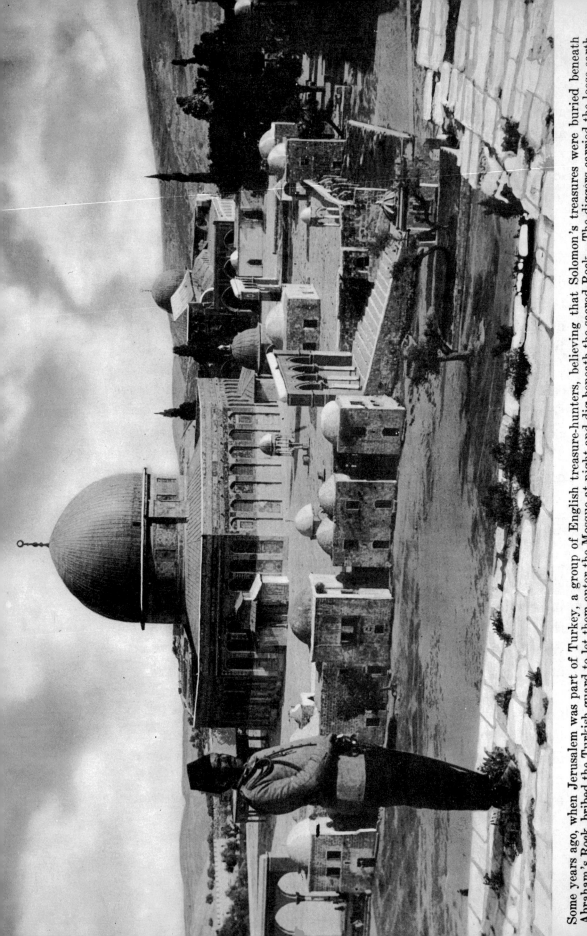

Some years ago, when Jerusalem was part of Turkey, a group of English treasure-hunters, believing that Solomon's treasures were buried beneath Abraham's Rock, bribed the Turkish guard to let them enter the Mosque at night and dig beneath the sacred Rock. The diggers carried the loose earth mosque floor close beside the Rock, dig a shaft straight down, and carry the loose earth away in baskets. Each dawn they would put the big stone back in place, and clean up all traces of their digging. If they found Solomon's treasure—which they were sure they *would* find—the Turkish guard would receive a present that would make him rich the rest of his life.

The guard, to whom nothing was sacred, agreed.

Choosing a dark night when all Jerusalem was sleeping, the Englishmen crept into the deserted court with their picks and shovels and baskets. In the darkness, the faithless guard unlocked the doors of the mosque and watched the robbers go to work.

For seven nights this dangerous, secret exploration continued. Deeper and deeper went the shaft. No one suspected, for every morning, just before sunup, the flagstone and rugs were put carefully in place again.

But on the eighth morning one of the Moslem priests, living in a house overlooking the temple enclosure, happened to wake up as the first light was coming into the sky. For a breath of fresh air he went to his balcony, facing the mosque. He noticed dim figures moving in the great courtyard . . . the figures seemed to be carrying heavy baskets from the mosque to the outer wall, and back to the mosque again. Suspicious, he went to find out who these people were, and what they were doing at such an hour in this forbidden place.

As the priest hurried across the court, the guilty Turkish guard saw him coming and gave the alarm to the robbers. At the same time the priest dimly guessed what was happening. He began to cry out, "Thieves—thieves—in the holy mosque!" His cries woke up the other priests. People, with daggers drawn, came running and shouting into the court.

The Englishmen knew, instantly, that they must flee. If they were caught digging away the very foundations of the sacred shrine, they would be torn to pieces by the outraged Moslems. They dropped everything—spades, picks, baskets, flagstones, rugs

—and ran for their lives. A motorcar, always ready, dashed with them down the Jaffa road. From the harbor, on their yacht, they escaped to England, followed by the curses of every Mohammedan in the Holy Land.

But the Turkish guard, who had helped the Christian robbers, did not get away in time. As he fled, too late, across the enclosure here before us, he was caught by the mob and stoned to death.

Do you believe the adventurers were on the track of untold treasure? Or were they just on a wild goose chase?

Perhaps we can find out. *I think I know another, secret, way to reach the caverns beneath the Rock of Abraham.*

To get there we'll have to do a little exploring of our own. Even if we fail to find the Ark, I promise you (if you're willing to go with me), an adventure even better than our visit to Salome's castle.

Everybody willing to take part, say *I*.

Good! Please follow me. . . .

CHAPTER XIV

TREASURE HUNTERS

First of all, let's go back to the market place.

We cross the great court, pass through the gate, and move on into a street lined with Arab shops. There we find a lumber merchant, and buy from him wooden poles and planks, long enough and strong enough to make a thirty-foot ladder. We also buy hammer and nails, rope, picks and shovels, buckets, candles, and flashlights.

These things we pile into a cart. Then we drag the cart outside the city, and down into the Kedron Valley. We can look back and see the walls of Jerusalem high above us.

We come to the brick-lined entrance of a cave in the valley floor. Through this entrance we can see stone steps leading downward through a tunnel deep into the ground. Up the steps come Arab women carrying water in gasoline tins.

At the bottom of these steps is a spring, called the Fount of the Virgins. We are going to explore this spring . . . it may lead to the caverns beneath Abraham's Rock, and to Solomon's treasures. . . .

I'll tell you why:

If we had lived 3000 years ago, and had come to visit this spring, we would have found the landscape around us very different from the landscape now. The spring, then, was on the top of the ground. Today it's fifty feet below the surface, buried under silt and trash that have been filling up the valley floor for long centuries. In the ancient days, just above the spring there rose a rock cliff. It, too, is now buried in sand. On top of this cliff stood a walled city called the City of the Jebusites. Not a trace of it remains. It was the original Jerusalem, though the place where it stood is now well outside the present walls, as you can see.

This Jebusite citadel, alone of all the cities in this part of the country, defied King David when, about the year 1000 B.C., he

127

sought to unite them into one nation. He tried to conquer it with his army. But the natural rock walls were too steep. The Jebusites drove back every attack, and mocked David from their strong rock battlements.

One thing puzzled the King more than anything else . . . where did the Jebusites get their water? He was sure there was no water on the top of their rock island. As for his own soldiers, they were well supplied, for at the bottom of the Jebusite wall was a spring—*this* spring—flowing out from a low grotto in the rocks.

Then one night, during the siege, a most surprising thing happened. About midnight one of David's officers, named Joab, went to the spring to drink. As he leaned down close to the water he heard the clink of copper buckets inside the grotto . . . Jebusite buckets, without doubt. Joab felt sure that the Jebusites had a shaft bored through the rock right down to an inner cavern of the spring, and were lowering their buckets by ropes into some pool which he could not see.

Acting quickly, he took off his clothes, slipped into the water, and began to explore the cave. And sure enough, after squeezing through a crack in the rocks, he came upon an inner cavity. Slanting down from above was a shaft, lighted by lamps, and down this shaft buckets were being lowered on ropes.

Greatly excited, he hurried at once to David's tent, reported the discovery and asked for a few brave companions to join him in a dangerous adventure. Joab's plan was to climb the shaft with a small company of soldiers, creep out at the upper end in the dead of night, kill the Jebusite guards, and throw open the gates to David's army. Joab realized he might fail, that he and all his brave comrades might be trapped and slain, but there seemed to be no other way of conquering the stubborn city.

Dragging their swords through the water, Joab, leading his men, reached the shaft about three o'clock in the morning. Stealthily they climbed up, aided by the cracks and ledges. At the top of the shaft they found a tunnel (fortunately deserted at such an hour) which wound upward through the rock. On tiptoe, scarcely breathing, they crept to the open upper entrance of the passage and came out into the citadel.

Except for the guards on the walls all the Jebusites were sleeping soundly. Not even the watchdogs gave the alarm. Joab rushed upon the guards and killed them before they could cry out. The gates were flung open, and David's army poured in upon the helpless city. From that night to this, Jerusalem—the City of the Jebusites—has been the capital of Israel.

I heard this story on a previous visit to Jerusalem. (Most of it is in the Bible.)

I also heard that, in 1907, German archeologists, working without the knowledge of the Turks, had crawled into Joab's spring, and found the Jebusite bucket-shaft up which Joab climbed. But before the Germans could find out where the shaft led, the Turks learned what was happening, and drove the explorers away. Since then no one had been near this mysterious passage.

Then I heard still *another* legend which said there was a secret tunnel (dug right through the rock on which Jerusalem stands) that joined the Jebusite shaft with the treasure-caverns beneath the Rock of Abraham—nearly a quarter of a mile away. This tunnel, people said, was built by King Solomon at the same time he built his great Temple. In case he wanted to leave Jerusalem secretly, or had to flee from his enemies, he could climb down into the treasure-caverns beneath the Rock, pass through the tunnel as it wound underneath the city walls, reach the Jebusite shaft, descend this by a ladder, wade through Joab's spring, and come out into the open air, well down the Kedron Valley.

The more I heard about the caverns and tunnel and shaft, the more curious I became about them. How exciting it would be if someone *could* explore the entire passage, the passage lost all these centuries. If someone found the tunnel, it would lead—if the legend turned out to be true—right into the treasure-caverns fron underneath. The reward of such an adventure might be the long-lost Ark of the Covenant, or the mummy of Israel's greatest king.

129

American Colony Photographs.

In the year 1000 B.C., Solomon built his famous temple on the flat summit of Mt. Moriah in Jerusalem. This picture is a model of that glorious group of buildings. The walls were of whitest stone and gleamed like snow. The roofs were all covered with gold. Each stone was fashioned outside the walls, and then put in place by the masons, so that the temple rose without "the sound of hammer or any metal instrument" to mar the sanctity of the place. Each court was held more sacred than the one outside it. The Holy of Holies (inside the tall arched entrance of the innermost building) was the most sacred of all. The Rock of Abraham rested just in front of the tall arch. For 3000 years people have said that Solomon dug caves beneath the Rock, and that in these caves the Ark of the Covenant and all the royal treasures were hidden when the Babylonians destroyed the Temple in 600 B.C. Legends also tell that secret tunnels lead from the caverns underneath the outer walls of the temple-grounds and down

The same temple-grounds as they look today (compare with picture on opposite page). From the ruins of Solomon's Temple, another temple rose in 570 B.C., after the Jews returned from captivity in Babylon. This was enlarged, shortly before the birth of Christ, by King Herod. Herod's temple, in its turn, was leveled to the ground—in 70 A.D., by the Romans. Six centuries later the Mohammedans captured Jerusalem and built the mosque (seen here) called the Dome of the Rock. This picture shows how the temple-grounds have looked since that time—for a period of 1200 years. Some day, if the Mohammedans ever give up possession of the Rock, archeologists may be allowed to dig beneath it, explore the caverns, and perhaps find the Ark of the Covenant and Solomon's burial place. We found the entrance to one tunnel (down in the valley outside the walls of Jerusalem) which people say leads to the caverns beneath the Rock of Abraham. But we soon came to a place in the tunnel where it was blockaded with sand, and could go no farther.

I resolved to be that someone myself.

There was certainly no hope of reaching the treasure-caverns by digging underneath Abraham's Rock! *That* had been tried with disastrous results.

Perhaps I could find the upper entrance of the Jebusite shaft— the place where Joab and his men crawled out to kill the Jebusite guards. But I soon learned that this upper entrance was buried under sand, trees, and houses.

The only possible entrance to the passage lay through Joab's spring.

And so, late one night, I found my way to this spring, to this very spot where we are now, ready for a great adventure. With me came my friend Moye Stephens. (Remember Timbuctoo?) We chose the night because the spring-grotto would be deserted. We went down these steps. . . . If you'll follow me I'll show you the way. Lend a hand here and we'll carry our ladder-lumber with us, and the hammer and nails. We must build the ladder in the grotto. The shaft is thirty feet high, and we'll never be able to drag a ladder that long through the entrance. Careful now, these old steps are slippery. . . .

We come to the spring, fifty feet below the surface of the ground. Here, Joab knelt down to drink on that famous night. Ten feet across the pool is a low and narrow crack in the rock. Through that crack Joab reached the Jebusite shaft. And through it we must follow.

We jump into the spring. The cold, clear water reaches up to our waists. Carrying our lumber and hammers and flashlights we wade across the pool, and find the historic crack. The crack leads us to the inner cave at the bottom of the Jebusite shaft. There it is, exactly as it was when Joab climbed it 3000 years ago! When I was here before, I had to go on alone beyond the crack, because Stephens, being a very big fellow, couldn't squeeze through.

It's pitch dark now. But with our flashlights we can look up the shaft for thirty feet and see the rock shelf from which the Jebusites lowered their buckets.

On my first visit here I had no ladder. But I was able, by going barefooted, to climb the shaft, using the same ledges Joab used. This system, for us, is needlessly dangerous and difficult. We'll use the ladder.

In half an hour our ladder is finished, and reaches to the top of the shaft. I'd best go first, since I'm the heaviest. If the ladder supports me, it's doubly safe for you. . . . Hold tight to the rungs, and don't drop those flashlights!

We reach the shelf, and climb out onto a level rock floor. Before us opens a great rock room, twenty-five feet across and domed high overhead. We wonder why the Jebusites went to so much trouble to dig this room so far down in the rock. Perhaps they stored grain here.

When I came to this room before, I had only a kerosene lantern for light. I was scared, too. I had no idea what lay up that winding rock tunnel there ahead. What would I find deeper in this ancient and forgotten gallery? Nobody had been here for perhaps 2000 years . . . yet through all these centuries the legend had lived, saying that secret tunnels led from Joab's shaft to the treasure-caverns beneath the Rock of Abraham. I had found the shaft—and the tunnel, too, leading *somewhere*. If I followed it, would a secret turning bring me to Solomon's tomb, or the Ark of the Covenant, as the legend said? Was I about to make one of the greatest discoveries in Bible history?

With my heart pounding I crept forward, holding my lantern before me.

But before I had gone very far—only around the curve in the tunnel there, just ahead—something very terrifying happened. Suddenly, from way down the black shaft here, there came a faint, far-off cry. It seemed to come from the other side of the world. In terror I started backward, slipped on the wet rock (you can see it's still wet), and fell with a crash. And as I fell the lantern struck against the wall and went out.

The cry was only Stephens' cry, asking me to hurry back. (He was still standing in the spring with water up to his waist—and had no lantern.) I soon realized who it was, shouting at me. Even so, I sat there in the darkness in complete panic.

I now had only one desire—to escape from this terrible place. I tried to re-light the lantern. I couldn't. *Stephens had all the matches.* And he could never crawl through the crack to bring them to me. I must get out by myself as best I could.

I turned about, and on hands and knees felt my way back to this shelf.

You can imagine how hard it was to climb down the pit again, in the blackness. In fact I found it impossible. So I lowered myself over the edge, right here, kicked away from the rock wall— and dropped.

It didn't take more than two seconds for me to fall twenty-five feet, but that blank instant in which I could neither see nor feel was one of the longest moments I've ever lived.

You noticed the mud and water at the bottom. I landed in that, and sprained an ankle. Luckily, I wasn't hurt worse.

Several days later, when my ankle had healed, I had to hurry off to Egypt, and never had a chance to come here again.

—Until today, with you.

What's around the curve in the rock gallery yonder—on past the place where I slipped and turned back? I don't know. I doubt if there is one person in Jerusalem today who *does* know. If we locate the tunnel that leads underneath Abraham's Rock, and if we find Solomon's mummy there, or the Ark of the Covenant—what shall we do with them?

You suggest less talking and more exploring?

Right!

We move forward again. The gallery winds upward. On the walls are the marks of the Jebusite picks, marks 3000 years old.

By the light of our flashlights we march 400 feet up the curving gallery. Then, abruptly, only a hundred feet on the other side of the place where I came to such grief before, we find our tunnel completely blockaded. The tunnel has turned sharply up a steep staircase, and the staircase is filled with sand.

We are prepared for this. With our shovels we dig away at the blockade. All afternoon we work—all next day. We have removed several tons of earth from the rock staircase . . . the passage behind is filling up. But as fast as we dig, more sand and gravel slide down on top of us, from above. After sixteen hours of labor we have not moved forward one inch.

We give up, and decide to let the Ark of the Covenant rest in peace.

But some day I'm coming back to Jerusalem with a million dollars, and a hundred workmen, and months of free time, and tackle this tunnel again, and keep on digging and digging away until I find out where it goes, and what marvelous secrets it may guard.

And when I return for the next attack—will you come, too?

135

One hundred and fifty years after the birth of Christ, the people of Syria, then a rich Rocolony, built a temple which, for might and majesty, has had few equals in history. It was
honor of Jupiter. The town where it rose was called Baalbek. Today only six of the temple's fi
eight columns still stand. But these six are so huge and so towering that they fill with awe ev
one who looks at them.

Gend

CHAPTER XV

BAALBEK

Do you recall, at the beginning of this book, how we followed the travels of Demetrius and Diomede to learn from them what were the wonders of the world 250 years before the birth of Christ? Now suppose, just for a moment, that we change the date to 250 years *after* the birth of Christ, and ask what the great sights were *then*. By this time the Roman empire had grown and grown until it covered all the western world and much of the eastern. And by 250 A.D. it boasted of new wonders such as little Demetrius, 500 years before, had never dreamed of.

A Roman citizen, answering our question about the great sights of his own age, would have thought, first, of the glories of Rome itself. He would have named the Circus Maximus, a stadium that held 200,000 people. He would have named the Colosseum, and the marble baths of Caracalla, and the marvelous dome of the Pantheon.

Outside Rome he would have named the Pyramids, of course, and the Pharos, and the Temple of Diana, all of which were still standing. (The temple was destroyed ten years later). He might even have included the Acropolis at Athens.

He *certainly* would have named Baalbek.

For every Roman schoolboy knew that between Rome and Babylon there was no work of man as mighty and as marvelous as the walls and temples of Baalbek. Only in Egypt could one find monuments as great.

And even today, when most of the wonders of the Roman world have disappeared, Baalbek's walls and temples still remain the mightiest and most marvelous ruins between Rome and Babylon —again not including Egypt.

In ancient times people traveled from the farthest corners of the Roman empire—sometimes 1000 miles away—to look upon Baalbek. As for ourselves—now that we're in Jerusalem—we need travel only 200 miles.

In Jerusalem we say good-by to our airplane and change to a motorcar. We speed northward to the Sea of Galilee, and on past its historic shores. Crossing the Syrian border, we reach the old city of Damascus. Thirty miles beyond, our road winds into a green valley. Above this valley rise the snow-clad Mountains of Lebanon. (From the forests on these mountain-sides came the cedar beams used in the building of Solomon's temple.) We notice, with sad hearts, the poverty of the people along the way, and the wretched mud villages they live in.

Then, as we are approaching an especially miserable village, I ask the driver to stop our car.

"Look at *that*," I say, pointing to a single block of quarried stone lying beside the road.

Your eyes open wide in astonishment. Never in your lives have you seen a building stone so large. Nor will you ever, anywhere on earth, see one larger, for this is the biggest stone block ever hewn by man. It's 68 feet long and 14 feet tall and 14 feet wide. It weighs 1200 tons. From this single block, masons could build three city houses, each 20 feet across the front, 40 feet deep, and five-stories high, with walls a foot thick.

It's been lying here over 1700 years.

The Egyptian obelisks—each a single block—were big, but not so big as this. The largest obelisk standing today weighs 500 tons. The one in Central Park, in New York, weighs 200 tons; the one before St. Peter's in Rome, 340. In ancient Egypt it took 5000 men to quarry and move these huge blocks. How they did it is a mystery. For even in modern times, with all our steel cables, and derricks, and machinery, and skill, engineers have the greatest difficulty in moving and erecting a 200-ton block.

Yet, here before us, we see a block *six times* as heavy.

But what— I know you're asking—is this gigantic stone doing all by itself 'way out here in the fields? We can only suppose that after working months, perhaps years, to quarry it and square it, the masons decided it wasn't just what they wanted. Or perhaps the building plans changed. Or perhaps the money gave out. Anyway, here it is, abandoned right beside the quarry.

a quarry just outside Baalbek we come upon this colossal building stone. It is the biggest block cut stone on earth. Apparently it was *so* big the masons were unable to move it. The stone mea- res 68 feet long and 14 feet tall and 14 feet wide. From it, masons could build three city houses, h five stories high with walls a foot thick. Steam and electric engines have the greatest difficulty moving stones weighing 200 tons. *This* monster weighs six times that much. It was never taken from the quarry, but others, only slightly smaller, *were* moved. (See page 143.)

But what was it for?

Here—climb up on top the block and I'll show you. . . . If this stone were not lying on a slope, the top-surface would make a fine dance floor, wouldn't it? Now look over there, about a mile away, above the trees. You'll see six towering stone columns looking like a great harp ready to catch the wind. Baalbek is there. Those giant columns mark the ruins of the Temple of Jupiter, one of the most famous buildings in history. This stone was to go in the wall surrounding the temple. When we get to that wall, as we will presently, we'll find, built into it, three other stones only slightly smaller than this monster.

Long before the birth of Christ, Baalbek had been a holy place in Syria. Temples and shrines to Baal, the greatest of the Syrian gods, stood there. But about the year 150 A.D., Syria, by this time one of Rome's richest colonies, had learned to worship the Roman Jupiter. In fact the Syrians became so devoted to this new god that they set their hearts on building a temple to him that would be greater than any temple in Rome itself.

Plans, on a gigantic scale, were drawn. Then the Roman-Syrians flung themselves upon the work. Never since the day of Ephesus had the world seen anything like it. Thousands of slaves were brought together to drag the enormous blocks from the quarry to the temple grounds. Thousands more were needed to lift these blocks in place. The architects demanded a certain rare marble for the huge columns. This marble could not be found in Syria—only in Egypt. So to Egypt they went, far up the Nile. Here the column-drums were hewn in sections twenty feet long, floated down the river to its mouth, and brought overland, 400 miles, on rollers that crept forward not more than a mile a day. From quarry to temple, the journey took three years.

What daring imaginations these early Syrians must have had, what skill and power!

First of all, in the center of the valley, they built up a platform 900 feet long and 600 feet across, made of great granite blocks. On top of this they raised their columns, 3 feet higher than those at Ephesus, and a foot thicker. Around this awe-inspiring building

140

Nesmith.

long as the Temple of Jupiter at Baalbek stood, people came from all over the Roman empire visit it. No temple in Rome itself was as great. The marble columns (of which these six remain) re quarried, in sections, far up the Nile, floated down to the river's mouth, and then dragged 400 les overland. Earthquakes have shaken the wreckage of the temple time and time again. But even in its ruin, Baalbek remains one of the wonders of the world.

they raised smaller shrines—smaller, but still built with blocks that weighed a hundred tons.

And then, with their energy and zeal still spilling over, they set to work to build a second temple, to one side, not as great in size as the first one, but even more beautifully decorated.

When the temples stood in all their glory, a large town spread out around them. Beyond the town were the orchards, watered by melted snow from the mountains. Baalbek's fruit came to be almost as famous as its temples. Its cherries were especially prized. One Egyptian pharaoh was so fond of them that at each cherry season he sent hundreds of carrier pigeons to Baalbek to bring the fresh fruit to him. One cherry, in a tiny basket, was tied to each of the pigeon's legs—and then the homing bird was freed and allowed to speed swiftly, 400 miles, back to the Nile. In this way cherries picked in the morning dew were on the king's table at noon.

Not a trace of the ancient town, and few of the orchards, now remain. Where the town once stood, present-day Arabs have built a poor little village that still bears the mighty name of Baalbek.

Passing through the village, we reach the front of the great temple-platform, and walk around the outer wall. Again, we stare in amazement at the size of the building stones embedded there. Over and over, the thought comes to us: Giants, giants, not men, did this.

In the rear of the wall, raised thirty feet above the ground, we find the three monsters I spoke of. They are each 63 feet long, 13 feet high, and 10 feet thick. (The block we saw at the quarry was 68 by 14 by 14.) In our mind's eye we try to see the picture of these colossal blocks being dragged in from the quarry by an army of slaves—thousands of men to each stone . . . one stone to go into the wall of the temple of the gods.

Climbing the steps, back at the entrance, we reach the top of the platform and wander into the midst of a sea of tumbled marble. Many of the fragments are richly carved with flowers and vines, with figures from the Greek and Roman myths. Only six of the towering columns from the Temple of Jupiter still stand. Fifty-two have fallen, and their broken pieces lie strewn about.

Wide World.

e beside the great Temple of Jupiter, we find this smaller Temple of Bacchus—smaller, but still mous in size, and even more beautifully carved than its gigantic neighbor. More than half the columns are intact. Note how small the two men seem, standing on the tumbled stones.

Wide World.

und the platform on which Baalbek's temples stand, runs this wonderful wall. To build it the ons used five of the biggest blocks of stone ever quarried. Two of these are only five feet shorter the super-giant we saw lying in the quarry. How the ancients ever moved such enormous weights, we'll never know.

The doorway of the Temple of Bacchus, at Baalbek, is fifty feet high, and is the most marvelous
fashioned doorway in all ancient architecture. Some years ago the keystone, over the door, w
shaken loose by an earthquake and fell to the ground. But archeologists have put it back in pla
again.

Much of the smaller, lovelier temple remains. The walls of its great central hall are still unshaken. The doorway, fifty feet high, is the most wonderfully fashioned doorway in all ancient architecture. The roof, alas, has caved in, and many of the roof-slabs are piled upon the floor. About half the columns of the colonnade outside have been hurled down. . . . What a roar there must have been when these huge pillars fell!

But there is a strange stillness now about the ruins. Left to ourselves and undisturbed, we wander where we please, speaking in whispers lest we disturb the silence that haunts the place. Here, there are no guides, no guards. Nobody tries to keep the ruins looking tidy. Grass grows soft and green underfoot. Moss and vines give color to the stones. Birds build their nests in the ancient eaves. In the sheltered corners adventurous cherry trees, sprung from the ancient orchards, still flower.

Yes, there is peace now for Baalbek. And how welcome this peace must be, for few other places in the world have seen such violence as has this place! Time and time again, the earthquakes have rocked Baalbek. One by one, the colossal pillars have crashed down upon the heaving earth.

And endless wars have caused even worse destruction. A hundred battles have been fought upon and around these stones. For fourteen centuries, pagans and Christians and Mohammedans, Crusaders and Arabs, Mongols and Turks, have hacked and burned and robbed this vast treasure-house of marble beauty.

But in recent years, with nothing left worth seizing or destroying, there have been no more battles amid these wonderful ruins. Shattered, but serene, the temples calmly watch the centuries come and go. By day they smile at the tiny mortals, like ourselves, who crawl, awe-struck, over the mossy stones. And at night in the starlight these broken giants, very old, very lonely, and forgotten by the world, sleep and dream of their mighty past.

CHAPTER XVI

ZENOBIA

Who is your favorite woman character in history?

How difficult it is to choose! Many of us would say Joan of Arc. Mary, Queen of Scots, would have a host of friends, and so would her rival, Queen Elizabeth. Perhaps Cleopatra, the glamorous queen of ancient Egypt, would be named; or Marie Antoinette; or Napoleon's wife, the Empress Josephine.

My favorite woman in history is Zenobia.

Zenobia? you ask. . . . But who was she?

She was one of history's greatest heroines. Let me tell you why:

The temples of Baalbek had been standing about sixty years when a baby girl named Zenobia was born in the deserts of eastern Syria. Her father, called Zabbai, was an Arab chieftain ruling over a tribe of Bedouins; her mother, a beautiful Greek woman, proudly claimed Cleopatra as an ancestor. Zenobia's early home was a camel's-hair tent, pitched now in the sands, now beside some oasis in the shadow of the palms.

While Zenobia was still a little girl her parents realized that she had been greatly blessed. Zabbai's people had never before seen such a beautiful child. She had the pale brown skin of the Arabs, and the radiant black eyes of the Greeks. "She's going to be as beautiful as Cleopatra," said her mother.

But she was more than just beautiful. She also had a strong body and a strong mind. By the time she was twelve years old she had learned to ride a camel as fast and far as any man. In her tribe she soon made herself a leader.

During this early part of Zenobia's life there was one oasis in the Syrian desert that stood out above all the others. It was called Palmyra. *This* oasis ruled over the entire eastern half of the country, for it lay right at the place where the great caravan routes crossed. To Palmyra the riches of the East were brought to be marketed and sent on again to the West. Greek and Arab merchants, Jews and Syrians, gathered here. They built luxuri-

Deep in the Syrian Desert, halfway between the Mediterranean and Bagdad, lies the ruined, but still queenly, city of Palmyra. In ancient times, the great caravans, bringing the riches of the East to the Roman West, all met at this oasis. Here, under the inspired rule of one of history's greatest women—Queen Zenobia—Palmyra grew so powerful that it became a rival to Rome itself. Leading her armies in person, Zenobia conquered and annexed all the lands from the Hellespont to Persia, and from Armenia to Egypt. She filled her capital with glorious palaces and temples. The Romans finally overcame Zenobia, and wrecked Palmyra, but the fragments that remain today are proud and beautiful as ever.

ous homes among the palms, and large storehouses for their silks and carpets and dates and grain.

For protection the citizens raised a wall seven miles long around the city. From gate to gate, inside, they laid out broad covered streets lined with rows of stone columns. More columns held up temples and palaces. Everywhere one looked there was a forest of these tall, slender carved pillars. Colonnaded, palm-shaded Palmyra, set in the middle of a desolate desert, found itself, in the year 250 A.D., proud and stately, and famous for its wealth across the world.

This wealth, however, soon aroused the jealousy of the Romans, and they were not willing to let such a queenly city remain free. So a Roman army seized the rich oasis, and made it a part of the empire.

But among the Palmyrans there were many Arabs—a race that loved freedom. They planned to revolt. Prince Odenathus, their young Arab ruler governing in the name of Rome, went secretly into the desert to train the tribesmen for a war of rebellion. There he met Zabbai, the chieftain—and Zenobia.

At once the prince fell in love with this beautiful, high-spirited, wild-riding Bedouin girl, and received Zabbai's consent to marry her. There was a fine wedding and a great wedding feast. Then Zenobia moved to Palmyra to live in a carved stone palace as the wife of Palmyra's ruler.

Rarely in history has a country been blessed with such a queen. In the first place she was very young—only eighteen. And as for her beauty—in a city famous for beautiful women, black-eyed Zenobia was the most beautiful of all. In affairs of state she astonished the ministers with her wisdom. In the army the generals marveled at her bravery.

From the very first day of her marriage to Odenathus, Zenobia, who hated Rome, took a leading part in his plots to free Palmyra from Roman rule. She learned to drill the Arab soldiers herself, to lead them in charges, to hold reviews, to make military plans. She learned to spend days at a time on a horse. She slept on the ground, ate with the officers.

Soon the chance came for her to lead into battle this army she had trained—though not, at first, against the Romans. To the east of Syria were the Persians, a strong and warlike people who were threatening to attack Palmyra. Zenobia, directed by Odenathus, decided to attack first. Led by her in person, the Palmyrans marched secretly across the desert and fell upon the unsuspecting Persian king. His soldiers fled, and the king became a fugitive.

With Persia at their mercy, Zenobia and Odenathus dared attack, next, an army of Rome itself, posted in the north of Syria. This army, too, they destroyed.

Amazed and frightened by these victories, all the states neighboring on the Syrian desert began to join forces with Palmyra. But at the very height of this success, Odenathus was murdered. Left to rule alone, Zenobia promptly named herself absolute monarch of her country, and then added the title "Queen of the East."

With this new title, Zenobia looked about for new worlds to conquer. There was Egypt, rich, civilized Egypt, the land of her ancestor, Cleopatra. She sent 70,000 of her soldiers to the Nile, and after one victorious battle they seized the whole country.

Nothing now seemed to be able to stand against Zenobia. Astride her white racing camel, her purple cloak flying, she led her Arab cavalry back and forth across the desert from battle to battle, from victory to victory. Syria, Palestine, Babylon, Arabia, Persia, Asia Minor, Egypt, all went down before this Bedouin Queen and accepted her as their supreme master. By the year 270, when Zenobia was forty years old, nearly half of Rome's former empire was in the grasp of Zenobia's strong brown hands. The world had never before seen such an all-conquering woman warrior. Nor has it since.

With so much homage, wealth, and glory pouring into Palmyra, the city promised to become the Rome of Asia. New palaces were built. Higher and more glorious rose the temples. In and out the city gates the camel caravans, laden with riches, moved in ever-swelling streams. To Zenobia's court came artists and poets from Europe and the East.

149

Over all this pomp and splendor Zenobia ruled with a proud hand. Wearing her gold helmet, armed with a spear, she rode fearlessly in her chariot about her marble capital. Everywhere the people cheered her—the soldiers most of all.

There was, however, a great black cloud moving across Zenobia's thoughts . . . her fear of Rome's power and Rome's pride. Zenobia knew that Rome, alarmed at Palmyra's rebellion, victories, and growing might, was preparing to fight and fight to regain the mastery of the eastern world.

So Zenobia prepared too. She increased the size of her army. She built fortresses on her frontiers. The whole country strained to arm itself against the day when the final clash must come.

And that day came at last. The Romans sent a general and their best troops to humble and kill Zenobia, and destroy her power. But the Romans did not know how great was Zenobia's military skill. When the two armies met it was the *Roman* general who was humbled, and the *Roman* soldiers who were killed.

Rome did not give up. A second army was sent against Zenobia. And this time the general was Aurelian, Rome's foremost soldier.

In Aurelian, Zenobia met her match. Face to face with his veteran troops, the Arab cavalry that had swept all before them from the Black Sea to the Nile, went down. Zenobia, fighting and retreating, moved back into the walls of Palmyra with what was left of her forces, and locked the gates against the invaders. And there she swore she would die rather than surrender.

Aurelian offered to spare the city and the Queen's life if she would open the gates peacefully. Zenobia mockingly refused.

So the siege began. The Romans attacked the walls savagely. Zenobia's troops, driven to desperate courage by fear, fought back. Their Queen marched defiantly along the ramparts, encouraging her soldiers, fighting with her own spear where there was need.

But courage was not enough. Food was necessary, too—and, before long, all the food gave out. Zenobia saw her army melting away from starvation. She realized that unless rescue came Palmyra was doomed.

150

Palmyra's architects liked to adorn all the city's public buildings with columns. Around the Central Temple courtyard they raised 370 columns. Here, in this picture, are a few that the Romans did not hurl down. (On the projecting stones, about halfway up the column, were once placed marble statues of Palmyra's great men). The city's Grand Avenue was lined with 1500 columns—two rows on each side. Everywhere one looked, there were forests of these tall, slender marble pillars. Though it was set in the middle of a desolate desert, Palmyra found itself, in the year 250 A.D., famous across the world for its wealth.

With so much homage, wealth, and commerce, Palmyra promised to become the Rome of Asi Higher and more glorious rose the temples. In and out the city gates the camel caravans, lade with riches, moved in ever-swelling streams. To Zenobia's court came artists and poets from E rope and the East. Rarely in history have the arts flourished as they did in Palmyra, during the reign of Zenobia.

She resolved to try to escape from the besieged city and seek aid from Persia.

Waiting for a dark night, she had herself let down by ropes from the walls, right into the Roman camp. A spy had several swift camels ready. Mounting one of these, the Queen, with a few followers, crept out past the Roman sentries. Then, with only the desert stars to guide her, she turned eastward toward Persia, and spurred her camel till it sped across the sands faster than a race horse.

All night Zenobia rode. At dawn, she and her little band hid in a ravine, and waited till darkness. Traveling only at night, dodging bands of Romans, avoiding villages, suffering from thirst, the heroic Queen rode on. And as she rode she kept thinking, Did the Romans know that she had escaped? Were they already in pursuit?

Dawn, on the fifth morning, broke in the east and revealed Zenobia, with the very life of her empire at stake, still flying forward. She had ridden many miles that last night without a stop. She was weary from the strain, but dared not rest.

Anxiously she peered ahead through the early light, searching for the Euphrates River. This river was her goal, for on the other side she knew she'd find the Persians, and they would help her.

The sun rose, and to her great joy Zenobia caught sight of a long line of palms two miles ahead . . . the palms along the river bank.

And then she looked backward. And there, only a few hundred yards away, she saw a troop of Romans racing after her.

With a cry of despair, Zenobia—not stopping to wonder how her enemies had learned of her flight—lashed her mount to the utmost speed . . . she must—she must—reach that river!

With every ounce of her strength she urged her weary camel forward—faster, faster—she could hear the shouts of her pursuers drawing ever closer behind. She prayed to her gods that there would be a boat waiting to receive her.

The river was now less than a mile away. In a few moments more, Zenobia and her companions reached the bank and flung themselves to the ground.

American Colony Photographs.

For miles across the desert we find the wreckage of Palmyra—as it was left in the year 275 by the vengeful Romans. After Zenobia's capture, the Romans left a small garrison to guard the town. This garrison the people of Palmyra slaughtered. Wrathful, the Roman general returned, once more fell upon the city, and this time showed no mercy. The entire population was killed. The palaces, temples, walls, and rows of columns along

Frantically they looked about for a boat. . . . The only boat in sight was a fisherman's skiff some distance from shore. Zenobia cried out to the boatman to come and fetch her—and in the name of heaven, *hurry*!

Puzzled by this handful of people shouting at him so violently from the bank, the boatman turned his boat and rowed toward them.

It had now become a race between the Romans and the fisherman. . . .

The Romans won.

Just as the boat touched shore, Aurelian's men dashed up to the bank, killed Zenobia's escorts, and seized the helpless Queen.

Sixty seconds more, and she would have been saved!

When the besieged people of Palmyra, now half-dead from hunger, heard that Zenobia was a captive in Aurelian's camp, they lost all hope. They opened the gates and surrendered the city.

Aurelian felt that with Zenobia in chains there was no need to punish the citizens who had merely followed her commands. He left a few archers in charge and turned toward Rome, taking Zenobia with him as his prize.

But just as he was crossing from Asia to Europe, word came that the Palmyrans had again revolted and massacred his entire garrison.

Wrathful, Aurelian faced about and rushed back to the treacherous city. Like a thunderclap he fell upon it. This time he showed no mercy. The entire population was slaughtered by the vengeful Romans.

And they were not content just to kill. In their rage they wrecked the palaces, the temples, the walls, the rows of columns along the avenues. They had found Palmyra one of the proudest and loveliest cities on earth. They left it a smoking waste.

And Zenobia? There are several legends about her end. One story tells that when she heard Palmyra had been destroyed she refused to touch food for thirty days, and killed herself by starvation.

But another story says Aurelian carried her, very much alive, on to Rome. And there, bound in gold chains, the unhappy Queen was forced to walk behind Aurelian's chariot as he rode through the streets in triumph. The same story tells that she was allowed to live on in the capital, as a Roman matron, and that she died there years later, honored by everyone.

Now—having read about this wonder-city in the Syrian desert—you say you'd like to go there?

Then so you shall.

We pass right through it on our way from Baalbek to Babylon.

In our motorcar we leave the fertile fields of western Syria behind, and roll eastward into the wilderness along the ancient caravan trail. For hours we meet nothing but sand. Then we climb to the top of a pass in the barren hills—and see below, rising close beside a forest of palms, Palmyra's ghostly ruins— ruins of palaces, ruins of temples, ruins of Zenobia's once-glorious city.

All day we explore the place. Unlike Baalbek, where everything is built close together on a single platform, the ruins of Palmyra spread for miles across the desert. But, as at Baalbek, there is a miserable mud village huddled against the wonderful tumbled stones. The Palmyra villagers have built into their mud huts carved blocks of marble from Zenobia's palace, and thirty-ton drums from the fluted columns of the Temple of the Sun.

This temple, built by Zenobia, must have rivaled Baalbek's in splendor. About half of it remains for us to see.

We climb the temple steps. Here Zenobia talked with her ministers. We pass beneath the Arch of Triumph. Beneath this Arch, Zenobia marched off to war, followed by her worshipful troops; and returned, laden with treasure and captives from a dozen conquered nations.

We walk down the Grand Avenue. It was once lined with rows of columns—1500 in all—two rows on each side. Scores of these columns, despite Aurelian and his Romans, still proudly stand. As we move along the colonnade we can picture the streams of

At the end of the Grand Avenue stood the Arch of Triumph. Beneath it Queen Zenobia and her all-conquering troops marched forth to victory after victory. Today the small colony of Arabs who dwell near the ruins refuse to go near the Arch at night. They say the ghost of Zenobia rides beneath it after dark.

people that once passed here—and the shops kept by Jews, Greeks, Arabs, selling all the riches of the eastern world.

But today, instead of piles of silks and carpets, we see only piles of sand, for sandstorms, blowing for centuries upon the wreckage of Palmyra, have half-buried it. What treasures might be found if the waves of sand were dug away!

In modern times, Syria is held by France, and a company of French Foreign Legionnaires are camped at Palmyra to guard the caravan trails that still cross here as in the ancient days. When the desert sun is hot in the sky, these Legionnaires (if there's no fighting to do) stay indoors to escape the heat. But when night comes with its cooling wind they wander through the ruins, through the Temple of the Sun, beneath the Arch of Triumph, down the sand-carpeted Grand Avenue. On my previous trip to Palmyra I often went along with them on these starlight walks. One wants company then, for Palmyra seems so full of eerie shadows at night . . . and there is such stillness everywhere.

The Legionnaires told me a story I quite believe. They said that no Arab from the village will go near the ruins after dark. And for this reason: Among them the legend has lasted through the centuries that often in the dead of night Zenobia's ghost, astride her ghostly camel, goes pacing down the Grand Avenue— her gold helmet faintly shining, her arms bare, her cloak flying in the wind, her black eyes pleading with everyone she passes to seize his spear and follow her to the walls and hurl back the attacks of Aurelian's men . . . and the Arabs are afraid.

Once, just from curiosity, I walked alone, late at night, along the columned street, hoping Zenobia would ride by, hoping I might see the ghost of my favorite woman character in history—hoping I might find out if the Arabs' legend were true.

The wind moaned through the columns—the bats flew past—a hyena howled in the distance. . . . But Zenobia never came.

Orient and Occident.

After riding for hours across the flat and barren wilderness, travelers are always surprised to come upon Palmyra's rows of ruined and lonely columns, springing, as if by magic, right out of the sands.

CHAPTER XVII

THE PRINCE AND THE FLYING CARPET

It's sunset.

Straight ahead of us, three miles away across the flat and heat-scorched desert, we see a cluster of domes and towers all covered with gold. The domes are shining so brightly they seem to be on fire. Groves of palm trees press close around them, trees that wave in the hot desert wind. A broad river, lined with gardens, flows near by. Overhead is the burning sunset sky.

You say: This looks just like a colored picture of Bagdad from the *Arabian Nights*.

Well, it *should* look like Bagdad.

It *is* Bagdad.

We have traveled on in our motorcar four hundred miles eastward from Palmyra, along the ancient caravan trail—the same trail Queen Zenobia followed when she was fleeing to the Euphrates River seeking aid from Persia. We crossed the Euphrates on a ferry boat, and rolled on toward the Tigris, one hundred miles beyond. For Bagdad is on the Tigris.

Alongside camel caravans we reach the city in the early twilight, and drive up to the market square. Here we park our car . . . we want to explore Bagdad on foot. We know that Bagdad, a thousand years ago, was one of the richest, most romantic, most glorious cities in history. . . . What would we find now?

Right away, to our delight, we find that all around the square are rows of little shops looking exactly like those described in the *Arabian Nights*. In each shop a merchant, large of waist, turbaned, bearded, colorfully gowned, sits cross-legged in the midst of piles of flaming silk and scarlet leather shoes and flowers and melons and dates and pomegranates. . . . "There was a certain merchant of Bagdad of a very jealous disposition, having a wife who was famous for her perfect beauty"—That's the way the *Arabian Nights* stories often began. Well, here is the merchant. We look around for the beautiful wife. We see several women in the square, but they all wear veils, so we can't tell whether they have perfect beauty or not.

159

Moving along the street, we come to a shop that sells only water-jars. Some are huge as a man and make us think of the story of Ali Baba and the Forty Thieves.

Next door is a lamp-seller. In his shop we see lamps of bronze and lamps of silver. No garish electric lights here, no smelly kerosene lamps with cheap glass chimneys—nothing so unbeautiful as that. Only lamps of graceful shapes made by the hand of an artist. These burn sweet oil of olives and give forth a soft and mellow glow. It was just such a lamp as one of these that Aladdin owned. Aladdin rubbed it, and made a wish—and *look* what happened! Remembering this, we buy a little blue lamp— and rub it—and make a wish. . . We wish that a white horse with wings would fly down from the clouds and take us for a sky-ride around the golden minarets. But instead of winged horses, two donkeys trot past the door, and bray. We give the lamp back to the dealer and tell him it's no good.

Such a clatter and hammering we hear down one narrow alley! We've come to the coppersmiths' market. Gleaming piles of copper trays, pitchers, boxes, fill the shelves in each shop. Bagdad's coppersmiths have been famous for a thousand years.

Everywhere are Persian carpets for sale—little ones hardly bigger than this book-page, used for prayer rugs; big ones fifty feet long, woven for the throne room of a king; but all of them rich in color and wonderfully soft.

What is that lovely fragrance floating toward us on the wind? We soon find out. We've wandered into the street of the perfume-sellers. The odor of perfume is so strong it makes our heads swim.

The people in the streets are mostly Arab men and boys, all dressed in long loose gowns. The few women we see wear heavy robes of silk that enclose them from head to foot. We're in a Moslem land again—that's why the women are veiled, with only their black eyes showing.

The streets themselves are narrow and unpaved. Clouds of dust rise up. Nobody seems to care. The men push and shout. The women cling close to the walls to escape from the lines of

160

As we approach Bagdad we see, ahead, a cluster of domes and towers covered with gold. The domes are shining so brightly they seem to be on fire. They rise above the greatest and most beautiful mosque in Bagdad. No Christian is allowed to enter even the courtyard. These golden minarets, the white Arab houses, and the palm trees, all bright beneath the desert sun, make us realize that we have come to the city of the Arabian Nights.

camels and donkeys plodding past. The donkey drivers all shout *ha-a-a* at their animals, which in Arabian donkey-language means *Keep moving.*

Had we reached Bagdad for sunset we would have heard another kind of cry rising across the city. Bagdad, like Jedda, has scores of mosques, and from their minarets, at the sunset hour, scores of muezzins cry, *Allah, Allah—God is great—come to prayer.*

The ways of the western world may some day destroy the romance of Bagdad. But that unhappy day has not yet come. When, later that evening, we see the starlight shining upon the Tigris River, and the golden domes and minarets gleaming softly overhead, it takes small effort for us to believe that we are still in the city of Haroun-al-Raschid—a city from the gorgeous past.

I have led you to Bagdad for two reasons: first, to see Bagdad itself; and next, to see the wonder cities from ancient times that lie close by. Bagdad is in the very cradle of civilization. All up and down the valleys of the Tigris and Euphrates are to be found the ruins of mighty capitals, some of them 5000 years old.

Two of the greatest of these once-proud cities—Samarra and Babylon—we must visit. I have a beautiful plan which, if it works, will enable us to see them with the best and most charming of guides—the young King of Bagdad himself. I know him well. He loves adventure. Perhaps he may be willing to take part in the adventure I am going to suggest.

I'll tell you, first, about him.

Up to 1918 all of Arabia, including Bagdad, was part of Turkey. But during the World War of 1914-1918 the Arabs, led by their great chieftain, Prince Feisal, revolted against Turkey and fought on the side of the Allies. When the war was over, the victorious Allies carved several new states from the defeated Turkish empire, and among them was one called Iraq (E-rack). To Iraq was given the valleys of the Tigris and Euphrates—the country ruled over, 2500 years ago, by ancient Babylon. Bagdad was made the capital, and Prince Feisal was made king. When last I visited this city, King Feisal still ruled there, and had won for himself the love and respect of all his people.

The King at that time had one son, sixteen years old, named Ghazi. This boy—the Crown Prince—was known as the Prince of Bagdad.

Ghazi, I soon found out, had become famous throughout the country as a young sportsman. He rode a horse better than any other boy in Bagdad. He swam, and boxed, with unusual skill.

But he had little interest in his books, and disliked to study.

So, on the boy's sixteenth birthday, King Feisal sent him to a military school where books were as important as sports.

The first month went by, and Ghazi brought home his report card to show his father. Printed upon it the King read:

Swimming	A
Rifle Practice	A
Football	A
Polo	A
Reading	X
Writing	Y
Arithmetic	Z

The King was very angry. "Can't you get at least a K or a Q in arithmetic?" he asked. "Is Z the best you can do?"

The boy's pride was hurt. The next month he studied very hard, and this month he brought back a B.

King Feisal beamed. "Ghazi," he said, "I'm so pleased over that B I'll give you anything you ask for, as a reward. And every month you bring back a B, I'll make you a fine present. What would you like to have *this* month?"

"That beautiful black Arabian race horse I saw at the races," said Ghazi.

The horse cost the King $5000. But he kept his promise, and the horse was brought to the happy young prince. Ghazi leaped upon it and went galloping down the garden lanes, riding like a wild desert Bedouin.

The next month went by, and Ghazi said to himself: "See here—if I can get a $5000 horse for a *B*—what can I get for an *A*?"

So he studied twice as hard and was rewarded with an *A*.

This time he said: "Father, don't be alarmed. I don't want a $10,000 present for my *A*. But I'll tell you what I *do* want:

"You don't know it, Father, but I've gone air-minded lately. I spend an hour every afternoon, after drill, at the airport, watching the army flyers go through all their wonderful stunts in the air. And yesterday, while I was watching, a beautiful foreign plane flew in from the west. Its colors were black and gold and scarlet. Painted on it was the name *The Flying Carpet*. When it stopped, two of the funniest-looking Americans climbed out. I hear they've come from California, and are flying around the world. Father, for my *A*, I want to meet those two Americans, and ask them how it feels to fly across oceans and deserts and mountains, aboard a flying carpet."

King Feisal was pleased to grant his son's request. So the two Americans were summoned to the palace.

One of the Americans—you've guessed it—was myself. The other was my flying companion named Moye Stephens. We had flown in from Palmyra and landed at the airport, but we had not known that the Prince of Bagdad was there to watch us land.

On meeting Ghazi we found him to be a most likable boy, quite small in stature, but agile and graceful as a young desert deer. He had fine black eyes and dark Arab skin. He stood very straight in his military uniform.

The Prince asked us in perfect English how we liked Bagdad.

"It's just as I hoped it would be," I replied. "Yesterday, coming in at sunset, and seeing the golden domes and minarets all shining, I knew I'd come to the city of the *Arabian Nights*."

"You two have been everywhere, I suppose," said the Prince. "No doubt you've met lots of kings and queens. But I'd like to ask if you've ever met another prince like *me*?"

"No," I answered. "You're the only prince like *you*, Ghazi, I've ever met."

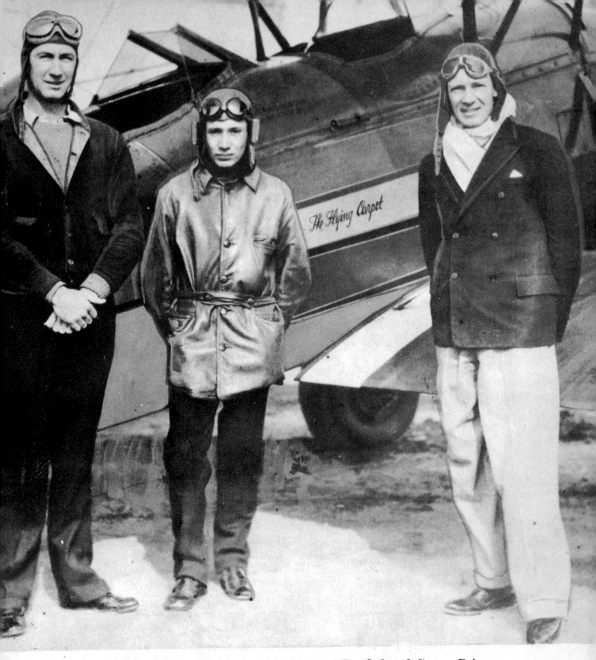

Prince Ghazi (center), the sixteen-year-old Prince of Bagdad and Crown Prince of Iraq, gets ready to explore his country aboard the Flying Carpet. Pilot Moye Stephens stands at the left, author Halliburton at the right. Not long after this picture was made, Prince Ghazi's father, King Feisal, died, and the boy became King Ghazi I of Iraq. On *our* visit to Bagdad we find that he is still king. With him as our guide, we visit Samarra and Babylon.

"Well," he said, "now that you've met me, I want to tell you about me. I want to fly. I want to be an aviator. Every day I watch the planes at the airport . . . flying must be the best sport in the world.

"And now," he added, with a twinkle in his eyes, "now that you've met me, and now that you know how keen I am to go flying, and now that you have an airplane out there in the hangar . . . what are you going to do next?"

I knew what I should say to *that*: "The next thing, Prince Ghazi, I intend to do, is to take the Prince of Bagdad aboard the Flying Carpet and show him Arabia from the air."

The boy's eyes danced with delight. "Oh, *will* you?" he exclaimed.

King Feisal agreed to let Ghazi go—the next morning—but made us promise, by our eyes, by our Prophet, by our beards, that we would have the boy back at his military school by six o'clock roll call.

We promised—by our beards—that we would have him back.

And so, next morning, Ghazi arrived at the airport in a royal motorcar. As he jumped out his face was shining. . . . His first airplane ride . . . and in such a gleaming golden plane.

He put on my flying helmet and goggles and jacket, and climbed in beside me in the front cockpit.

With the throttle wide open, Moye raced us down the field and into the air. In a moment all Bagdad was spread below.

"Oh, look!" shouted Ghazi above the motor, pointing down to the city, "there's the palace, and the gardens, and the river, and the race track!" I had to hold onto him by the pants to keep him from leaning too far overboard.

In a moment more, Ghazi suggested that since we had seen Bagdad he would now like to go somewhere else.

"Let's go to Babylon," he said. "I'm the Prince of Babylon, too—and I've never seen that city from the air. It's only sixty miles away."

Happy to obey, we turned south toward the Euphrates, and flew on till we reached the ruins of the greatest city in ancient history. For miles and miles, 2500 years ago, its marvelous walls and gates and palaces stretched along both sides of the river. (Since then the river has moved a half-mile away, and left the city high and dry.)

Below, we could see the endless ruins scattered about on every side.

Leaving Babylon, we flew next to a beautiful grove of palms on the river bank, a grove which marks the site, so people say, of the Garden of Eden.

And from the garden we sped on to a dozen other places of interest. In fact there were so many things to see in this wonderful country that we forgot about our promise—by our beards—to have Ghazi home by six. And the first thing we knew the sun was touching the horizon—and Bagdad was fifty miles away.

Pilot Stephens, realizing how late it was, turned the plane about, and raced with the gathering night, home to Bagdad.

The city came in sight—there was the airport. Stevens prepared to land . . . it was twenty minutes to six.

But Ghazi, seeing us headed toward the earth, seized my arm in alarm. "Please don't land yet," he begged. "What's the hurry? We still have twenty minutes. That's just time enough for one last favor I want you to do for me."

"All right," I said, "But please hurry up and tell me what it is . . . twenty minutes is very little time. King Feisal will never forgive us if we're late."

"It's this," he said. "Do you see that big building down there by the river? That's my military schoolhouse. Now please, please, let's climb way up in the sky and do a *zoom* at my schoolhouse . . . because I've told all my fellow students that if they hear a red and gold airplane zooming overhead, they must all go out and look, because up there in that airplane, that's *me*!"

Stephens—the best zoomer in the world—agreed. He spiraled up to 3000 feet and dived back down over the roof of the school. And just as Ghazi hoped, his fellow students all came rushing out to behold their Prince roaring overhead aboard a flying carpet.

We landed just in time. As the bugle was blowing six o'clock at the military school, our motorcar dashed up to the front gate. The Prince jumped out. He had not one moment to lose. Even so, he turned to bid us good-by: "Oh, Mr. Halliburton, Mr. Stephens," he said, "that was the most fun I ever had in all my life. . . . Let's go every day! The Prince of Bagdad aboard the Flying Carpet—it was just like the story book. Good afternoon."

167

Courtesy Royal Flying C

A thousand feet below our airplane we see the ruins of the ancient city of Samarra. The ri of sand that were once walls and houses make a vast checkerboard across the desert. In center of the ruins is a small modern town. In the foreground rise the crumbling walls of a o great mosque. Beside these walls we notice a curious tower spiraling upward. It's built in same form as the Tower of Babel. The trenches zigzagging across the picture were dug in 1 by the Turkish army trying to defend Samarra against the English invasion.

That night in the darkness I climbed up to the flat roof of our hotel. Overhead arched the starry Arabian sky. And across the sky there sailed the crescent moon—the symbol of Arabia and of all Moslem lands. I looked up at that crescent moon and I wondered to myself if that crescent might not be the spirit of the ancient, original flying carpet come back again. . . . I wondered if, aboard that carpet, there might not be, riding across the sky, the spirits of Haroun-al-Raschid and Scheherezade themselves, come back from the *Arabian Nights* to bless Bagdad, the city they have made immortal; and to bless, sleeping in his hard military bed, little Prince Ghazi—Prince Ghazi, the heir to all the glories of Arabia's past, who for one lovely day had lived a story from the story book.

168

CHAPTER XVIII

BABYLON

My flight in the Flying Carpet with Prince Ghazi took place several years ago. Not long afterward, King Feisal died very suddenly. "The old King is dead," cried the people. "Long live the new King!" The Prince of Bagdad became King Ghazi I of Iraq.

And on our present visit to Bagdad we find that he is still king.

I'm going to be very bold and ask him if he remembers his first airplane ride, with Stephens and me. My beautiful plan, mentioned in the last chapter, is this: If he *does* remember, I'll ask him to ride again, aboard a private passenger plane with all of us, and act as our guide when we visit the wonder cities of his country.

Through his secretary, I am able to tell King Ghazi of our plan. To our delight he sends word back that he does indeed remember the Flying Carpet and his flight aboard it. And he says that he will be happy to go with us in our air-liner and show us whatever we wish to see.

Next morning we meet him at the airport. He looks older and far more serious than when I saw him last. But there is the same twinkle in his eye. He is still small and slender in stature, and still wearing a military uniform.

The King's own pilot sits at the controls.

"Samarra first," commands King Ghazi—and away we go to the north, toward the famous city of Samarra.

Samarra is as old as recorded history. Several thousand years ago it covered forty square miles. Now it's only a small walled town in the center of a sea of ruins. We fly over it before landing, and look down at the miles and miles of crumbled streets that make a gigantic checkerboard upon the desert. Standing by itself, off to one side, we notice the decaying walls of an ancient and once-vast mosque. The ruins of the mosque itself hold no interest, but the tower rising above them is one of the most wonderful towers ever built by man. To get a good look at it our pilot circles twice around. We see a tall, cone-like structure 160 feet

169

high, with a roadway spiraling up the outside. It is called a zig-gurat, and is the only tower from Babylonian times that has survived the centuries and still stands.

We land. The King, walking between lines of salaaming Arabs, leads us to the ziggurat and up its circular ramp.

It is an exciting and dangerous climb. There's no railing, and the paving is full of holes. The King tells us that he once wanted to ride his horse up this spiral path. A cavalry officer, testing the safety of the path for horses, reached the peak on horseback. There a hawk flew out from a hole in the masonry. Startled, the horse reared, slipped over the edge, and, still carrying the rider, crashed to the ground. Both horse and rider were killed.

The King's attendant has brought along a big lunch basket. Perched on the top of this high tower we open it. Out comes roast chicken, and olives, and peaches, and melons. The citizens of modern Samarra have also prepared a feast for the King and his guests. Several of them struggle up the dizzy incline carrying platters of rice and curried lamb. We are soon bulging with these delights.

We could spend all day exploring Samarra, but the ruins of a city much greater than Samarra await us. We follow King Ghazi down the ziggurat, climb into our plane again, and fly on south across the desert.

Both Bagdad and Samarra are on the Tigris River. This river is soon left far behind, and the Euphrates comes in sight ahead. In a few minutes more, King Ghazi asks us to look down at the jumble of sand hills and trenches on the ground below. "There's Babylon," he says.

Babylon! What romance and wonder that name holds! Some 600 years before the birth of Christ, Babylon the Great had several million people. It was New York and London and Paris and Rome, all put together, in the ancient world. Its wall ran for *sixty miles* around the city. This wall, made of sun-dried bricks, was 300 feet high, 80 feet thick, and had 250 towers. It was pierced by 100 gates made of brass.

city of Babylon crumbled into dust many centuries ago. But this one single monument from
ylonian times still stands—at Samarra, 70 miles from Bagdad. Though made only of sun-dried
k, this 160-foot tower has withstood the assaults of man and nature for 2500 years. It too
ld have crumbled, like the other Babylonian buildings, had not the Mohammedans, when they
t over this country 1200 years ago, decided to turn the tower into a minaret and build a
que at its feet. And so for another thousand years the tower was kept in a good state of
ir. For ten centuries the muezzins each day trudged up the spiral path to give their call to
er from the summit. Within the last two hundred years the mosque has fallen into decay,
the great tower has once more been abandoned. Even so, we can still climb to the top by means
he spiral path. Notice the black hole in the tower-wall, just beneath the summit. This is a
way through which a flight of inside steps climbs to the roof. On our visit to Samarra, King
hazi guides us up the path, and at the summit of the tower shares with us his royal lunch.

To this imperial city, the Babylonians dragged the people of Jerusalem after the destruction of Solomon's Temple.

In this city Daniel was thrown into the lion's den. But from this den—if you remember the Bible story—Daniel, having the Lord's protection, came forth unharmed. We wonder which one of these holes in the earth below was Daniel's den of lions.

In this city King Belshazzar held his famous feast, and saw the handwriting on the wall.

In this city was the Tower of Babel built; and the Hanging Gardens, always numbered among the Seven Wonders of the ancient world.

Twenty-five hundred years ago, this Babylon, this Golden City, was the center of the universe, feared and envied by every race of people on earth.

How far has this mighty Babylon fallen!

Again we land, on the desert outside the city. We ride back to the ruins on donkeys. Ghazi rides on a donkey too—the King of Iraq on a donkey! But he laughs so merrily we soon forget that he's the King.

Archeologists have spent years uncovering Babylon's buried glory. Avenues down which conquerors rode in their chariots have been restored. Walls covered with colored tile figures of lions have been brought to light. The ruin of each temple and tower and palace has been marked.

Led by our young King, we walk down the walled avenues. We know that down these same streets there once flowed throngs of people—soldiers, priests, princes, pilgrims, merchants, slaves—who had traveled to Babylon to enjoy the astonishing sights of this world-capital.

We come to the ruins of the Tower of Babel. Only the foundations remain. This tower was built in the form of our Samarra ziggurat—but many times higher. Its builders dreamed of mak-

...y we find Babylon, once the greatest city on earth, a sea of ruins and sand dunes. Five hun-
...years before the birth of Christ, these sand dunes were magnificent palaces and temples.
...nd Babylon ran a wall sixty miles long and *300 feet high*. Scarcely a trace of this wall re-
...s. But by digging away the covering of sand, archeologists have uncovered splendid build-
...like these. This one was probably a tower guarding the entrance-gate to one of the Grand
Avenues.

ing it so tall that its summit would reach unto heaven. The Bible
tells that the Lord became angry at this challenge and decided to
punish the builders. So He caused each group of masons to speak
a language which no other group could understand. Then all
work on the tower had to stop.

The King takes us next to the palace of Babylon's most famous ruler—Nebuchadnezzar. It's only a hole in the ground now,
but 2500 years ago it was perhaps the largest and costliest
building in the world. Upon one of the walls of this building
Belshazzar saw the words—MENE, MENE, TEKEL, UPHAR-
SIN—which Daniel said meant, "God hath numbered thy

kingdom, and finished it, Belshazzar. Thou art weighed in the balance, and art found wanting. Thy kingdom is divided, and given to the Medes and Persians." ... And that same night was Belshazzar slain.

King Ghazi takes us, last of all, to the site of the Hanging Gardens.

When Demetrius and Diomede, in 250 B.C., were on their Grand Tour of the world and were visiting the great sights of their day, the Hanging Gardens, like the Temple of Ephesus, the Colossus, and the Pyramids, were considered one of the Seven Wonders. And Diomede would have liked his son to see the Gardens. But Babylon was too far away from Greece, and Diomede could not spare the time for such a long journey. Even so, he hoped that some day Demetrius would go to Babylon and see this Seventh Wonder.

What made the Gardens so wonderful? Did they really hang? I'll explain.

When Nebuchadnezzar became king of Babylon he married a princess from Media. Media was a country to the north, and famous for its fruits and flowers. In flat, rainless Babylon the Princess longed for the green beauty of her native hills.

So, to make his wife happy, Nebuchadnezzar resolved to build for her a garden more beautiful than any garden ever dreamed of in Media.

First of all, in the center of the palace grounds, he raised a great platform, a quarter of a mile on each side and fifty feet high. Then on this platform he piled up a series of terraces that grew smaller as they climbed. The topmost terrace was only 200 feet square, but it rose to a height of 350 feet—as high as a thirty-story skyscraper. So the Gardens didn't really "hang," as you see. They were just built high in the air.

When, at last, the terraces were finished, Nebuchadnezzar had thousands of tons of rich earth carried up to them. Deep flower beds were made along the broad balconies, and, in these beds, flowers and vines and fruit trees were planted in such numbers that the whole pyramid was half hidden under a green blanket of foliage.

After a drawing by Joseph Boggs Beale, courtesy Modern Galleries, Philadelphia.

e Hanging Gardens of Babylon—the seventh of the Seven Wonders of the ancient world. Baby-
's greatest ruler, Nebuchadnezzar, wishing to please his wife, raised this enormous pile of stone
races beside the Euphrates River. And upon these terraces he planted a forest of tropical trees
d flowers and vines. Water was pumped from the river to the top terrace and allowed to flow
wn into the flowerbeds below. In this picture the artist shows Nebuchadnezzar escorting his
een about the marvelous garden. Notice the elephants and camels that have been able to climb
the inclined ramps to the second and third terraces. In the days of Babylon's glory, the
phrates flowed through the center of the city. (Later the river changed its course, and now
ws a half-mile away from the ruins.) On the opposite bank we see the famous Tower of Babel
ring into the clouds. We know from the Bible that this mighty Tower was never completed.
en so, in this picture it seems 1000 feet high. Beyond, on the horizon, loom the military towers
of the city wall.

But how was the King going to supply water to his Gardens, in this hot, dry climate?

This problem, too, he solved. On the top terrace he had a huge tank built, and into this tank he pumped water from the Euphrates River. In pipes, this water flowed down from terrace to terrace. Overhead sprinklers gave an artificial rain. To keep the water from leaking through the floors, each flower bed was lined with lead. Inside the terraces were beautiful apartments where Nebuchadnezzar and his Queen spent their days, surrounded by their flowers and trees and birds.

History does not tell us whether the Hanging Gardens cured the Queen's homesickness for her native land. But we know that Nebuchadnezzar certainly did his best.

We are sorry to leave these famous ruins, but we must not tarry longer, for it's getting late. The pilot requests us to return to our plane at once, in order that he may deliver the King safely home before dark.

We speed back to the Bagdad airport. There King Ghazi, the modern King of Babylon, seems as happy over the day's adventures as we ourselves are. With a gay smile, he says good-by, But before he goes he signs a picture of himself for each of us, and invites us to call on him if ever we come again to Bagdad.

We watch him get in his big motorcar and ride away. And every one of us is thinking the same thing . . . if all kings were as human, as charming, as friendly, as *that*—what a wonderful world this would be!

CHAPTER XIX

HOME OF THE NIGHTINGALES

We're now on our way to Isfahan—the home of the nightingales.

If you'll look at the map on page 96, you'll find Bagdad and Babylon marked upon it, and King Ghazi's country of Iraq. To the east of Iraq you'll find Persia. In the center of Persia is Isfahan.

Isfahan is one of the romance-cities of the world. Throughout all the Orient, Isfahan is famous for the turquoise-colored domes of its wonderful mosques. The city is also famous for its rose gardens, and orchards, and fields of flowers. In the spring— and spring has come now to Persia—Isfahan is half hidden in blossoms, and perfumed with lilacs and violets. At this time the nightingales go there by the thousand to build their nests in the trees and hedges of the gardens, and sing their hearts out all night long.

Did you ever see a nightingale? I never had until I went to Persia. Just to *look* at one you'd never believe that such a colorless little bird could have such a golden voice. The head and back and wings of a Persian male nightingale (the females only listen) are a dull reddish-brown. Its breast is gray. No one would notice him were all the birds to pass by in review. But wait till this dull-colored bird begins to sing! Then all rivals are forgotten. Such marvelous melody comes from that tiny voice! His song is a love song to his mate, a song filled now with joy, now with tears. In whatever garden a nightingale builds his nest, that garden is blessed and made beautiful. Every tree from which he sings falls in love with the singer. The rose bushes and the jasmine bowers burst into flower when, on moonlight nights, he pours forth the magic of his serenade.

We're lucky to reach Persia in the month of May. Most of this country is on a high and rather barren table-land. All winter the land is bleak and frozen. In summer it becomes a rocky desert. But now, in May—what loveliness! Look at this flat

177

plain we're motoring across. Did you ever see so many flowers? Here carpets of scarlet poppies wave in the wind. There a whole hillside is covered with purple iris. Yonder, near the village, that splash of white is a pear orchard. Of course, this sea of flowers lasts only a few brief weeks. But during this time the blossoming countryside, and the rose gardens of the town, turn Persia into a paradise of color and perfume and poetry.

No wonder the nightingales—in May—think that Persia is the best land in the world.

We left Bagdad by motor car three days ago. Over towering mountain passes we have climbed, down into deep valleys. The road has been fearfully bad—suited for camel caravans rather than automobiles.

But now, at last, we are approaching a city. Surrounding it are groves of flowering trees and gardens. And rising over everything, from out of the trees, is a huge and swelling dome. The dazzling blue-green color of the dome seems to have come from the blue-green depths of some tropical sunlit sea.

We have reached Isfahan. The dome marks the Royal Mosque, the most beautiful mosque, I think, in all the Orient.

I once spent several weeks in this lovely city, so I know my way about. One of the first places I want to take you is to the nightingale shop. If you like, you can buy a nightingale there. Bird-trappers catch these divine little singers in nets, and put them in cages, and sell them to people who want a songbird in their homes. In western countries we keep canaries in cages—in Isfahan it's nightingales.

Leaving our baggage at an inn, we set out on foot toward the market.

Along the way we pass an enclosed court surrounded by a high wall. We look through the gate and are spellbound by the beauty we see inside. We see a garden overflowing with iris and narcissus and blossoming plum trees. In the center are a fountain and a marble pool. And at the far end rises the arched entrance of a famous Mohammedan college called the Madrasa.

Photograph Pope—Courtesy American Institute of Iranian Arts and Archeology.

In the Persian city of Isfahan (the home of the nightingales), we find this beautiful domed building. It's a Mohammedan college called the Madrasa. The dome and minarets are covered with green tiles. We look through the arch and see the college students and teachers wandering about this flowering courtyard. In this same courtyard we later liberate our hundred nightingales.

Above it rise two slender turquoise minarets and a graceful turquoise dome. We can't decide which is the more beautiful—the garden or the building. We notice several boy students wandering with their teachers along the garden paths. Surely, we think to ourselves, any boy who goes to school in such an enchanting place as this would grow up to be a poet.

I lead you down more streets. We turn a corner and come suddenly upon another astonishing sight. It's really one of the great sights of Asia—the Royal Square of Isfahan.

Before us is an enormous plaza, *one-third of a mile long and 500 feet across*, framed in trees. And there, on the far side, we see again that heavenly beautiful, sea-green mosque soaring up into a vividly blue, springtime sky.

This glorious mosque has been standing 300 years. It was built by the greatest of Persian kings, Shah Abbas. (He ruled in Persia at the same time that Queen Elizabeth ruled in England. Isfahan was his capital.) When his workmen had finished the mosque he felt that he had never beheld anything so colorful and so perfect. So, in order that his people might have the best possible view of it, and learn to love it as he did, he swept away acres of houses before the front entrance, and made the Royal Square we're standing in now. This mosque is very sacred to the Persians. Since they are strict Mohammedans they will not allow Christian "unbelievers," like ourselves, to go inside.

Moving on to the end of the square opposite the mosque, we walk beneath an enormous gate. This gate leads into a covered street lined with little shops. Such a street, in oriental countries, is called a *bazaar*.

The Isfahan bazaars are much like those we saw in Bagdad, with one exception. In Bagdad they had no nightingales for sale.

Passing the silks, the camel bells, the silver goods, the shawls, we come at last to the front door of the nightingale-shop, and look, fascinated, upon the rows of cages inside. There, for sale, are a hundred male nightingales. All our lives we've heard of these supremely sweet singers. But they have never seemed real like sparrows or robins. They belonged rather to oriental fairy tales. And now, before us, all at once, are a hundred!

Courtesy Dr. Schneider—Isfahan.

the center of Isfahan is found the Royal Square, one-third of a mile long and 500 feet across.
the far end, rising against an intensely blue sky, looms the turquoise-colored Royal Mosque.
om the columned porch at the right, the kings of Persia used to watch their courtiers playing
lo in the Square. The two stone polo goal-posts (about six feet high) can be dimly seen before
the arched mosque gate.

Six young princes of Persia, each adorned with a fortune in jewels. Most of the people of modern Persia are very poor, but the nobles and the royal family are rich enough to dress their sons in diamond headdresses and pearl necklaces. One of the most dazzling collections of jewels on earth belongs

They are not singing at this hour. It's midday. Also they are very sad, for it's spring, and they are yearning for their mates and nests and rose gardens. Even so, they are chirping, fluttering, pecking at their birdseed. We feel so sorry for them. To keep a nightingale in a cage seems such a cruel thing to do—it's like keeping an angel in a cage, or a rainbow, or a star. Through an interpreter we learn, from the owner of the shop, that a number of these little prisoners were caught only yesterday, and have been caged just twenty-four hours . . . perhaps their wives and children have not yet given up hope of their return.

We ask the price. It is surprisingly cheap, much less than we would pay for a canary back home. I decide to buy one just to set him free. We'll take him to the loveliest garden in the town, and open the cage door, and watch him fly away to seek his nest and mate, and sing and sing again because he's no longer in prison.

But why—we ask ourselves—be content with freeing just one? There are so many others also longing to escape. I decide to buy, for myself, not one, but *six*—no, twelve! . . . I want to free *twelve* nightingales. To buy them I'll go without lunch, and dinner, too. I had planned to buy a small Persian carpet . . . I'll buy twelve nightingales instead.

Did someone else say he also wants to buy and free one? Oh, it's five you want. And you—ten? And you—what? Not *twenty!*

See here—I've a grand idea. Let's buy *all* the nightingales in the shop—every single one. Let's not allow one of them to stay another minute in these hateful cages. I'll take another twelve—I don't care how much they cost.

You say I can't have that many? All right, you buy a dozen each, and I'll take what's left.

The shop-owner thinks we've lost our minds. Just the same, he rejoices in having such customers as ourselves . . . all hundred of his birds sold in a few minutes!

Now—where will we go to set them free? I know—the Madrasa College garden, the garden with the iris and the fountains and the plum blossoms. It's the very homeland of spring. It's just the place.

We pay the shop-owner for our nightingales, and lift the hundred bird cages down from the shelves. The Madrasa is half a mile away. We can't begin to carry so many cages that far. Four porters appear. We carry all the cages we can manage, and the porters take the rest.

The poor little birds are frightened by all this jostling. . . . If they'll only be brave a little longer. . . .

Back across the Royal Square we go, each of us laden down with nightingale cages. Soon we reach the Madrasa gate. The students and teachers there, seeing a group of foreigners entering the garden with a hundred bird cages, stare at us in alarm. Our interpreter explains. The students had always heard that westerners did foolish things, but they had never supposed it was as bad as *this* . . . buying a hundred nightingales just to turn them loose.

Seeing there is no stopping us, the students decide to help. We open the first cage. In a flash the poor little prisoner darts through the door. With a loud chirp and a whir of wings he flies to the top of a blossoming plum tree . . . free, free. Then out of the garden he goes, away to his mate and his nest. Good luck, nightingale. May Allah speed you and send you safely home.

Then we all begin to open cages—you, I, the students, the teachers . . . nightingales, nightingales, nightingales. They are darting about the garden, up into the sky, around the turquoise minarets. We empty the entire prison. A hundred golden, glorious voices we set free.

And tonight, when the moon shines down upon this flowering land, there will be love songs and spring songs again in Isfahan.

184

Photograph Pope—Courtesy American Institute of Iranian Arts and Archeology.

Persia is justly famous for its beautiful architecture. In many of the mosques and public buildings we find tall arched doors like this one, rising before marble pools of water. This is another view of the Madrasa College. How happy the nightingales must have been to be set free in such a lovely place!

Afghani

KHYBER PASS

KASHMIR

TIBET

HIMALAYA

Indus River

PUNJAB

BALU-
CHISTAN

MOUNTAINS

MT. EVEREST

L.

NEPAL

MT. KINCHINJUNGA

24

DELHI

AGRA

DARJEELIN

RAJPUTANA

22
23

OUDH

BOMBAY

CHITOR

20
21

UDAIPUR

INDIA

Ganges

BENARES

BIHAR

BEN
River

CALCUTTA

GUJARAT

From Bushire

CENTRAL
PROVINCES

PRESIDENCY

BOMBAY

HYDERABAD

Bay of Bengal

Arabian Sea

MADRAS PRESIDENCY

MAP *showing location
of Marvels
in India and Tibet*

MYSORE

MADRAS

MADURA

27

Chapters
20 and 21. Udaipur
22 and 23. Agra
24. Mt. Everest
25 and 26. Lhasa
27. Madura

To Singapore

CEYLON

CHAPTER XX

WONDERLAND

When I was a boy I once received, as a Christmas gift, a beautiful book of oriental fairy tales. The stories all took place in India. They told of mighty kings riding to war on elephants; of marble palaces with golden domes where lovely princesses were kept imprisoned; of magic music that came at midnight from an enchanted grove in the jungle.

The stories were wonderful enough. But the colored pictures! These were twice as wonderful. In the pictures I saw elephants covered with silver cloth, and draped in ropes of pearls. The rajahs who rode them had fierce white beards. They wore huge black turbans on their heads, and orange jackets studded with jewels. Their guards were dressed in brocade coats, shoes that turned up at the toes, and baggy trousers of scarlet silk. Each carried a long curved sword aflame with gold.

In the pictures the artist sometimes painted dream palaces of alabaster and pink marble, with ivory balconies looking out over dark-blue lakes. There were islands in the lakes where shining white temples rose out of the green trees. Upon the blue waters white swans swam among the lotus blooms.

And such lovely ladies adorned the pages of this book—ladies with soft black eyes, and little gold rings in their noses, with gold bracelets on their arms, and gold anklets on their feet; ladies dressed in veils, shawls, robes, all the most dazzling colors.

How often, as a boy, I read these stories, and looked at these pictures. . . . I would close my eyes and try to see myself, with a turban on my head, a curved sword by my side, riding on an elephant—out from the gates of the marble palaces. Or perhaps in an ivory boat I floated over lotus-covered lakes, with a dark-eyed Hindu princess by my side.

How I longed to find such a fairyland as I saw pictured in that book!—a land that was all romance, beauty, wonder.

Well—will you believe me?—I found it!

We'll be there in three days.

187

Isfahan and its nightingales are far behind. We've traveled by motorcar south to the Persian Gulf, and taken a steamer to Bombay, the great port on the west coast of India. From Bombay a train carries us north to the Indian state called Rajputana.

In Rajputana we come to the town of Udaipur. And here we find the land that has stepped straight from the pages of the fairy tales.

It bursts upon us all at once. We've come to the edge of the most beautiful lake we've ever seen. Tropical trees, splashed with scarlet blossoms, grow along the shore. The still waters mirror the clouds floating upon an indigo sky. Marble shrines, half hidden in flowers, rise up from little islands. Behind us soar the jungle-covered hills. And before us—across the lake—is a sight that makes us rub our eyes. It simply can't be true!

Did I say fairy palaces? There they are. Tier on tier they climb, blue palaces, yellow palaces, pink palaces, white palaces, with ivory balconies looking out upon this enchanted lake. They do not seem to have been built, but dreamed. They seem made not of bricks and stone, but of music and romance and rainbows. Perhaps some magician first drew pictures of them with paints from the flowers in the spring, and then waved his wand—and behold!—they rose up, real.

Eagerly we go on into the town. We find the streets lined with flower-bedecked temples, and filled with throngs of people in holiday dress. We learn it's the Rajah's birthday.

Did I promise you elephants? Look at the wonderful monster coming across the square. It bears the Rajah himself. Draped over the elephant's body is a canopy of silver cloth. Around each foot is a bracelet of bells. Its toes and tusks are painted gold.

The Rajah sits in an ivory chair, high on the elephant's back. His turban sparkles with rubies. The long dagger in his belt has a diamond case. Upon his yellow velvet coat are sewn a thousand pearls.

Did I say picture-book people? Look at the Rajah's guards . . . turned-up shoes, great curved swords, scarlet coats. And look at the girls and women! They can scarcely walk, so heavy

European Pictures.

western India, in the state of Rajputana, we come to the town of Udaipur, and find the land
at has stepped straight from the pages of a fairy tale. It bursts upon us all at once, across a
e tropical lake. On the far shore we see tier on tier of fairy palaces—blue palaces, pink palaces,
ite palaces. They seem to be made not of bricks and stone, but of music and romance and
rainbows.

Udaipur seems a city that has been dreamed rather than built. Its many-colored palaces a
temples, rising out of the tropical trees, shine along the shores of the beautiful lake. Part of
city is edged with marble docks, part protected by marble walls. High over everything is
castle of the King. The lake is dotted with green little islands on which the rich families have b
white marble pleasure grounds and summer palaces. Around these islands, lotus flowers float u
the water, and swans swim among the blossoms. The people of this romantic city are as colorfu

he buildings. The men wear huge bright turbans, brocade coats, turned-up shoes, curved swords. The women array themselves in veils and shawls and skirts of brightest hue, and wear all the rings nd anklets and bracelets and necklaces they can carry. To visit Udaipur is to go back hundreds f years into an Oriental dream-land untouched by modern ways—into a land that is all magic, beauty, wonder.

are their anklets, bracelets, and necklaces. Each has a ring in her nose and a hundred more upon her fingers. Veils, shawls, skirts, are all dyed the brightest colors they can find. They have dark skins, these girls of Udaipur, but I think many of them are very beautiful.

Bright-clad and jangling with jewelry, crowds of the Rajah's subjects are hurrying along behind the elephant. We follow the throngs to see where everybody is going in such a happy mood. Presently the elephant stops. The Rajah dismounts with the help of a ladder and walks to a grandstand that overlooks a sunken court.

In honor of the Rajah's birthday a curious duel is taking place below—a battle between two huge male elephants.

They have been chosen for this battle because there has long been a fierce hatred between them. They are separated by a low stone wall. Over this wall they seize each other with their trunks. They stab with their tusks. Trumpeting with rage, they strain and struggle, each trying to kill his enemy. One elephant finally sinks down from exhaustion. The other gets a medal—and an extra bale of hay.

Now an enormous pair of scales is brought to the Rajah. He sits in one cup of the scales and has his guards pour silver coins into the other cup until the scales balance. Then the Rajah flings all this money—his own weight in coins—to his subjects. This is his annual birthday present to Udaipur. His people wish for him long life and good health, and hope that he'll grow fatter and heavier each year.

We wander along more streets of this story-book city, and soon come to the lake again, close beside the palaces. White pigeons by the thousand fly about us. Peacocks spread their bright feathers on every wall and terrace. Sacred white cows and tame deer eat from our hands along the marble shores.

Moving up and down the lake are scores of small boats beautifully carved and colored. In these boats we see gaily-clad young Hindus, with wreaths of flowers around their heads, playing harps and mandolins, and feeding the swans. Farther out rise the green islands, covered with little temples shining in the sun.

Courtesy Colonel P. T. Elberton.

Each year, in Udaipur, in honor of the Rajah's birthday, the people of the town are invited to an elephant fight. The fight takes place across a wall. Otherwise the angry beasts would kill each other. They stab with their tusks, wrestle with their trunks, and trumpet with rage. They struggle until one elephant sinks down from exhaustion. The other gets a medal, and an extra bale of hay.

We, too, decide to hire a boat, row out upon the lake, and look back at the castled city on the shore. We all pile in one boat. I take the oars and begin to row away very bravely. But before we've gone a half-mile I'm *tired.* So I think it would be a nice idea if we just drifted for a while and watched the clouds. I've been wanting to tell you a story—a true story—about a Hindu princess I once took riding on this very lake, and now's my chance.

You say you'll listen for just five minutes, but no more?

Right-o. That's all the time I need. My story starts off very sad, but it has a comical ending. . . .

193

CHAPTER XXI

MY HINDU PRINCESS

Once upon a time there dwelt in India two great kings. One was the ruler over the Mohammedans; the other ruled over the Hindus. These two peoples, though they were of the same race, had differing religions, and they feared and hated each other, as they still do even today.

The Mohammedan king had his capital at the city of Delhi, in the north of India. The Hindu king's capital, called Chitor, was right here in Rajputana, only forty miles distant from Udaipur.

The Hindu king had a daughter, his only child, named Padmini, who was famed for her beauty throughout the land. The year she was sixteen, suitors came from all over Asia to ask for Padmini's hand in marriage. But she loved only her father and his people in Chitor, and refused to marry anyone.

Before long, the Mohammedan king, far away to the north, heard about the beauty of the Hindu princess. He, too, asked her to be his bride, and vowed that if she refused he would march upon Udaipur and burn it to the ground.

Padmini's father sent back a mocking reply . . . and the Mohammedan king began to prepare for war.

Down from Delhi marched a hundred thousand Moslem soldiers, and flung themselves against Chitor's walls. The Hindus resisted with all their strength. But they could not stop the onrush of the invaders. The Moslems broke through the gates and seized the city.

Padmini, watching the terrible battle from a tower, saw her father killed, saw her city set on fire. She knew that she, herself, if she were captured, would be dragged off to Delhi and flung into the harem of the Moslem king.

Such a shameful fate this Hindu princess was unwilling to endure. Quickly—with the fires of the burning city filling the sky—she summoned her twelve serving-maids. To each of them she gave a bundle of sticks, a jar of oil, and a torch. Then she

Galloway.

In order to get a good view of the Udaipur palaces along the castled shore, we hire a boat and go for a ride upon the lake. We feed the swans, and make chains of the lotus blossoms. Suddenly it sweeps down upon us and we are drenched before we can reach the dock.

led them down into a stone room beneath the palace, and locked herself and all her maids inside.

In a moment more the Moslem king was beating on the door, eager to seize Padmini. . . . Soon he would take captive this flower-like princess for whom he had killed 50,000 men. . . . On his war elephant he would ride with her, in triumph, back to Delhi.

The door, being made of iron, held fast. The King brought up his battering-rams. These pounded the hinges to pieces—and the door fell with a crash. And as it fell, a cloud of flame and smoke came pouring out. Padmini and her maids had been true to the first commandment of all Hindu women: "Choose death before dishonor!"

This tragedy took place over 400 years ago. Ever since that day, Padmini, who burned herself to death rather than surrender to the Mohammedans, has been the national heroine of the Hindus —a symbol of courage and fidelity, known throughout the nation to every child.

Chitor never rose again from its ashes. The people—those who did not perish in the disaster—fled from the smoking ruins. Looking for a new place to live, they came here to this very lake. On the shore, over there, they built the city that you see.

I was just about your age when I read the history of Padmini, and it made a very deep impression upon me. One of the first things I did, on reaching India some years ago, was to visit Chitor. I wandered among its ghostly temples and tumbled palaces. Leading down beneath the ruins of the largest palace I found a stone staircase. At the bottom of these steps I found the entrance to a small stone room. Across the entrance was a sign. And on the sign I read these words: "Stranger, do not tread here. This is holy ground. This is Padmini's tomb."

I pick up the oars. No one speaks. I begin to row quietly across the lake again.

And then somebody says: But you told us your story had a happy ending that would make us laugh. We haven't laughed once. The tale of Padmini is all tragedy. . . . And what about

early kings of Udaipur must have been poets, or artists, for they loved beauty. Their favorite
mer residence was this marble palace on this enchanted little island. Trees with scarlet blos-
shade the walls. At night the odor of jasmine flowers perfumes the gardens. The lake, and
marble island, and the turbaned Rajah who lives here, all seem like a tale from a story-book.

the Hindu princess you said you took boat-riding on this lake?
Where does *she* come in the story?

Oh, my story isn't finished. I've just told you the sad part.
Now comes the happy part . . . I think you'll like this part the
best. . . . But you said I mustn't talk more than five minutes,
and I've already talked six. So I thought I'd better stop.

You say I can have five minutes more?—if I make it *very*
funny?

All right.—Quiet, please.

Well, having seen Chitor, I naturally wanted to see Udaipur,
too. The day I got here was much like this one—they must have
a holiday every week in this town. The same crowd of young
people, with their jewels and shawls and swords and turbans,
were parading up and down the lake-shore, just as they are now.

I wandered around for a while, looking at everything, and
then I came to the lake. I saw a lot of people out boating, so I
hired a boat—smaller than this one—at the same dock where we
got ours. But I was alone. And I knew it wouldn't be much fun
boating by myself. All the other men I saw, out on the lake, had
each a girl companion. In each boat there was a man and a girl,
a boy and a girl, a man and a girl. But in my boat there would
be just a man—*no* girl. So I thought I'd try to find *me* a girl,
just to sit beside me and decorate my boat.

I looked up and down the dock. It seemed to me I'd never seen so many pretty girls—big girls and little girls, schoolgirls and grown girls. They passed by in throngs, with their clothes (all made of cheesecloth) flashing in the sun, and their anklets jangling on bare feet . . . *you* know—you've seen them today.

Presently I noticed, coming down the line, the flashiest cheesecloth flash of all. I could have seen her a mile away . . . scarlet veil, purple shawl, green bodice, yellow skirt. Her bracelets and necklaces must have weighed ten pounds. And she seemed like such a *little* girl to be wearing so much jewelry.

When she came close enough, I could look beneath the scarlet veil. Half-hidden behind her nose ring was the cutest, prettiest little face I almost ever saw.

And how old was she?

Eight!

But, as you know, I'm a fatherly soul, and just love children. I thought it might be fun taking this little Hindu girl for a boat ride.

My walking rainbow was not alone. Her mother walked beside her. I knew this would help, because I always get along fine with mothers.

This happened on my first trip to India, and I was just learning to speak a little Hindustani. I could say *how much,* too *much, what time, good-by,* and count from one to ten. And that was about all. I realized none of these words would be right for a boat-ride invitation. So I tried gestures. I stepped in front of the little girl, made a low bow, and pointed first to her, then to me, and then to the boat, all the time smiling my very best.

She understood. At the same time she felt a little frightened. This was the first time a white *sahib* had ever spoken to her. She held back.

But her mother seemed to like me. She spoke to daughter and said—I suppose—"Daughter, it's all right—I think it would be just lovely if you went for a ride with the *sahib*. He looks like a pleasant sort of fellow. Go ahead—I'll wait for you right here."

Seeing I had the mother's support (which is a big help, I tell you!), I took the child by the hand and began to pull her toward the boat. Mother was delighted, and helped me by pushing daughter from the rear—like this. . . . Don't think daughter didn't resist. She certainly *did* resist. But not too much.

It was the most public kidnaping in the history of Udaipur—and the merriest. I was laughing, the child was laughing, mother was laughing, and so were a score of friends who had stopped to watch.

As we started rowing gayly away, I felt I must talk to my fair passenger. So I said *how far, what time, good-by,* three or four times, and counted to ten. And that was the end of my conversation.

Then the child tried to talk to me in Hindustani. I couldn't understand one word even when she shouted.

Before I knew it, I had rowed into the center of the lake—out past the island over yonder—when, all of a sudden, there was a clap of thunder and a flash of lightning.

I looked up . . . the sun had gone—heavy black clouds filled the sky—and here came a rainstorm borne on by a sudden wind.

It was two o'clock, and every day, here in Udaipur, at two o'clock the sun disappears and the rain comes down, all in a few minutes. If your watch says it's five minutes to two when the rain begins, then your watch is five minutes slow. *Everybody* knows about the two-o'clock rainstorm. Even *I* knew about it—only I'd forgotten. I'm sure, now, that's what the little girl was trying to tell me when she shouted. She was saying, "Look behind you, stupid, here comes the rain!" But I just kept on smiling agreeably, and saying *how far, good-by,* and counting to ten.

Anyway it was too late now. I turned about and rowed like mad for shore. But we hadn't gone a hundred yards when the rain hit us. In one minute we were both half-drowned. I took off my sun helmet (I didn't need it much now) and gave it to the dripping child. This would keep the ring in her nose from getting rusty.

When the Rajah of Udaipur goes for a ride upon the lake, he does not dash around in a mod
speedboat, but instead moves slowly, and in state, aboard one of these royal barges. The Ra
sits on a raised throne under a canopy. Fourteen oarsmen furnish the power. An orchestra pl
while guards in bright uniforms stand at attention.

The entrance to the Rajah's palace is through this marble gate. The lower part of the palac
white marble, the upper part pink marble. Out from this gate, each year on his birthday,
Rajah rides forth on an elephant to scatter to his people his own weight in gold coins.

I had on a khaki shirt and shorts. These were soon besodden and sticking to me.

But if I was rain-washed, what about my little cheesecloth passenger! She was melting fast. Her scarlet cheesecloth veil began to stream all over the purple cheesecloth shawl; the purple shawl and the scarlet veil over the green bodice; the green bodice and scarlet veil and purple shawl over the yellow skirt; and the yellow skirt and purple shawl and green bodice and scarlet veil all over the boat, all over the lake, all over everything. And the only gesture I could make to help my streaming, melting, weeping little companion was to row harder than ever into the teeth of the rainstorm.

When we got back to shore we certainly were a mess. But at least the rain, which was still beating down, had driven everybody indoors so that there was no one on hand to see our shameful return.

Dripping water at every step I crawled up on the dock. Holding my wet hand, the little girl, trailing her soggy cheesecloth glory behind her, came sloshing out of the rain-filled boat—the most pathetic picture you ever saw . . . her gay veil—her party dress . . . Weeping and wretched, shivering with cold, she just stood there leaving red puddles and yellow puddles and purple puddles of raindrops on the pavement.

I didn't know what to do, what to say. I felt, for her sake, so terribly unhappy. I wanted to say: "My dear child, I'm *so* sorry—I promise never to let this happen again. Will you ever, ever, forgive me?"

But I couldn't say it. All I could say was *how much, how far, what time,* and count to ten. Again this didn't seem to be the right thing.

And then I had a sudden flash of inspiration. I knew just what to say:

"Good-by, PADMINI."

Padmini! This she understood in *any* language. In astonishment she looked up through her tears. Was it possible I had really called her *that?* Padmini—the most glorious girl-name in Hindu history! She'd never been called anything so wonderful in all her eight years. It was like saying to a small boy in America: "Good-by, little George Washington Teddy Roosevelt." She felt sure now that despite her clammy clothes and chattering teeth, the white *sahib* still thought her beautiful and brave, like the heroic Princess of old Chitor. She felt sure I still liked her even though she was all wet.

This one lovely word changed everything. She stopped weeping. The sunshine came back into her eyes. She pressed my outstretched hand, then turned and darted through the rain into a grove of palms. There she turned and waved. I saw one last flash of yellow and purple and red and green, through the trees—and my Princess Padmini had gone. . . .

Now, children, wasn't that a nice story?

You say yes, but it's going to rain.

Going to rain! It's raining right this minute—and here we are a mile from shore! Why didn't you notice the clouds coming up? Why did you let me talk on so long? Why didn't you watch the time? I *told* you it always rains at two o'clock. Here, give me those oars—and tuck away your nose rings. . . . We're going to get very, very damp.

My little Princess Padmini of Udaipur wasn't half as wet as we are when our boat, struggling through the deluge, reaches shore.

You ask me what we are going to do? You say you've no dry clothes?

Well, I suggest you hang your wet clothes on the palace gates. I'll get each of you a nice pink cheesecloth veil to wrap up in. And while your clothes are drying off, I'll tell you another story of magic and romance . . . it's about how I once killed a dragon.

You say you'd rather stay wet?

Oh, all right. But if you all catch pneumonia, don't say I didn't try to save you.

The
TAJ MAHAL

CHAPTER XXII

A LOVE STORY

We're in Agra, a city in northern India—one of the most famous and wonderful cities in the Orient.

The hour is early morning, and the season is spring. The morning wind, sweet with the perfume of springtime blossoms, brushes past. Soon the hot tropical sun will rise high in a burning sky. But at this hour there is still dew on the grass and flowers.

On foot we leave our hotel. Before us stretches a road lined with trees. I lead you along this road as it winds out of the city into the countryside. For two miles we walk on through the cool air, shaded by pines and palms, and serenaded by the bright-winged tropical birds that sing in the treetops.

You know where we are going! You know why we have come to Agra! You know that in Agra is the most heavenly beautiful poem in stone ever built by man—and that we have traveled half-way around the earth to see it. You know it's called the Taj Mahal.

In a few minutes more we shall stand before this Marvel. In these few minutes let me tell you the story that led to the building of the Taj, in order that you may better understand its beauty and its wonder. This story—a love story—is one of the undying romances of the world. . . .

The name of Shah Jehan is perhaps not known to you, but it has a place high among the really great names in history. He was a mighty king who, 300 years ago, once ruled a vast Moslem empire in India. Agra was his capital. His marble palaces still adorn the city. At the same time that Shah Jehan reigned in Agra, King Charles I reigned in England, and the earliest European settlers were crossing the Atlantic to found the American colonies.

Shah Jehan, true to the custom of all great Indian emperors, lived in unbelievable splendor. It was he who first sat upon the famous Peacock Throne, a throne studded with the most enormous

The Taj Mahal, the most beautiful building in the world, is a monument to a great love. It was built over 300 years ago by Shah Jehan, one of the emperors of India, as a tomb for his wife. It was his desire to make the tomb as beautiful, as delicate, as graceful, as the Empress, to make it the image and the soul of her beauty. The Taj Mahal is the most perfect tribute ever paid to a woman. *Black Star.*

and dazzling jewels ever seen. From every country he brought celebrated artists and architects to build his marble palaces and his marble city. He possessed huge chests of rubies, roomfuls of gold. In his royal stables were thousands of horses and hundreds of elephants. Under his rule India reached the peak of its glory, and became a rich and happy land.

But of all the great Shah's treasures, one treasure alone really held his heart—his beautiful and devoted wife. Other Indian princes had many wives. For Shah Jehan, there was only the Princess Arjemand. When she became his empress he called her Mumtaz Mahal—the Chosen of the Palace.

The proud young prince was twenty-one when he first set eyes on this enchantingly beautiful nineteen-year-old girl. From that hour, Shah Jehan had loved her with a love that was almost worship. And Arjemand had returned this adoration with her whole soul. To please Arjemand, his bride and queen, he ruled over his people with justice and mercy. To please her, he filled Agra with flowering gardens and noble buildings. Whenever he traveled about his empire on affairs of state, he always took the Empress with him. Even on the battlefield Mumtaz Mahal rode by her husband's side. It is said that not once, for the eighteen years of their married life, did they ever spend a single day apart.

And then, alas, this great, this perfect, royal romance was turned to tragedy. The Chosen of the Palace was stricken with a fatal fever. Sick unto death, the Empress, pale with suffering, lay on her couch, too weak to raise her hand. In a torment of anxiety, Shah Jehan watched by her side. When the end came, his anguish was so great that his court feared he too would die, of heartbreak.

For days the grieving King refused all food. Not even his own children dared speak to him. In these desolate hours he yearned to give up his kingdom, since, without Mumtaz Mahal, his power and his glory had turned to ashes in his heart. Only a sense of duty to her, to the people she had loved and served, made him return to the throne.

Longing and longing for Arjemand, he began to plan a tomb that would be a monument to his love for her and his grief for her. He summoned his greatest architect, a Persian named Usted Isa. "Build a tomb where I may bury her body," commanded the unhappy Emperor. "Make it as beautiful as she was beautiful. Make it as delicate as she was delicate, as graceful. Make it the image and the soul of her beauty."

And in a dream Usted Isa had a vision of a tomb that was as lovely, yet as majestic, as the face of Arjemand. This dream he drew on paper, and when the design was placed before the King, Shah Jehan embraced his architect with joy. Never, in a drawing, had the King seen such perfection. Here, ready to be re-created on earth again, was the spirit of Arjemand, in stone.

In a frenzy, Shah Jehan—as great an artist as he was a lover—pushed forward the building of the tomb. He would call it the Taj Mahal—the Crown of Mahal. He chose, as the proper place for it, the most fragrant garden in Agra, a garden overlooking the placid Jumna River.

In this garden, close beside the river bank, upon a marble platform, the great pearl of a tomb began to rise, white as ivory, harmonious as music, soft and delicate as a summer cloud. From the roof, a huge white dome swelled upward. At each corner, a slender, graceful minaret was placed, a minaret where the muezzins could call the faithful to come and pray for Arjemand.

In the Shah's burning desire to make his Taj supremely beautiful he searched the world for the purest of milky marble. From France and Italy came jewelers and sculptors to do his bidding. From Persia came shiploads of silver for the great doors. The shores of Arabia supplied ten thousand pearls. These pearls were woven into a canopy and folded over the casket that held the body of Arjemand. All thought of the price he was having to pay was flung aside. Into the hands of his architects he poured out his riches.

At length Usted Isa began to wonder if the building of the Taj would not bankrupt the royal treasury. Fearfully the architect exclaimed to his master: "Sire, the Taj Mahal has already cost *ten million rupees!*"

"Make it cost ten million more!" replied the heartbroken Emperor. "The Crown of Mahal must be the one perfect thing."

But the Great King spent upon the Taj more than just his treasures. Into the building of it, also, went his grief and his tears. Thus it has come to pass that the tomb seems to have a soul, which, so legends tell, can be seen on moonlight nights. Legends say that if a man and a maid greatly love each other, and have only goodness and mercy in their hearts, and if they come to the garden together to watch the full moon rise, they may chance to see the sepulcher fade into mist and moonbeams. And in the mist they may see the image of the Queen, revealed for one magic moment—all beautiful and radiant.

We walk along in silence. Then someone asks, What happened to the King?

I wish I could tell you that the builder of so wonderful a monument, to so wonderful a woman, lived on, loved and honored by his people. But this is not the way the story goes. It has a most unhappy ending. . . .

For seventeen years Shah Jehan devoted himself, ceaselessly, to the building of his Taj Mahal. At last the Crescent, the symbol of the Mohammedan faith, was placed upon the summit of the great central dome. The tomb, enthroned in the park, adorned with fountains, framed in trees, stood complete, ready to bless and purify everyone who looked upon its dazzling loveliness. Shah Jehan himself came each day to gaze at its gleaming walls and soaring glory—and was content. For here was perfection beyond praise. Here was beauty beyond belief.

Into this white vision of a sepulcher the King, certain that Arjemand's spirit was there to bless him, brought the body of his wife.

But scarcely were the Great King's building labors at an end, when his own son led a rebellion against the empire. Shah Jehan, now aged and helpless, was driven from his throne, seized by the rebel soldiers, and put in prison. There, through seven long years, he waited for death, waited for the moment when he would join his Chosen of the Palace once more. When death was at last upon this lonely and desolate old man, he pleaded, not in vain, to be carried at dawn to a balcony in his prison, where his dying eyes might rest upon the distant domes and minarets of the mausoleum. There his heart and soul already were, there he knew his body was soon to be, beside her for whom he had created the one perfect thing. With fading sight, he watched the eastern horizon brighten with light, watched the first beam of sunrise strike the Taj. Then his heavy weary eyes closed forever—and the soul of the King went to meet the soul of Arjemand, waiting for him in Paradise.

211

The burial tombs of Shah Jehan and his wife, Mumtaz Mahal, rest side by side
under the dome of the Taj.

Courtesy Indian State Railways.

...s the proper place for the tomb of the Empress, Shah Jehan chose the most beautiful garden in ...gra, a garden overlooking the placid Jumna River. It was the Emperor's plan, just before he ...as dethroned, to build a tomb for himself, on the opposite bank of the river, which would have ...xactly the same shape as the Taj. But his own tomb was to be made of black marble instead of ...hite. And he dreamed of joining the two mausoleums together by means of a silver bridge. We ...an be glad these plans were never carried out. As it stands now, all alone, the white marble spirit of the Queen is perfect and complete.

...he Taj Mahal is seen in all its shining glory from the roof of the entrance gate. Here is perfec-...on beyond praise. Here is beauty beyond belief. The Taj itself is milk-white, and after 300 ...ears seems as fresh and fair as a summer cloud. It soars up into a sky of intense and tropical ...lue. The trees and flowers of the park, flooded each night with water from the river, remain ...merald-green, no matter what the season. The setting of the Taj—the garden, the river, the sky —is as lovely as the Taj itself.

CHAPTER XXIII

THE GLORY OF ASIA

Before us now rises a high stone wall. In the center of the wall is an arched gate. We walk through this arch—and there, beyond, in the springtime sun, we see it . . . that miracle of a tomb, built by the King of India in honor of the woman he so greatly loved. Rising from a sea of fresh green grass and flowers into a sky intensely blue, the Taj, at this first breathless moment, seems to be all the dreams of beauty in the world suddenly come true. We feel we behold not a building made of stone, but a vision made of sunlight and clouds, floating against the turquoise sky, yonder at the end of the cypress-tree avenue. We stand silent in the presence of such overpowering loveliness.

Drawn forward toward this shining white jewel, we move down the marble pavement that leads into its very heart. Fountains, in a long row, splash beside us. Trees and flowers, all in blossom, grow about us. And at the end of the pavement soars the ivory temple.

We come to a raised lily pool, halfway along the cypress aisle. Marble steps lead up to it, and down the other side. Upon the surface of the pool, huge white lotus blossoms float.

We climb to the marble platform on which the Taj is built. The wondrous sepulcher seems to float like a magic bubble of sunlight above us. We know that Shah Jehan built this tomb 300 years ago. And yet it seems to have been built just yesterday. After three centuries it still appears as fresh, as fair, as a temple built of snow. Time leaves no mark upon its face, but stands aside unable to touch such perfection.

We cross the platform and pass through a carved marble doorway that leads into the central room of the Taj itself. How cool and still it is inside! Before us rest the two marble burial tombs —one for Arjemand and one for Shah Jehan. Encircling the tombs is the most wonderful screen, made of pierced marble slabs —slabs that look more like delicate lace than stone. Far overhead, in the half-light, arches the carved marble ceiling. In this peaceiul room, every whisper echoes. A note of music seems to drift up into the soft gloom above. There it is repeated in endless harmonies, and then falls back in sweet misty sounds upon the marble floor.

All about us are the inlaid walls, delicate as the embroidery on the bridal gown of the Chosen of the Palace. The silver doors, the canopy of pearls, long ago disappeared, but a treasure house of beauty still remains.

Hardly daring to speak in such a holy place, we move slowly about, wondering at everything. Outside, we cross the pavement and climb to the top balcony of one of the four minarets—the "four tall court ladies tending their Empress." Descending, we wander over to the platform's river edge. From here we look down upon the Jumna flowing serenely by. Across this river, on the other bank, is the place where Shah Jehan once planned (just before his imprisonment) to build his own mausoleum. It was to have exactly the same shape as the Taj Mahal, but to be made of black marble instead of white. And he dreamed of joining these two mausoleums together by means of a silver bridge.

I'm glad these plans were never carried out. As it now stands, all alone, the white marble spirit of Arjemand is perfect, complete, and at peace.

All day we linger in the enclosure. Every hour brings new light, new shades, new beauty, to the fairy palace of the Taj.

The sun sinks in the west. The wind dies down. The domes and minarets cast perfect reflections in the still water of the lily pool.

Twilight falls, and a soft lilac veil enfolds the garden.

Night is at hand, but not one of us even thinks of going home . . . we've never been so close to heaven as this. . . .

Early in the evening a huge full moon rises out of the treetops and smiles down upon our breathless dreamland. We look toward the Taj. It has turned into a pale pearl ghost, touched by the moonlight, and perfumed by the spring blossoms flowering on every side. We wonder if it is going to melt into moonlit mist, as the legend tells, and reveal to us the image of the Queen. . . .

When the full moon rises and floods the Taj Mahal, a time exposure on our cameras gets th
magical effect. The moonlight turns the tomb into a pale pearl ghost. We find seats on the marb
benches beside the raised lily pool. All about us the crickets begin to chirp, the night-birds
sing . . . we've never been so close to heaven as this. There is a legend told by the people

Keystone.

gra, which says that if a man and a maid greatly love each other, and have only goodness and
ercy in their hearts, and if they come to the garden together to watch the full moon rise, they
ay chance to see the sepulcher fade into mist and moonbeams. And in the mist they may see the
image of the Queen, revealed for one magic moment—all radiant and beautiful.

We find seats on the marble benches beside the raised lily pool. All about us the crickets begin to chirp. From flame-of-the-forest trees, from the bowers of honeysuckle, come stirs and flutters of the night birds, softly singing.

This is a new and magical adventure for you. And magical for me, though I have been here before. Something very strange happened to me on my first visit to the Taj. I was twenty-two years old then, and on a vagabond journey through India. I spent the entire day here, just as we have—and half the evening. In those days the entrance gate was closed at midnight, and no one was allowed to remain within the walls. (Now, you see, the place is open all night long.) But when twelve o'clock came I couldn't leave this magic garden. It seemed to me I'd never known anything on earth a thousandth part as beautiful. The waning moon, that night, rose well after the closing hour . . . and I did want to see the Taj floating in the moonlight. Indeed, for this I'd come to India.

As the guards came forward to drive out all visitors, I was standing in the dark shadow of a tree. I was so much under the spell of the Taj, I didn't, I *couldn't,* show myself to them . . . and the guards passed on. In a moment more the great gates boomed shut . . . I was locked inside . . . and the only other living person in the enclosure was the sentry who slept on the platform at the entrance to the tomb.

For a brief moment I felt afraid. Then I decided to accept, gratefully, this strange adventure.

Outside the walls the sound of voices died away. Within the luminous garden, only the leaves rustling in the breeze broke the stillness. Now I could walk forth from the shadows and answer the call of the moonlit Taj.

Leaving the tree I tiptoed up the steps to the platform. The solitary sentry was so deep in sleep, and so unused to visitors at this late and forbidden hour, that he did not wake. Creeping on around him, I crossed the threshold very softly, and stood beside the faint-lit tombs of the Great Shah and Arjemand. I remember the bronze lantern and the soft shadows its pale light cast on the carved walls. I remember how sad I felt that I had no offering to place upon the Empress' grave. Then it came to me that I did have, in my wallet, a twig from a myrtle bush, brought all the way from the Alhambra, the old Moslem palace in Spain. So I placed these fragile, faded leaves on her tomb. The wind, just then, brushed gently through the corridors, and slowly swung the lantern to and fro, and I fancied that this was a blessing, sent by the spirit of the Queen.

The sentry still slept as my shadow moved down the platform steps again, and back here to this same pool. On that night, as on this, there were great white lotus blossoms drifting on the water— just as you see them now.

I remember sitting on this very marble bench . . . It must have been about three o'clock in the morning. The moon was well up in the sky, shining as it is now. I was all alone—more peacefully alone than I have ever been. The whole garden—*my* garden —seemed truly enchanted. (Doesn't it seem enchanted now?) The pool looked so cool and inviting, and the tropical summer night was so warm—the season was later than this—that I took off my clothes and lowered myself into the pool's dark five-foot depths, here at this corner, and swam among the lotus blooms. I meant no harm. I felt that the Princess Arjemand would not object . . . she had no more faithful worshiper than I. And there was no one to see me, or to know, except her own merciful spirit.

I must have stayed in the pool half an hour. Then I remember resting and dreaming on the marble rim, right here, for a long time. After a while I looked over the edge again—and I saw a reflection looking back at me from the water. It didn't seem to be my face at all. It *wasn't* mine. It was a perfectly strange face. I couldn't explain it. Perhaps the strange reflection was just my foolish imagination—or a ripple on the water. Anyway I remember I was frightened. A crow cawed . . . I looked up, and noticed

221

that the light of dawn was in the east. That's how I was able to see a reflection. The moonlight alone isn't strong enough. Look for yourselves—lean over the edge here. All you can see is the black shadow of our heads. But in that first gray light I saw something else. I've often wondered—strange things can happen in this mystic garden—if the face I saw was me in some life I lived a long time ago . . . the people of India firmly believe, you know, that after death we are born again in a new body, generation after generation. Or maybe the image I saw was the me that I'll be a hundred generations hence. I wish I knew.

Don't you think it's time for us to go home now? . . . we still have a long walk ahead. I know how hard it is to leave this heavenly place. But remember, the Crown of Mahal will be here tomorrow, and for a hundred years of tomorrows, waiting, as radiant and beautiful as it is tonight, for your return.

The Empress Mumtaz Mahal.   The Emperor Shah Jehan.

Stretching across the garden from the entrance gate to the Taj itself, there is a long, narrow, shallow canal, adorned with fountains. In the center of this canal is a raised lily pool made of marble. This pool is five feet deep and thirty feet square. When the author first visited the Taj, he found himself, one moonlit night, locked inside the garden—alone. The pool looked so inviting, he went for a swim in its cool dark depths.

Black Star.

Surrounding the tombs of Shah Jehan and Mumtaz Mahal there runs this screen made of pierced marble slabs. Imagine the skill, patience, and devotion needed to carve these lace-like panels from solid stone.

The Taj is enthroned upon an enormous platform paved with marble. On this platform visitors ca walk entirely around the tomb, and admire all four sides at close range.

At each corner of the marble platform on which the Taj is built rises a slender, graceful, marbl
minaret—"a tall court lady tending her Empress." At sunset a muezzin climbs one of thes
lovely towers, and calls the faithful to come and pray for the soul of the Queen.

CHAPTER XXIV

THE TOP OF THE WORLD

Do you like to climb?

If you had an apple tree in your back yard, would you climb to the highest branch for the biggest apple? Or would you just stay on the ground and knock it down with a rock?

And what about hills and mountains? Does a mountain, with a glorious view from the summit, offer you a challenge? Or would you rather sit on the front porch, down in the valley, and play casino?

If climbing trees does not interest you, if the struggle up a mountain gives you no joy and no thrill—then you might as well skip this chapter. It's only for boys and girls who love treetops, and mountain-tops.

From the time I could walk I've always had an urge to climb. That's what steeples and trees and cliffs and hills were *for*, I thought—climbing. When I was nine my father and I climbed Mount Mitchell in North Carolina, the highest point in eastern America. When I was twelve we trudged up the footpath to the summit of Pike's Peak. On the way, we were caught in a snowstorm, and I got very cold and breathless. But I loved it. The view from the summit was worth anything.

When I was sixteen I slipped from the top of a tall steel windmill, and was in the hospital for months after. The doctor said it might be a year before I could climb again. But he also said that if I would follow his directions, by the time I was twenty-one I could *climb the Matterhorn*. To him the Matterhorn, the Tiger of the Alps, was one of the most difficult mountains on earth to conquer. This put ideas in my head. And so, when I was twenty-one, I *did* climb it!

And then, having found the joy of mountain-climbing, I reached the summits of Mount Olympus in Greece, and Etna in Sicily, and Popocatepetl in Mexico, and Fujiyama in Japan. Someday I hope to climb Mount Ararat in Armenia—the mountain on which Noah's Ark came to rest after the Flood.

And after Ararat? There remains the overtowering giant of giants—the highest, most famous, most deadly difficult mountain on earth—Mount Everest, the Queen of the Himalayas, the top of the world.

Because of my love of climbing, one of my heroes has always been that bravest of mountaineers—George Mallory.

George Leigh Mallory was born in England in 1886. From early childhood, every mountain beckoned to him and seemed to say, "I'll wager you can't climb *me*." But the mountain always lost the wager. All his holidays this boy spent in the Alps looking for the most difficult and dangerous peaks. He could go anyplace where mountain goats could go—and many places where they couldn't.

It wasn't long before the Alps became too easy. He wanted a *hard* mountain, the hardest he could find.

In 1921 Mallory and a party of eight other Englishmen left England for India and the Himalayas. They had found the hardest mountain. They planned—they *dared* to plan—to climb Mount Everest.

At that time no white man had ever been near this terrible all-highest of peaks. It rises 29,145 feet, over five and one-half miles high, on the boundary between Nepal and Tibet. The southern slopes of the mountain are in Nepal, the northern slopes in Tibet. (See map on page 186). Up to 1921 few European explorers had been allowed by either country to cross their territories. This was because both countries fiercely disliked foreigners. Furthermore, the Tibetans worshiped the mountain. To them its vast pile of glittering spires seemed holy and unearthly. They called it Chomo Lungma, which means the Goddess Mother of the World. And for anyone to climb to her snowy crown would be an offense against the gods.

But in 1921 the Tibetans agreed, fearfully, to allow George Mallory and his companions to approach the sacred peak.

The Queen of the Himalayas, and the top of the world, is Mount Everest—29,145 feet high. This all-highest of mountains rises on the boundary between Nepal and Tibet. Until recent years no foreigners were allowed by either country to explore the great peak. Not till 1921 did any white man set foot upon its slopes. From the summit of Mount Everest a never-ceasing cloud of snow and mist, blown by the hurricane winds, streams like a great white banner.

Galloway.

The Englishmen entered Tibet with high hopes. But they soon found themselves in difficulties . . . there were no maps, no roads, no guides. They spent days in the wilderness of ice-armored giants, just trying to *find* Mount Everest. One way they knew they could spot the mountain was by the cloud of ice-fragments and snow that streamed, like a long thin banner, eternally from the summit. Everest alone, the Goddess Mother of the World, wore this swirling plume.

And when, at length, they did find the peak with the cloud-banner, they had to spend more weeks looking for a route that might lead to the top.

Mallory and his friends and their strong Tibetan porters pushed their way upward on the northern, Tibetan, side. Mallory, struggling ahead, reached 23,000 feet above sea level—nearly 8000 feet above the summit of Mont Blanc, the highest peak in the Alps. There, with the thermometer far below zero, he could look toward Everest's summit still 6000 feet above him. He saw the eternal swirling plume of snow being lashed from the dome by the raging blizzard, and he wondered if a rest-camp, which would be needed on the upper slopes, could be made to stand against such a hurricane.

But an even more serious problem! The higher above the earth we go, the thinner the air becomes. Could human beings breathe, much less climb, at 29,000 feet? Even at 23,000, Mallory was so faint and dizzy he could hardly stand.

Before these questions could be answered, the climbing season came to an end. Storms swept down from the snowbound mountain and drove the climbers from the slopes.

The following year, 1922, they came back again. And now the party knew the route, and lost no time. Mallory and two of his comrades, slowly becoming used to the thin air, reached 26,000 feet—the highest any man had ever climbed in history. They

230

The first five attempts (all by Englishmen) to climb Mount Everest ended in failure. In the second attempt, in 1922, seven Tibetan porters were killed by an avalanche. On the third attempt, in 1924, two climbers, within 600 feet of the summit, disappeared behind a veil of mist, and were never seen again. They may have reached the top before the terrible winds froze them to death. This is the type of rest-camp from which they set out upon their fatal climb. Mount Everest rises 5000 feet above. Note the plume of snow.

Courtesy Daily Telegraph, London.

passed 26,000 feet. But their lungs and hearts were enduring the most terrible torture. The climbers were gasping for breath, frozen by the screaming wind, staggering with every step, advancing 200 feet an hour—up to 26,800! They could go no farther—and the summit still loomed 2300 feet above.

Next day two other members of the party took up the fight, this time carrying oxygen tanks on their backs. With a tube from the tanks to their mouths they could breathe enough of this canned air to keep alive.

They reached 27,100 feet. There one of the tanks ceased to flow. The climber collapsed unconscious in the snow. His companion had to drag him back to their sheltered camp.

And then came a terrible avalanche, flung down the slopes from the summit by Chomo Lungma's guardian demons. Seven Tibetan porters were hurled upon a glacier in the valley far below, and dashed to pieces.

Again the climbing party retreated to India, with Chomo Lungma still unconquered.

But the challenge of Mount Everest remained as strong as ever. In 1924 the climbers returned a *third* time. And once again George Mallory led the way. With him came a young man, 22 years old, named Andrew Irvine, a student at Oxford University.

Back at the old camp-site the party prepared for a supreme effort. It was to be now or never.

On the first clear day, two of the climbers, without oxygen tanks, drove themselves to 28,000 feet—with the top only 1000 feet above. There they sank down almost dead before the hurricane. They were lucky to get back to camp alive.

Mallory and Irvine, throwing soul and body into the fight, now started up *with* oxygen. They carried their tent on up to 27,000 feet, and resolved to make the dash for the top next morning.

The morning broke fair. Watching anxiously from the base-camp half a mile below, all eyes saw the two specks creeping forward up the towering top-slopes of the iceberg. The specks reached 28,000 feet—28,500 feet—only 645 feet to go. Was there ever a more dramatic moment in the history of exploration?

In the dizzy altitudes of the Himalayas, the air is so thin, the cold so intense, and the wind so furious, that climbers suffer from torments of pain and exhaustion. They must wear fur-lined clothes to keep from freezing. The Everest climbers felt they were moving forward rapidly if they were able to climb 500 feet up the slopes in an hour.

Black Star.

Those two specks were suffering the most terrible tortures, but the summit drew them on. . . .

And then a cloud drifted across Mount Everest's peak, and Mallory and Irvine were blotted out of sight.

Forever.

What happened that they never came back? No one knows. Did they reach the top, only to be struck down by the fury of Chomo Lungma's guardian demons? Were they blown by the hurricanes over the precipice into Nepal? No one has ever learned. We only know that Chomo Lungma, a jealous goddess, behind a veil of mist slew those two brave men who challenged her, and left no trace.

This defiant mountain we must see, for where, in all the world, is there a Marvel more marvelous than this? It's certain we can't climb it, nor come within even a hundred miles of it on foot. But there is one way we *can* visit Mount Everest—we'll fly!

I've telegraphed ahead. A plane is waiting for us at the southern boundary of Nepal.

Don't be surprised. Mount Everest has seen planes before. The first plane ever to approach her slopes was my own Flying Carpet. Moye Stephens and I met the Maharajah of Nepal during one of his visits to India. He gave us permission to fly across his country and explore Chomo Lungma from the air.

With a ceiling of only 18,000 feet (as high as the Carpet would go), we couldn't hope to do much "exploring." At this altitude we flew up to the face of the Nepal-side precipice . . . but the pinnacle of the peak still towered another two miles above. Wishing our plane had more power, we had to turn back. Just as we turned, I took a picture of the Goddess Mountain. It wasn't very good—the straining engine almost shook the camera out of my hands. Even so, it was the first picture of Everest ever made from the air.

Shortly afterward, a group of English flyers, improving on the Everest adventures of the Flying Carpet, came to India bringing two super-powerful planes. With these—and with the permission of Nepal—they planned to rise 30,000 feet, and sail right over the summit of Chomo Lungma.

And they did! But it was a very dangerous flight. The hurricane-winds, tearing at the peak, were blowing from west to east at *120 miles an hour*. The speed of the planes was likewise 120 miles an hour. When the planes, flying from east to west, crossed the summit, they stood still! It was necessary to retreat, and try the crossing from another direction.

And even then the blast of ice-fragments and snow, which form the plume, was so violent it broke the glass windows in the closed cockpits when the planes flew through it. The fifty-below-zero blizzard swirled in and almost froze the cameramen and the pilots.

At 30,000 feet each man aboard the planes had to breathe from his oxygen tank. With oxygen—life. Without oxygen—death. Lashed by the winds, tortured by the cold, gasping for more and more oxygen, the flyers—for those desperate moments over the summit of Mount Everest—gambled with death.

The Himalayas, seen from an airplane at 20,000 feet, make a glorious sight. In 1933 two English airplanes flew over the summit of Mount Everest. During the flight, the flying photographer, riding swift and treacherous winds, took this wonderful picture. The curiously-formed armchair mountain in the distance is Makalu—27,790 feet high. Mount Everest is just off the left edge of the page. No climbers have ever tried to climb Makalu. About 7000 feet of the peak is showing above the clouds.

Courtesy Houston-Mount Everest Expedition.

To the Mount Everest flyers, four miles above Nepal, the world's highest mountain looked like t
(The large black spot is the shadow of the airplane's wing.) Guided by the everlasting plume
snow, the pilots could fly straight toward their goal. Since Everest soars more than 29,000 f
the planes had to rise well above 30,000 feet to sail—with a safe margin—over the top. The w
at the pinnacle was found to be blowing, from west to east, 120 miles an hour. The airplan
when they tried to fly from east to west over the peak—also at 120 miles an hour—stood s
They had to retreat and attack the peak from another direction. Even then, one plane was hur
dowwnard 1000 feet toward the fang of ice, and escaped only by inches. The pilots could not h
lived without their oxygen tanks. Lashed by the winds, tortured by the cold, gasping for more a

Courtesy Houston-Mount Everest Expedition.

re oxygen, the flyers—for the few desperate moments over the summit of Mount Everest—gam-
d with death. The peak on the right-hand page is Makalu. It is twelve miles to the east of
erest. In this picture, about 9000 feet of Everest is above the clouds—20,000 feet below. On
r own early-morning visit to the mountain, our plane rises just above the clouds to enable us to
one of the most dazzling pictures on earth. The mighty wall of the Himalayas stretches for
les and miles before our eyes. The giant peaks, made of snow and clouds and spires of ice,
rn purple and gold in the sunrise. Mount Everest stands out boldly. With her great precipices,
r glittering glaciers, her royal streamer, her court of gods and demons, her deadly beauty—what
glory crowns this Goddess Mother of all mountains!

One plane almost lost. A sudden whirlwind caught it as it struggled 1000 feet above the pinnacle, and flung it downward 1000 feet. The pilot fought frantically to escape the fang of ice that seemed to be leaping up at him. He escaped by inches.

So the Goddess Mother of the World has seen men from earth fly above her head—and live.

We leave Agra and the Taj far beyond. Traveling on east we arrive at the English airport near the borders of Nepal. Here we find our big passenger plane waiting. It can climb with us, to 20,000 feet—no more.

We must put on our heavy overcoats. It's blazing hot on the ground, I know. But at 20,000 feet it will be zero and below. We must wear woolen helmets, warm mittens, heavy stockings. If anybody has a weak heart—please stay behind. You may faint at four miles high.

Just at sunup we roar into the sky. We climb rapidly—15,000 feet—17,000—19,000. Our heads begin to throb, our hearts to pound. But when we look to the north, the dazzling sight we see is worth the misery. There is the mighty wall of frozen Himalayas stretching for miles and miles before our eyes. A hundred peaks appear, made of snow and clouds and spires of ice, all purple and gold in the sunrise.

Far to the east is Mount Kinchinjunga thrusting its towers 28,225 feet into the clear cold sky. The early morning light falls upon its shining pinnacles. Seeing such blinding whiteness, we wonder if Mount Everest itself, though 1000 feet higher, can be half as beautiful.

Next to Kinchinjunga, and only 400 feet lower, comes Makalu, formed in the shape of a gigantic armchair.

And then, about twenty miles away, we see Chomo Lungma herself, the most wonderful of all. We know it's Everest because we note the magnificent white plume floating from the glittering

238

peak. Her cascades of ice, her royal streamer, her court of gods and demons, her deadly beauty—what glory crowns this Goddess Mother of all mountains!

As we look, fascinated, toward the terrible spire above us, we all have one thought: Where are Mallory and Irvine? Buried under snow up there, on that last high point? Down here at the foot of the precipice? We wonder how long it will be before other climbers, supermen, reach the summit on foot, and plant a flag of conquest on the topmost crest of this defiant mountain. This victory is certain to come some day—perhaps soon. Each summer new attempts are made to climb the peak, and each year the climbers reach a point higher than the year before. Mount Everest can not hope to hold out much longer.

We are now nearly four miles high—and that's high enough for *us*, even though the mountain still rises another 9000 feet above. With all our heavy clothes we are shivering from cold. Our hands and feet feel frozen. Our teeth chatter. Our heads are bursting. We struggle to get our breath. Our plane, caught by the blasts from Everest, is being driven upward, blown downward. Were it not for our safety belts we'd be flung from our seats.

It's too dangerous to go nearer. The pilot turns our ship about. And just in time! The angry peak hurls down an extra-violent wind that almost rips the plane apart.

The pilot flees, as fast as he can go, back across Nepal. We spiral down, and land, still dazzled by the mighty mountain we have seen, upon the good flat earth of India.

This dazzling mass of rock and snow is Kinchinjunga, the third highest mountain in the worl[
28,225 feet. (Mount Godwin-Austen, in the Himalayas, but several hundred miles to the west c
Everest, is the second highest.) Kinchinjunga is only a few miles away from the Indian borde
and can be seen at close range by all travelers who visit the summer-resort town of Darjeelin
Kinchinjunga has greater snowfields than Everest and is more blindingly white. It ranks belo

Galloway.

Everest in height and in majesty—not in beauty. On our expedition into Tibet our route leads us over a high pass near this mountain. We suffer from the altitude. But always hanging over us is Kinchinjunga's glittering glory—and one look at the shining giant makes us forget that we are half-dead from the thin air.

CHAPTER XXV

LAND OF MYSTERY

Attention, please! I have an important announcement to make.
In order to visit the next Marvel on our list, our party must be
broken up. This marvel is completely out of range for the average
traveler. To get to it, one must endure so many hardships that
I do not dare invite you all to go there with me. I can take only
two of the oldest and strongest boys. I've chosen Tommy Davis
and Billy Wing.

It's too bad that we must leave the rest of you behind, for this
is something many people would rather see than anything else in
Asia. Thousands of travelers have dreamed of visiting it, or read
books about it, or been astonished by photographs of it. But out
of each hundred thousand visitors who come to behold the marvels
of Asia, only the merest handful have ever looked upon this truly
wondrous sight.

Few places in the world are as difficult to reach. It is located
far away on the other side of the Himalayas. There are no roads,
only mule-trails that climb to a height of 15,000 feet in order to
cross the mountain passes that lead from India. In these passes,
even in August, the snow sometimes lies waist-deep, and the freezing wind blowing down from the icy peaks drives back all but
the hardiest travelers.

Then, once the pass is conquered, a barren and frozen plateau,
12,000 feet high, stretches ahead. It takes fourteen days, on foot,
to cross this desert of rock and ice.

But even when a traveler is rash enough to face the physical
hardships of the trip, the people who live in this grim country
will stubbornly bar the way. They live in a nation tightly sealed
from the rest of the world. They hate and fear all outsiders. They
are ready, with gun and knife, to kill anybody who dares approach.
In the last thirty years scarcely a dozen white men have been able
(mostly in disguise) to reach the capital of the country and get
back alive to India to tell about the strange things they have seen.

This country is Tibet. The capital is Lhasa. And just outside Lhasa, on a hilltop, soars one of the most amazing buildings on earth, called the Potala. It's the Palace of the Buddhist Pope, and in Tibet the Pope is the King. He is also a living god.

This marvelous palace, this Potala, is another wonder of the world, and Tommy Davis and Billy Wing and I may be fortunate enough to see it.

But how—you say—are *we* three going to get there—fly? What about the guns and knives?

No—we must go on foot. No plane has ever flown to Lhasa . . . they are strictly forbidden by the rulers. But we need not be afraid—there will be no danger, this time, from attack. I've just had the good fortune to meet the members of a telephone company who have been summoned to Lhasa by the Pope-King. He has requested them to install—of all things!—telephones in the Potala. They will allow me to go along, and say I may take two sturdy boys. No more. And no girls at all. I sincerely wish we could all go. But that's impossible. Tommy and Billy and I will be back in about five weeks. The rest of you will stay here in Darjeeling. This is a very beautiful town—right at the foot of Kinchinjunga. You can sit on the porch, drink lemonade, and gaze at the Himalayas, while we three are walking 700 miles to Lhasa and back.

Our caravan is soon ready to depart. It consists of the six members of the telephone company, the two boys and me, twenty Tibetan porters, and a dozen yaks. The yaks, a kind of long-haired buffalo, are the favorite pack-animals in Tibet. On their strong backs we have loaded most of our provisions and baggage.

Almost at once the steep climb to the top of the 15,000-foot pass begins. For two days we struggle along the trail that leads forever upward. At night we sleep in frozen little mountain villages far above the timber line. The thin air is tormenting us again. We thought our hearts would pound out of our chests when we visited Mount Everest by plane. Now, our hearts are beating even harder. We can't walk fifty feet without stopping to get our breath.

243

But always hanging over us is the glittering glory of Kinchin-junga. One look at this dreaming giant and we forget that we are half-dead from the thin air.

At the top of the pass—nearly as high as Mont Blanc—a snowstorm beats upon us. We have to fight our way through drifts that have piled six feet high.

At such a time as this we are grateful for our yaks. They act as snowplows, plunging ahead and making a path for us to follow. Protected by their long thick hair, they do not seem to mind the cold at all. In fact they thrive best in cold weather and in high altitudes. Without the yak, the Tibetans would all soon die. The yak is their beast of burden, their motor truck and their freight train. They also eat its meat, drink its milk, wear its skin, make cloth of its hair, make fuel from its fat.

Tommy and Billy find a new use for the yak. They grab the tail of one of our animals and allow it to drag them through the snow, over the stormy pass, and down the other side.

We reach the Tibetan border where armed guards stop us. But the soldiers, learning that we have come to put telephones in the Potala, let us go on.

The barren plateau, 12,000 feet high, now lies before us—for some 350 miles. As we trudge across it we see no trees, little grass, just rock and gravel. Only in the protected valleys do we find fields of barley—and these valleys are few and far between. Across this plateau the cold wind never stops blowing. We pass other caravans of yaks carrying barley and wool to India. The yak-drivers look at us in astonishment—seven men and two boys—all *white*. If we bow to them and say "Good morning," they push forward one ear with their hand and stick out their tongues. This is the Tibetan way of saying "How do you do?" They would be very angry if we laughed at their curious courtesy.

We notice that the Tibetans have almond-shaped eyes like the Chinese, and dark-brown leathery skin. Indeed they *are* a branch of the Chinese race. On all maps, Tibet is marked as part of China. But the Tibetans say the maps are wrong, that Tibet is an independent country. Any Chinese official who comes to rule them, or gather taxes, gets killed.

244

In every town in Tibet, the most important building is always a monastery perched on some hill above the houses. These monasteries shelter thousands of red-robed and yellow-robed Buddhist monks called lamas.

The yak-drivers, porters, travelers, we meet on the road are dressed alike in long, loose, gray-wool gowns, grimy with dirt. Everybody, men as well as women, wears several pounds of crude jewelry. Brass ear-hoops reach to their shoulders, colored necklaces hang to their waists, silver bracelets jangle on their arms. Even so, they seem extremely poor—poor but happy. They laugh and sing all day.

Every twenty-five or thirty miles we come to a dirty little mud village where we rest and sleep. We are always fed the same thing —a soup made of yak butter, tea, and barley. The barley is home-grown, the tea comes from India. This soup has a terrible taste. But we are almost always cold and hungry, and ready to eat anything.

The inns where we sleep are usually owned, we soon find out, by one woman and several men. The men are all brothers, and all husbands of the one woman. There are several countries where one man has several wives, but Tibet is the only country where one woman has several husbands.

This strange custom began centuries ago. From the earliest times Tibetan men have made a living by trading in distant towns, and by driving yak caravans to India. For this reason most of the men remained away from their families months at a time. But the homes needed to be guarded, and the children needed the care of a father as well as a mother. So the women, by marrying several husbands, could hope to have at least *one* man at home. This means many Tibetan women can have no husbands at all.

At every town we notice that the most important building is always a monastery, perched high on some near-by mountain crag. Tibetans are Buddhists—that is to say, they are followers of the teachings of Buddha, a religious leader who lived in India some twenty-four centuries ago. These monasteries shelter thousands of red-robed Buddhist monks called lamas. In fact, *every third man* in Tibet becomes a lama. They usually enter the service of Buddha while still little boys. They do no work, but spend their time reading holy books and saying their prayers.

Tibet is governed from these monasteries. All taxes, all wealth, go to them. As the lamas grow richer the people grow poorer. But the people cannot protest, for the heads of the church are the rulers of the nation. Among the many wonders to be found in this country, the monasteries are the *first* wonder. They were built centuries ago, and always on some upsurging spire of rock. Some of them are located as high as 18,000 feet above sea level. Remembering how we suffered from the thin air in crossing the snow-bound pass at considerably less than this altitude, we wonder that people are able to live at such dizzy heights. But somehow the lamas *do* live there, thousands of them, and often reach a very old age.

246

Some of the monasteries in Tibet are built on crags 18,000 feet above sea-level —3000 feet higher than the tops of the Alps. Many people, living at low altitudes, faint when they come to such heights. But in Tibet, monks spend their entire lives on these frozen and cloud-capped mountain-tops.

Keystone.

Even down here on the 12,000-foot plateau we find the climate far from pleasant. At noon the thermometer soars up to 110 degrees, and we almost suffocate from heat. Smoked glasses and broad hats must be used to protect our eyes and faces from the scorching sun.

But as soon as night comes, the thermometer drops seventy degrees—down to forty, only eight degrees above freezing. In winter it may be zero after sundown on the very day when at noon it had been ninety. We spend a good part of our time putting on clothes and taking off clothes and putting on clothes and taking off clothes, trying to keep pace with the up-and-down weather.

For fourteen days we tramp on across the plain. Then, one afternoon, we turn a corner, and suddenly catch sight, ahead, of a hilltop flashing with what seems to be gold fire. We look again. The flashing comes from the golden roof and golden pinnacles of a vast and haughty palace soaring from the summit of the hill.

It's the Potala!

Three Tibetan lamas pose for their picture. The center figure is wearing a mask used to frighten evil spirits from the monastery. In the distance rise the snowy Himalayas.

CHAPTER XXVI

PALACE OF THE LIVING GODS

Nearer and nearer we move toward the towering Potala. It grows in size and splendor as we approach. It seems to sweep up the mountain-side like a mighty cliff of shining stone—a cliff four hundred feet high and a thousand feet long. We notice that the central section is painted brilliant red, the wings white. Green bushes cover the rocky slopes leading up to the castle walls. Overhead in the deep-blue sky rise the glittering roofs of gold. Along the zigzag entrance steps move streams of lamas in bright red and yellow robes.

What a magical vision! Here, having struggled for days across this desolate and frozen land, we have come, all of a sudden, upon a magnificence beyond all our dreams.

We hurry on into Lhasa. We find it to be a town of about 40,000 people, of whom *nearly half* are lamas. We are shocked to find the streets so filthy, the houses so wretched. There are no wheeled vehicles anywhere. No one in Lhasa has ever seen an automobile, or an airplane, or a train, or a bicycle—not even a cart; and how the Pope-King even *heard* of telephones is a mystery to us.

As we walk along looking for the inn, a few people throw rocks at us, and call us "foreign devils." Packs of savage dogs snarl at us. Half-naked beggars, lying in the mud, wake up as we come in sight, and ask for alms. Ragged, grimy children, caked with dirt, stare as we pass by.

Such squalor and filth and poverty, here below!

Such majesty, such grandeur, there above us on the hilltop!

Right away we want to visit the Potala. Leaving our baggage with our telephone-friends, Tommy and Billy and I follow a friendly lama as he guides us up the zigzag steps of Potala Hill. And as we climb, along with dozens of Tibetan pilgrims who have come here to worship, I tell the two boys what I know about the history of this amazing palace:

249

The Potala, built on a hilltop above Lhasa, is one of the most magnificent and commanding buildings on earth. The outer walls are white—the center section red—the roof gold. Here the Tibetan parliament meets, and here the Dalai Lama, the Tibetan Pope, lives.

It was begun in the year 700 A.D.—over 1200 years ago—as a residence for the Pope-King, called the Dalai Lama. Part of it was made into the Tibetan House of Parliament, part into a Buddhist college, part into a great national temple, part into a fort. What St. Peter's and the Vatican, in Rome, are to the Catholic religion, the Potala is to the Buddhist. For about a thousand years—up to 1750—the Dalai Lamas continued to work upon the Potala, and to pour into this work most of the wealth of the country. The palace has 500 rooms, 1400 windows. A thousand priests, students, and soldiers, who serve the Pope-King and his court, live under the wide-spreading golden roof.

Now, by means of the outside steps, we have reached the great central red section of the Potala, and can enter the front doors. Inside we find endless halls and rooms, all adorned with painted Chinese demons. We stumble through black tunnels, up stairs, through a mystic maze of passages, and come to the innermost, holiest, shrine. Here we find the sacred images of Buddha, some of them forty feet high, sitting and smiling down at us. The images are made of wood, bronze, and sometimes gold.

We hear the babble of many voices drifting from a dim-lighted room ahead. We move forward and come upon a group of red-robed lama students, chanting from their sacred books. Most of them are youngsters the age of Tommy and Billy. Seeing, for perhaps the first time, white boys of their own age, the students all stop chanting to stare.

More steps and we reach the golden roof. The glitter of the sun upon the masses of gold leaf is half-blinding. Just over there (where we cannot go) are the apartments and roof garden of the Dalai Lama himself. Up here in this realm of holiness, far above the people, he can walk along the edge of his golden roof, and look down upon the in-leaning slopes of this gigantic palace, down upon Lhasa, and out upon the snowy Himalayas.

I must explain to you that the Dalai Lama is worshiped by the Tibetans as a god. The people believe that his spirit has dwelt in all the Dalai Lamas who have ruled before him, and that, when he dies, his soul returns to earth again in a newborn baby. The

In the city of Lhasa itself we see squalor and filth and poverty. But we need only raise our eyes to the Potala, rising above the city, to see majesty and grandeur beyond belief. This vast building has 500 rooms, 1400 windows. It houses a Buddhist college, the great national temple, a fort. A thousand priests, students, and soldiers live in it. Few white travelers have ever looked upon this magnificent Potala, for Tibetans, fearing and hating foreigners, do not want them to visit their sacred city. And the few who *are* allowed must walk, or ride horseback, 350 miles from India to reach Lhasa, since in Tibet there are no railroads and no motor roads.

church officials are led (by divine guidance they say) to the home of the newborn Dalai Lama. The infant is brought to the Potala, and cared for by the priests until he is old enough to be crowned king. He must never marry, so he never has a son to follow him to the throne.

Also, in the Potala—perhaps over there in one of those white wings—there dwells a Living Buddha. He is even holier than the High Lama, for *he* is believed to have within him the soul of Buddha himself, handed down, in the same manner as the soul of the High Lama, through the generations. When the Living Buddha dies, his soul, too is born again in another child. The Tibetans say this Living Buddha has died, and been born again, about fifty times.

And now, Tommy, if you'll sit here beside Billy—here where you can see the city, but be out of this cold wind—I'll tell you both a story about one of these living gods I once met—a really true story:

The living gods aren't all here in Lhasa. In almost every monastery in Tibet there's some holy saint—usually the head priest, called the abbot—whose soul has lived for centuries . . . that is, if you believe these Buddhists. I once saw the coronation of such a god while he was still just a baby. It wasn't in Lhasa, but in a town in western Tibet. By good fortune I arrived there on the day the abbot of the local monastery was being crowned—for the thirtieth time! His first coronation had been twenty-nine lives before.

This present abbot was just four years old. He'd been born about a year after the previous abbot's death, and the dead abbot's soul had gone into this baby. Anyway, that's what the priests said. As you might expect, on the day the baby was crowned, the town had a holiday and a festival. Thousands of people came from miles around to parade and dance before the new god.

I never saw a sweeter child. He had pale brown skin, big innocent eyes, and very fat, very red, cheeks. He wore a yellow silk robe, and sat, for the ceremony, on a big wooden throne piled high with yellow silk cushions.

For a whole hour, with a solemn face, he watched the ceremonies from a high platform. And then, as the sun sank in the west, His Royal Highness began to nod—with 10,000 people worshiping at his feet.

His guardian carried the sleepy little saint back to the monastery. I followed—and no one seemed to mind. In the throne room, with hideous demon-masks all around, the guardian-priest let me take the baby's picture. (You'll see it on page 256). Next I asked if I might undress him and feed him his supper. And this, too, I was allowed to do, in the nursery.

International News Photos.

In Tibet every third man becomes a monk. They usually enter the service of Buddha while still little boys such as these. They do not work, but spend their time reading holy books and saying their prayers.

A Tibetan baby god dressed in his coronation robes. Tibetans believe that the soul of a person is reborn, after death, in a newborn baby. When the head-abbot of a monastery (who is often a saint) dies, the priests look about for the baby with the abbot's soul. When this baby has been found, the priests take him to live in the monastery. When he is four years old he is shown to the people of his district. They come for many miles around to honor and worship him. The baby in this picture has been abbot—so the priests believe—twenty-nine times before. He is a beautiful child with pale yellow skin and very red cheeks. His guardian (the priest at the left) let me feed the little god his supper, and put him to bed.

For a nightgown the child had just a warm woolen shawl. I put this around his brown little body, and held him in my lap till the porridge came. Before giving him the porridge I first tasted a spoonful myself, to see if it had the right seasoning. It had *no* seasoning—no salt, no sugar, no milk, no nothing—just cold, boiled, barley porridge. It almost choked me. But the little fellow *loved* it and ate it from the wooden spoon just as fast as I fed him. This was the only kind of food he'd eaten in four years. But he was the fattest, healthiest, best-natured child I've ever filled full of porridge.

He was ready for bed now. Near by stood an ancient blackened cradle that had nestled this same abbot in many babyhoods before. Into this cradle I lifted the heavy-eyed cherub, gave him his wooden doll, and covered them both with a shaggy sheepskin. Then as the sun went down behind the Himalayas, and the darkness came, I was allowed to stand beside His little Holiness and softly rock the baby god to sleep.

CHAPTER XXVII

THIRTY MILLION IDOLS

It's early evening. The moon is rising from the eastern hills. But the heat, tropical and damp, still lies like a steaming blanket on the land.

It is too hot to stay indoors. Leaving our hats and coats behind, we walk out into the streets, and stroll toward a curious cluster of great dark towers that loom high above the housetops into a starry sky. From the direction of these towers drifts the beat of drums and tom-toms, and the chanting of many voices. We follow the throb of the drums, pass through an arched gate, and find ourselves in a big stone court.

Here we come upon a most astonishing sight—several thousand frenzied people prayer-dancing and chanting to the rhythm of the drums. This shouting, pushing mob completely fills the court. Their half-naked, dark-skinned, sweating bodies shine in the lamplight. Their faces are painted with streaks of white. Their waving arms and bobbing heads cast weird shadows all about. Tom-toms beat—hands clap—gongs clang—horns blow—voices wail. . . .

Look at the walls? They are lined with statues of plaster demon-gods who, like the shouting multitudes, are also writhing and dancing. Some of the gods have twenty arms, some have heads of bulls, some have monkey-tails, some have wings, some have horns, some are giants, some are dwarfs, some are colored red, some wear crowns of gold. All the gods glisten and reek with a coating of rancid butter. They, too, seem to be moving to the music of the drums.

More half-naked people are rushing through the gate. We are pushed forward into the struggling throng. Underfoot we slip on the trampled blossoms of lilies and moonflowers brought as offerings to the sacred cows. The cows themselves, snow-white and wreathed in garlands, are wandering here and there in the midst of the tumult, or lying calmly on the pavement.

Above our heads strange birds, attracted by the flickering oil lamps, dart about in the half-light. No—they are not birds—they

258

On our first evening in Madura—a holy city in southern India—we see a curious cluster of dark towers looming high above the housetops into a starry sky. From them drift the beat of drums and the chanting of many voices. We follow the sound of the drums and come upon a great crowd of prayer-dancing people holding a night festival in this Hindu temple.

are huge bats with wings a foot across. They fly so close to us that we can see their devilish little faces.

In our effort to dodge the bats we stumble over one of the sacred cows. As we gain our feet again, an enormous writhing snake thrusts itself into our faces. We cry out in terror and leap back. But again our eyes deceive us. It's not a snake—it's the twisting trunk of a sacred elephant plodding through the crush of people and asking to be fed.

In panic we fight our way through a demon-guarded door into a less crowded corridor. Here beggars covered with sores and rags stretch out their hands and whine for alms. Somebody bumps into us. We turn, and gasp. There stands a bearded man, stark naked, and smeared from head to foot with a coating of white ashes. Wild black eyes shine through his ashen mask of a face. A blow from a grinning ghost could not have frightened us more.

Look—there are naked ash-men all around. One is lying on a bed of pointed nails. One has long needles stuck through his cheeks. One is holding his arms straight above his head. In this position he has held them so long they have grown stiff and cannot be brought down.

In the jostling throngs somebody, on hands and knees, pulls at our clothes. We glance at the crawling figure. And our eyes meet those of an old woman nearly dead from leprosy.

Over there in the glow of lights we see the food-stands selling ice cream and lemonade. . . .

What *is* this dreadful story? you ask.

Is it a nightmare?

Are we in a madhouse?

Nothing of the sort. We are attending a night festival in the Hindu temple of Madura.

Madura needs a little explaining.

India, as you know, has some 350,000,000 people. Of these, about 15,000,000 follow the Buddhist religion, and worship the same gods as the people of Tibet. Another 80,000,000 are Mohammedans. Agra and Delhi are their strongholds—the Taj Mahal

Courtesy Indian State Railways.

bout 300 years ago a great Hindu king named Tirumala, ruling over southern India, built a mon-
er temple to the glory of the Hindu gods. The outside walls of the temple-grounds were 1000
et on each side. The walls had ten great gates, and over each gate Tirumala built one of these
00-foot towers of stone and plaster. Beneath this gateway, throngs of pilgrims, from starving
beggars to rich rajahs, pass in and out.

their greatest shrine. Mohammed is their Prophet and Mecca their Holy City. Most of the remaining 255,000,000 are Hindus. They have many gods—great gods and small gods, demon gods and gentle gods. Few Hindus themselves know the names and natures of all their deities. For Hindus, the Sacred City is Benares, on the Ganges River. After Benares, the next holiest is the south-India town of Madura. Benares has no temple worth visiting. But in Madura there is a temple fantastic beyond belief, a temple we must not fail to see—the greatest Hindu temple in the world.

To reach Madura, Tommy Davis and Billy Wing and I have tramped back from Lhasa, across the cold Tibetan plateau, and over the Himalayan pass. At Darjeeling we had a reunion with the rest of our party. Then, all together once more, we traveled by train south to Calcutta, and 1200 miles on down the east coast of India to the very toe of the peninsula.

Here we found Madura.

About the same time that Shah Jehan, a Mohemmedan, was building the Taj Mahal in Agra, there came to the throne of the south-India Hindus a great king named Tirumala. Like Shah Jehan he set his hand to the building of great monuments. But unlike Shah Jehan, instead of building a white pearl of beauty in memory of a great love, Tirumala built a monster temple to the glory of the Hindu gods—a vast stone crazy-house. Over 1000 feet long on each side, his temple is adorned with 30,000,000 garish and terrifying statues of gods and demons, and guarded with ten pyramid-like towers that rise 200 feet above the ten gates.

These towers are among the wonders—and curiosities—of architecture. Made mostly of stucco, covered with nightmarish plaster images, and painted hideous hues of green and red, these pyramids cannot be called beautiful. And yet, when first we see them at a distance, rising high above the palms, we must confess that they have a strange kind of splendor.

We decide to put this temple on our list of Marvels, along with the Taj Mahal. One belongs there because it is so perfect and so beautiful we will always remember it. The other belongs there because it is so full of amazing ugliness and monsters and horrors that we'll never be able to forget it.

Inside the temple courtyard at Madura we find this sacred pool, called the Pool of the Golden Lotus. It is not well named. The pool is not golden, and there is not a lotus in sight. The water is stagnant and filthy. But to Hindu pilgrims this pool holds the most sacred of water. To bathe in it washes away all their sins. On certain hours on holy days they stand about in it by the hundred, pour it over their heads, drink it. The pool was deserted when this picture was taken.

Spread over the walls and towers of Madura's temple are *30,000,000* images of Hindu gods and demons. It would take an entire lifetime just to count them. What an insane jumble they make! We see goddesses, painted green, riding on red cows the size of dogs. We see blue monsters with heads of elephants and bodies of men. We see all the heroes and demons from all the terrible and fanciful Hindu legends. The jumble makes our heads swim.

We come to a tower-arch. Throngs of pilgrims, from starving beggars to rich rajahs, stream in and out. Along with them wander sacred bulls, sacred cows, goats, deer, monkeys, dogs, elephants. Most of the pilgrims have traveled many miles to visit this holy place. Having arrived, they are shouting for joy. Filth and flowers, devils and children, lepers and saints, men and gods, fill to overflowing the passage through the demon-carved gate.

We find a guide who offers to take us to the top of the tallest pyramid—the very place we want to go. Inside the pyramid we find the stone staircase so dark we can scarcely see, and so narrow and steep we have to feel our way upward. The stagnant odor of bats almost stifles us. For three centuries they have swarmed here. Now, hundreds of them, disturbed, dart and squeek about our heads.

But we stubbornly keep on, reach the top, and walk out on the roof. We startle the flocks of birds that use the plaster images for nesting places. At the base of the towers, pigeons and crows keep house. Halfway up come the colonies of parrots. But at the top the pyramid is ruled by the hawks and the eagles. A great flock of hawks launches out into the air, and wheels around us with sharp cries of anger and alarm.

Rippling down the tower-sides in terraces of plaster are the images and idols. Such an insane jumble! We pick out goddesses riding on cows the size of dogs. We see popeyed monsters. We see all the heroes and devils from all the terrible Hindu legends. We wonder how even the eagles dare nest and raise their young among such troops of demons. Someone told us there are 30,000,000 images carved on the walls and towers of this temple, and that in an entire lifetime we could not count them all. Such an enormous figure—*thirty million*—seemed unbelievable when we heard it. But we believe it now.

Down in the enclosure below, we notice the labyrinth of courts, halls and colonnades. And every court and corner is crowded with people.

Back to earth once more. Our guide takes us from one holy shrine to another. They all reek with rancid butter, and are occupied by sacred cows. Again, on every side, we see the bearded men covered with white ashes and lying on beds of spikes. By going naked, and by tormenting themselves, they show their disdain for the world, and thus hope to gain the good will of heaven.

We come to the stable of the sacred elephants. A dozen of these great beasts, covered with gold cloth, are driven about the temple grounds day and night, to ask for food and money with their snouts. The elephants promptly eat any food a pilgrim gives them. If it's money, they suck the coin into their snouts and blow it out, over their shoulders, into the laps of the drivers.

At length we reach the treasure room of the great god Siva. To this room, for 300 years, pious pilgrims have been bringing their offerings to the god. The collection of treasures is now worth millions and millions of rupees. The guards proudly show us baskets full of gold coins, ropes of glittering emeralds big as walnuts, strings of pearls woven into a shawl for the great god when his statue is carried in processions, seated on his golden horse.

The golden horse, life-size, glitters there in an ivory stable. To keep it company there is a golden cow and a golden peacock. And on guard over the stable stands a solid silver lion.

Our heads begin to swim from the jumble of beautiful and dreadful things we have seen—glittering emeralds and rotting lepers; sacred cows and golden horses; strings of pearls and rancid butter; dancing demons, trampled flowers, shouting pilgrims, throbbing music, naked ash-men, elephants and lemonade! We wonder if, at any moment, we are not going to wake up and find that all this heathen pageant is only a wild dream. . . . We wonder if it's possible that this group of white people, standing here wide-eyed, can be really *us*.

On the way back to our hotel, Tommy Davis remarks that Madura seemed to him more like a circus side-show than a holy place. Sally says the lepers and rancid butter made her sick, but that she'll never forget this Marvel as long as she lives. Billy Wing says that Tirumala must have been a very crazy king. And *I* say that any religion which builds a church like Reims Cathedral, or a tomb like the Taj Mahal, must be a greater and finer religion than one which builds the Temple of Madura.

The carved plaster towers of Madura are among the wonders—and curiosities—of architectur[e]. Made mostly of stucco, covered with nightmarish images, and painted bright hues of red and gree[n], these pyramid-like towers can not be called beautiful. And yet, when first we see them at a di[s-]tance, rising high above the palms, we must confess they have a strange kind of splendor. The[y]

ers, inside, are the home of vast colonies of bats. Outside, birds by the thousand make nesting
es among the plaster images. At the base of the towers, crows and pigeons keep house. Half-
way up come the parrots. The top is ruled by the hawks and the eagles.

Mongolia

Siberia

G O B I DESERT

Manchukuo

VLADIVOSTOK

JAPAN

Inner Mongolia

TOKYO

Sea of Japan

FUJIYAMA 30

Korea

GREAT WALL 29 • Peking

TIENTSIN

GRAND CANAL River

Yellow

SHANGHAI

CHINA

NANKING

HANGCHOW

Yangtze River

FORMOSA

TIBET

MAP *showing location of Marvels in China and Japan*

chapters
28. Angkor
29. Great Wall
30. Fujiyama

CANTON

HONGKONG

BURMA

Irrawaddy R.

FRENCH INDO-CHINA

PHILIPPINE ISLAN...

South China Sea

SIAM

Mekong R.

BANGKOK

28 ANGKOR

CAMBODIA

SAIGON

Gulf of Siam

From Madura

BORNEO

MALAYA

SUMATRA

SINGAPORE

CELEBES

CHAPTER XXVIII

A TALE FROM THE JUNGLE

Suppose—just to help me tell this story—that the city of Washington were five times as big as it is now, with five times as many people. And suppose the great public buildings—the Capitol, the Library of Congress, the Supreme Court, the Lincoln Memorial, were likewise five times as big as they are today. Suppose, instead of a dozen or a score of such huge buildings, there were a hundred. Suppose one of them—a great national temple—was the largest and finest temple ever built by man . . . *Think* what a magnificent city that would be . . . spread for miles across the land, and towering in the sky.

Now please keep on imagining. . . .

Instead of having smooth white stone walls and smooth white columns, the walls of *this* imaginary Washington are flooded, down to the last inch, with the most delicate and wonderful carving—and above all the walls rise towers and spires of carved stone lace.

This city—if you're still keeping up with me—swarms with 2,000,000 people. It has wealth, and luxury, and power, and fame.

And then, suddenly, at the height of its power, a terrible disaster falls upon it. A plague kills off every man, woman and child—all 2,000,000 inhabitants—within a month. Or perhaps a civil war arises and the people kill each other. Anyway, they all suddenly disappear. Every stone of this mighty city is left uninjured, but not one human being is left to live there. It becomes a vast stone corpse, intact but dead. With no one to defend the corpse, the forest marches in upon it. Trees sprout from the stone towers, roots twine themselves around the carved stone columns, vines block the doors, the streets become fields of grass. The city is swallowed up in a flood of foliage, and completely lost from the memory of man—for 500 years.

And then a naturalist, in quest of rare butterflies, comes to this country, and is hacking his way through the forest. He comes to an open glade, and looks ahead across the treetops. He rubs

The great temple at Angkor, in Indo-China, is the largest and finest temple standing in the world
ished race of master-builders called the Khymers, this mammoth temple has been wonderfully pr
it. It is the biggest building in Asia, yet no coral cameo was ever so delicately fashioned as eac
centuries in the depths of the forest, Angkor was re-discovered, accidentally, in 1861 by a French na

his eyes . . . it must be an attack of fever . . . for there before
him, springing right out of the jungle, are five great towers of
stone lace. With a pounding pulse he rushes forward toward those

...more than 500 years ago by a van-
... the efforts of the jungle to destroy
...building stone. After being lost for
...g for butterflies.

Lionel Green.

towers and, in a moment more, comes face to face with the greatest and most gorgeous temple his eyes have ever beheld. Most wonderful of all is its perfect preservation. Unlike the ruins of Greece, and Rome, this temple has almost every stone in place. Even the forest that has blanketed wall and pinnacle has been unable to dislodge the massive blocks.

With increasing wonderment the naturalist creeps up the carved stone steps. Snakes lie in his path. Panthers slip noiselessly from their carved stone dens. Bats and owls fly about his head. Whole colonies of monkeys chatter at him as he moves along the carved corridors.

But he pushes on and finally reaches the supreme central tower. From this high point he looks back down upon the miles and miles of waving forest-tops. In this sea of trees he spots a hundred other great and beautiful buildings lifting their heads above the branches.

And the naturalist knows that he has made one of the greatest discoveries in history—that he has stumbled upon the ruins of a lost city, the city that was once the proud capital of an empire, a city as big in area as Paris, and with far finer buildings. And not one human being lives in this city. And only he, of all the millions of people on earth, knows that it exists.

273

The naturalist hurries home to tell the world what he has found. But back in France, his friends, hearing him insist that he has discovered a lost city more wonderful than Paris, just tap their heads and suppose the heat has weakened his brain. Indeed, in a very short time some kind of jungle fever does bring about his death. But, to the end, he keeps raving about the miraculous city and temple.

Now—if you have imagined all *that*, I'll tell you the next chapter in the story. . . .

You say it's nice of me to try to amuse you with my tall tales of adventure and romance . . . didn't the naturalist also find a white princess chained in the temple, and guarded by gorillas? . . . but you would like it better if I told you something more useful—something, for example, about our next Marvel—what is it going to be—and where. . . .

But I *am* telling you about our next Marvel. The city I've asked you to try to picture in your mind's eye did actually exist. And it still exists. It *was* a great capital, like the city of Washington, only five times as big. It did and still does have a hundred gigantic buildings—temples, palaces, libraries, monuments. And they are all adorned with the most gorgeous carving, just as I said, and have beautiful towers 250 feet high. The great central temple is the biggest building in all Asia. Yet no coral cameo was ever so delicately fashioned as is each block of this mammoth monument.

And just as I said, the city, about the year 1350, actually had 2,000,000 people, and they all suddenly disappeared as if by magic. The forest, as I explained, crept in and swallowed the place, and it was completely lost to the memory of man for 500 years.

Then in 1861 (the year the American Civil War began), the French naturalist was wandering in the jungle, and bumped right into this marvelous ruin. As I said, he found not one human being living in it.

His name was Henri Mouhot.

The city's name is Angkor.

Angkor, before it got lost, was the largest city in the Orient, and the finest city in the world.

Look here—I'll show you where it is on the map, and how we are going to reach it:

You remember we left Madura and went past the island of Ceylon, off the southern end of India. (See map page 186.) Aboard a ship we crossed the Bay of Bengal to Singapore at the tip of the Malay Peninsula. (See map page 270.) From Singapore we continued by sea north to Saigon, the port of Cambodia, which is part of French Indo-China. Saigon is near the mouth of a huge tropical river called the Mekong.

Now, in a river boat, we are traveling 300 miles up the Mekong and into one of its largest branches. Soon the river will broaden out to make a lake. Near the banks of this lake, sunk deep in the forest, lies this Marvel we have come to see.

Early in the morning we leave our boat and go ashore. A narrow road, pressed on either side by the dense, dark jungle, leads us inland. Jungle, jungle, for several miles smothers the earth. And then, all of a sudden, we come to a glade, and look over the trees—and see what Henri Mouhot saw . . . five magical towers rising out of the forest—the towers of the Great Temple!

Like Mouhot, we hurry forward. We come to the Temple grounds, and look up at the stone miracle before our eyes. With wonderment we stare at the enormous mass of the thing—it blots out the whole horizon. And then we stare with just as much wonderment at the richness of detail—at the acres of delicate stone carving, at the hundreds of carved windows, at the miles of carved galleries, at the towers thrusting upward to meet the sky—all powerful and beautiful and desolate beyond belief.

But no use trying to describe it. It can't be described. We just stand there at the edge of the glade in silence and amazement.

Then somebody finally asks our native Cambodian guide: "Who built this mighty temple?" And we quite believe him when he says: "The gods."

Where did the Khymers who built this gorgeous temple come from? Where did they go? What made them disappear? No one knows. When we ask the people living today in Indo-China: "Who built Angkor?" they say: "The gods." The enormous size of the temple is difficult to comprehend even from this air-photograph. The top of the central tower is 250 feet high. The outer gallery, lined inside with the most exquisite carving, is over half a mile around.

With a feeling of awe we move on toward the carved stone mountain. To reach the entrance we walk along a raised stone causeway, 1200 feet long and 40 wide. This causeway leads over what was once a sacred lake. The balustrade is made of the long stone bodies of huge seven-headed stone cobras. We notice that the pavement is rutted by the passage of ancient chariot-wheels— chariots that once bore the king and his nobles to worship at this god-built shrine.

We climb the steep steps that lead through the entrance door into the lowest gallery. (Look at the picture on pages 276 and 277.) Inside we find ourselves in the midst of the most marvelous stone tapestry. The Egyptians might have raised this vast pile of stones in place, but only these ancient Cambodians—called Khymers by historians—could ever have carved them with such lavish beauty. Every inch of this giant building is covered with decorations. Kings and cobras, smiling deities, chains of dancers, riot over wall and tower. They rioted likewise at Madura. But there they were hideous, made of plaster, painted pink, and gave us a headache. The Angkor carvings are all stone—such stone beauty as the world has never seen before, and may never see again.

Only one thing at the Angkor temple reminds us of Madura— the bats. These same evil-smelling little beasts swarm by the million in the silent halls of this empty building. Whenever we walk along the galleries, the bats, as at Madura, squeak and tumble about our heads. For some 500 years these glorious stone rooms and terraces were the homes of monkeys, panthers, and bats. The monkeys and panthers have been driven out by the French archeologists. But the bats cling to their temple, and squeak with rage at everyone who comes to visit it.

When I was here once before, I happened to glance, one day just at twilight, toward the peak of the central tower, and I saw what looked like a great plume of smoke pouring out of the tower-top. I thought: The Temple is on fire! And then I saw that the smoke was bats—millions and millions of bats, pouring out of the tower, and in a black cloud spiraling into the sky.

e city of Angkor is protected by a high wall. Piercing the wall are five magnificent Victory
tes like this one. Each gate is 65 feet high. At the top are four heads of the greatest Khymer
d, facing the four points of the compass. When the French naturalist came upon the gate, at the
ne of the discovery of Angkor, the jungle had covered all the lower tiers of stone, so that the
explorer saw only the huge stone faces peering at him from the treetops.

To the Khymers, who built Angkor, snakes were sacred. On every side one sees images of cobras with seven heads. Leading to one of the great Victory Gates is a roadway bordered by two lines of stone giants, each eight feet tall, holding the long body of a huge seven-headed stone cobra. A Chinese traveler who visited Angkor when it was the living capital of a rich empire wrote about this amazing snake-monument: "On each side of the road there are 54 genii who look like gigantic and terrible generals turned to stone—108 statues all together. They hold the body of a sacred cobra. The

This Temple is called Angkor Vat. The city surrounding it is called Angkor Thom. We must see the city, too. The French government has cleaned all the weeds and trees from the walls and towers of the Temple. (Henri Mouhot would hardly recognize the place if he came back today.) But the other hundred wonderful buildings, strewn about the city, are still in the grip of the jungle.

We spend eight hours wandering from one of these magnificent structures to another. We walk ten miles, and late afternoon comes, and we have not seen half of Angkor Thom. Half?—we have not seen a tenth. We would need a week to see it all. The number and size of Angkor's ruins are staggering—more temples, more palaces, more libraries, baths, walls, gateways, monuments . . . all gorgeously carved, all but a few drowned in the jungle.

Let's rest here on this big stone—I'm tired. But first, look well at the stone! The cobras are thick around these ruins—let's not sit on one!

You've asked me what happened to the Khymers, what made them disappear. You've asked me why this heavenly city, with its huge population, its armies, its palaces, its temples, its might and glory, should suddenly be deserted and turned over to the forest.

History itself would like to know the answers. Some people say a plague came and killed all the inhabitants. Some say an enemy conquered the city, and dragged every one of the 2,000,000 citizens away into slavery. Still others say—and I think this is the true answer—that the Khymers' *own* armies of slaves, who had been driven like beasts to work in the quarries and on the walls, found a leader. And the leader led them in a murderous rebellion against their overlords. For many years, thousands upon thousands of slaves had died of torment and despair in order that these glorious temples might rise; in order that stones might be piled on stones to quench the kings' mad thirst for beauty.

Then came the day of reckoning. The slaves turned on their cruel masters, and slaughtered them in every horrible fashion they could think of. The nobles, fleeing for their lives, hid in the jungles, only to be tracked down and slain like beasts. Every house that would burn was set on fire. Every child of a noble family

281

was killed. The slaves, in an orgy of hate and vengeance, butchered everybody who was not a slave.

And then the rebels, with no one left to feed them and clothe them, began to wander away from the corpse-strewn city, until soon not even a slave remained.

And scarcely were they out of sight when that hungry fiend, the jungle, rushed upon the helpless and deserted capital and suffocated all but a few of its greatest monuments. It remained deserted and lost in the forest, for five long centuries. Perhaps it might be lost still, had Henri Mouhot not come along on that famous day.

Slowly and wonderingly we crawl on, like ants, about these lonely ruins. The sun sets behind the western treetops, and twilight creeps through the jungle. Every bird has become hushed; not even a cricket breaks the silence that sinks upon this mighty graveyard. In a few moments more, it's almost night. We begin to see ghosts of murdered Khymers in the shadows. We draw closer together for protection against the terrors of the darkness.

I suggest we stay here in the jungle till morning . . . it might be nice to sleep in a ruined temple along with a few ghosts and cobras.

You reply that *I* can stay here, if I wish, but *you* are going out of this dark jungle, and away from these snaky ruins, and back to the river-boat, as fast as your legs will carry you!

I say! Wait a minute! In the name of all the Khymer gods, don't leave me behind!

CHAPTER XXIX

THE GREAT STONE SERPENT

Does anybody here live in Topeka, Kansas?

No?

Well, let's pretend, for a moment, that we *all* do. And let's pretend that school's out, and that we are spending our vacation on a motor trip to New York.

We leave Topeka in the morning and reach Kansas City—100 miles away—in time for lunch. We have cousins we want to see in Little Rock, Arkansas. So we motor south, 400 miles, and arrive there the next day.

Leaving Little Rock we wander across country to call on friends in scattered cities. We go into southern Illinois, and then down to the Kentucky-Tennessee border and turn north to Louisville. Six hundred miles more.

Our next stop is Pittsburgh—another 400 miles. Then we cross northern Pennsylvania, and on to New York—400 miles from Pittsburgh. Our speedometer shows 1900 miles traveled since leaving Topeka.

Now stretch your imagination as far as it will stretch, and pretend that right beside our motor road, all the way from Topeka to Little Rock, to Louisville, to Pittsburgh, to New York, there had been not just a line of telephone poles, but a massive stone wall as high as the poles and fifteen feet thick, with strong stone towers strung along, about twelve to the mile.

If you can imagine such a wall, then you will have some idea of the Great Wall of China.

If transferred to America it would stretch from Kansas to the Atlantic Ocean.

Nothing else on earth, created by man's hand, even remotely approaches the Great Wall in sheer size, in amount of masonry piled up, in amount of labor required.

From the material in the Great Wall, a smaller wall, eight feet high and three feet thick, could be built entirely around the world at the equator—25,000 miles.

If the Great Wall of China were rebuilt in the United States, it would stretch from Topeka, Kan
to New York. With all its extra loops, it measures more than 1900 miles long. At one p
it climbs to a place 5000 feet high. The wall was first built about 200 years before the b
of Christ. It has been enlarged and strengthened several times since.

The same material would build *thirty* Great Pyramids.

The walls of Babylon, famous throughout all ancient history, were sixty miles around. But they were built on level ground. The China Wall, with all its extra loops, is 1900 miles long— thirty-two times as far—and at one place climbs to a point 5000 feet above the sea.

Astronomers say that the Great Wall is the only man-made thing on our planet visible to the human eye from the moon.

Here is something truly wonderful—something that must go near the very top of our list of Marvels.

But let's not talk so much about this wonder-wall. Let's go see it.

The journey from Angkor requires several days. We travel back down the Mekong, and at Saigon board an ocean liner which takes us north to Hong Kong, and on up the China coast to the Chinese city of Tientsin, the port for Peking.

Peking, for several hundred years, was the capital of China. It's full of wonderful palaces and temples. But these things, we know, will seem small and unimportant compared with the stupendous stone monster crawling over mountain and valley, thirty miles to the north of the city.

A train ride into the mountains—a short steep walk—a climb up crumbling stone steps—and we reach the top of a heavy, square-built watchtower perched on the top of a hill. We look over the battlements. All about us spreads an expanse of wild and rugged mountains. And there, writhing across this pitched and tumbled land, is the Great Wall.

It leaps downhill to either side of us. It ripples and twists through the valleys. It swoops, like an angry python, up the far mountainside. It races along the topmost mountain rim. It dodges and dips and disappears, to reappear at the summit of the next wave of peaks. It seems to seek the hardest way, to challenge the wildest pinnacle, to defy heaven and earth. It reminds us of a gigantic stone roller-coaster. If there were a track along the stone wall-top, and we could drag a car to the 5000-foot high-point, we could roller-coast for several days and nights nonstop—if some of the thousand-foot up-swoops and thousand-foot down-swoops didn't wreck our car.

We can see twenty miles of Wall twisting to the west, and as many more miles twisting to the east. We can count a hundred towers. But in all this vast wilderness of crags and gorges we cannot see a house or a human being or a tree (the railroad is hidden behind a hill)—just Wall, Wall, Wall, on and on and on, until both Wall and mountain fade into the distant haze.

And most amazing of all, we realize that this section of Wall before our eyes is only a tiny fraction of the whole. We can see forty miles of it—there remain one thousand eight hundred and sixty miles of it we cannot see. We can count perhaps 100 towers, but almost 24,000 towers are out of sight.

We leave our high battlement, and walk for a mile along the roller-coaster grass-grown Wall—up and down, up and down. Along either edge there is a parapet to protect the Wall's defenders from arrows shot from below. Between these two para-

Pix Publishing Company.

The Great Wall could not cross rivers, but had to stop at the river bank, and start off again on the other side. Invaders, no doubt, were able to sail through these gaps in the Wall in boats.

pets there runs a road, once paved—twelve feet wide and 1900 miles long. But it's a road no vehicle nor even a pack-animal can use. Only a man, and a sure-footed one at that, can climb some of the slopes—slopes so steep that the road becomes a stone step-ladder. The road tunnels right through the watchtowers. No precipice, no crag, no canyon, can stop it—only rivers.

In crossing rivers there is a break in the Serpent. The Wall ripples down to the river bank and stops at a battle-tower right at the edge of the water . . . then from the opposite bank soars off into the mountains again. Whatever kept enemies from sailing down the river in boats, through this gap in the Wall, I don't know.

By now, after a steep climb, we've reached another towered hilltop, twelve towers away from where we started. When we've rested a bit, somebody asks me who built this monster-Wall, anyway; and why was it built; and how was it built; and when. . . .

Well, I've been reading all the books I could find about the Wall. It's had a marvelous history . . . I'll tell you what I've learned:

286

You've all heard about Hannibal. He was the great general from ancient Carthage who crossed the Alps with his war-elephants for an attack on Rome. (We had a story about him in our first Book of Marvels.)

This took place 218 years before the birth of Christ.

Well, about the time Hannibal was crossing the Alps, a powerful emperor with the difficult name of Chin Shih Hwang Ti came to the throne of China. The Chinese at that time (as they had been for centuries before) were a very highly civilized people, and their luxurious cities invited attacks from plunderers.

This danger always came from the north, from Mongolia and Manchuria, where the barbarians lived—the Tartars and the Huns. These barbarians came swooping down, every time they felt like it, upon China's richest provinces, burning the cities and robbing and murdering the people.

To keep the Tartars on their own side of the fence, the Emperor decided to build one, so strong and so tall and so long and so well-guarded, that the barbarians could never break through into China. The wall would begin at the sea and march on into the Gobi Desert. It would need a million laborers. Several hundred thousand men would have to die in the struggle to build it. The cost might bankrupt the nation.

But Chin Shih Hwang Ti let none of these things stop him.

He built his wall.

From the sea the Emperor drove the great barrier westward, always choosing the hardest, most difficult, route for the Wall to go—always up the steepest mountain-side. Why did he do this? There is a Chinese legend which tells that the Emperor didn't choose the route at all, but left the choice to his magic winged horse which led the way. (The horse *must* have been magic, for no ordinary horse could have climbed some of the crags which the Wall climbs.) Wherever the winged horse went, the workmen had to follow—up hill and down dale, over mountains, across deserts.

More and more laborers were needed, as the work went forward. The Emperor forced all the soldiers in his army to put aside their swords and become masons.

Nothing on earth, created by the hand of man, even remotely approaches the Great Wall of Chin
in sheer size, in amount of masonry piled up, in amount of labor required. Twenty to forty fee
high, fifteen feet thick, and 1900 miles long, it contains enough material to build *thirty* Grea
Pyramids. Astronomers say that the Great Wall is the only man-made thing on our plane
visible to the human eye from the moon. Starting at the sea, it twists and writhes its way into th
deserts of western China—up hill and down dale. It ripples through valleys, swoops up the mour
tain-sides. It races along the topmost mountain rim. It dodges and dips and disappears, to re
appear at the summit of the next wave of peaks. Legends say that a winged horse chose the rout

The horse *must* have been winged, for no ordinary horse could climb some of the slopes the Wall climbs. History tells that every third man in China was forced to work on the Wall. So many laborers died that the Wall became known as the longest cemetery in the world. In this picture we can see, looking to the east, about ten miles of Wall. There remain about 1890 miles we can *not* see. We do not envy the Chinese soldiers who, when they received the beacon-fire signals, had to hurry along this galloping roller-coaster—a hundred miles east, or a hundred miles west—to meet an attack from the Tartars. We walk for just *one* mile along the up-and-down Wall top, and our legs begin to ache.

He emptied the prisons and drove the prisoners to the mountain-tops to pile up bricks. Anyone who criticized him was promptly sent north to the stone quarries.

It is said that every third man in China was ordered by the Emperor to work on the Wall.

Unhappily for all these hundreds of thousands of workers, the route chosen by the magic horse twisted through the most barren part of China, through land where there were no villages, no food, no water. Water and food had to be brought for miles, up to the tops of the cruel peaks.

No wonder that thousands upon thousands of laborers died. Their bodies, we are told, were flung mercilessly into the trench between the two stone facings of the barrier, and covered over with dirt. The Great Wall of China has properly been called the longest cemetery in the world.

And, after all this, it really never succeeded in stopping the barbarians. Their armies continued, almost at will, to break through the Wall at some weakly guarded point. Someone has well said: "The cost of the Great Wall, in life and treasure, was so heavy that the Chinese never got over it—but the Tartars did!"

For 1600 years—from 218 B.C. to 1400 A.D.—the Tartars *kept* coming over the Wall, and then, about the year 1400, the Chinese resolved that something had to be done. So they went back to work and rebuilt the Wall from end to end. This time it was made twice as strong as before. More beacon-towers were added. Brass cannon were placed behind the parapets. And another hundred thousand workmen perished. . . .

But all this labor, as before, was wasted. In 1644, not many years after the Pilgrims landed in America, the Manchus from Manchuria hurled themselves against the barrier, determined to seize the riches of China. The brass cannon boomed; the Chinese armies fought bravely. But they could not stop the onrush of the invaders. The Manchus captured Peking and made it their capital. And from this city they ruled over the entire nation right up to the time when China became a republic—in 1912. The Manchus naturally had no desire to defend themselves against their own fellow countrymen in Manchuria. And so, ever since 1644, the Wall has been abandoned, and allowed to fall into decay. For stretches of a hundred miles, toward the western end, the Wall sees no human being for years at a time. The jackals and the wolves make dens in the tumbled stones. Antelopes graze upon the grassy parapets. Eagles nest in every tower. And in these days of airplanes and big guns, there is little chance that the Chinese will ever build up their Great Stone Serpent again. It will gradually crumble away until, in some far-off time, the Wall will be just a twisting ridge of sand, 1900 miles long.

Those are all the facts I know about the Wall—and they're probably all the facts you want to hear about it. But I've learned how much you like stories—you're always asking me to tell you a *story* about the wonders we see. So, as we walk back to the station, I'm going to tell you just a little story that may interest you, a story about the Wall and the last emperor of the Manchus:

You remember I said that the invaders from Manchuria broke through the Wall and conquered China in the year 1644?—and that they ruled the country up to 1912? In 1912 the Chinese rebelled against the Manchus, stormed the imperial palace, killed all the members of the royal family they could find, and declared that China, henceforth, would be a republic like the United States.

The Manchu emperor at that time was a little boy just seven years old. He, too, would have been killed had his nurse not changed his rich clothes for rags, and smeared his face with dirt. This ruse saved his life, since the rebels never thought that this dirty child could be the Royal Prince.

Later, the new Chinese government allowed the boy to live on as a state prisoner in one corner of the palace, and hold the courtesy title of "Emperor."

The years passed, and the little prisoner, supported by the government, reached his seventeenth birthday. On this date the guardians of His Imperial Highness chose for him a wife, a young Manchu princess whom he had never seen.

The bride was just fifteen.

At four o'clock on the morning of her wedding day, the little girl was escorted in her curtained sedan chair to the prison-palace where the Boy Emperor awaited her.

And I was one of the fortunate people standing on the side lines, watching the procession move by.

Richly dressed noblemen in embroidered robes led the way. Then a forest of pennants, and hundreds of swaying lanterns, blazed and fluttered past. Last of all came the bride's sedan chair, hung with yellow silk brocade, and borne along by sixteen porters.

I followed close behind the curtained chair, and wondered about the girl inside. Fifteen years old! Married to a boy she'd never seen—a boy who was a prisoner of the State. Now she would be a prisoner too . . . I felt sure the child inside that covered chair was not a happy bride.

The procession reached the entrance of the palace. The great gates opened wide, and the trembling little girl, hidden in her flowered box, was carried on into the throne room where her lord and master waited to make her his Empress.

Before I left Peking the young couple had settled down to married life in the imperial prison. The Emperor felt he needed exercise, and asked for a horse. Instead of getting an energetic animal, the Chinese officials brought him the fattest, whitest, gentlest pony they could find. Then, having been lifted into a cushioned saddle on the pony's broad back, the young Emperor was led, with two gigantic groomsmen clinging to the white silk bridle, solemnly round and round the courtyard.

This was the imperial exercise.

The little Queen also needed to be amused. She had an American tutoress whose fingernails were always pink and glossy. The Queen said she also wanted pink fingernails. So one day the tutoress brought along scissors and file and gave the Bride of Heaven a manicure. This simple beauty treatment made the poor little Manchu prisoner the happiest child in China.

The more I heard about the child Empress and the prison life she led, the sorrier I felt for her, and the more I wanted to help her. There didn't seem to be much I could do. . . . And then I thought about the tiger's tooth I always carried in my pocket. The tooth came from a tiger I'd helped to kill some months before in

roadway—once paved—along the top of the Great Wall is about twelve feet wide. But it's ad only a man, and a sure-footed one at that, can climb. The road tunnels right through the ch towers. No precipice, no crag, no canyon, can stop it. Along the northern edge of the wall find a four-foot parapet behind which archers could shoot at enemies attacking from below.

India. I carried the tooth with me everywhere, and it had brought me nothing but good luck. I'd send it to the Empress—it might bring her good luck too.

And I did. I mailed it to the "Empress of China, Imperial Palace, Peking."

I like to think the little Queen received my gift. At least her good luck returned. For after several years of imprisonment, and then of exile, she and her royal husband were brought back to Manchuria, the land of their warlike ancestors. There the Boy Emperor was made the royal governor of Manchukuo (as Manchuria is called today) by the Japanese, who had seized this province from the Republic of China.

293

I do not know by what route the young couple traveled to Man-chukuo. But if they went by train from Peking, they passed through a gap in the Great Wall—a gap where the bricks and stone have crumbled and left an opening for the railroad tracks. If the young King did travel by this route, what a dramatic moment it might have been, had he stopped the train at the gap, and climbed to the top of the Great Wall! Through this Wall his forefathers had once fought their way south to conquer China. And now, through this same Wall, after 300 years of Manchu rule, the last Manchu Emperor was retreating north again, back home to Manchuria.

This must have been a bitter moment for the young King. However—he had a great deal to be thankful for. He and the little Empress were free again—and they had been asked to gov-ern the land of their ancestors. . . . Perhaps this good luck was brought them by my tiger's tooth. Otherwise—who knows?—the little Bride of Heaven might still be living in a Peking prison, with nothing more important to do than lean out the window of her prison apartment and wave a magnificently manicured hand at her imperial husband riding on his milk-fed pony below her in the courtyard.

In places the slope of the mountain-side up which the Wall climbs is so steep that the road on the Wall-top becomes a stone stepladder. *Wide World.*

CHAPTER XXX

THE MAGIC MOUNTAIN

Through the blue summer seas our ship, coming from China, steams along the coast of a new and beautiful land. Past rocky little islands, covered with pine trees, we sail; past little bays where the water is emerald green, and the beach gleams white. Floating over the land is a pale blue haze that half-conceals the hills.

From the rail we watch the flying fishes dart across the waves. Then one of us happens to glance up—it's Tommy Davis. He suddenly catches sight of something in the clouds, and stares in such wide-eyed astonishment we wonder if he sees the gates to heaven.

"Look! Look!" he cries.

We follow his gaze, and we see it, too—something floating far above the mist-hidden earth and soaring like music up into the sky . . . a snowy vision of peace and purity dreaming in the sunshine.

It's Fujiyama—the Magic Mountain.

Over there, that misty shore—is Japan.

From the first moment we behold Mount Fuji we've only one thought, one desire—to climb it, to answer the call of that beckoning, beautiful snow-queen in the clouds. And climb it we shall—all 12,400 feet of it, and from the summit watch the sun rise in glory from the sea.

Before we make the climb, let's explore Japan a bit, and learn more about this country, and its Magic Mountain.

If you'll look at the map on page 270, you'll see that Japan is a collection of large islands, strung along the eastern shore of the mainland of Asia. The islands are very rugged and very mountainous. High over all the other peaks rises the one supreme peak—the perfect cone of snow-clad Fuji. Like most of the high mountains of Japan, Fuji is a volcano, sleeping, but far from dead. Compared to the Alps and the Himalayas, Fuji isn't especially high. Yet it seems high because it rises in one superb sweeping curve right from the shore to the sky, a curve that can be seen for a hundred miles on every side.

295

Sailing along the coast of Japan, we look up from the waves toward the clouds, and see somethin
floating far above the mist-hidden earth and soaring like music up into the sky . . . a snowy visi
of peace and purity dreaming in the sunshine. It's Fujiyama, the Magic Mountain. Mount Fu
is a volcano, with a deep crater in the top. But it has been sleeping since the year 1707. Hig
above all the other peaks of Japan rises this one supreme peak—a perfect cone, and always sno

...ad. It's 12,400 feet high—not high as mountains go. Yet it seems high because it rises in one ...uperb sweeping curve right from the seashore into the clouds. This curve can be seen from seven ...rovinces in Japan. People aboard ships crossing the Pacific from America can see the snowy vol-...ano, too, long before they can see the shore of Japan. Could there be a more wonderful welcome to any country?

From the beginning of Japanese history the people of Japan have loved this mountain. They have more than loved it—they have *worshiped* it. They have a fanciful legend about the creation of Fuji. They say that a long time ago, when the gods dwelt upon the earth, the goddess Fujisan quarreled with the other gods. Unhappy, she resolved to live alone in peace. And so, in the midst of a wooded plain, she changed herself, in a single night, into a perfect volcano that soared more than 12,000 feet into the farthermost clouds. In the morning the other gods looked up and saw Fujisan, gleaming and triumphant, smiling down at them. And they felt very small and very angry.

To the Japanese this legend is truth, and Fujisan is the Goddess of Beauty in mountain form. To them she is not a terrible and deadly goddess, like Chomo Lungma of Tibet, but a loving and gentle friend. They see in her a white and sacred angel enthroned in snow high above the realms of the other gods—an angel ready to bless and purify whoever looks upon the shining wonder of her face.

Fuji is the very symbol of the entire Japanese nation. Japan's artists and craftsmen draw and paint and carve images of the mountain on almost every object of art and industry they make. No house is complete without a colored print of Fuji hanging on the wall. The cone-shaped bamboo hats worn by the peasants are called Fuji hats. If a pretty girl has a smooth white forehead, she is said to have a Fuji brow. The greatest poetry of Japan has been written in praise of Fuji's graceful lines and crown of snow. Children are taught from their cradles that it is their duty to climb Fuji and pay homage to the goddess. No good Japanese feels his life has been well-lived, or that his soul, after death, will rest in peace, unless he has made a pilgrimage to the summit of the great volcano.

I have climbed Fuji once before. (I love her as much as the Japanese.) So I know the climb ahead of us is not very difficult—at least not for Tommy Davis and Billy Wing and myself, who have crossed the 15,000-foot pass into Tibet. But it's a long climb. We must take our time and see everything. Yes, the girls can go

298

mong the Japanese there is a fanciful legend which tells that Fuji is the Goddess of Beauty—
med Fujisan—in mountain form. This goddess quarreled with the other gods at a time when
ey all lived on earth. Wishing to be alone, and at peace, Fujisan changed herself in a single
ght into a perfect volcano more than 12,000 feet high. The other gods were very jealous, but the
people of Japan began to worship the mountain—and they have worshiped it ever since.

as well as the boys. They *couldn't* have gone not so many years ago, because no girls or women were allowed to ascend the sacred mountain. There was a legend that Fujisan disliked her own sex, and that when a girl or woman started to climb, terrible storms arose. Then, one day, a few stubborn girl-climbers refused to be frightened by the legend. They started up the slopes . . . and at once the thunder rumbled and the lightning flashed. The girls would not retreat. Through rain and storm they fought on—and reached the top. And there, Fujisan had a good look at them and saw that they were just as nice and just as respectful as the boys (indeed nicer!—those that had Fuji brows like hers). After this the goddess decided not to hate girls any more, but to welcome them and give them fair weather when they came to call.

Having heard this story, we *beg* the girls in our party to go with us. Then we can be sure of sunshine.

We're lucky to reach Japan during the climbing season. It's only six weeks in midsummer. (My climb was in January, but everybody said I was crazy.) During these six weeks Japanese come from all parts of the empire to pay their respects to Fujisan.

On our early-morning train going south from Yokohama there are several hundred fellow pilgrims. At the little town of Go-temba, where the climbing trail begins, we get ready for the battle. We have decided to be *real* pilgrims, and wear pilgrim clothes, and follow all the ceremonies.

The first thing a pilgrim has to do is take a bath. No matter if he has just had one an hour before—he must take another before starting up the sacred trail. So we find a bathhouse. There all of us—the boys in one room, the girls in another—get into huge wooden tubs, eight feet square, filled with the hottest water we can stand. In this water we must boil for at least an hour.

Then, our hearts and pores purified, we put on our pilgrim garments. These must be new, all white, and spotlessly clean. A cone-shaped bamboo Fuji hat goes with it. Thus arrayed we march to the little shops run by the Buddhist priests in the sacred shrines. (Buddhism is one of the chief religions of Japan, having come from Tibet by way of China.) At the shrines we buy a string

is the religious and the patriotic duty of every Japanese to climb Fuji. Children are taught in the cradle that, once in their lives, they must stand on Fuji's summit and say their prayers the sun rises out of the Pacific. The climbing season is six weeks in mid-summer. At that time as many as 50,000 pilgrims may trudge up the trails to the top of the great mountain.

of sacred beads to put around our necks, and a necklace of little bells. Without the beads and the bells no pilgrim is properly dressed. We are supposed to wear sandals. But I balk at this. The lava ash, I know, will work its way into the sandals and cut our feet. This is being *too* holy. We'll keep on our stout boots. We do not forget food and water for our knapsacks. One thing more—a climbing staff. These are especially made just for the Fuji climb. No, there is still *another* thing I almost forgot—the sacred pilgrim-chant which we must repeat every few minutes all the way up. It goes like this: *Rokkon sojo O yama keisei. Rokkon sojo O yama keisei.* It means: "May our six senses be pure, and the weather on the honorable mountain fair." Got it?

Now—is everybody present? Are we all purified? Please check up on your sandwiches, beads and bells—hat, staff and chant. . . .

All set? Here we go—*ROKKON SOJO O YAMA KEISEI!*

We are only one group of many groups of pilgrims. During the six-weeks season as many as 50,000 people may climb Fuji, an average of over 1000 a day. Gotemba is a favorite starting point. We see strings of pilgrims in front of us, and more strings following us—young pilgrims and old pilgrims, boys and girls, rich and poor, all musical with bells, all chanting the request that their six senses be pure and the weather fair.

We look ahead. Above us the glorious mountain shines in a cloudless sky. It looks like a long climb to the top. It *is* a long climb—thirteen miles long and 12,000 feet *up*!

The first stretch of trail leads through beautiful forests of pine. As the slope increases in steepness we stop often to rest and get our breath. Several Japanese speed-demons pass us, almost on the run . . . the slope higher up will slow *them* down! We pass a few pilgrims ourselves, mostly the old and feeble. We pass one old man—he must be eighty—with his son and grandson. They are pushing him along—he's determined to say his prayers on the mountain-top before he dies.

Along the trail, about a mile apart, are little rest-houses where pilgrims can sleep. Some of the oldest pilgrims take an entire day to climb from one rest-house to another, and perhaps ten days to arrive on top.

At last, forcing ourselves forward with our staffs, we reach the timber line, at about 5000 feet. Here the forest gives way to slopes of lava. This lava has been here since 1707, when the last eruption of the volcano took place. Fuji has been asleep well over 200 years. However, she's not dead, for there are still wisps of steam in her crater. Fuji may have a clear cool head, but despite this she also has a warm heart—a heart *so* warm it may explode some day and again rain destruction upon Japan.

Steadily we trudge along up the ever-steepening slope—resting and climbing, resting and climbing. The lava ash is ankle-deep. How glad we are we didn't wear those sandals! We look behind us. Zigzagging up the lava trail comes the long white line of chanting pilgrims, moving like an army of great white ants.

We reach 10,000 feet. Here we strike the snow. The wind turns cold, and our eyes ache from the white glare. The mountain-side, too, slants ever more sharply upward. It's like climbing steps.

By the time we reach 11,000 feet the sun is going down on the other side of the peak. The whole cone floats in glowing light. The sky has turned crimson, the snow-fields deep violet. We look down into the darkening valleys far below. There the villages "are being tucked in by the mists for the night." Beyond, the Pacific has faded into dreams.

We decide it's time we tucked *ourselves* in for the night. But the 11,000-foot rest-house is jam-packed with pilgrims. There isn't an inch, even of floor-space, for us to sleep on.

No hope of rest here. We decide to push on through the snow, right to the summit, and spend the night there. It's only 1400 feet above, and on such a clear summer evening as this there will be the glow of starlight to brighten the trail.

As twilight fades into luminous darkness we keep up the struggle. Our muscles are aching, our hearts pounding. In an effort to cheer ourselves we sing at the top of our lungs: *ROK-KON SOJO O YAMA KEISEI....*

303

At about seven o'clock we reach 12,000 feet. Here we come upon a group of laughing, shouting Japanese coolies standing beside the trail. They hold up a wide leather belt for us to see—and smile—and point to the summit—and say "One yen." They are the extra-power boys. For one yen they'll strap the leather belt around a weary climber's waist, and, by means of ropes, drag him, in a wild burst of shouting and energy, right to the top.

We all might *like* to have the coolies drag us the rest of the way, but we're too proud to admit it—all except Sally and Pat. They have sense . . . their feet are blistered, and wet from the snow; their legs are wabbling. They say *yes* they'll use the coolies—with pleasure. We help them strap the harness over their white pilgrim gowns. And then, whish!—up they go in a whirl of snow like galloping ghosts to the top.

The rest of us plod on. Nobody is chanting *Rokkon sojos* any more. Our entire thought is bent on the struggle to get up this last steep slope.

Three hundred feet to go—it seems like three thousand; two hundred—Sally and Pat see us and shout down from the summit to be brave; one hundred—the gleaming white slope seems almost straight up; one last heroic push. . . And we're there!

We sink down in a heap on a snowbank, and wonder if we're going to live.

When we can move again we begin to look around. To our surprise we see that we're on the edge of a deep crater. The great hole, a thousand feet across, appears to be bottomless. We hope it doesn't start erupting tonight—we're just too tired to dodge flying boulders and streams of lava.

The few crude little inns and sacred shrines on the summit again offer us no place to sleep. They, too, are bursting with pilgrims, several hundred of them, who have reached the top that afternoon. But we are able to buy a big basket of firewood. We find a sheltered spot protected from the wind, and fairly free from

305

Fuji, clouds, and moonlight. On our climb up the sacred mountain we start from the base station about noon. But we do not reach the top till well after dark. The last few thousand feet are covered with fields of snow. Up these snow-slopes, in the starlight, we find our way. Once at the summit, we spend the rest of the night on the edge of the crater.

snow. Here we make our fire, eat our supper, dry our shoes, thaw out our cold, stiff legs—and wait for the dawn.

On one side of us the wall of the starlit crater falls sheer. Without much trouble we could roll right off into it. On the other side the pale snow-slopes swoop down into black space below. Off to the north, toward Yokohama and Tokyo, are clusters of tiny lights trying to brighten some faraway world.

Once we've eaten our chocolate and sandwiches, and been warmed by the fire, we decide we're not quite as dead as we thought. In fact, *I* feel quite happy again. . . . I've a lovely idea—we can't sleep, and there's not much else to do . . . how about a story?

"Yes!" say Sally and Pat and Billy Wing.

"No-o-o!" say Peggy and Tommy Davis.

The ayes have it, so a story you're going to get! And—hoo-ray!—it's about *me*!

You remember I told you I climbed this mountain once before —in January? And was *that* a climb! I did it to celebrate my twenty-third birthday. January was the worst possible season. I couldn't help this. So far as I knew then, this might be my last chance the rest of my life. Before making the climb I tried for days to find somebody to go with me. Nobody would.

And so I climbed alone.

There had been two Englishmen, the previous year, who had reached the top in midwinter—the first midwinter climb in Fuji's history. They had made many midwinter climbs in the Alps, and knew how to rope themselves together. Even so, they were driven back three times by the blizzards. Clear weather, on the fourth attempt, allowed them to succeed.

These same climbers were very kind to me. They supplied me with an ice-ax, and sharp iron cleats for my boots, but they never dreamed I'd get even halfway up . . . the mountain was blanketed with ten feet of snow and ice, from Gotemba to the summit— and I was all alone.

I didn't have much hope myself.

306

In Gotemba I had to do without the purification bath, for the bathhouses were all boarded up. The shrines were closed. There were no priests, no guides. I was the only pilgrim in sight.

For a costume I had a sweater and a fur jacket. Instead of a bamboo hat I wore a woolen flying-helmet. Also, in case I slipped and began to slide down the iceberg, I had put on three pairs of pants.

Finally (by paying half his wages in advance) I was able to persuade a Japanese coolie to escort me to the base station at the edge of the forest. We had to wear snowshoes to get even this far. Here, at the timber line, about four o'clock in the morning, I bade farewell to Katsu. Our parting was very touching; the coolie never expected to see me again, and I still owed him six yen.

I really didn't need a guide, as there was no trail. I could just help myself to any path I pleased. The things I *did* need, I had— the nail-like spikes in my shoes, and my ice-ax. The ax was attached to my wrist by a six-foot rope. If it slipped out of my hand, it wouldn't be lost. Without these aids I couldn't have moved a single yard upward.

With them I was able to chop and stamp my way up to the 11,000-foot rest-house. I sat down on the roof—the rest of the house was buried under snow.

Here the wind began to blow—*really* blow. And in January these winds were howling blizzards that would have frozen my face had I not kept rubbing it. From here on I had to struggle up that last terribly steep slope—*you* know! Only I didn't have a nicely marked zigzag trail ... all I had was the side of an iceberg, slick and hard as glass. I didn't dare slip. (If I had—well, I wouldn't be here.) I just kept on crawling up, inch at a time —chop, chop, chop with the ice-ax; stamp, stamp, stamp with the ice-cleats.

The last few hundred yards was a grim battle with Fuji's blizzards. More than once I was on the point of retreating before I was frozen to death. But each time some demon inside urged me higher and higher into more dangerous territory. "To the peak! To the peak!" So I wound my muffler tighter, and crawled on.

In winter, Fuji is covered from base to summit under ten feet of snow and ice. There are
climbers then. Richard Halliburton made the climb in January—alone, because no one would
with him. On top he found the cold very intense, and a blizzard howling past. To help him up
slick slopes he had ice-spikes on his boots, and an ice-ax.

When I *did* reach the rim—right along here somewhere—the
blasts struck with such force I had to lie flat on the ice and fight
to keep from blowing off the top of the mountain. The sky was
clear, and there was sunshine, but the only views I had from the
summit were merely blurs of flying snow-clouds lashed into fury
by the screaming winds. I felt sure the winds couldn't blow
harder than this on the summit of Mount Everest!

Up here, not even the *roofs* of these shrines and inns were
showing. Everything was completely buried under ice. So there
was no place I could go to escape from the blizzard.

I knew I couldn't stand the cold for long, now that climbing had ceased. So I had to think quickly about taking photographs of the crater, and get down.

I'd lugged a camera all the way up. I knew that if I didn't have pictures of the crater to prove my story, nobody would believe it. Working quickly as I could, I unpacked my faithful camera, and crawled over to the edge of the crater. The swirl that met me there almost dashed the camera out of my hands. But somehow I managed to take a picture of the great hole—and fled. It was the first picture ever made on Fuji's crown during the ice season.

Later on, the English newspaper in Tokyo published my story in full. The crater picture, that proved I'd reached the top, was put on the front page—upside down!

Descending the mountain was just as dangerous as climbing up. I had to use my ice-ax every minute. Reaching the 11,000-foot mark I was out of the worst of the winds, and decided to rest a little . . . I hadn't stopped a minute since four o'clock that morning. I drove my ice-ax deep into the ice, propped my iron-shod boots against this support, and lay back on the steep slope.

Now, almost for the first time, I had a really good look at the wonderful picture of snow and sea below me. I agreed, whole-heartedly, with the first part of the Japanese proverb which says: "You are a fool if you do not climb Fuji." And then, feeling my aching legs and frostbitten face, I agreed just as heartily with the second part of the same proverb which says: "But you are a worse fool if you climb it twice." . . . And now I've climbed it twice!—and I'll do it the third time if I ever have a chance. But the *next* time I'm going to have the coolies drag me all the way to the top, right from Gotemba—and then ride back down on a bicycle.

Today, seeing our mountain covered with lava ash for half the distance up the slope, you can't imagine what a perfect shoot-the-chutes this mountain-side is in January. As I rested on the ice, propped up by the ax, I couldn't resist a childish urge to send something dashing and skating down the slopes, just to see how far it would go. All I could spare was my thermos-flask. This I launched forth as hard as I could. Like a streak of lightning it leaped and slithered . . . down, down, down . . . until in a few seconds it disappeared into the white hem of Fuji's skirts.

And in a few moments more I almost went slithering after it. As I tried to shift my clumsy shoes, they slipped off the ice-ax support, and instantly, with my ice-cleat brakes turned skyward, I began to slide toward Gotemba with all the speed of the thermos-flask.

I didn't travel very far. Almost before I knew what was happening, the rope connecting my wrist with the firmly-secured ax became taut, and I was stopped dead. Good old rope! I'd tied the ax to me to keep from losing the ax. And now the rope had kept the ax from losing *me*.

I was so frightened by this little drama I decided to stop daydreaming and hurry on to safety. I didn't have a moment to lose . . . twilight comes early in January. Even then, the light was beginning to fade.

This brought me face to face with another danger. In the darkness I would not be able to find Katsu and the trail to Gotemba. But again I was lucky. Just as the last trace of day was departing, a speck of light appeared in the darkness below . . . it was a signal bonfire the faithful Katsu had lighted to guide me home.

On seeing me still alive with his six yen, Katsu's face beamed with delight—and so did mine, especially the frozen, swollen part of it.

Take my advice, children, and never climb Fuji in January!

Well!—I must say, I don't seem to be a very good story-teller. Look at Pat and Peggy—they've gone fast asleep! We'd better put a coat over their feet . . . and more wood on the fire. We'll wake them in time for the sunrise. . . . You may as well all sleep. I'll act as watchdog and protect you from the wolves.

But the next thing *I* know, a fearful racket wakes *me*. Such a banging of gongs, and blowing of horns! The priests are rousing the pilgrims—there is a streak of dawn in the eastern sky— the sun is soon to rise out of the Pacific.

The author and two of his Japlet friends photographed, with all his climbing equipment, soon after he had made a January ascent of Fuji. Snowshoes were useful along the lower slopes. The little Japanese boy holds the all-important ice-ax. The camera was necessary, because without pictures of the snow-blanketed crater no one would have believed that a midwinter climb had been made alone. In the distance is Fuji, turned by the wintry weather into an iceberg.

Just before dawn, on the summit of Fuji, the priests blow horns and beat drums, to rouse the pilgrims sleeping there and tell them that the sun is about to rise out of the Pacific. Soon from the ocean there springs a streak of fire—and then the glowing sun comes riding forth. Often at dawn a sea of clouds enfolds the lower slopes of the peak. To one standing on the summit, Fuji then becomes an island in an ocean of mist. Silent and awed, with bare heads bowed, the pilgrims face this sublimely beautiful picture of sunrise, and worship the Creator who has touched with such glory the heaven and the earth.

Nesmith

This is the sacred moment to which the pilgrims have been looking forward all their lives.

Instantly the crater-rim begins to stir with life. White-clad bundles of pilgrims stand and walk about. We stand up, too. Oh—what stiff legs! Oh—what aching backs!

We turn to the east. The whole sky is gold-spangled now, the sea a silver mystery. Out of the far Pacific springs a streak of fire—and then the great glowing sun, the King of the Day, comes riding forth to wake the world.

Silent and awed, with bare heads bowed, the pilgrims face this sublimely beautiful picture of sunrise, and worship the Creator who has touched with such glory the heavens and the earth. Some stretch out their hands—out to the rose-hued clouds, the island-studded ocean—and beseech all the gods they know to accept their surrender to the divine powers. Some, whispering their prayers, fall on their knees and humbly ask for the blessings of the goddess Fujisan.

Lifted up into this holy realm, on the white crown of the magic peak, we too stand there, as moved, as lost in rapture, as the kneeling, praying pilgrims. And as we watch the miracle of the morning unfold, each of us, after his own fashion, gives thanks to the Master Hand that made the beauty and the wonder of the world.

THE END

PROPER NAMES PRONOUNCED

Acropolis	ak-KROP-o-lis	Eiffel Tower	EYE-fel tower
Ægeus	E-je-us	El Mashnaka	el-mash-NAH-ka
Ægean	e-JEE-an	Ephesus	EFF-e-sus
Agra	AH-gra	Everest	EV-er-est
Akaba	AH-ka-ba	Euphrates	you-FRAY-teez
Alhambra	al-HAM-bra		
Al Mamoum	AL-ma-MOOM	Feisal	FY-sal
Angkor Vat	ANG-kor-WOT	Fujiyama	foo-jee-YAH-ma
Ararat	AIR-a-rat		
Arjemand	AHR-je-mahnd	Ghazi	GAH-zi
Artemisia	ahr-te-MIZZ-i-a	Gibraltar	ji-BRAWL-ter
Aurelian	aw-REEL-yan		
		Hadji	HAJ-ee
Baalbek	BAHL-beck	Halicarnassus	hal-i-kahr-
Babel	BAY-bul		NASS-us
Bedouins	BED-oo-ins	Haroun-al-	hah-roon-ah-rah-
Belshazzar	bel-SHAZZ-er	Raschid	SHEED
Benares	ben-AH-rehz	Helios	HE-li-us
Buddha	BOOD-a	Hellespont	HELL-es-pont
		Herod Antipas	HER-ud-ANN-
			ti-pass
Cæsar	SEE-zer	Herodias	her-OH-di-as
Cairo	KI-ro	Himalayas	him-a-LAH-yas
Calcutta	kal-KUTT-a		
Candia	KAN-di-a		
Caracalla	kair-ah-KAL-a	Ibn Saud	ih-ben-sah-OOD
Carthaginian	kahr-tha-JIN-i-an	Icarus	IH-ka-rus
Chares	SHAH-reez	Iguazu	ee-gwa-SOO
Chitor	chi-TOOR	Isfahan	is-fa-HAHN
Chomo Lungma	CHO-mo-	Istanbul	ih-stahn-BOOL
	LOONG-ma		
Circus Maximus	SIR-kus-MAK-	Jebusite	JEB-you-zite
	si-mus	Joab	JO-ab
Cleopatra	KLEE-oh-		
	PAY-tra	Kaaba	KAH-ba
		Kedron	KEE-drun
		Kheops	KEE-ops
Dædalus	DED-a-lus	Khephren	KEFF-ren
Damascus	da-MASS-kus	Kinchinjunga	kin-chin-
Darjeeling	dahr-JEE-ling		JOONG-ga
Dalai Lama	DAH-lie-LAH-ma	Knossos	NAHS-us
Delhi	DEL-ee		
Demetrius	de-MEET-ri-us		
Diomede	DIE-oh-meed	Lhasa	LAH-sa

Macedonian	mas-e-DOH-ni-an	Rajputana	RAHJ-poo- TAH-na
Madrasa	ma-DRAH-sa	Reims	reemz
Madura	mad-OO-ra	Rhodes	rodz
Manchukuo	man-CHOO-kwo		
Marie Antoinette	mah-REE-ahn- twa-NETT	Saigon	SIGH-gone
Masada	ma-SAH-da	Salome	sa-LOH-meh
Matterhorn	MAT-er-horn	Scheherezade	shuh-HAY-ray- ZAH-da
Mausolus	maw-SO-lus	Shah Abbas	shah-ab-BAHS
Medina	ma-DEE-na	Shah Jehan	shah-je-HAHN
Minos	MY-nus	Sidon	SIGH-done
Minotaur	MINN-oh-tor	Siva	SEE-va
Moriah	mo-RY-a	Smyrna	SMUR-na
Mosi-oa Tunga	MO-see-OH-a- TUN-ga	Sudan	soo-DAN
Moslem	MAHZ-lem		
ˋMouhot	moo-OH	Taj Mahal	TAHJ-ma- HAHL
Mumtaz Mahal	MUM-tazz- ma-HOLL	Theseus	THE-si-us ("th" as in "thing")
Nebuchadnezzar	NEBB-you-kad- NEZZ-er	Tibet	tib-ETT
Nepal	nee-PAUL	Tientsin	tin-tsin
Niger	NY-jer	Tigris	TIE-gris
		Timbuctoo	tim-buck-TOO
Odenathus	oh-de-NA-thus	Tirumala	tih-roo-MAH-la
Olympus	oh-LIM-pus	Tuareg	TWAH-reg
Padmini	pad-MEE-nee		
Palmyra	pal-MY-ra	Udaipur	OO-die-POOR
Parthenon	PAR-the-non	Usted Isa	OO-sted-EE-sa
Petra	PEE-tra		
Phœnician	fuh-NISH-an	Zabbai	ZAB-bye
Piræus	pie-REE-us	Zambezi	zam-BEE-zee
Popocatapetl	po-po-kah- TAY-petl	Zenobia	zeh-NOH-bi-a
		Zeus	zoos

316